THE LONG WAR

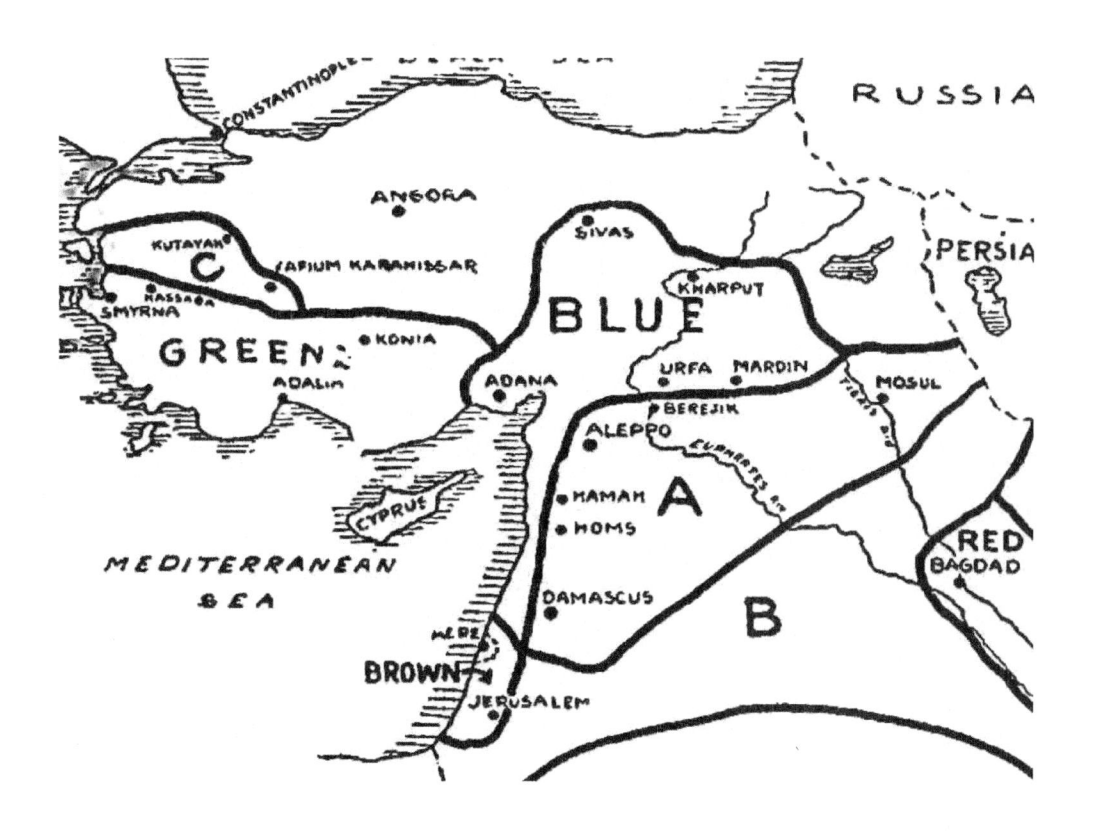

S.E. Al-Djazairi

MSBN Books

S.E. Al-Djazairi: *The Long War;* Published by MSBN Books; 2020
Website: msbnbooks.co.uk
Email: info@msbnbooks.co.uk
ISBN: 9781549941047

© S.E. Zaimeche Al-Djazairi

No resale, reproduction, or downloading of this work on the internet is allowed. Use of extracts from it is permitted as long as such extracts do not exceed what is necessary to make an argument.

Design and Artwork: N. Kern

About The Author: Salah Eddine Al-Djazairi lectured and researched at the University of Constantine in Algeria. He also tutored at the Department of Geography of the University of Manchester, and worked as a research assistant at UMIST (Manchester) in the field of History of Science.
He has published papers on environmental degradation and desertification as well as politics and change in North Africa, and problems of economic and social development. He has also contributed historical entries to various encyclopaedias.

Recently Published works by the same author:
Islam in China (3 vols).
The West, Islam, Barbarism and Civilisation.
The Destruction of the Environment in/of the Muslim World.

CONTENTS

INTRODUCTION	1
A CENTURY OF DEMISE, 1806-1910	8
LIBYA, 1911-1912	55
THE BALKANS, 1912-1913	104
THE FIRST WORLD WAR, 1914-1918	165
THE WAR OF INDEPENDENCE, 1919-1922	225
CONCLUSION	302
BIBLIOGRAPHY	306

'The injection of the poison of hatred into men's minds by means of falsehood is a greater evil in wartime than the actual loss of life. The defilement of the human soul is worse than the destruction of the human body.'
Arthur Ponsonby[1]

'The central problem from the standpoint of history remains the sources on which the Western historical narrative is still being written. The Ottoman archives remain largely unconsulted. When so much is missing from the fundamental source material, no historical narrative can be called complete and no conclusions can be called balanced...... The search for 'truth' will probably remain chimerical but is more likely to lead somewhere if left to historians rather than politicians and lobbyists.'
Jeremy Salt[2]

---

[1] Arthur Ponsonby: *Falsehood in Wartime*, New York, 1971, p. 18.
[2] Jeremy Salt: The Narrative Gap in Ottoman Armenian History; *Middle Eastern Studies*, vol 39, No, 1, Jan 2003, pp. 19-36, at p. 35.

INTRODUCTION

> It is a testimony that is due from British Christianity. Last month the Churches, established and disestablished, were worked up to an extraordinary pitch of excitement in order to prevent one black man beating one white man in a boxing match.
> But when a nominally Christian nation (Italy) carries fire and sword into the territories of its neighbour (Libya) in order to seize a province, the Christian Churches preserve an ominous and sinister silence.[3]

Indeed, this reality caught by Stead in 1911 when the Italians were killing Turks and Libyans is the same caught by Gordon in 1821 when the Greeks were committing terrible atrocities on the Turks in the Morea;[4] by Alison Phillips over the same incident;[5] by the various British diplomats when the Turks were being eradicated in Bulgaria and throughout the Balkans in the 1870s;[6] by Loti when the Turks were suffering some of the worst excesses in history in the Balkans, again, in 1912;[7] the same reality also witnessed when the Greeks were slaughtering the Turks in İzmir in 1919; and the same accounts of Greek atrocities committed towards the Turks between 1919 and 1921, as seen and reported by Toynbee.[8] In all instances, what was being done to the Turks was generally passed in silence. All, except these voices and other silenced witnesses, connived directly or indirectly with those busy removing the Turks.

Among the witnesses just cited, Toynbee, like many other British before him or after him, never liked the Turks in the first place. In fact, there were fewer people who abhorred the Turks as much as he initially did. When working for the British Ministry of War Propaganda during the First World War (1914-1918), he was commissioned to write *The Murderous Tyranny of the Turks*, which was prefaced by Viscount Bryce.[9] In this work, Toynbee, just as Bryce, attributed to the Turks bestial behaviour and systemic massacres Christians. To this day, in fact, Western scholars, media, and opinion makers, widely refer to this work by Toynbee to demonstrate "Turkish bestiality towards humanity in general, and Christians in particular." Yet, with the rarest of exceptions, none has used or referred, or refers, to Toynbee's second work on the Greek crimes perpetrated against the Turks, which he himself witnessed. This second work (*The Western Question in Greece*

---

[3] W.T. Stead: *Tripoli and the Treaties or Britain's Duty in this War;* London; 1911; p. 6.
[4] T. Gordon, *History of the Greek Revolution,* 2 vols; Edinburgh, William Blackwood, 1832.
[5] W. Alison Phillips: *The War of Greek Independence 1821-1833*, Charles Scribner's Sons; New York; 1897.
[6] See sources in Turkish work, include also journalists or correspondents
[7] P. Loti: *Turquie Agonisante*; Calman Levy; Paris; 1913.
[8] A.J. Toynbee: *The Western Question in Greece and Turkey*; Constable; 1922.
[9] A.J. Toynbee: *The Murderous Tyranny of the Turks*; Hodder and Stoughton, London, 1917.

and Turkey), published in 1922,[10] in fact is hard to know about. For writing it Toynbee paid the price: He became shunned, including by those who were kind to him before, and he lost his chair at the university of London.[11]

Twenty or so years before Toynbee, the British war correspondent, Ernest Bennett, who eventually rose to some of the leading positions within the British establishment, was reporting from Crete during the Greek uprising of 1896-1897.[12] Like Toynbee, and many others, initially, he had no particular sympathy for the Turks, but once he saw the reality in Crete, which was then being cleansed of Turks, he was nearly shot by the Greeks for what they considered was his excessive zeal or sympathy towards the Turks.[13] What Bennett did was to offer water and other humane assistance to the Turks, and just like Toynbee, in good gentlemanly British fashion, he ran to protect undefended Turkish refugees as they were being hounded by Greek mobs. It was absolutely the same scene in 1897 in Crete as in 1921, both Bennett and Toynbee and a few British, mainly soldiers, being the only barrier in front of Greek mobs seeking to hack, bludgeon, and bayonet (and do other nasty things besides) to terrified Turkish crowds of women, children, and the old as they were being ferried to safety by mainly British troops.

Another witness in a former Turkish territory, Libya, who also saw mass-murder on a large scale, was the Dane Knut Holmboe. There, following the Fascist arrival to power after 1923, they engaged in a policy of mass-cantonment and mass-murder that nearly wiped out the whole Libyan population, which Holmboe witnessed and reported. He was mysteriously murdered not long after his book appeared.[14]

Years earlier, after the Italians had invaded Libya in 1911, McCullagh, the veteran British war correspondent, who was then in Tripoli, wrote about the horrors he witnessed, and despatched to London some of the most hard-hitting photographs of the war-crimes committed by the Italians. When his work was put in print, his publishers began:

> NOTE BY THE PUBLISHERS
> SOME photographs of the Oasis Repression taken by Mr. McCullagh and submitted to us have been found unsuitable for publication in a work intended for general circulation, and have not, therefore, been reproduced in the present volume.
> The Publishers are not necessarily committed to the views on the war expressed by the Author.[15]

---

[10] A.J. Toynbee: *The Western Question*; op cit; p. 233.
[11] A. Mango: *Ataturk;* John Murray; London; 1999; p. 329.
[12] *Among the Cretan Insurgents*, Ernest N. Bennett, Blackwood's Edinburgh Magazine, February 1898; p. 166.
[13] Ibid
[14] K. Holmboe: *Desert Encounter*, London, 1936.
[15] F. McCullagh: *Italy's War for a Desert;* Herbert and Daniel; London; 1912; opening page.

Then, the author himself, McCullagh, informs us:
> While writing the present book (on the Italian invasion of Libya and their crimes) in an isolated house on the Surrey Downs (in the south of England), I was interrupted one day by the arrival of three gentlemen who had come from London in a motor-car and wanted to speak to me.
>
> They were Signor F.T. Marinetti, who calls himself a "poet," and who said that he had just come from Tripoli and was staying at the Savoy Hotel; Signor Boccioni, who is, I believe, a "futurist" painter; and another gentleman who did not give his name, but whom I suspect to be the London correspondent of the "Giornale d' Italia." The object of these gentlemen in motoring all the way from London was to fight a duel with me, and they managed to find me at home when there was nobody else in the house, save a maid-servant. This was the second invitation of the kind I have had since my return from Italy. I told them that I would communicate with them in due course; whereupon one of them threatened to attack me there and then.[16]

Italian crimes in Libya horrified many amongst the British, including parliamentarians of 1911-1912. In one session, Mr. McCallum Scott, a member of parliament, asked whether,
> '...in view of the fact that the Italians are conducting the war in Tripoli by barbarous methods, contrary to... the law of nations... [what's Britain's position?]'

The Speaker of Parliament replied:
> 'I do not think a question of that sort ought to be put in these terms with reference to a country with which we are on friendly terms. Before the honorable member asks such a question, perhaps he will kindly let me see a copy of it.'

Mr. Mason, another member, called attention
> 'to a definite matter of urgent public importance, namely, the events in Tripoli in their relation to the Hague Conference.'

The Speaker:
> 'The honorable member must be definite. The honorable member has not named anything definite.'

Mr. Mason:
> 'The atrocities in Tripoli are a matter of definite and urgent importance.'

The Speaker:
> 'That is altogether too vague. The Government is not responsible for the so-called atrocities in Tripoli.'

Mr. Mason:
> 'As regard our treaty obligations...'

The Speaker:

---
[16] Ibid; p. xxii-xxiv.

> 'The hon. member should at least have taken the trouble to prepare the matter.'[17]

Move forward 80 years, in the early 1990s, when the Bosnians were being massacred and mass-raped, the leader of the British Liberal Party, Paddy Ashdown, today Lord Ashdown, at each parliamentary session raised one issue and one issue only: the mass-slaughter of the Bosnian Muslims and the complete indifference of the world, urging Britain to do something. Without fail, the same replies as made by the Speaker to Mr. Mason and Mc Callum Scott in 1911-1912 in relation to Libya (i.e to stop referring to the massacres of Libyans) were made by John Major, British Prime Minister, to Paddy Ashdown. At times, John Major tried to turn Lord Ashdown's interventions into derision, and definitely showed utmost irritation at Ashdown's continually raising the Bosnian issue.

A step back to the past and the Balkan Wars of 1912, and there was the Frenchman, Pierre Loti, who wrote one of the most poignant works on the terrible crimes being committed on the Turks by all Christians, that is Bulgarians, Greeks, Montenegrins, and Serbs. Loti collected accounts, photographs, letters, all sorts of documentation and evidence from tens, maybe even hundreds of witnesses: French, British, Jews, Austrians, Germans; he cried, pleaded, cajoled, did all that was humanly possible to draw attention to the crimes committed against the Turks and to seek to stop them. For his pains, Loti, one of the greatest men of French literature and culture ever, was not just ignored by most and insulted by many, he was threatened with death, he himself expecting his murder any time; which did not dissuade him from pursuing his campaign.[18]

> In vain [writes Loti] all of us who had lived in the East: diplomats, men and women of religion, engineers, businessmen, people without distinction, all have been trying to raise the alarm regarding the subject of suffering of the Turks; nobody cares or bothers to listen, or even to print these witnesses' accounts; all the witnesses are writing to me, telling me about the conspiracy of silence, how truth is being smothered, the media stripped of freedom, whilst at the some time terrible calumnies are said about the Turks.[19]

Indeed, on the last point (terrible calumnies), it was not just that the Turks were being massacred in their tens of thousands, as Loti and others noticed, it was they, the Turks, who were then being accused of committing the massacres. A macabre irony that lasted from 1821 till 1922 on the ground, and that still lasts in scholarship, the media, fiction, the cinema, and other quarters to this day, a macabre irony the Turks have lamentably failed to deal with to this day (2017-18).

---

[17] W.T. Stead: *Tripoli and the Treaties or Britain's Duty in this War;* London; 1911; p. 75.
[18] P. Loti: *Turquie Agonisante*; Calman Levy; Paris; 1913. 73-4.
[19] Ibid; 139-140.

At the same time as Loti, the German scholar, Jäckh, witnessed the same atrocities against the Turks in that same conflict, and gathered plenty of evidence, which he summed up subsequently in his book (*Deutschland im Orient nach dem Balkan-Krieg – Germany in the Orient after the Balkan War*) which included some such evidence.[20] He cried of despair:

> Isn't there in Europe any will; any helping hand for humanity, no voice in support of civilisation? Why is it that all that happened; proved by documents, photographs, evidence of all sorts, is being ignored? Why all the silence?[21]

To the calls for an international enquiry late in 1912 over the crimes being committed in the Balkans, hopefully to stop the mass-slaughter of Turks, a call led by Loti, Jäckh, the Turkish government, and the countless witnesses of the atrocities, only the Italians, to their credit, answered favourably. Everyone else refused to hear or budge. So the mass-killing of, and atrocities towards, the Turks continued, and only when those who inflicted terror and death on the Turks turned against each other with the same frenzy of killing in the Second Balkan War of 1913, then, we suddenly had a commission of enquiry, the semi-farcical Carnegie Enquiry of 1914 sent to the ground,[22] when it was too late for the Turks.

We step briefly into the years 1919-1921; Toynbee, who was seen as the voice of civilisation and humanity, of truth and good, when he wrote his *Murderous Tyranny of the Turks* from London in 1917; now that he wrote his *Western Question* from the ground, and reported what he witnessed: the Greek war of extermination of the Turks, his accounts were met with scorn, hostility, and eventually he lost his chair, as already stated. And what he met with was the same as that by others such as Monsieur Lebouvier, a Dutch Pastor. He saw, and he reported

> The hideous bloodshed, the saturnalian orgies, and the riot with which the Greeks celebrated their triumphal entry into Smyrna [İzmir] (on 15 May 1919).

He wrote such as to *The Times* in London, but his account was everywhere suppressed.[23]

We move forward to our day, or more precisely the 1990s, and we have Justin McCarthy, who in his *Death and Exile*, demonstrates through the use of contemporary data, mostly archives from Western diplomatic missions, that rather than the Turks massacring everyone from 1821 till 1922, it was they, in fact who paid the heaviest price, millions of them massacred by the cruellest

---

[20] Ernst Jäckh; *Deutschland im Orient nach dem Balkan-Krieg;* Chapter 7: Deutsche und französische Augenzeugen von christlichen Massakers. (Die Balkangreuel des 30 jährigen Krieges); Martin Mörikes Verlag, Munich,1913; pp. 83-98.
[21] P. Loti: *Turquie Agonisante*; op cit. 242.
[22] Carnegie Commission of Investigation. *Report of the International Commission to Inquire into the causes and the Consequences of the Balkan Wars*; Washington DC; 1914.
[23] G. Ellison: *An Englishwoman in Angora* (London, 1924)., p. 26.

methods, their bodies generally mutilated; whilst the survivors were expelled from their homes. McCarthy had dared not just say the unsayable, but also provided powerful evidence for what he said. That is the wrong stuff to write and say these days. On his visit to Australia in November 2013, the venues where he was booked to speak were locked up on the ground of public and staff safety, and McCarthy was, instead compared with holocaust denier David Irving and portrayed as 'a tool of the Turkish government.'[24]

Like McCarthy, Stanford Shaw and Ezel Kural Shaw committed the same crime in their *History of the Ottoman Empire and Modern Turkey*. And so, they got the same retribution. Colin Imber who reviewed their work noted that it was 'so full of errors, half-truths, oversimplifications and inexactitudes that a non-specialist will find them positively misleading.... When almost every page is a minefield of misinformation, a detailed review is impossible.'[25]

Imber is, as a rule, a kind person anyone who knows him can tell, and his criticism remained tame.

Another reviewer of the Shaw's work, Victor L. Ménage, Professor of Turkish at the University of London, counted over 70 errors in the work and concluded, 'One "prejudice" that has vanished in the process is the respect for accuracy, clarity, and reasoned judgment.'[26]

Speros Vryonis went further, amongst other, accusing the Shaw (husband and wife) of wholesale plagiarism,[27] whilst Eric J. Zürcher of the University of Leiden stated that the work's last one hundred years it covers suffers from a 'Turkish-nationalist bias.'[28] The second volume caused immense anger among Armenian students, and on the night of October 3, 1977, a bomb placed by unknown assailants exploded at the doorstep of the Shaw's home at 3.50 a.m.[29] S. Shaw said that Armenian and Greek students had threatened him over the previous two years and cancelled the rest of his classes for the remainder of the quarter.[30]

Oddly though, Oliver Stone, who wrote the script for the film Midnight Express, where the Turks are depicted in the most vile manner, years later regretted this and admitted he had exaggerated the evil he had attributed to the Turks in the script of the film. At the time when the film was released, however, Oliver Stone

---

[24] *The Sydney Morning Herald*: 23 November 2013.
Not a genocide: Visiting professor's views on Turkey and its historic role anger Australia's Armenians
[25] Imber, Colin. 'Review of History of the Ottoman Empire and Modern Turkey.' *The English Historical Review*; 93 (Apr., 1978): pp. 393-395.
[26] Ménage, Victor L. 'Review of History of the Ottoman Empire and Modern Turkey.' *Bulletin of the School of Oriental and African Studies, University of London* 41 (1978): pp. 160-162.
[27] Vryonis. Speros: *Stanford J. Shaw, History of the Ottoman Empire and Modern Turkey, Volume I: A Critical Analysis*. Thessaloniki: Institute for Balkan Studies, 1983, pp. 88-112.
[28] Zürcher, Eric J. *Turkey: A Modern History*, 3rd. Ed. London: I.B. Tauris, 2004, p. 360.
[29] Manoukian, Socrates Peter; Kurugian, John O. (1977-10-04). 'Crude Bomb Explodes at UCLA Professor's Home;' *Los Angeles Times;* pp. D1 (Part II). Retrieved 2008-07-10.
Manoukian, Socrates Peter; Kurugian, John O. (1977-10-18). 'Shaw Bomb.' *Los Angeles Times*. pp. C6 (Part II). Retrieved 2008-07-10.
[30] *Daily Bruin*. October 4, 1977, p. 1.

was granted the film industry's ultimate award.[31] He is not alone to be awarded fame and fortune for a work that vilifies the Turks.

So then, how to write the story of the Long Turkish War in this climate of intimidation and intellectual and artistic blight and crookedness? Very simple: Just ignore the oncoming onslaught by the voices of crookedness and mind police, and ignore them in the writing of this work as well. One is not going to waste any time on today's 'scholars' of Turkey, whose writing, with exceptions, is utter trash. Reliance, instead, is primarily placed on the accounts of those who saw or participated in the Long War. Some of these witnesses were war correspondents, others photographers, many officers or soldiers, countless more just writers who captured the events raw. It is not important at all whether some of these accounts were by those who did not have any liking of the Turks. What are important are the facts they relate to us and how they saw things. It is very easy to reconstruct the Long War by relying on those who were there, from the Turks' war in Libya in 1911-1912 until the War of Independence in 1919-1922. We have the likes of Abbot, Bennett, Ostler, Mc Cullagh, and others who wrote in Libya; Elis Ashmead Bartlett, Seppings Wright, Grant and Gibbs in the Balkans; Sir Ian Hamilton, General Townshend, and Philips Price, who were present in the fields of the First World War; Toynbee and Halide Edib, who witnessed the War of Independence, and many others. Regarding secondary sources, the likes of Shaw, who used Turkish archives, and Llewellyn Smith who did the same for the Greek side, are much relied upon. Military historians, especially the likes of E.J. Erickson, G.S. Patton, M. Uyar, and a few others are also much relied on to clarify the military angle where and when needed.

In this work, all the witnesses and participants will be given the space to let us know about things as they saw them and lived them. Here there won't be the usual Western scholarly practice of massaging facts, and stating the opposite of what contemporaries said. Instead, these contemporaries are left to say it by themselves, the likeable and the dislikeable. So somehow, with the exception of chapter one, which deals with the century-long background to the Long War (1806-1910), this work is simply a work by those who saw the Long War in relation to Turkey or were involved in it. There will only be recourse to other (secondary) sources to connect in between facts, or when needed.

---

[31] Oliver Stone in I. Karlsson: The Turk as a Threat and Europe's Other; in *International Issues and Slovak Foreign Policy*; issue 1, 2006; pp. 62-72; at pp. 69-70

One

A CENTURY OF DEMISE, 1806-1910

When we consider the terrible list of wars which Turkey has had to fight in the last century, and when we consider that her armies have been almost entirely recruited from among the Mohammedan subjects of the Empire, we no longer wonder that the country is backward and misgoverned, our only surprise is that the Turkish race has not ceased to exist.
(E. Ashmead Bartlett, 1913) [32]

Writing just at the eve of the new century, in 1798-1799, the Frenchman Volney, held:

> I swear that by the ruin of so many empires destroyed: the Empire of the Crescent shall suffer the fate of the states whose scheme of government it copied. A foreign people shall chase the sultans from their metropolis; the throne of Orkhan shall be overturned; the last relict of his race shall be cut off, and the hordes of Oguzians (the Turks by their pre-Ottoman designation), deprived of their head, shall be scattered.[33]

At the same time, the French minister Choiseul who was 'so much carried away, through his admiration of ancient Greece,' as to see in the Turks only 'persecutors of the descendants of the Hellenes,' drew attention of Christendom 'to the miserable condition of the Greeks.'[34] He stated that the Morea should be made an independent state under the protection of France:

> To regenerate the Ottomans is an impossibility, was an assertion heard on all sides; they themselves believe that the moment of their destruction has arrived. The alliance of the Porte can no longer enter into combinations for the equilibrium of the Great Powers. Ought we, in order to aid such a people, to carry the theatre of war as far as the Black Sea, and ourselves cover the capital of that Empire? Could we make such efforts in face of the rival Powers interested to destroy our commerce in the Levant? Should we not rather, since a dismemberment is certain, take possession of the best Turkish ports, and seize upon, in Egypt and Syria, the true sources of abundance and of commerce?[35]

---

[32] E. Ashmead Bartlett: *With the Turks in Thrace*; George H. Doran Company; New York; 1913; pp. 33-4.
[33] Volney: *Les Ruines*; Paris; 1798-9; chap ii; in N. Daniel: *Islam*; op cit; p. 72.
[34] Sutherland Menzies: *Turkey Old and New*, 2 vols; Allen Lane; London; 1880; vol 2; p. 88.
[35] Choiseul in Sutherland Menzies: *Turkey Old and New*; p. 88.

The dismemberment, carving up, or partitioning of Turkey and its realm, regardless how it was called, stood at the source of the Long War. The Long War itself had origins early in the 19th century when the carving up of the Ottoman realm began.

1. The Beginnings of a Long War

In 1806-7, the Serbs rebelled at the instigation of Russia, the uprising being carried by pig farmers who were led by another pig farmer: Georges Petrovich (Georges the Black). So, in Serbia, consequently, there was 'No more lucrative or more honourable calling than that of the dealer in swine.'[36] During the war of 1787, that is twenty years earlier, Georges had put himself at the service of the Austrians against the Ottomans.[37] The Emperor Joseph of Austria had already put the Serbian Patriarchate under his protection when, in that same year he declared war on the Ottomans with the purpose 'of driving them out of Europe, to revenge mankind on those barbarians.'[38]

In order to accomplish this aim, he armed and organised a strong force of Serbs, who, in a climate of rising nationalist feelings, now nurtured the idea of Greater Serbia.[39] Further support to the Serbs came from Russia, ever keen to foment disorder within the Ottoman realm and to supply arms to the rebels, whether Serbs, Montenegrins, or Mainotes.[40] Kara (Black) Georges was known to his own countrymen as Tzerni Georges, 'the bold creation of wild countries and troubled times, a man with an impetuous courage, iron strength, original talent, and doubtful morality.'[41] During the revolt of 1806-7, Black Georges seized the city of Belgrade and besieged the citadel, forcing the Pasha of Belgrade, Suleiman, to capitulate; allowing the latter to retire safely with his troops first, before some distance away, massacring all of them.[42] Once the army was disposed of, there followed what would occur repeatedly between 1806 and 1922 in the wake of every Turkish defeat or Christian retreat: the mass-killing of Turkish civilians. The Serbs first cut the men, then the children to pieces, then finally disemboweled the women or reduced them to slavery.[43]

Following their success against the Ottomans, the Serbs turned their land into independent principalities under various warlords. The two leading ones were Black Georges who ruled in Schumadia; the other was Milosh Obrenovich, who

---

[36] E.L. Clark: *Turkey*; P.F. Collier &Son; New York; 1878; p. 388.
[37] E. Driault: *La Question*; op cit; p. 90.
[38] See an able and valuable Consular Report in the *London Mail* for December 15, 1875.
[39] E.L. Clark: *Turkey*; op cit; p. 382. E. Driault: op cit; 90.
[40] Sutherland Menzies: *Turkey Old and New*, op cit; p.111.
[41] Ranke, p. 131, note; in E.L. Clark: *Turkey*; p. 382.
[42] Sutherland Menzies: *Turkey Old and New*, op cit; p.140.
[43] Ibid.

ruled over Eudnik, from Vonitza to Semendria; and in the end, whilst the country was freed from the Ottomans, it found itself sank in anarchy.[44]

In 1813, the Ottomans concluded one of their countless wars with the Russians. Once that was done and in reminiscence of Serb atrocities, the Ottomans returned to Serbia with a vast army. Kara Georges issued a proclamation in which he said:

> The Turks have sworn to decapitate every Serb above seven years of age, and to carry into slavery the women and children, and to make Mussulmans of them in order to colonize Servia with other people; but are not these the same Turks that we have defeated unarmed, whilst now we possess 500 cannon, seven fortresses, and forty redoubts steeped in Ottoman blood?[45]

In the fighting that ensued, the Ottomans crushed the Serbs wherever they encountered them, and the Serbs, including Kara Georges, fled in every direction

> The cowardice and defection of his civil and military servants, who were stealing in crowds across the Austrian frontier for safety [says Clark] seemed to have filled him with deep and hopeless despondency... Without one effort for the preservation of the imperilled freedom of his native land, he too joined the swelling current of fugitives, and stole ignominiously across the Danube.[46]

And so the Ottomans were back in control in Serbia.

Two years later, on Palm Sunday 1815, another uprising occurred at Takovo, led by Milosh Obrenovich, the other main warlord.[47] The revolt spread fast, and soon the fortress of Passarovicz was captured and, once more, the Ottomans were expelled from the country. Kara Georges returned from exile eager to take a leading part in the movement, but Obrenovich had him murdered and sent his head to the Pasha of Belgrade.[48] Sultan Mahmud, under pressure from Russia, granted terms to the Serbs and met their claims, including retaining their army, the right to collect their own taxes, and to share in the administration of justice.[49]

Russia was now amongst the club of the big powers, France, Britain, and Austria to a lesser degree, which henceforth increasingly dictated Ottoman policy, meddling in the affairs of the realm to such a degree, it gradually became impossible for the Ottomans to undertake any coherent set of measures. The following highlights the problem: Napoleon, who had risen to great power on the continent, in 1806, sent as his emissary to Istanbul, Sebastiani, a monk turned diplomat. Sebastiani demanded in the name of the Emperor that the Bosphorus should be closed to all Russian ships that carried troops or armament, and insisted that to leave that passage open to the Russians would be

---

[44] Ibid.
[45] Ibid; p. 142.
[46] E.L. Clark: *Turkey*; P.F. Collier &Son; New York; 1878; pp. 394-5.
[47] W.E.D. Allen: *The Turks in Europe;* John Murray London, 1919, p. 108.
[48] Ibid.
[49] Ibid.

> A violation of neutrality, and to give the French the right of passing over Ottoman territory to attack them upon the shores of the Dneister, and any renewal or even any continuation of alliance with England or Russia would be considered as an accession to the war against France. The French army in Dalmatia had no other object than to maintain the integrity of the Ottoman Empire; but should the Sublime Porte unite itself with the enemies of France, the Emperor would be constrained to give to that army a destination quite opposite to that which it had had hitherto.[50]

As they were being remonstrated by the French, the Ottomans were soon warned by the Russians, also in no uncertain terms. Italinski, the Russian ambassador at the Porte, demanded the conclusion of a defensive and offensive alliance against France, and the recognition of the Tsar as Protector of the Ottoman Christians.[51]

Not to be left out, at precisely the same time, the British ambassador, Sir Charles Arbuthnot, boldly demanded the expulsion of Sebastiani, the cession of Moldavia and Wallachia to Russia, the giving up of the Ottoman fleet to England, as well as the forts and batteries of the Dardanelles, and threatened an expedition against Istanbul if the British demands were not accepted.[52]

The Ottomans, of course refused. In earnest, Admiral Duckworth, on 19 February 1807, at daybreak, taking advantage of a favourable wind and the Feast of Bayram, which made the Turks careless in guarding the batteries, forced the Dardanelles, anchored before Istanbul, and delivered an ultimatum, demanding the immediate expulsion of Sebastiani, a declaration of war against France, an alliance with Britain and Russia, and the cession of the Danubian principalities to Russia, otherwise Istanbul lay at the mercy of the British guns.[53] As the Ottomans were slow to yield, the British found the Ottoman fleet near Nagara Point (Gallipoli), and there, totally annihilated it, with only one brig escaping.[54]

That same year (Summer 1807), Napoleon and Tsar Alexander met at Tilsit to 'form an Imperial Duumvirate of the world,' the partition of the Ottoman Empire one of the chief subjects of discussion.[55] Napoleon agreed that Russia could annex all the Rumanian lands and Northern Bulgaria; Austria was to be silenced by having Bosnia and Serbia whilst France would have Albania, Thessaly, the Morea, and Crete, which would give it command of the Eastern Mediterranean, and Syria and Egypt, which would open the road to India.[56] From the correspondence of Napoleon with Sebastiani, the partition would have been a little bit more different: France would get Bosnia, Albania, Epirus, all Greece, Thessaly, and Macedonia; Austria would receive Serbia; and Russia would obtain Wallachia,

---

[50] Sutherland Menzies: *Turkey Old and New;* op cit; vol 2; p.112.
[51] W.E.D. Allen: *The Turks in Europe*, op cit; p. 98.
[52] Sutherland Menzies: *Turkey Old and New*, op cit; p. 116.
[53] W.E.D. Allen: *The Turks in Europe;* op cit; p. 98.
[54] Sutherland Menzies: *Turkey Old and New*; op cit; p. 117.
[55] W.E.D. Allen: *The Turks in Europe*, op cit; p. 103.
[56] ibid.

Moldavia, Bulgaria, and Thrace, as far as the Maritza; this would have left Ottoman Turkey (in Europe) with Istanbul and the portion of Thrace comprised between Bourgas (Burgas) and Enos (Enez).[57]

It just happened that at that precise juncture, in Istanbul, there was great chaos following the deposition of Sultan Selim III in 1807, his replacement with Mustafa IV, who ruled for just over a year from May 1807 until July 1808, before he was removed in favour of Mahmud II (1808-1839). Russia used 'the deplorable condition into which the empire of the Osmanli had fallen,' asking for the prompt partition of the Ottoman Empire. 'Turkey,' said Tsar Alexander, 'is a succession which cannot fail to fall to Russia, in failure of heirs.'[58] And, because of that, he was no longer happy with what had been agreed with Napoleon, but also asked for cession to him of Istanbul and the Straits. The French Ambassador at St. Petersburg tried to explain to the Tsar that this was impossible, for should Russia's demands be met, it would control the commerce of the Levant and even of India, and she would, when she desired it, 'be at the gates of Corfu, Toulon, and anywhere.' Alexander replied that 'Constantinople would merely be for Russia a provincial city at the extremity of the Empire, that geography gave it her, that it was necessary that he (the Tsar) should hold the key of his house.'[59]

On hearing this, Napoleon, we are told, placed his finger on that spot on the map, and passionately exclaimed:

'Constantinople! Constantinople! Never! for it is the empire of the world!'[60]

Then Napoleon concluded,

> We ought to delay the ruin of that (Ottoman) Empire until the moment at which the partition of those vast remains can be effected without having to fear that England may come to appropriate, by the acquisition of Egypt and the isles, the richest of the spoils.[61]

The matter of Istanbul and the Straits would in fact remain the main point of contention between France and Britain on one side, and Russia on the other, and until the First World War. In fact, it was this contention which saved Turkey from being wiped out in the 19th century. Only late 1914-early 1915 would at last France and Britain agree for Russia to have Istanbul and the Straits following what they were hoping to be their victory at Gallipoli in the early Spring of 1915. Gallipoli, instead, proved to be an Ally disaster. And then, in 1917, there took place the biggest ever shift in history: following the Bolshevik Revolution, the new Soviet Russia not only renounced all her previous claims (including over 'Constantinople'), but even denounced the partitioning of the Ottoman realm.[62] It was not just one of the greatest U-turns in policy, it was also one of the most

---

[57] Sutherland Menzies: *Turkey Old and New*; op cit; p. 129.
[58] Ibid; p. 135.
[59] Ibid; p. 136.
[60] W.E.D. Allen: *The Turks in Europe;* op cit; p. 104.
[61] Sutherland Menzies: *Turkey Old and New*, op cit; p. 136.
[62] See chapter on war of independence.

ironic: Russia which had fought countless wars to get Istanbul, now that it was at last offered to her, she no longer wanted it.

Greece, throughout the 19th century, became the main instrument for the gradual break up of the Ottoman realm for the benefit of both the great powers and Greece herself. Initially, and remembering the perennial hatred between the Western and Eastern Churches, as Sutherland Menzies expresses it, the Greeks,

> Who had preserved in slavery all their hatred of the Latins, turned themselves hopefully towards the barbarians of the North (i.e the Russians), whom they regarded thenceforward as their liberators, from whom they received secret presents, and whose agents they welcomed.[63]
>
> "The Greeks," says the English historian, Rycaut, who wrote in 1670, "hold the Muscovite in great consideration, and have more friendship for him than for the other Christian princes; they commonly call him their Emperor and protector; and, according to all their prophecies, ancient and modern, he is destined to be the restorer of their church and of their freedom."
>
> "They flatter themselves," says the Frenchman, Tournefort, who travelled in the Archipelago in 1700, "that the Grand Duke of Muscovy will some day extricate them from the misery in which they now are, and that he will destroy the Empire of the Turks."
>
> "They are persuaded," says the Jesuit Souciet, missionary at Thessalonica in 1708, "that the Czar will deliver them one day from the domination of the Ottomans."[64]

Already during his rule, Tsar Peter the Great of Russia (1672-1725) announced to the Greeks 'The approaching restoration of the Byzantine Empire.'[65]

When Catherine II came to power in 1762 (r.till 1796), she revived Peter's plans. Russian agents stirred Greeks and Montenegrins into anti-Ottoman uprisings in 1768, whilst a Russian fleet largely commanded by Englishmen sailed to the Peloponnese, received the submission of 18 islands in the Archipelago, and even threatened Istanbul itself.[66] Russian agents continued to stir up the Greeks, and, in the Spring of 1790, Catherine received in St. Petersburg a deputation of Greeks, who demanded her assistance 'to free the descendants of Athens and Lacedaemon from the tyrannous yoke of ignorant savages.'[67]

Some wealthy merchants fitted out a fleet of thirteen frigates, under the command of Lambros Caviziani, but he was defeated by a Turco-Algerian squadron, and the Greek cause was soon abandoned by Russia at the Treaty of Jassy in 1792.[68]

---

[63] Sutherland Menzies: *Turkey Old and New*; op cit; p. 4.
[64] Ibid.
[65] W. Miller: *The Ottoman Empire 1801-1913*; Cambridge University Press; 1913, p. 6.
[66] Ibid, p. 7.
[67] W.E.D. Allen: *The Turks in Europe;*, op cit; p. 109.
[68] Ibid.

A few years later, prospects seemed brighter, when once more the idea of a restoration of the Byzantine Empire with Napoleon's help became general among the Greeks, and Napoleon began to be seen as 'a deliverer of the Hellenic race.'[69]

Then, in 1814, the Philike Hetairia, or Friendly Society, dedicated to the idea of greater and independent Greece, was founded at Odessa, and during the following six years, its agents worked strenuously to prepare the great uprising throughout the Morea and the Islands.[70] The movement attracted the support of the Great Powers, of course, but also the nobles, and even Ali Pasha of Janina.[71] A Phanariote noble, Prince Alexander Ypsilanti, who was also a general at the service of Russia, was appointed by the Society 'General Commissioner of the Supreme Authority.'[72]

By early 1821, the Greeks were shipping arms and gunpowder into the Peloponnese, and whilst the Ottomans were at war with Persia and besieging Ali of Janina, the Greeks began a revolt in the Morea in late March 1821.[73] At an agreed signal, the Greeks rose and massacred all the Turks — men, women and children — on whom they could lay hands.[74] The massacres of Turks were horrific, and although witnessed by many Europeans, they remained largely concealed from general knowledge, to this day in fact. As far as historical narrative goes, it was the Turks, instead, who were responsible for the outrages.

Whilst the Greeks were killing civilians en masse, the Ottomans were engaged in one of their endless wars with the Persians.[75] Here, it ought to be noted that the Persian army was being strengthened by the British, whilst the Russians were prompting the Persians to take advantage of Ottoman problems in order to compensate for their losses to Russia by taking some territories from the Ottomans.[76] Consequently, as a Persian army captured Bayezit (Sept 1821) and advanced on Erzurum, a second took Bitlis and marched toward Diyarbakır, both armies threatening to tear away eastern Turkey until an epidemic of cholera devastated their ranks.[77] Following that, the Russians themselves invaded Persia, captured Erivan and even Tabriz (1827), which curbed Persian military actions.[78]

Elsewhere, after they terminated the military power of Ali of Janina, the Ottomans returned to the Greek business. The Greeks had rebelled with Franco-British assistance (with arms, finance and political support) and propaganda, too.[79] Many

---

[69] W. Miller: *The Ottoman Empire 1801-1913*; op cit, p. 4.
[70] W.E.D. Allen: *The Turks in Europe;* op cit, p. 110.
[71] Ibid.
[72] Ibid.
[73] S.J. Shaw and E.K. Shaw: *History of the Ottoman Empire and Modern Turkey*; vol 2; Cambridge University Press; 1977; p. 18.
[74] T. Gordon, *History of the Greek Revolution,* 2 vols; Edinburgh, William Blackwood, 1832.
[75] W.E.D. Allen: *The Turks in Europe;* op cit, p. 112.
[76] S.J. Shaw and E.K. Shaw: *History of the Ottoman Empire;* op cit; p. 16.
[77] Ibid.
[78] Ibid.
[79] Details in E. Driault: *La Question*; op cit; and A. Sorel: *The Eastern;* op cit.

leading figures from the West brought in cash (which the Greek leaders stole and fought over), arms, and other forms of support. Quite famed amongst these figures were the poet Byron and Colonel Heideck, the agent of the King of Bavaria; also Lord Cochrane, Sir Richard Church, the Italian Santa Rosa, and the French Colonel Fabvier, all doing their best for the Greek cause.[80] However, by 1825-1826, the Ottomans, assisted by the Egyptians, were crushing the Greeks on all fronts, pushing them back to Missolonghi, which finally was taken after a long siege (April 30, 1825-April 23, 1826).[81] This was not to the liking of the Great Powers. The Duke of Wellington, subsequently British Prime Minister, in earnest journeyed to St. Petersburg and came to an agreement with the Emperor Nicholas, which developed later into the Treaty of London of 6th July 1827, which also included France.[82] By the terms of the Treaty, France, Britain and Russia agreed to send a fleet to the Mediterranean to fight the Ottomans, which, on 20 October 1827, ended in the burning of the Ottoman-Egyptian navy at Navarino.[83] This meant not just the destruction of the whole Ottoman fleet, it cut off Ibrahim Pasha, the son of Muhammad Ali of Egypt from reinforcements and supplies from home, and secured the Greek rebels ultimate victory.[84]

> In a sense [say S.J. and E.K. Shaw] it also it provided the pattern for a series of European interventions in Ottoman affairs that was to reduce the empire to what appeared at times later in the century to be a puppet dancing at the end of an imperialistic string.[85]

Whilst the fleet was being destroyed, French troops, under Marshal Maison, were completing 'the deliverance of the Greek territory.'[86]

The destruction of the Ottoman fleet served Russia immensely, and so it declared war on the Ottomans in April 1828. Promptly, the Russians crossed the Balkans, and, on the 19th of August, after a string of victories, General Diebitch found himself under the walls of Adrianople, thus forcing the Ottomans to agree terms. Amongst such terms, the Ottomans agreed that the Dardanelles should be open to ships of all nations, as well as to recognise Russia's protectorate over Greece and the Danubian Principalities, and all the Turkish fortresses established on the left shore of the Danube were to be rased to the ground.[87]

Even more crippling, the Ottomans were to pay about 16,000,000 Francs to 'the Russian merchants who had experienced losses in the war,' and also a war indemnity of 125,000,000 Francs, to be paid in ten years at the rate of 12,500,000 Francs annually.[88] After the payment of the first instalment, Adrianople would be

---

[80] W.E.D. Allen: *The Turks in Europe;* op cit; p. 117.
[81] S.J. Shaw and E.K. Shaw: *History of the Ottoman Empire*; op cit; p. 19.
[82] W.E.D. Allen: *The Turks in Europe;* op cit; p. 117.
[83] H. Inalcik: Chronology of the Ottoman Empire; op cit; p. 101.
[84] S.J. Shaw and E.K. Shaw: *History of the Ottoman Empire*; op cit; p. 30.
[85] Ibid.
[86] E. Creasy: *Turkey*; The H.W. Snow and Son Company; 1910; p. 425.
[87] A. Gilson: *The Czar and the Sultan*, Harper and Brothers, Publishers; New York; 1853; p. 39.
[88] Sutherland Menzies: *Turkey Old and New*, op cit; p. 177.

evacuated; after the second, the Russians would cross back to the Balkans; after the third, they would re-pass the Danube; finally, at the last payment they would entirely leave Ottoman territory.[89]

> Thus, that treaty [Sutherland Menzies remarks] was calculated to deal the final blow to Turkey, already mortally stricken by the battle of Navarino: in the state of exhaustion in which that empire was, the war contribution of 125,000,000 francs, made it an impossibility for the Sultan to create anew a fleet and an army.[90]

Also amongst the terms of the treaty, Russian subjects

> Residing or travelling in Turkey would solely depend upon the jurisdiction and the police of the ambassadors and consuls of Russia; no Russian vessel might be boarded by the Turkish authorities, whether at sea or in the harbours belonging to the Sublime Porte.[91]

Of all the treaties between Russia and the Ottomans, the Treaty of Adrianople was the most favourable to the nationalities: Wallachia and Moldavia preserved the rights and privileges recognised by the preceding treaties; no Muslim subject was to reside in the two principalities, and eighteen months were given to the Turks who were dwelling there to sell their properties and depart.[92] The autonomy of Serbia was also recognised, and France took advantage of all this to colonise Algeria and throw the Turks out of there in 1830.

2. From One War to the Eve of Another (1831 till 1875)

The new decade began with the very resentful Muhammad Ali of Egypt seeking his dues. He deemed himself badly rewarded for his services to the Sultan (or those of his son Ibrahim more properly) in Greece in the mid 1820s, and so made great many demands.[93] In truth, all he could see was an Ottoman realm with its power broken, and he, too, wanted some spoils just like everyone else. And so, he prepared himself well, and then when all was ready, in 1832, he picked a quarrel with the Pasha of Syria, and pretending to make war against him and not against the Sultan, he sent an army under Ibrahim across the desert into Syria. The army effected precisely the reverse course of what Selim I did in 1517, whether in terms of its march or in the effects of it. It first captured Gaza and Jerusalem without much effort, and then marched on to Acre, where the Egyptian fleet met it and co-operated in a successful attack, before sweeping through Syria and capturing Aleppo and Damascus defeating two Ottoman armies en course.[94]

---

[89] Ibid.
[90] Ibid.
[91] Ibid; p. 176.
[92] Ibid.
[93] For the best of Muhammad Ali's rule, policies and wars, there is the unsurpassed and impossible to equal work by the Frenchman G. Hanotaux on the history of Egypt: *Histoire de la Nation Egyptienne*; Plon, Paris, 1936. Vol vi Egypt from 1801 to 1882; absolute exquisite reading.
[94] Lord Eversley: *The Turkish Empire, its Growth and Decay*; Dodd, Mead & Company; New York; 1917; p. 281.

Ibrahim then crossed the mountains into Asia Minor, fought another great battle at Konya on 27 October 1832, defeated a large Ottoman army, then marched onto Bursa, his progress causing great alarm.[95] Oddly, the only support the Ottomans got was from Russia, obviously not that it suddenly became fond of the Turks, but simply, here Muhammad Ali had emerged as another competitor for the spoils. In February 1833, a Russian fleet issuing from Sebastopol conveyed an army to the Bosphorus for the defence of Istanbul.[96] This obviously alarmed both France and Britain, thus starting a wrangle between the powers and Muhammad Ali, who now realised they might all get together against him, forcing him to come to an arrangement with the Sultan in 1833. Whilst he was temporarily satisfied with Syria and Crete, his ambitions were far from quelled though. So, in 1838, having built an even stronger army, he provoked another war driving Sultan Mahmud to send to Syria a land force and also a large fleet in 1839.[97] It all ended again in yet another Ottoman disaster: The army was crushed in Syria on 25 June 1839 whilst the fleet's commander simply sailed to Alexandria and handed over his ships to the enemy.[98] The only fortunate thing for Sultan Mahmud was that he died on 1 July 1839 before learning about the two disasters, thus ending the reign of a sultan who surely had shown vision and great grit, but in whose favour events were not. As for Muhammad Ali, his ambitions were finally quelled by the great powers as they were not too glad to see the rise of a force that might disturb their long-term schemes; and so, under the powers' pressure, the Sultan passed, on 13 February 1841, a firman (decree) establishing Muhammad Ali as governor of Egypt, with the position to remain thereafter in the hands of his family, under more or less symbolic Ottoman suzerainty.

Whilst on Egypt, briefly, this arrangement did not last. Egypt was gradually brought under firm Western control. The rising Western influence soon turned into widespread looting of the country's wealth thanks to the policies of Ismail Pasha, the Khedive, who was put in charge of the country in 1863 by Western powers.[99] He was extravagant, spending as if there was no tomorrow on entertainments, palaces, failed schemes...[100] Western banks were obliging and lent him money at exorbitant rates which plunged Egypt into heavy indebtedness which threatened its independence.[101] Revolted by this state of affairs, Egyptian officers, led by Arabi, removed the Khedive from power in 1882, prompting French and British consuls to deliver a joint note to the Egyptian government demanding the return of the Khedive.[102] Egyptian refusal was met with a bombardment of Alexandria on 11 July 1882, a landing of British forces, the occupation of Cairo on 14 September 1882, the removal of Arabi, and 'bringing things back to order' by

---

[95] Ibid; p. 282.
[96] Ibid.
[97] Ibid; p. 284.
[98] Ibid.
[99] Viscount Milner: *England in Egypt*; Edward Arnold; London; 1907; p. 176.
[100] Ibid; p. 177.
[101] M Morsy: *North Africa*; op cit; p. 173.
[102] J.C.B. Richmond, *Egypt, 1798-1952*, Methuen & Co Ltd; London; 1977; p. 128.

putting Egypt under British control.[103] And so was gone another Ottoman province.

The Crimea War 1853-1856

> Réveillés en sursaut de leur long sommeil par le péril de leur race et de leur nom, attaqués en pleine paix par envahissement de leurs mers et de leur territoire, insultés dans leurs foyers, outragés dans leur indépendance, incendiés dans leurs ports, submergés de toutes parts par des armées... les Turcs, debout sur ce qui leur reste de frontières, les armes du désespoir à la main, combattent sans regarder devant eux ni derrière eux pour savoir si la Turquie ressuscitera dans son sang ou pour mourir avant le dernier jour de leur patrie.
> Translation: Startled from their long slumber by the perils to their race and name, attacked in the midst of peace by an invasion of their seas and territory, insulted in their dwellings, murdered in their ports, overwhelmed on all sides by armies... the Turks, standing fast upon what's left of their frontiers, the arms of despair in their hands, are fighting without looking in front of themselves or behind to know whether Turkey shall be regenerated in its blood, or for them to die before the last hour of their nation. (Thus wrote Lamartine at the height of the Crimean War, in 1855.)[104]

It was in fact a fire in 1808 which was at the origin of the Crimea War. This fire sparked into life again the old demon: the perennial hatred between the Western and Greek Orthodox Churches. The fire in question devastated the Church of the Holy Sepulchre in Jerusalem, and the Greeks, maybe because wealthier, or more caring, or faster, did all the repairs, and consequently deemed themselves worthy to seize control over all the Holy Places.[105] Now that Russian power had become more assertive, Russian pilgrims gradually flooded Jerusalem especially after Czar Nicholas rebuilt two old Orthodox monasteries for their use (1841).[106] All this was looked on with disquiet by the traditional foes. The French, whose protection of the Holy Sepulchre and other sacred edifices were the symbols of they being the leaders of the Crusades (1095-1291), and also the protectors of Catholic Christians in the East, were not particularly happy.[107] Accordingly, the French government demanded from the Sultan, who ruled over Palestine, new privileges for Latin clergy (1850), which triggered a three-year period of

---
[103] Ibid; pp. 129-31.
[104] A. De Lamartine: *Histoire de la Turquie*, Paris, 1855, tr., as *History of Turkey*; 3 vols, tr., from French; D. Appleton and Company; New York; 1855; vol 1. Preface; p. 2.
[105] Sutherland Menzies: *Turkey Old and New*, op cit; p. 200.
[106] S.J. Shaw and E.K. Shaw: *History of the Ottoman Empire*; op cit; p. 137.
[107] See Rear-Admiral Sir Adolphus Slade: *Turkey and the Crimean War*; Smith, Elder &CO; London, 1867; chapter IV.

demands and counter-demands on the Sultan by Catholics and Orthodox straining the wits of the poor Sultan, who wished to antagonise neither side.[108] Among the demands were those made in May 1851 by Louis Napoleon, who, after having invoked the capitulations of 1740, insisted on the possession of the Holy Places, including: the Holy Sepulchre, the Great Cupola built above the Holy Sepulchre; the Tomb of the Virgin, the Seven-Arched Vaults of the Virgin; the Upper Church of Bethlehem, with the gardens and cemeteries dependent thereon; and declared, moreover, that the Latins 'consented to make particular concessions to the other communions, but renewable annually.'[109] The Emperor of Russia, Nicholas, was left livid, and was even more annoyed to see that France had just obtained a favourable answer and that the Ottomans authorised the Latins to build an ambry in the cave of Bethlehem.[110] Of course the Tsar could not act alone against France, including declaring war, especially if France went into alliance with Britain. So, he decided on another course and tried to restore the old cooperation with Britain (as against Napoleon Bonaparte in 1815) by reaching an agreement for division of the spoils once the Ottoman Empire was broken up.[111] At St. Petersburg, in 1853, the Tsar had a private conversation with Sir Hamilton Seymour, the British Ambassador, an exchange whose substance is excellently summed up by the contemporary Lord Eversley.[112] During the conversation, the Tsar said:

> Now, I desire to speak to you as a friend, and as a gentleman. If England and I arrive at an understanding in this matter, as regards the rest it little matters to me. It is indifferent to me what others do or think. Frankly, then, I tell you plainly that, if England thinks of establishing herself one of these days at Constantinople, I will not allow it. For my part, I am equally disposed to take the engagement not to establish myself there— as proprietor, that is to say— for as occupier I do not say; it might happen that circumstances, if no previous provisions were made, if everything should be left to chance, might place me in the position of occupying Constantinople.[113]

The British ambassador did not apparently commit himself, or maybe he did, but this we don't know. What is certain is that the Tsar was convinced he had London's support for efforts to counter the French in the Holy Land.[114] Hence, in earnest, he sent to Istanbul his envoy, Prince Mentschikoff, who demanded the guardianship of the Holy Sepulchre, in opposition to that of France, with further demands regarding the protection of the Greek Church throughout the Ottoman

---

[108] S.J. Shaw and E.K. Shaw: *History of the Ottoman Empire*; op cit; p. 137.
[109] Sutherland Menzies: *Turkey Old and New*, op cit; p. 201.
[110] Ibid; p. 201- 203.
[111] S.J. Shaw and E.K. Shaw: *History of the Ottoman Empire*; op cit; p. 137.
[112] Lord Eversley: *The Turkish Empire, its Growth and Decay*; op cit; p. 294 ff.
[113] Ibid; pp. 295-6. The conversations are reported in Parliamentary Papers, 1854, Eastern Question, House of Commons, 84.
[114] S.J. Shaw and E.K. Shaw: *History of the Ottoman Empire*; op cit; p. 137.

realm.[115] He moreover, demanded an answer in five days and insisted that should the Ottomans fail to reply satisfactorily, harsh retributions would result.[116]

The Turks refused to reply, and on 18 May, Mentschikoft, after having renewed his threatening demands, declared his mission terminated: 'The refusal of a guarantee for the Orthodox worship,' he said, 'would henceforth impose upon the Imperial Government the necessity of seeking it in its proper power.'[117]

On 21 May, a note from Count Nesselrode, Minister of the Czar, declared that the Russian armies were about to enter the Danubian Principalities in order to occupy them until the Porte agreed the demands laid down by Prince Mentschikoff.[118]

> The right claimed by Russia [he said] is similar to that which France has exercised over the Catholics of the Ottoman Empire for centuries; it confers no right of perpetual intermeddling in the interior affairs of that Empire.[119]

The Ottomans refusing to give in, Russian troops crossed the Pruth on 3 July 1853, and at once entered Wallachia and Moldavia. This prompted Turkey to declare war.[120] And so began the Crimea War, perhaps the bloodiest conflict of the 19th century.[121] The Ottomans fought alone for the rest of 1853 and the first months of 1854, the most notable event of this period being the utter destruction of the Ottoman fleet at Sinop on 30 November 1853.[122] Then, in the spring of 1854, once the conditions became right, the French and British agreed with the Ottomans an offensive and defensive treaty and went in.[123] The immense superiority of their navies allowed them to attack Russia in all the seas, beginning with the bombardment of Odessa (22 April 1854), before the conflict entered its bloodiest phase.[124] It was a war of attrition, perhaps the first truly modern war, involving all forms of warfare from cavalry charges, to naval battles, costly sieges, trench warfare, assaults and counter-assaults, besides diseases, cold and hunger assisting in the work of death.[125] The conflict lasted until the Treaty of Paris of 30 March 1856, which caused Russia to lose both the domination of the Black Sea and the protectorate of the Eastern Christians, thus literally extinguishing the gains made by all previous Russian rulers, besides ruining the fleets and naval

---

[115] Lord Eversley: *The Turkish Empire, its Growth and Decay*; op cit; p. 298.
[116] For the development of the issue, see Rear-Admiral Sir Adolphus Slade: *Turkey and the Crimean War*; op cit; chapters IV and V.
[117] Sutherland Menzies: *Turkey Old and New*, op cit; p. 202.
[118] Ibid; p. 204.
[119] Ibid.
[120] For Turkish preparations and refusal to bend to Russian pressure, see Rear-Admiral Sir Adolphus Slade: *Turkey and the Crimean War*; chapters VI; VII; VIII, and also IX for early military engagements.
[121] The Literature on this conflict is vast, and includes:
C. Badem: *The Ottoman Crimea War*; Leiden; Brill; 2014.
O. Figes: *Crimea the last Crusade*; Allen Lane; 2010.
A.J. Taylor: *The Struggle for Mastery in Europe, 1848-1918*; 1954.
[122] Rear-Admiral Sir Adolphus Slade: *Turkey and the Crimean War*; see chapter X for all the details; the author was involved to a large degree in the sea operations; also chapter xi.
[123] W.S. Monroe: *Turkey and the Turks*; L.C. Page and Company; Boston; 1907; p. 37. Sutherland Menzies: *Turkey Old and New*, op cit; p. 205.
[124] See the older works such as J. Ladimir: *La Guerre en Orient;* Renault Editeur; Paris; 1855.
[125] C. Badem: *The Ottoman Crimea War*; op cit; O. Figes: *Crimea the Last Crusade*; op cit.

arsenals created by previous Russian admirals. 'The imprudent policy of Nicholas,' says Sutherland Menzies, 'had compromised the work of two centuries of successful efforts.'[126]

But this was not the only consequence. An Ottoman force under Omar Pasha was sent to Eupatoria, where it was attacked by a much stronger Russian army early in 1855.[127] Protected only by earthworks it fought with such great resolve and courage, it completely repulsed the Russians. It was said that 'the humiliation of this defeat of his troops by the despised Turks,' was the immediate cause of the death of Emperor Nicholas on 2 March 1855.[128]

Although the Crimea War seems to have ended rather positively for the Ottomans, it was just an interlude, and much worse, it witnessed the beginning of a trend which is unique in History: The Turks entered a phase whereby they soon became the most displaced people in history. Indeed, it is not just in their numbers that the Turks became uprooted from their lands of settlements, but also in the frequency of their displacements. Some Turks, as will be seen further on, were displaced four to five times in succession in their lifetime. Toynbee, the British historian, would find in 1921 in Istanbul families of Turks who had been displaced six times.[129] Some, he would also find, had been living in the courtyards of mosques for more than a decade.[130] It was the scenes of distress of refugees which subsequently deeply affected people such as Halide Edib[131] and Mustafa Kemal, who saw people from his native Salonika massed together in the courtyards of the mosques, ragged and destitute, in the cruel winter weather, his own mother and sister among them.[132] The problem for Ottoman Turkey was not in not taking care of its refuges, the problem was that as soon as it resolved one crisis, or before it even resolved it, hundreds of thousands more of expelled or fleeing Turks arrived. Why they fled will be explained in the final heading of this chapter and throughout this work.

The problem began precisely in the wake of the Crimea War; and the Ottoman authorities responded very quickly when in 1857 they introduced the Refugee Code *(Muhacirin Kanunnamesi)* of that same year, whereby immigrant families and groups with only a minimum amount of capital (stipulated at 60 gold *mecidiye* coins, about 1500 French Francs at that time) were given plots of state land with facilities of diverse sorts to help them.[133]

Here, it is important to take note of another fact of importance, unique to Ottoman Turkey. Long before any other nation, it had opened its lands to most

---

[126] Sutherland Menzies: *Turkey Old and New*, op cit; p. 214.
[127] Lord Eversley: *The Turkish Empire, its Growth and Decay*; op cit; p. 304.
[128] Ibid.
[129] A.J. Toynbee: *The Western Question in Greece and Turkey*; Constable; 1922; p. 139.
[130] Ibid; p. 169 ff.
[131] Halide Edib: *Turkish Ordeal;* p. 65 ff. Halid Edib: *Memoirs*; pp. 285-295; and also chapter xiv, the Balkan war; 329 ff.
[132] Lord P. Kinross: *Ataturk: The Rebirth of a Nation*; Weidenfeld and Nicolson; London; 1964; p. 54.
[133] S.J. Shaw and E.K. Shaw: *History of the Ottoman Empire*; op cit; p. 115.

refugees: Christian minorities who were persecuted for their beliefs;[134] the Jews who were being persecuted everywhere for who they were;[135] in fact, in 1454 Isaac Sarfati, a Jew born in Germany of French descent, sent a circular letter to the Jews of the Rhineland, Swabia, Styria, Moravia, and Hungary depicting their good fortune 'under the Crescent in contrast to their yoke under the Cross;'[136] likewise Muslims who were expelled from al Andalus;[137] then many Algerians including leaders of the anti French resistance, such as Emir Abd al Kader, who settled after 1852 in Bursa until the earthquake there,[138] or Bou Ma'za, who died fighting alongside the Ottomans in the Crimean War;[139] and countless others who would keep on seeking shelter under the umbrella of Othman.

In 1860, in order to help process the requests and settle the refugees, a Refugee Commission *(Muhacirin Komisyonu)* was established, at first in the Ministry of Trade and then as an independent agency a year later.[140] These measures were in response to an influx of Turkish Tatars and Circassians who were losing their lands to the Russians north and west of the Black Sea and the Caspian.[141] Prior to that, tens of thousands of Muslims had fled from diverse places from the repressions that accompanied and followed the Nationalist revolutions of 1848, especially from Hungary, Bohemia, and Poland.[142] Then, following the Crimean War, the situation simply exploded as the Russians abandoned their previous relatively tolerant policy toward the Tatars and Circassians into one of active persecution and resettlement from their original homes, pushing them to desolate areas in Siberia and even farther east.[143] As the Russians encouraged flight, this led to the Russianisation and Christianisation of the southern parts of their empire.[144] These measures might have affected around 176,700 Tatars from the Nogay and Kuban, who arrived between 1854 and 1860, and another million, who came in from 1860 to 1876, from the Crimea alone; 1.4 million Tatars migrated into the Ottoman Empire.[145] Then, as will be seen further on, soon after, another few millions came fleeing from Greece, the Caucasus, and most especially from the Balkans.

---

[134] S. Faroqhi: *Subjects of the Sultan*, I.B. Thauris Publishers, London, 1995, p. 7. J. Delumeau: *Naissance et Affirmation de la Reforme*, Paris, PUF, 1973; 1977. T. Arnold: *The Preaching of Islam*; M. Ashraf Publishers; Lahore; 1979; p. 149 ff. G. Finlay: *A History of Greece*; Oxford; 1877; vol 3; p. 502. T.B. Irving, Dates; Names and Places; The End of Islamic Spain; in *Revue d'Histoire Maghrebine;* No 61-62; 1991; pp. 77-93, p. 90.
[135] J. Davenport: *An Apology for Mohammed and the Koran*; J. Davy and Sons; London; 1869; pp. 126-7. F. Babinger: *Mehmed the Conqueror*; op cit; p. 106.
[136] Ibid. 107.
[137] T.B. Irving, Dates; Names and Places; The End of Islamic Spain; op cit; pp. 77-93.
[138] J.M. Abun-Nasr: *A History of the Maghrib*, op cit, p. 247.
[139] W. Blunt: *Desert Hawk*; Methuen & Co Ltd; London; 1947; p. 201.
[140] S.J. Shaw and E.K. Shaw: *History of the Ottoman Empire*; op cit; p. 115.
[141] Ibid.
[142] Ibid.
[143] Ibid; p. 116.
[144] Ibid.
[145] Ibid.

Muddling Matters and The Turkish Tartars

Two crucial issues need to be addressed at this juncture: The central one is the issue of the Turkish Tartars, and the other is how their history, just as that of the Tartars in general and the links between Turks and Mongols, is muddled today by scholarship.

Without going into complex matters, this not being within the scope of this work, let us first raise the issue of muddling of this piece of history, and then in point two deal with the Crimean Tartars.

First, countless people, including scholars who do not have a firm grasp of medieval or Mongol history, unfortunately, keep making claims, often contradictory, which turn things upside down. One, for instance reads that the Mongols killed millions of Muslims, destroyed their towns and cities, and yet also reads that the Muslims served the Mongols or were their allies. One reads that all Turkish dynasties whether in India, in the Arab East, or in Asia Minor, fought the Mongols, and yet one also reads, sometimes in the same paragraph or a few paragraphs down, that the Turks were Mongols and vice versa; one reads the Turks were 'fanatic warriors for Islam,' and then one reads the Turks were shamanists; one reads the Muslims were servants of the Mongols in China, and then one reads the Muslims played a major role in the removal of the Mongols from that same country; one reads Timur the Lame was a Ghazi of Islam, and then one goes through his life and deeds, and all one finds are his mass-killing of Muslims, mass-rape of their women, destruction of mosques, his soldiers stabling their horses in mosques, and not a single service to Islam by conquest or anything, his only attack against Christians, as will be seen further down, being against the Venetians community in order to ruin the Khanate of the Golden Horde. Then one reads that these descendants of the Golden Horde were Tartars, and so was Timur who broke their power, and that he was a Turk, and they too were Turks, and then nobody explains the difference, or why did Timur destroy their khanate. And things under the pen of some authors of today become even more muddled that in the end nothing whatsoever makes sense at all. Then, some amongst these modern scholars, the most competent amongst them being Peter Jackson,[146] repeat the unfortunate mistake one finds with most Western authors of today, who make claims which contradict fundamentally those made by tens, if not hundreds, of contemporary sources, of six or so centuries ago. Those contemporary sources, all of them that is, claim that the Mongols of the south, i.e. based in Iran, or Timur, were allies with the Christians and had great hatred for Islam, regardless if outwardly they professed the faith of Islam. Instead, modern scholars elaborate a number of theories to contradict these contemporaries, not realising that surely they cannot today, in 2020, be right in their views and claims,

---

[146] P. Jackson: *The Mongols and the West*, 1221-1410; Pearson Education Ltd; London; 2005.

and those who wrote at the time of the events, and saw things, and lived through them, all be wrong in their tens or even hundreds.

It is, indeed, a systemic practice by today's scholars to reinterpret Islamic/Turkish history as noted by this author in most of his work. We give a couple of instances here. All contemporary Christian sources or witnesses during the Crusades rejoiced at the killing of Muslims, whilst today's scholars talk instead of the humanity and devotion of the Crusaders.[147] Centuries later, colonial army officers spoke of their own murderous deeds, whilst modern scholars instead tell us about the civilising role of colonisation.[148] The widespread massacres of Turks were witnessed by contemporaries whilst modern authors claim the opposite.[149] In fact, such is the capacity of today's scholarship at reinterpreting history, Wilfried Madelung, writing in the 1990s, claims to know the secret thoughts of Prophet Mohammed.[150]

In regard to the Tartars of the Crimea, or Turkish Tartars, if we may call them by this name, they are related to the Golden Horde Mongols, that is the Mongols of the North (based in southern Russia) as opposed to the Mongols of the South (based in Tabriz, modern Iran).[151] The Golden Horde had become Muslim early in the 13th century; then they entered into conflict with the Mongols of the South because of the massacres of Muslims by these southern Mongols.[152] It ought to be reminded, that whilst the Mongols of the North and their leadership, i.e. Berke, were Muslims, and allies of the other Turkic people, including the Mamluks, Seljuks, and the Ottomans, the Mongols of the South, under the leadership of Hulagu, Mongke, Kithbukha, Kubilai (who became emperor of China), and their descendants (Abaqa, Ghazan, and so on,) converted in large measure to Christianity, or their wives or mothers were Christian.[153] In the medieval context this meant great enmity to Islam and thus their 13th century devastation of Syria, Iraq, and the Muslim East.[154] These Mongols were in continuous alliance with the

---

[147] See Chapter one of this author: *The Crusades*; Institute of Islamic History; Manchester, 2007.
[148] Contrast, for instance, the works and letters by French army officers during the colonial war in Algeria, Montagnac in particular, with writing by Hisketh; of Julien, Mantran, and even French National Assembly decision February 2005.
[149] See chapter one *Decisive Victories* by the same author.
[150] W. Madelung: *The Succession to Muhammad; a Study in the Early Caliphate*, Cambridge University Press, 1997; p. 18.
[151] P. Pelliot: *Mongols and Popes; 13th and 14th Centuries;* Paris; 1922.
-P. Pelliot: Les Mongols et la Papaute; In *Revue d'Orient Chretien*; 1923-1924; and 1931-2.
-P. Pelliot: Mellanges sur l'Epoque des Croisades; *Memoires de l'Academie des Inscriptions des Belles Lettres;* 44; 1960.
Baron G. d'Ohsson: *Histoire des Mongols*; 3 vols; La Haye et Amsterdam; 1834.
H.H. Howorth: *History of the Mongols,* London, 1927.
For an easier work, far more entertaining to read, but with less depth, see J. Curtin: *The Mongols; A History*; Greenwood Press Publishers; Westport; 1907.
[152] For the best on Mamluk Golden Horde relations, see A.A. Khowaiter: *Baibars the First;* The Green Mountain Press; London; 1978; pp. 43 ff.
[153] John of Plano Carpini: *History of the Mongols*; IV; tr. by a nun of Stanbrook Abbey in *The Mongol Mission*, C. Lawson; New York; Sheed and Ward; 1955. F. Nau, *L'expansion nestorienne en Asie*, Musée Guimet, tom. 4o, 1913-14. There are two brief German studies: W. Barthold, Zur *Geschichte des Christentums in Mittel-Asien*, Tubingen, and E. Sachau, *Zur Ausbreitung des Christentums in Asien*, Berlin, 1919. See also K.S. Latourette, *A History of the Expansion of Christianity,* vol. II, London, 1939, ch. V.C. Brunel: David Ashby, auteur meconnu des 'faits des tartares' in *Romania*, LXXIX, 1958, pp. 39-46.
[154] Baron G. d'Ohsson: *Histoire des Mongols*; 3 vols; La Haye et Amsterdam; 1834.

Christians, most particularly the French king Louis IX, who led the Crusade of 1248-50, and also with the Papacy; Iran based Mongol envoys being frequently found in the Western courts and in the Vatican.[155] The power of these southern Mongols was broken by the Turkic Mamluks at the battle of Ain Jalut in Palestine in September 1260, and after that, principally, by Baybars who was a Kiptchak Turk from the Caucasus.[156] Finally, even when amongst such southern Mongols, leaders such as Arghun and Ghazan supposedly turned Muslim, they remained in alliance with the Crusaders or with Byzantium.[157] Arghun (Ilkhan 1284-1291), in particular, is described by the Dominican missionary Ricoldo of Montecroce, who was in Baghdad in 1290, as 'A man given to the worst villainy, but for all that a friend to the Christians.[158]' The Armenian Hayton, who was the main link between the papacy and the southern Mongols, states that Ghazan (Ilkhan 1295-1304), two years after being proclaimed sultan, that is in 1297, became pro-Christian and anti-Muslim.[159] Ghazan was an ally of the Byzantines against the Ottomans.

Regarding Timur, his devastation of Islam and the Ottoman realm has been considered at great length by this author elsewhere for it to be repeated here.[160] In just few words, it was this same Timur who destroyed the power and prosperity of the Khanate of the Golden Horde. In fact it was his destruction of the Khanate which made the rise of modern Russia at their expense possible. Timur's only action against a Christian nation was precisely against the Venetians based in southern Russia, when in 1395 he destroyed Tana, on the Sea of Azov, including the Venetian outpost there.[161] This attack was the result of his desire to destroy the economy of the Golden Horde and not out of hostility towards Christians.[162] Together with the flames ended the privileges conferred on the Venetians granted by successive khans of the Golden Horde.[163] And in the flames also ended the Khanate prosperity.

Here one must add that unlike Mongol territory elsewhere, a section of the former Golden Horde territory passed under Ottoman rule in the time of Mohammed II (sometime after 1460), which led so to speak to the Turkisation of

---

H.H. Howorth: *History of the Mongols*, London, 1927.
[155] J.M. Fiey: *Chretiens Syriaques*; op cit. J.J. Saunders: *Aspects of the Crusades*; University of Canterbury; 1962; J. Richard: *La Papaute et les Missions d'Orient au Moyen Age*; Ecole Francaise de Rome; Palais Farnese; 1977
[156] See P. Thorau: *The Lion of Egypt*.
[157] See d'Ohsson: *Mongols*; vol 4; Delaville Leroulx: *La France*;
[158] Ricoldo of Montecroce, Liber peregrinationis, ed. J.C.M. Laurenr in *Peregrinatores mediiaevi quatuor*, 2nd ed (Leipzig, 1873), p. 121: *homo pessimus in omni scelere, amicus tamen Christianorum*. Cf. also 'Gestes des Chiprois', p. 843, §591 (tr. Crawford, p. 149).
[159] Hayton, iii, 39, Fr. text p. 191, Latin text p. 316. The version of events in 'Gestes des Chiprois', p. 844, §§593-4 (tr. Crawford, p. 150), is very similar.
[160] Se chap I Decisive Victories by this author.
[161] Andrea de Redusiis de Quero, 'Chronicon Tarvisinum' (down to 1428), *RIS*, XIX, cols. 802-4. More generally, W. Heyd, *Histoire du commerce du Levant* au moyen age; tr. Raynaud, 2 vols (Leipzig, 1885-6), II, pp. 374-6.
[162] See Z. Kedar, *Merchants in Crisis. Genoese and Venetian Men of Affairs and the Fourteenth-Century Depression* (New Haven, CN, and London, 1976), p. 130, for references
[163] *RDSV*, I, p. 217 (no. 927, 20 Feb. 1397).

former Mongols, but of Mongols of the North (Golden Horde), not those of the south (Ilkhan/Iran).

Therefore, people need to be perfectly clear about these very important distinctions, which, unfortunately, tend to confuse many, including Turks, whose scholarship, just like that of the rest of the Muslim world, does not shine with brilliance. This confusion and muddling of history was even used during the First World War by the British Ministry of Propaganda, when it made Turks into Mongols in order to divide Arabs and Turks by putting in the mouth of Turkish officials that it was the Turks who had destroyed Baghdad in 1258.[164] This is a confusion of the first order which has affected scholars, lay persons, and imams in their Friday sermons as heard by this author himself. For, indeed, not everyone can spend years of study on the Mongols and see the differences between them; including the difference between what Timur did, i.e, his destruction of Islam, and what is alleged about his Ghazi status; the vast difference between his apparent Islamic faith and his strong alliance with the Christian West in particular; and finally, and more importantly, being careful about the scholarly machine, and how its muddling of history serves many purposes far beyond scholarship.

3. Through the Troubled Rule of Sultan Abdul Hamid to the Eve of the Long War (1876-1910):

It did not last too long for the Ottomans to enjoy stability after the Crimean War; in fact they hardly ever had it. And here it ought to be reminded that the Turks did not start one single war throughout the 19th century and only responded when attacked. Whether the Serb rebellions from 1806 onwards; or the Greek uprisings from 1821 onwards; or the destruction of the Ottoman fleet at Navarino in 1827; or the wars that Russia unleashed on the Ottomans, whether in 1828 or at the Crimea; or the wars by Muhammad Ali, and subsequent ones until the First World War, including the 1877 war by Russia and its allies; the Cretan uprising of 1896-1897; the war in Libya in 1911; and the Balkan Wars of 1912, none of them was started or initiated by Turkey. In fact reading through the history of the period, one is astounded by the lengths to which the Turks went to try and avoid conflict, for they had realised that they needed peace and stability most of all in order to recover. But when you want something too badly….

Towards the mid-1870s there flared up a series of violent disturbances throughout Bosnia Herzegovina amongst Christian populations. The revolt began in several small villages in Herzegovina, the discontent this time arising around

---
[164] I. Karlsson: The Turk as a Threat and Europe's Other; in *International Issues and Slovak Foreign Policy;* issue 1, 2006; pp. 62-72; at p. 68.

tax issues.[165] Then followed that same scenario as before and after, whereby Christians massacred Muslims so much until the Ottoman authorities were forced to intervene to restore order and security for all.[166] This, as usual, prompted the customary outbursts of Western opinion, which S.J and E.K Shaw note, ignored Muslim deaths while the deaths of Christian rebels 'were trumpeted as massacres.'[167] Christians, whether politicians, writers, priests and archpriests, opinion makers, and whomsoever could stir a mob, called for Christian Holy War in revenge.

Abdülhamid became sultan (1876-1908) precisely at this time, commonly known as the Bulgarian Crisis. The political antecedents of this crisis go back to the Bosnian uprising of 1875 and the Serbo-Ottoman war of 1876.[168] After several failed attempts, the Bulgarian Revolutionary Central Committee took the opportunity of Ottoman involvement in dealing with the Bosnian rebels to start the uprising throughout Bulgaria.[169] The Ottomans, once more, were forced to intervene (May-June 1876) to bring back order and protect the local Muslims from being entirely wiped out, thus triggering the usual massacres and counter-massacres between Muslim and Christian villages.[170] In the end, whilst a much vaster number of Muslims were slain, the killing of 4,000 Bulgarians was turned into the 'Bulgarian horrors.'[171] American missionaries spoke of 15,000 Christians slaughtered; the Bulgarians themselves raising the figures to between 30,000 and 100,000;[172] others made it the horror of the century. Amongst them, the previous, and subsequently also, British Prime Minister, William Gladstone, gave up his religious studies to devote his all to this 'holocaust of a Christian nation.'[173] From all corners of the Christian world, Turkish 'barbarism' led to calls for Crusades against the Turks.[174] Then, to add fuel to the fire, there was an incident in Salonica on 6 May when a Bulgarian Christian girl who had converted to Islam was seized upon by a group of Greeks at the railway station and had her veil torn; Muslims intervened on her behalf, and in the ensuing violence, both the French and German consuls were killed; now war was unstoppable.[175]
Russia declared war on the Ottomans on 24 April 1877. With its allies it went on the offensive; the Ottomans, attacked from all sides, had little chance.[176] Lootsk was stormed by the Russians on 3 September; Niksic was captured by the

---

[165] Pinar Ure Immediate effects of the 1877-1878 Russo-Ottoman War on the Muslims in Bulgaria, in *History Studies* vol 13; pp. 153-170.
[166] S.J. Shaw and E.K. Shaw: *History of the Ottoman Empire*; op cit; p. 162.
[167] Ibid; p. 158.
[168] Pinar Ure: Immediate effects of the 1877-1878 Russo-Ottoman War; op cit; p. 157.
[169] Ibid; p. 158.
[170] S.J. Shaw and E.K. Shaw: *History of the Ottoman Empire*; op cit; p. 162.
[171] Ibid.
[172] Ibid.
[173] W. E. Gladstone, *Bulgarian Horrors and the Question of the East*, London: John Murray, 1876.
[174] C. Grossir: *L'Islam des Romantiques*; (Maisonneuve; Larose; Paris, 1984); p. 103.
[175] S.J. Shaw and E.K. Shaw: *History of the Ottoman Empire*; op cit; p. 162.
[176] W.S. Monroe: *Turkey and the Turks*; L.C. Page and Company; Boston; 1907; p. 43.

Montenegrins on 8 September; then more successes followed between October and December including the capture by the Russians of Kars and Plevna.[177] The year 1878 opened with the capture of Sofia by the Russians, of Nish by the Serbians, and Antivari by the Montenegrins, whilst Adrianople fell on 20 January, thus opening the way for the Russians to begin marching toward Istanbul.[178] The Ottomans sued for peace; an armistice was declared; and the treaty of San Stefano, signed on 3 March 1878, concluded the war.[179]

That was the military side. There was yet the other that always follows Turkish-Christian fighting and Turkish defeat: the wiping out of Turks. There was no exception here, the levels of atrocities being some of the worst in history.[180] Foreign observers noted the pillage and generalised massacres of Muslims and burning of their villages.[181] Muslim villagers desperately seeking flight with the retreating Ottoman army were often caught up with and there submitted to whatever their slayers felt pleased to do.[182] Bulgarian irregulars and Cossack cavalries attacked many refugee convoys, in some cases totally annihilating the fugitives, women and children included, as in the Bjala forest on 12 September 1877.[183] Confidential official Western reports spoke of systematic destruction of Turkish areas, mass-immolations of populations, and also mass-conversions to Christianity under the threat of arms.[184] Writing on 19 November 1878, the British Consul, Calvert, said:

> The Bulgarian hatchet, knife and club are meanwhile busy everywhere. It is a literal fact that every Christian is free to violate any Turkish girl or woman at will, and that the Christians exercise to the full the license accorded them, adding in the recent case of Slimnia, insult and derision to outrage, by publicly parading the victims of their brutality to the sound of bagpipe.[185]

Then there was the perennial refugee issue, which became a dominant feature of Ottoman-Turkish life for the whole period from 1853 until 1922-1923. In this instance, those who managed to escape from the massacres in their towns and villages or from attacks on refugee convoys in the countryside, there awaited them other woes. Their flight during the late autumn and through the winter

---

[177] Ibid.
[178] Ibid; pp. 43-4.
[179] Ibid; p. 44.
[180] Pinar Ure: Immediate effects; op cit; pp. 153-170. J. McCarthy: *Death and Exile: The Ethnic Cleansing of Ottoman Muslims*; op cit
[181] M. Jacquot to *Journal des Debats* in Paris. 2 July 1877.
The extermination of Turkish people by Russia, and the true policy for England (London, 1878), pp. 1-4. *Russian atrocities in Asia and Europe during the months of June. July, and August 1877* (Constantinople, 1877), p. 12.
[182] Governorate of Tulca to the ministry of interior, 23 June 1877, Justin McCarthy: *Death and Exile*; p. 157.
[183] F.O. Layard to Earl of Derby, 26 July 1877,
[184] See Foreign office reports; also R. Millman: *Britain and the Eastern Question*; Oxford; 1979; pp. 125-89.
[185] F.O. 195-1185; No 73.

seasons exposed them to the extremes of weather, famine, and epidemics which the Ottoman government could hardly deal with effectively.[186] According to a report by British Major F. de Winton written in 20 November 1877, there were about 8,000 fugitives in Edirne; 4,000 in Filibe; 30,000 on the road between Botevgrad and Sofia, and a further 23,000 in the Sofia sub-province.[187] The British ambassador Layard reported that in early 1878 there were around 200,000 fugitives in Shumla, Pravadi, and Osmanpazar, and in the surrounding countryside without proper shelter, clothing, and food.[188] By the end of the war, there were approximately 40,000 fugitives around Drama, 200,000 in Sumnu (Shumen), 200,000 in Istanbul, 150,000 around the Rhodope Mountains, 50,000 in Gumulcine (Komotini), and 60,000 in Xanthi.'[189] The incessant migratory waves of Turks and other Muslims of various ethnic affiliations came about just as the state was already fighting for its economic survival, thus presenting it with what seemed to be an insoluble problem.[190]

It was only one aspect of the drama. Refugees, as pictures in this book show, for the most part, fled on their oxen-carts, or simply by walking, or, if fortunate, by train.[191] Or maybe not. In a letter to British ambassador Layard, Colonel Waiter Blunt, an English officer in the Turkish Gendarmerie, depicted the misery of the fugitives in trains:
> I inform you that at each station crowds were wailing with their orders signed, ready to jump into any nook or corner they could find. On this account women and children were afraid to leave the carriages, lest they should lose their places, even for the calls of nature. The air, therefore, in some of the closed wagons, was beyond conception and probably was the cause of much of the mortality that occurred and the sickness now existing. Nearly every disease was represented from small-pox downwards.[192]

The numbers of Muslims affected by this disaster, between the killed and exiled exceeded the million, about two thirds, if not more, of the Muslim population of Bulgaria.[193]

The congress convened at Berlin on 13 June 1878 in order to amend the Treaty of San Stefano in March, signed July the 13th, 1878, stipulated amongst others, that Russia should retain Bessarabia and other places; the independence of Serbia, Montenegro, and Rumania, the placing of Bosnia and Herzegovina under the protection of Austria; and greater territorial gains for both Bulgaria and

---
[186] Pinar Ure: Immediate effects; p. 163.
[187] Major de Winton to Layard. 20 Nov. 1877; pp. 232-5
[188] Layard to earl of Derby, Jan. 9, 1878.
[189] D. Turan, *The Turkish minority in Bulgaria. 1878-1908* (Ankara. 1998); pp. 144-5.
[190] B. Pekesen: *Expulsion and Emigration from the Balkans*, originally published in German, 2012; available of the web, accessed Aug 2014; p. 17.
[191] Pinar Ure: Immediate effects; op cit; at p. 163.
[192] Blunt to Layard, I Feb. 1878.
[193] J. McCarthy: *Death and Exile*; pp. 59-109.

Greece.[194] The Ottomans ended up with just over a third of territory in Europe as they had before Berlin but half the population.[195]

There were other gainers elsewhere, too. France took her share, wresting Tunisia from the Ottomans in 1881, whilst Britain used the Arabi "Rebellion" to take Egypt.

As the Ottoman realm shrank rapidly, Turkey's very survival was now in question. Writing in the wake of this Russian-Ottoman war, A.J. Schem foresaw events that were to happen decades later with an uncanny exactitude:

> The review of the condition of the Turkish Empire in the light of the events which are now taking place, clearly indicates that all of the European provinces will, at no distant period, be converted into European, Christian States; that Constantinople will again become a European city; that the African dependencies will pass into the condition either of independent States or of European dependencies; that Armenia will become Russian; that the Arabs will fall away soon after Turkey has been sensibly weakened and attempt an independent sovereignty of their own; and that the Turks will be driven to their home in Asia Minor, where, hemmed in on one side by the Russians, and on another by the future owners of Syria, and crowded by the enterprising Greeks on the sea-coast, they will live out what remains to them of national life, an insignificant State, without power to molest any one seriously and exposed to a process of gradual wearing away by the pressure and friction of the enterprising States which will surround them.[196]

Sultan Abdülhamid endeavoured with all his might to stabilise the condition of the realm, but simply faced an impossible task.[197] He had first of all to protect Istanbul against an attack by the Bulgarians. He had only a very limited amount of money to spend, and all this money was required for the reorganisation of the army, for the purchase of arms and ammunition, mines, and other equipment, for the Dardanelles and the Bosphorus.[198] The troubles in Albania and Arabia and the expenses for their suppression hampered further state policies. Time, money, stability, everything was lacking.[199] Then to compound the situation, the Armenians suddenly unleashed a reign of terror, tearing Istanbul throughout the 1880s and 1890s.[200] In the years 1890-1893, bombs were exploded in public places; officials were murdered at their desks, and even postmen along their routes.[201] Muslims were slaughtered in their villages en masse.[202] However, as

---

[194] W.S. Monroe: *Turkey and the Turks*; L.C. Page and Company; Boston; 1907; pp. 44-5. H. Inalcik: Chronology of the Ottoman Empire; op cit; p. 103.
[195] W.S. Monroe: *Turkey and the Turks*; L.C. Page and Company; Boston; 1907; p. 46.
[196] A.J. Schem: *The War in the East between Russia and Turkey*; H.S. Goodspeed & Co; New York; 1878; p. 571.
[197] See Great Turk book; Chapter 7.
[198] F. McCullagh: *Italy's War for a Desert*; Herbert and Daniel; London; 1912; p. 33.
[199] Ibid
[200] H. Inalcik: Chronology of the Ottoman Empire; op cit; p. 104.
[201] S.J. and E.K. Shaw: *History*; op cit; vol 2; pp. 162 163; 203; 204; etc.

would become customary, during the year 1893, Armenian publicists established committees in the chief cities of Europe and began the agitation of Armenian grievances against 'the barbarities of the Turks.'[203]

As the Ottomans grappled with these problems, yet another uprising took place, in Crete this time, but following precisely the same scenario as in 1821. On 3 February 1897, a Greek force of 10,000 men, led by Prince George, sailed into the island cutting a swath of devastation, slaying thousands of Muslims, thus, forcing the Ottomans to intervene once more to protect the people.[204] But again, as the Shaw remark, it was this act alone that seemed to catch the eye of the West,[205] and the usual hysteria of Turkish atrocities burst out again. Which contradicted reality on the ground as the British war correspondent, Ernest Bennett, witnessed

> After the surrender of Candanos a combined force of international troops was employed to escort the Mussulman inhabitants down to the coast at Selino, and it was found necessary to drive off by force the Christians, who, in violation of the terms of capitulation, persisted in plundering and maltreating the miserable refugees. A file of marine infantry suddenly halted, fired a volley at long range, and knocked over some dozen Cretans with their Lee-Metford bullets. This put an effectual stop to the brutality of these ruffians, who, but for this volley and a well-placed shell from the Rodney, would doubtless have repeated their infamous behaviour at Sitia and Daphne by massacring the helpless men, women, and children who were unarmed and at their mercy.[206]

Bennett had also this to say:

> Frequently on these excursions to the extremity of the military lines, and sometimes beyond them, we were brought into contact with Turkish officers and soldiers, who invariably treated us with the utmost courtesy and kindness. In fact, go where you will in the world, you will not find a better fellow than the Osmanli soldier. Not a penny had been paid to the troops in Crete for six months, yet I never heard a murmur...
> I have sometimes seen four or five of them sit round a pot containing a few beans and cabbage-leaves and a lump of bread, and while this queer mess of pottage was boiling, they laughed and joked in the best spirits possible...
> In short, a more shabby and dilapidated crew than the Turkish garrisons of Crete would be hard to find. Yet how these fellows fight! How loyal and good they are! I spent some time one afternoon with an old Turkish bimbashi (major, Turkish: binbaşı) in command of a detachment on the Platania road. He had one or two fine Turkish rugs to sleep on, and his bell-

---

[202] S. Shaw: *History;* op cit; vol 2 pp. 162 163; 203; 204; etc; Justin McCarthy: *Death;* op cit;
[203] W.S. Monroe: *Turkey and the Turks*; L.C. Page and Company; Boston; 1907; p. 48.
[204] S.J. and E.K. Shaw: *History*; op cit; vol 2; pp. 207.
[205] Ibid.
[206] *Among the Cretan Insurgents*, Ernest N. Bennett, Blackwood's Edinburgh Magazine, February 1898; p. 166.

> tent was littered with copies of various European newspapers with which he whiled away the time. The bimbashi was a delightful old gentleman with big gold-rimmed spectacles, and had fought at Plevna with Edhem Pasha, under Ghazi Osman, amid the awful carnage of the Grivitza redoubt. He was one of the older school of Turkish officers, but spoke French fairly, and was extremely proud of his troops. His fine old face lit up with pride as he spoke of his dear soldiers... Yet poor as these troops were, sometimes on the verge of starvation, I always found the greatest difficulty in persuading them to take a trifling "tip" for any services rendered me e.g., holding my horse or escorting me from one military post to another. This was certainly in marked contrast to the general behaviour of the poorer Christians in the interior, who worried me incessantly for money on the most flimsy pretexts.[207]

In Crete, the Greeks had begun a war which was ending in disaster for them, pushed back at Monastir, losing at Thessaly, losing Terhala, Larissa, and Tirnovo, thus raising the possibility that Greece itself might fall.[208] Just as seventy years earlier, in 1827, seeing this, the Great Powers intervened, and put an end to the fighting by forcing a peace agreement by which the Ottomans agreed to leave Thessaly, and the Greeks promised to pay a small war indemnity as well as allow Muslims to emigrate to Ottoman territory, starting yet another flow of refugees.[209] All in all, as Pekensen sums it up,

> In the 19th century, the Ottoman Empire experienced one of the most serious systemic crises since its inception. Starting in the 18th century various symptoms of crisis began to accumulate which led to a long period of great peril for the multi-ethnic empire.[210] The state was bankrupt, uprisings tore it from within, wars never ended, more territories were being lost; all this causing a crisis of political legitimacy; then to make things even worse, over one million Muslim refugees streamed in from the Caucasus and the Balkans region.[211]

The new century, the 20th, began just as the previous ended. Serbs and Greeks soon set up terror organisations in Macedonia, backed by the consuls of their nations with the supply of cash, arms and ammunitions, and other forms of support.[212] Muslim villagers were massacred, as per usual, and so were Christians who refused to follow the line traced by the terror gangs. The Ottomans offered all forms of inducements for peace: mixed police and gendarmerie forces, special new departments to deal with public works and foreign affairs, mixed courts, a

---

[207] *Among the Cretan Insurgents*, Ernest N. Bennett, Blackwood's Edinburgh Magazine, February 1898; pp. 169-70.
[208] S.J. and E.K. Shaw: *History*; op cit; vol 2; p. 207.
[209] Ibid.
[210] B. Pekesen: *Expulsion and Emigration*; op cit; p. 17.
[211] Ibid.
[212] S.J. and E.K. Shaw: *History*; op cit; vol 2; p.. 209.

Christian governor, and amnesty for the gangs and their members.[213] It was to no use. Once more, thousands of terrorised Muslims fled toward Istanbul, the Great Powers became involved, and all Sultan Abdülhamid could do was to try and steady the boat if he could, and most of all, watch the realm being torn; and not just that,

> He observed the ambitions and intrigues of the politicians on all sides and the Parliament's delaying role in the legislative process, imposed as it was on the existing structure between both the Council of State and the Council of Ministers. It was difficult to unify various groups whose interests often clashed, in the sultan's opinion, with the interests of the empire as a whole. Abdulhamit was also disillusioned by the attitude of the powers, which ignored the sufferings of the thousands of Muslims being persecuted and massacred in Bulgaria and Bosnia while presenting the suffering of Christians as evidence of Muslim barbarism, and by their exploitation of the ambitions of the Balkan states more as instruments of their own imperial goals than to meet the needs of the people of the area. The rise of groups within the Parliament that used the war disasters to put forward their own views and needs rather than supporting the war effort.[214]

And so there took place the much-publicised Young Turk revolution in 1908. Of course this work is not concerned one iota with the Young Turks Revolution and its sources, aspects, or impact. The main reason for this is quite simple: tens, if not hundreds of authors have dealt with it. As the Shaw put it, 'The Young Turk era more than any other, has attracted scholars of modern Ottoman history, and it has been studied in such detail that it is difficult to believe that it was so short.'[215]
This work is not going to bring anything new to it except this: It is certain that besides the personal ambitions of many of those behind the revolution there was also a patriotic urge and great desire to improve the situation for Turks and non-Turks alike. The fact though was simple: The Young Turks could have created the dream state on earth; the greatest brotherhood and sisterhood in history, even fulfilling the dreams of the greatest political idealists, it would still not have worked. The reason was simple: Nobody but the Turks was interested in the survival of Turkey. Everyone saw a realm that, true, was trying its best to survive, but simply there were too many forces tearing it; so everyone wanted their share or morsel of that dying empire. The Ottoman realm at the time could be compared to a noble but wounded creature, caught in the woods and surrounded by hyenas, ready to tear it apart. The creature could do what it liked — fight, make imploring sights and sounds, run, thrust forward, jump, do anything — the hyenas would not budge. In this respect, nobody puts the situation of Turkey at the eve of the Long War as admirably as McCullagh:

---

[213] S.J. and E.K. Shaw: *History*; op cit; vol 2; p. 210.
[214] Ibid; 213.
[215] Ibid; p. 273.

> The Young Turk Revolution in Constantinople did not improve matters so far as the Turks were concerned. If anything it made them worse... The Powers felt as justly irritated with the Sick Man of Europe as greedy heirs might feel with a rich uncle who, after making a will in their favour, going mad, and falling sick to the point of death, suddenly recovered his health and the use of his reason.[216]

Lines that only a brain as McCullagh's could yield.

By now, indeed, what mattered was the final carving up of the ex Ottoman realm piece by piece and to grab one's share, or the choicest piece before it was too late; and nothing else mattered. Nobody expressed this sense of urgency better than Lapworth an apologist for Italian claims in Libya, who made the following argument:

> "When decay has proceeded for so long a period," [says Mr. Bryce,] "and is so plainly due to deep-seated maladies, there remains no hope that decay can be arrested." He talks of "facilitating, with as little strife and bloodshed as may be, that extinction of the Ottoman Empire which is plainly inevitable," and adds that "Britain, France, and Italy have no interest in a policy of delay in the breaking up of Turkey."
> The other Powers had led Italy to believe that the disintegration of Turkey was a consummation devoutly to be desired by the whole civilised world. The forces of disintegration were already silently at work. Why then should Italy have been expected to show any compunction in accelerating this disintegration.[217]

The Italians would go in, first, in 1911, beginning the Long War, to be followed by others, and one conflict leading to the other, until it ended with the War of Independence (1919-1922). This is what will be looked at in this work. This is after examining the final and central issue, which explains all that has preceded and all that will follow.

4. Why What Happened to the Turks Happened? How Was it Made to Happen? And What Happened?

> The Turks of Greece left few traces [says William St Clair.] They disappeared suddenly and finally in the spring of 1821, un-mourned and unnoticed by the rest of the world... Upwards of 20,000 Turkish men, women and children were murdered by their Greek neighbours in a few weeks of slaughter. They were killed deliberately, without qualm and

---
[216] F. McCullagh: *Italy's War for a Desert;* Herbert and Daniel; London; 1912; pp. 31-2.
[217] In C. Lapworth: *Tripoli and Young Italy*; Swift and Co Ltd; London; 1912; pp. 103-4.

scruple, and there were no regrets either then or later. Turkish families living in single farms or small isolated communities were summarily put to death, and their homes burnt down over their corpses... In the smaller towns, the Turkish communities barricaded their houses and attempted to defend themselves as best as they could, but few survived. In some places, they were driven by hunger to surrender to their attackers on receiving promises of security, but these were seldom honoured. The men were killed at once, and the women and children divided out as slaves usually to be killed in their turn later. All over the Peloponnese roamed mobs of Greeks armed with clubs, scythes, and a few firearms, killing, plundering and burning. They were often led by Christian priests, who exhorted them to greater efforts in their holy work.[218]

This is one amongst hundreds of similar instances of what happened to the Turks between 1806 and 1922, i.e. over a century.

What happened to the Turks over the period just cited (1806-1922) can easily be retraced by anyone by relying on British contemporaries who saw and reported what happened; the British, it would seem, being the only people who felt the most of humanity towards the Turks. Which is extremely odd, as one can see from their views of Turkey and Ottomans, all of them (with the exception of Seppings Wright and Pickhtall), whether Grant and Gibbs,[219] Toynbee, Ashmead Bartlett, and all the others, absolutely none of them had any liking of Ottoman Turkey or Turks initially. And yet, all of them without any exception, even if they were all tough men hardened to human suffering, were moved at times to extreme emotions by what they saw being done to the Turks. Whilst Gordon, a Scotsman, saw and reported his experience in 1821,[220] others such as the English surgeon Charles Ryan saw and described scenes from 1877-8 in Bulgaria.[221] The terrible suffering of the Bulgarian Turks and all that was being inflicted on them then was also seen and reported by many British war correspondents especially those of the Daily Telegraph, London, and the Guardian of Manchester. Twenty years later, in 1897, E. Bennett saw and reported what was happening in Crete.[222] Grant and Gibbs, Ashmead Bartlett, Seppings Wright, and Pickhtall saw and reported what happened in 1912-1913 in the Balkans;[223] and Toynbee saw and reported the Greek atrocities and destruction in 1921.[224] Also, of all diplomatic reports, the most poignant were by British envoys, whose correspondence ceaselessly

---

[218] William St. Clair, *That Greece Might Still Be Free - The Philhellenes in the War of Independence*, Oxford University Press; 1972 pp. 1-2.
[219] See Grant and Gibbs feeling towards Ottoman Turkey page 4; p. 11, and many others how they had no sympathy for Turks, their rule, or policies.
[220] T. Gordon, *History of the Greek Revolution*, 2 vols; Edinburgh, William Blackwood, 1832.
[221] C. Ryan: Under the Red Crescent; Charles Scribner's Sons; New York; 1897.
[222] *Among the Cretan Insurgents*, Ernest N. Bennett, Blackwood's Edinburgh Magazine, February 1898; p. 168.
[223] E. Ashmead Bartlett: *With the Turks in Thrace*; George H. Doran Company; New York; 1913. Gustav Cirilli: Journal du siege d'Adrianople; Paris, 1913. M. Pickthall: *With the Turk in Wartime*; J.M. Dent &Sons; London; 1914. H.C. Seppings Wright: *Two Years Under the Crescent*; Small, Maynard & Company; Boston; 1913.
[224] A.J. Toynbee: *The Western Question in Greece and Turkey*; Constable; 1922, Chapter war of Extermination.

highlighted Muslim Turkish suffering.[225] These British men not only saw and reported, thus leaving the truth of what happened for posterity, by doing this they saved many lives as will be explained further down. In many instances, in whatever capacity, they even put their own lives at risk and rescued, helped, and at least comforted Turks who were about to be murdered.

These witness accounts can be complemented by the works of McCarthy, principally, and also to some extent by those of the Shaw, Salt, and Wheatcroft.[226] However, regarding the Balkan Wars of 1912-1913, and the atrocities inflicted on the Turks by Bulgarians, Serbs, Greeks and Montenegrins, there are no better works than the German Jäckh's,[227] and above all, the Frenchman, Pierre Loti's.[228] At the height of the war, the latter compiled accounts of witnesses who saw what was being done to the Turks behind the front lines by the same murderers who were at the same time accusing the Turks of massacres of Christians. Loti's work remains, indeed, the most powerful account of the tragic trickery the Turks were the victims of, and would remain the victims of for quite long, in some respect to this day.

In the remainder of this chapter, the plight of the Turks will only be briefly outlined, for this book has no intention to stir the filth of history, nor is it within its scope anyway. This is a task for the Turks themselves. And whether they wish to do it or not, that's their business, and this author is not going to cover up for their perennial incompetence at dealing with the tragedies their people and their nation suffered. The focus here is on two other central issues little examined anywhere else:
1. Why were the Turks massacred and mass-expelled in their millions?
2. How was it made to happen?

There is a third question that one can ask, which is: Why is so little known about this? The answer here is quick: corruption of Western historians and incompetence and feebleness of Turkish historians/media/artists/intellectuals (with a couple of exceptions for both).

Why What Happened Happened

The mass-killing of Turks and the brutalities that have been inflicted on them between 1806 and 1922 are not the result of revenge over Turkish brutal occupation. The evidence is that Turkish rule over the centuries was far from

---

[225] See J. McCarthy: Death and exile for the huge amount of correspondence and reports by British diplomats on the terrible deeds inflicted on Muslims from the earlier times till the post World War One.
[226] J. Salt: *The Unmaking of the Muslim World; A History of Western Disorder in the Arab World;* University of California Press; 2008; p. 31 f. A. Wheatcroft: *Infidels*; Penguin Books; London, 2004; pp. 249-54. J. McCarthy: *The Ottoman Peoples and the end of Empire;* Bloomsbury; 2001. J. McCarthy: *Death and Exile;* op cit.
[227] Ernst Jäckh; *Deutschland im Orient nach dem Balkan-Krieg;* Chapter 7: Deutsche und französische Augenzeugen von christlichen Massakers. (Die Balkangreuel des 30 jährigen Krieges); Martin Mörikes Verlag, Munich, 1913; pp. 83-98.
[228] P. Loti: *Turquie Agonisante*; Calman Levy; Paris; 1913.

despotic, cruel, or damaging to the Christians. Gibbons, von Hammer, Arnold, Babinger, Lewis, Courbage and Fargues, or anyone who studied or touched on minorities under majority rule accepts that Ottoman rule was far more lenient, humane, protective, and equalitarian than any other worldwide.[229] Compared to Christian countries, the Turks never burnt en masse some religious groups because of their faith, and they never had an inquisition. Christians have been at it for centuries, even in the 1990s. For centuries, whoever was persecuted fled to the land of Othman, whether in North Africa, the Middle East, or Turkey proper. It is just one of the lamentable states of the scholarship of today, whether on the part of Westerners or Turks, that these simple facts are erased from knowledge whilst in the 19th century and early 20th everyone was aware of them.

Of course there were deficiencies within the Ottoman realm, deficiencies which regularly affected the relations between the central authority and its subjects, including Muslims. Of course, it would be silly for anyone to claim that the Turks, or Muslims for that matter, have always been acting humanly, that their history is not tainted by anything, or that the Turkish character is nobility itself. This would be the most stupid claim to make, for Turks, just like everyone else, have their vile people, their vile practices, and their vile features. Likewise, goodness is by no means a Turkish or Muslim preserve but is shared by all races, peoples and entities, and only sick minds and souls believe in the moral or humane superiority of their own folk. The point is, or expressed differently, all that this work rants against is the attribution to the Turks the evils that have been attributed to them, not because they are giants of humanity, but simply because it is historically false. Should one push things further, any historical study that would bother comparing the legacies of empires relying on facts and facts alone and not on historians' or other opinion makers' claims, would find, without a doubt, that of all empires, none was as humane as the Ottoman's. And should one decide to have a quick look at the legacy of other empires, then let them examine some of the works by Howitt,[230] for instance, or Alleg,[231] or Ward Churchill,[232] and then let them see whether the Ottomans were ever capable of, or performed, such acts as described by these authors.

It is the view of many who studied the Turkish question, that it was in fact the softer attitude of the Turks which drove the hatred and mass-killings of them. As Allison Philips puts it:

> It is a mistake to suppose that it was the intolerable tyranny of the Turk which forced the Greeks into rebellion. All history and experience indeed prove that a people will bear without murmuring the most crushing burdens; and it is only when the cords have been relaxed, and the load

---

[229] Babinger: Mehmed, op cit; T. W. Arnold: *The Preaching of Islam*; Lahore: Sb. M. Ashraf, 1961. Y. Courbage, P. Fargues: *Chretiens et Juifs dans l'Islam Arabe et Turc*, Payot, Paris, 1997.
[230] W. Howitt: *Colonisation and Christianity*: Longman; London; 1838.
[231] H. Alleg; J. de Bonis, H.J. Douzon, J. Freire, P. Haudiquet: *La Guerre d'Algerie;* 3 vols, Temps Actuels; Paris, 1981.
[232] Ward Churchill: *A Little Matter of Genocide*; City Lights Books; San Francisco; 1997.

> lightened, that the oppressed will feel the energy to turn upon the oppressor. It was the conscientious efforts at reform of the government of Louis XVI., which directly produced the French Revolution. It was the lessening pressure of Turkish rule, and the growing prosperity of the Greek population, that rendered the Hellenic revolt possible and inevitable. The rule of the Ottomans is indeed harmful rather for what it leaves undone than for what it does; it is intolerable rather for what it implies than for what it is. The Christian subject of the Sultan, even before modern capitulations, was free to exercise his religion, to accumulate wealth, to educate himself as he pleased; he could even rise to high office in Church or State, become Dragoman to the Porte, or governor of a province. The status of the peasantry under Ottoman rule was, in the eighteenth century, far more tolerable than in most parts of Europe. Serfdom, still almost universal throughout Christendom, had disappeared; and, in many parts of the Turkish dominions, the cultivators of the soil enjoyed a prosperity unknown to the peasantry of some nations accounted more civilised.[233]

Also as odd as it may seem, countless British war correspondents, especially during the Balkan Wars, blamed Turkish excessive humanity for their plight. Reproducing some of what some of them said or wrote is truly not appropriate here, for it verges on the extreme towards some ethnic groups who repaid Turkish kindness with immense ingratitude. But briefly here, quoting Ashmead Bartlett late in 1912 during the Balkan Wars:

> One day at the height of the crisis, when the Bulgarians were said to be on the eve of entering Constantinople and of setting up the cross on St. Sofia, we watched a Greek religious procession passing through the streets of Pera. A priest dressed in robes of silk and gold went before, carrying high the cross, while others in gaudy raiment followed after, chanting a solemn hymn as they went. And no attempt was made by the Turks to molest these Greeks. We wondered what would have happened in Piccadilly if, when the army of a Roman Catholic nation, which had invaded England with the avowed intention of stamping out Protestantism, was on the eve of entering London, the Roman Catholic Archbishop of Westminster had gone in procession through the streets carrying the Host. We remembered the outcry in the Press, when he had mooted doing such a thing in a period of profound peace, and trembled for the fate of him and his priests.[234]

M. Pickthall, an English writer, at the height of that same conflict, witnessed something worse, the Greeks of Istanbul jeering the returning wounded Turkish soldiers:

> About three hundred wounded Turkish soldiers, walking two and two, and holding hands; dragging their feet along, with drooping heads. One or two, more stalwart, kept up some kind of a song to cheer the rest. War-stained,

---
[233] W. Alison Phillips: *The War of Greek Independence 1821-1833*, Charles Scribner's Sons; New York; 1897; pp. 7-8.
[234] E. Ashmead Bartlett: *With the Turks in Thrace*; George H. Doran Company; New York; 1913; p. 249.

> travel-stained, their honest peasant faces each with its look of pain, they took no heed of the amusement of that fashionable throng, trudging along with their grave patience — Anatolian Turks, the most long-suffering and kind of races, to which no Power of Europe gives a thought. Therefore they are dirt to the "aristocratie perote," who feed on them. Because they pray to God five times a day they are fanatical; because they have not been to mission schools they are barbarians; and when they come back wounded in their country's cause, their condition is fit theme for gibes and laughter. They had the presumption to fight for their own land against superior, civilised Christians who desire to take it. It is a joke to see how well they have been hacked about. The Christians line their Via Dolorosa. They are jeered at in the streets of their own capital. Ah, the fanaticism of the Turks, dear Christian brethren![235]

Seppings Wright, as he felt immense sorrow at the plight of the Turkish refugees fleeing from Christian terror during the terrible days of the Balkan Wars, went even further: 'Their (the Turks') generous faith and belief in the good in human nature has helped to bring about the present state of affairs.'[236]

Whilst acknowledging that excessive kindness to the underserving does bring out the worse in them, still it leaves us to find other answers for all the brutalities and crimes committed against the Turks. Here, one has to raise the point that human corruption being what it is, weakness has its price. Once Ottoman Turkey went into decline, it opened the door to all: the petty, the greedy, the blood thirsty, the vile, the evil, and whoever belongs to those categories of human scum, and whoever their historians and Western historians call patriot, to arm themselves with anything that was blunt or sharp, and search for any unarmed Turk and slaughter them.

The weakness of the realm opened a great door of opportunity to all. Everyone sought a morsel of the empire, and all served themselves. In this regard, there is no better quote than this one by the American Commodore Beehler, who writing about the Turkish Italian War in 1911-1912 and quoting some Christian religious text, concluded his work with the main lessons learnt from that conflict:
> The lesson is that of the history of all nations in all the world in all ages. This experience is merely another illustration of the infallible teaching of our Saviour, viz.:
> "When a strong man armed keepeth his palace, his goods are in peace.
> But when a stronger than he shall come upon him, and overcome him, he taketh from him all his armor wherein he trusteth and divideth his spoils."
> St. Luke XI, verses 21 and 22.

---

[235] M. Pickthall: *With the Turk in Wartime*; J.M. Dent &Sons; London; 1914; pp. 19-20.
[236] H.C. Seppings Wright: *Two Years Under the Crescent*; op cit; p. 200.

> Eternal Vigilance is the price of Liberty.[237]

Indeed, then, as before, or as now, only the inept and cretins believe in the rule of law and right as far as world affairs are concerned. All that rules is brute force. It is the only law, the only right, the only logic, the only humanity; and this applies not just to military affairs, but also to culture, economy, and intellect. The strong win in all; the inept lose in all.

So, in regard to Turkey, when the power and strength of Othman ruled, peace and safety ruled, too. When the inept, the corrupt and the imbeciles ruled on behalf of Othman, Turkey's power faltered, and the Turks paid the price in blood and misery. This is all there was.

Of course, when the time came to tear Turkey apart and clear its people away, there had to be justifications, for never in history did Christians inflict bloodshed and suffering, whether during the Crusades, or by the deeds of the Inquisition, or the burning of "heretics," or burning of "witches," or the slave trade, or colonisation, or the hundreds of wars, and now the partitioning of Ottoman Turkey, without presenting the legal, moral, and other justifications for these acts, first. And, indeed, in respect to the mass-clearing of Turks, the excuse was always the same as expressed here:

> Italy has taken Tripoli, Bengasi, Derna and Tobruk, with the force of arms, and with the force of arms will keep what she has taken, at the dear cost of her noble children's blood, and if necessary she will take more of the Turkish Empire, in the name of justice, in the name of moral, in the name of humanity and civilization.[238]

And, indeed, as will be seen further on, in the last chapter, it was in the name of civilisation that the removal of Turkey off the map and Turks off the ground were justified, and were deemed Right.[239]

The concept of barbarism has definitions and situational contexts, and both these aspects, besides historical backgrounds and precedents, will be looked at in greater detail further down to explain how the genocide of people and nations works. Here, it is necessary to first list other reasons for the removal of Turks as people and Turkey as a nation.

As much as Western scholarship of today tries to deny it, the central fact is that all the military campaigns launched against the Ottomans were launched as wars of the Cross against the Crescent, whether to 'Free the Holy Sites,' 'Redeem the Cross,' or avenge the 'Blood of Christians,' or whatever else of similar sort. When in 1911 the Italians launched their invasion of Libya, the religious element was central, not only to regain Libya, which in the past was a Christian land, but also

---

[237] Commodore W.H. Beehler: *The History of the Italian Turkish War*; Annapolis; 1913; p. 107.
[238] Dr Paolo de Vecchi: *Italy's Civilising Mission in Africa*; Brentano's; New York; 1912; p. 40.
[239] Such as: A. Mandelstam: *The Sort de l'Empire Ottoman*; Lausanne, Imprimeries Reunies; 1917. A.J. Toynbee: *The Murderous Tyranny of the Turks*; Hodder and Stoughton, London, 1917. E. Driault: *La Question d'Orient*; Paris; 1920; 8th edition. Henry Morgenthau: *Ambassador Morgenthau's Story*; Double Day, Page & Company; 1919.

as here expressed by the leading theoretician of the Italian campaign, Dr de Vecchi:

> And worst yet, it is surprising that the same Nation should have been able to misrule one of the most prosperous part of Europe, in spite of the continual protest of its population, the continual rebellion of its people, oppressed, outraged, massacred, under the very eye of their brethren of the same race and of the same religion...[240]
>
> Only one third of the population of Turkish Europe is Mussulman, and yet the two thirds of them, being Christians, have to suffer the tyranny and the abuse of Islam, under the eyes of their indifferent brethren.
>
> And this outrage is possible in this twentieth century of civilization and progress, only because there is not a man who would lead the willing crowd with that pennant of the Cross, which has been once the glory of Christianity.
>
> The time is ripe, and this is the great opportunity of a really Great Ruler, who would thus send down to posterity his name as that of the greatest Reformer after Christ.[241]

Political, religious, and intellectual elites played a central role in Ottoman Turkish woes. And when a figure has the religious fanaticism, political ambitions, and enough intellect, the combination is always lethal. W.E. Gladstone — British Prime Minister recurrently, religious zealot, chief distorter, and maybe a few other qualifications — certainly, played the leading role in the greatest mass-killing of Turks in history. It happened as follows. In the mid 1870s, as he was plunged in his religious studies, perhaps meditating, and certainly cursing the unfairness of this world that demoted him from the post of Prime Minister and brought in his stead that loathsome figure of Disraeli (I.e. Gladstone's view), there took place the miracle. Suddenly, there came the news of troubles in Bulgaria, and wherever there is trouble involving Turks, it is without a doubt in any zealous Christian mind that the Turk is massacring; whether the dead are Muslims or Martians, the Turk is at it again. And hurriedly, Gladstone interrupted his theological studies to complete a 60-page pamphlet in which, thanks to the inspiration of his Holy surroundings, he could see through the distance the horrific deeds being committed by the Turks.[242] Throughout his pamphlet, only one theme prevailed: that of Christians being slain en masse by 'Mahometan fanaticism.'[243] 'We have been authoritatively warned, that the condition of the Christians in Turkey is now eminently critical,' he barked.[244]

---

[240] Dr Paolo de Vecchi: *Italy's Civilising Mission in Africa*; op cit; pp. 63-4.
[241] Ibid; p. vii.
[242] W. E. Gladstone, *Bulgarian Horrors and the Question of the East,* London: John Murray, 1876.
[243] Ibid; p. 22:
[244] Ibid; p. 23:

As his contemporary M. Hynes put it, Gladstone resembled 'A sleeper who after having fallen from office (in 1874) woke up and Turkish rule with its abominations for the first time met his astonished gaze.'[245]

Another figure, Alfred Austin, wrote to Gladstone, inviting him

> To ask himself with merciless scrutiny whether, had the name of his pamphlet been regulated either by what it contains or by the emotion which lately invaded his retirement, he would not in candour have been compelled to call it, "Tory Horrors, or the Question between Lord Beaconsfield and Myself."[246]

Gladstone was, indeed, strongly implying and playing on the other favourite theme: a Jewish British Prime Minister, i.e. Disraeli, standing by "his murderous Ottoman chums," slaughtering Christians with gusto as the two have always done; a claim guaranteed to win any elections in those days.[247]

Then, to the less fanatically and less anti-Semite inclined, he presented another argument: winning the heart and soul of Eastern Christians:

> In European Turkey, it cannot too often be repeated, the Christian element is the growing, and the Turkish the decaying one. If a conviction can but be engendered in the Christian, that is for the present purpose mainly the Slavonic mind of the Turkish provinces, that Russia is their stay, and England their enemy, then indeed the command of Russia over the future of Eastern Europe is assured. And this conviction, through the last six months, we have done everything that was in our power to beget and to confirm.[248]

With all this, Gladstone won himself a new Prime Ministerial position in 1880.

More importantly, with his 60 pages pamphlet of Turkish horrors, he gave everyone enough material to also rant about the Bulgarian horrors; he gave the moral legitimacy to the Russians to unleash fire and destruction on the Turks, and he also gave legitimate and moral right to Christians in Bulgaria and the Balkans to also unleash fire and destruction on the Turkish civilian population. And thus took place one of the greatest mass-slayings of history:

> The inexcusable cruelty of the Bulgarian massacres [Baumgart remarks] was preceded by the Bulgarian Christians' equally gruesome massacres of Muslim settlers – these, however, were not reported to the European public at that time, neither by the Russians, who relayed only the information that was useful to them, nor by the English Atrocity Meetings. Moreover, for the estimated 25,000 murdered Bulgarians, the Turks paid

---

[245] See M. Hynes: The Story of Russian Aggression and Turkish Defence: Being a Reply to Gladstone and Bright's Recent Utterances on the Eastern Question (Liverpool: Author, 1877, p. 29.

[246] See Alfred Austin, Tory Horrors or the Question of the Hour, A Letter to the Right Hon. W. E. Gladstone (London: Chatto and Windus, 1876) p. 4.

[247] For Gladstone political manoeuvring within this context, see R. T. Shannon, *Gladstone and the Bulgarian Agitation 1876*, London: Thomas Nelson and Sons,1963.

[248] W. E. Gladstone, *Bulgarian Horrors* op cit; p. 27:

with some 1.5 million casualties in the subsequent war against Russia, not counting the hundreds of thousands of refugees who fled the Russians in the winter of 1877/1878 to Constantinople, before dying there of typhus, smallpox and other epidemics.[249]

How did what happened happen?

What happened to the Turks was a repetition of the same from 1806 until 1922. This has been explained by this author in his other work,[250] and therefore he will not add too much to it here, except the briefest of outlines on the pattern of how Turks were mass-slaughtered and some central themes that are common to all genocides.

Regarding the pattern, it went like this:
Christian populations start a bloody mass-uprising where they inflict terrible atrocities on their Muslim neighbours. The Ottoman authorities intervene and inflict retribution, but which in no instance surpasses what the Turks suffered. As a result of the latter, there arises an outcry from all over the West, as with Gladstone's pamphlet, that Muslim Turks are massacring Christians, a cry which boils opinion so much that invariably it ends in four recurrent effects:
- Wider war followed by 'revenge' massacre of Turks in their tens or hundreds of thousands.
- Loss of Ottoman territory to the benefit of their slayers.
- Huge war indemnities to be paid by the Turks, which cripple them for the foreseeable future.
- A prevailing image of the Turkish mass-slaughterer, which justifies the previous three effects and prepares for the next round of the same.

Here we have to seize on the last point, and elaborate a little on how genocides work. Throughout history, and to this day, the trick has remained the same: demonise your foe, especially if you control opinion directly or by the help of your allies, and then inflict whatever you like on him (without forgetting his progeny, of course). A brief look at a few instances in history helps:
When the Western expansion in Africa began in the 15th century, Black people were depicted by Catholic intellectuals, such as Zurara, 'like beasts, with no law of reasonable creatures... nor knowledge of good, only of surviving in animal sloth.' In the previous generation, according to him, they seemed 'drawn from bestiality.'[251]

---

[249] Baumgart, Winfried: Die "Orientalische Frage" redivivus? Große Mächte und kleine Nationalitäten 1820–1923, in: Tel Aviver Jahrbuch für deutsche Geschichte 28 (1999), pp. 33–55; p. 43
[250] See Chapter One of *Great Turks*.
[251] G.E. de Zurara: *Chronica do Descobrimento e Conquista da Guiné* (Paris, 1841; Eng. version by Edgar Prestage in 2 vols. issued by the Hakluyt Society, London, 1896-1899: *The Chronicle of Discovery and Conquest of Guinea)*; chs 79-82; I; pp. 295-310.

He found the first slaves directly shipped from Africa 'so deformed in their faces and bodies as almost to resemble shadows from the nether world.'[252] This literature, not Zurara's alone, but by hundreds of works similar to his by Western intellectual elites, justified Black and American Indian mass-enslavement, and mass killings in their millions if not tens of millions over the centuries.[253]

Throughout the so-called Renaissance period (15th-17th centuries), the Christian West burnt millions of women, but only after they were declared as witches.[254]

During the colonial period, the French arrived in Algeria in 1830 in order to civilise the 'Barbaric, Inferior, Algerians,' and in doing so, killed millions of them.[255]

Recently, the Jews could only be suppressed if they were depicted as inferior; and once they were deemed sub-creatures, killing millions of them was made acceptable.

The Turks, likewise, have been singled out as the most barbaric people in history, barbarism as defined in its two senses: incapable of civilisation and bestial. Without exception, every single mass-slayer of the Turks, from the early stages until the Greek invasion after the First World War, has used "Turkish barbarism and their massacres of Christians" as the pretext for their mass extermination of Turks.

The Italian apologist de Vecchi thus put it in 1912:

> The world has progressed in these 450 years, the civilization has advanced, and humanity has regulated and attenuated the barbarities of war, but the Turks have maintained their valor and their barbarity of old.[256]

Chevalier Tullio expressed it thus:

> The Turks have done nothing but devastate, and there is not today a single Turkish province which was not much more prosperous before the advent of the Turks. In fact, the whole Turkish history is nothing but an orgy of assassinations, robbery, misgovernment, and general destruction. During the last four years the Young Turks have been in power assassinations, massacres, robberies, and misgovernment have continued to the same extent as before. The world owes to the Turks nothing but distress.[257]

Gladstone again:

> The elaborate and refined cruelty — the only refinement of which Turkey boasts! — the utter disregard of sex and age — the abominable and bestial lust — and the utter and violent lawlessness which still stalks over the land.[258]

The Duke of Argyll, in the 1890s, remarked:

> One of those appalling outbreaks of brutality on the part of the Turks which always horrify but need not astonish the world. They are all

---

[252] Ibid; Zurara pp. 107-12.
[253] Howitt: Christianity, op cit.
[254] A. Dworkin: *Woman Hating*; (New York; 1974); p. 130.
[255] H Alleg et al: *La Guerre d'Algerie*: op cit; vol 1; p. 69.
[256] Dr Paolo de Vecchi: *Italy's Civilising Mission*; op cit; p. 63.
[257] Chevalier Tullio Irace: *With the Italians in Tripoli; the authentic history of the Turco-Italian War*; John Murray; London; 1912; p. preface ix.
[258] W. E. Gladstone, *Bulgarian Horrors*; op cit; p. 18:

according to what Bishop Butler would call "the natural constitution and course of things;" that is to say, they are the natural results of the nature and government of the Ottoman Turks. The cruelties of their rule are not accidental, but chronic and inherent. Their revenue system is, to the last degree, corrupt and oppressive. Their judicial system is not only corrupt, but involves besides an open denial of justice to their Christian subjects. Their executive system of armed ruffians... Thus in all great leading departments of administration, the causes of oppression are as obvious as they are grinding and desolating in their effects.[259]

McDonald tells us more:

Thirty years have passed since Professor Freeman exposed the deceptive character of such words as "Turkey," "State," "nation," "subject," "government," "representative," when applied to the rule of the Ottomans... Freeman the hard-hitter would make short work of a Turkish ambassador who, at a European Conference, instead of being put in the criminal's dock, should sit in judgment upon his victims. Every Turk, soldier or civilian, was one of the army of occupation. He alone, of all the Sultan's subjects, was permitted to go about armed. Of the army of occupation, conquest and tax-gathering have been the main business; it has shown no aptitude for any other...

We can see how unavoidable were all those massacres from Chios and before it, to the Kotchana butchery, in the summer of 1912, which some weeks later made the Bulgarians spring to arms, how the Turk must massacre, or perish; how naturally it came about that the Turk conquests in Europe were to a great extent the achievement of the Turk's own victims; why the decline of the Turk Power began at the time it did (the last years of the seventeenth century); why reforming Sultans were either deposed or assassinated; why projects of reform that deceived a credulous, uninstructed Europe, not only never were introduced, but intensified the inherent tyranny in a word, never could be introduced, so long as the Turk remained the Turk we have known in history.[260]

In conclusion, if we read through every single account (not just in those days but also in today's scholarship or media), the Turks are evilness and barbarism personified. In relation to evidence/proof of their massacres of Christians, it is always the same trick: A refers to B who speaks of such massacres, whilst B refers to C who speaks of such massacres, whilst C refers to A. It is also somehow like when Westerners arrived in America, they declared the natives cannibals and mass-slaughtered them on this account. Nobody eaten by the cannibals could of course be found to give the evidence of their cannibalism. It was the same with the Turks: They had killed everyone, and so there was nobody to give the

---

[259] W.S. Monroe: *Turkey and the Turks*; L.C. Page and Company; Boston; 1907; pp. 50-51.
[260] J. McDonald: Turkey and the Eastern Question; T.C. & E.C. Jack; London; 1913; pp. 11-12.

evidence of their crimes. So, evidence came via claims (A, B, C, etc), and repeated claims are strong enough evidence.

There remains, indeed, the fact that there were witnesses on the ground who saw the very reverse: that rather than the Turks massacring (as it was being claimed,) it was they who were being massacred en masse, regardless of age or gender. E. Bennett, who was a war correspondent in Crete in 1897 thus states:

> On my return to Candia I was met by several Christians, who declared in excited tones that some Bashibazouks had made a foray upon a neighbouring village and brought in three Christian heads. These ghastly trophies were so, every one said, being carried about in a bag and displayed at the coffee-houses. Nevertheless, I could find no one who had actually seen the heads, and a little cross-examination revealed the fact that the whole story of the bag and its contents was absolutely without foundation. I mention this incident to show how careful one ought always to be with respect to alleged atrocities, especially in the case of Cretans, Armenians, et hoc genus omne.[261]

In Libya in 1911 and during the Balkan Wars, Seppings Wright:

> The more I have seen of Turkey and the more I know about her and her people, the more I am attached to her cause. Europe has treated this fine, generous race with a callous brutality that fills my soul with indignation. The Turks are being consistently and grossly misrepresented and maligned.[262]

McCullagh, a war correspondent in Libya, for his part notes:

> We are accustomed to think it an awful thing for Christian women to be left to the mercy of the Turk. On the present occasion there were hundreds of Christian women at his mercy, and not one of them was molested. On the other hand, the Turk knows from experience stretching back to the time of the Crusades that it is not quite safe to leave the women of his harem to the tender mercies of the Christian.[263]
>
> Ever since the beginning of the war, indeed, it was 'unspeakable Stamboul' which had been prudent, careful of life, merciful; it was Holy and Royal Rome which had been addle-headed and inhumane.
>
> Towards the end of September last it was confidently predicted in the English Press that the Turks would poison the wells along their line of retreat, and thus make it impossible for the Italians to follow them. They did no such thing. They did not even cut the water-supply at Bumeliana nor burn the town behind them, though they might very easily have done both. Seldom, indeed, in modern times has a retreating army shown so much consideration for the civilian population and even for the enemy as the

---
[261] *Among the Cretan Insurgents*, Ernest N. Bennett, Blackwood's Edinburgh Magazine, February 1898; p. 168.
[262] H.C. Seppings Wright: *Two Years Under the Crescent*; Small, Maynard & Company; Boston; 1913; p. 143.
[263] F. McCullagh: *Italy's War for a Desert;* Herbert and Daniel; London; 1912; p. 63.

army of Nesciat (Neşet) Bey exhibited on its evacuation of Tripoli in October last.[264]

If so, the wish was father to the thought, for at the beginning of the war the Italian papers were continually reporting massacres of Italians by the Turks in Tripoli probably in the wild hope that some of these massacres would really come off. First, we had the massacre of some Franciscans at Benghazi. It was announced and deplored but it did not happen. Then, we heard of the massacre of an Italian scientific mission, which had been probably spying out the land in the interior. With a deplorable lack of patriotism this mission also failed to get massacred. Then, the Italian Consul at Derna was in difficulties. The Arabs wanted to murder him and all the rest of the local Italian colony, but the Turks prevented a single life being lost, and eventually, after guarding them for four days, handed the Consul and his party over to the commander of an Italian gunboat. Naturally, on reaching Augusta, the Consul used the vilest language about the very Turks who had saved his life and left it to be understood that he had terrorised the whole Derna garrison with his revolver.

When their turn came to show mercy, the Italians burned Arab villages, butchered the strong, and threw out the sick people to die like dogs in the street.[265]

Another scene, the Balkan War in 1912, and another statement by a war correspondent there, Baldwin:

Here let me say that throughout the time which I spent in the Thracian battle-zone I saw no single instance of that ferocity and cruelty with which the Turks have too often been falsely charged. I am not, of course, in a position to refute every allegation that has been levied against the men of the Ottoman army, but I have seen their conduct under conditions of a character which might be expected to put a severe strain on the morale of the best European troops, and I cannot recall having witnessed, even during the panic, any single outrage or atrocity, or to have heard of any through other correspondents, English or foreign.[266]

Moving forward another decade, in 1921-1922, Toynbee, formerly a hater of Turks when he was employed by the British Ministry of War Propaganda, now on the scene, in north west Turkey, writes:

The Turkish troops on their side consisted of three categories — regulars, volunteers, and local chettes. I had a glimpse of all three from the 29th June to the 2nd July 1921 at Ismid [İzmit], and was impressed by their discipline. The chettes were undoubtedly under the Army's control. The volunteers, who came like the regulars from distant parts, were properly organised

---

[264] F. McCullagh: *Italy's War for a Desert*; op cit; p. 164.
[265] Ibid; p. 165-6.
[266] H.F. Baldwin: *War Photographer in Thrace; An Account of Personal Experiences During the Turco-Balkan War 1912*; Fisher and Unwin, London, 1913; pp. 148-9.

units. The regulars themselves, in spite of their miscellaneous uniforms, were unmistakably fine soldiers. I saw them in circumstances of extreme provocation, but they stood the test. There had been no retaliation upon the churches for the state in which the Greeks had left the mosques; no wrecking of the deserted Greek and Armenian shops, though the sign of the cross still remained chalked on their shutters to distinguish them from the Turkish shops, which the Greeks, before they left, had systematically looted; no violence against the few native Christians who had remained, in revenge for the previous massacre of Turkish civilians. The sale and consumption of alcoholic liquors had been effectively prohibited by the military governor. At night the town was quiet, the troops sober and orderly, and a Westerner could walk the streets in the dark with no adventures except courteous challenges from sentries and the offer of a lantern to light him on his way.[267]

The American Rear Admiral, Chester, who for years had been an observer of world affairs, Editor, who had visited and stayed in Turkey regularly from the late 19th century (when in 1896, he was sent on a war mission against the Turks, and was in command of the first American battle ship sent to the region) until the early decades of the 20th century, at the time when Turkish massacres of Christians were supposed to have reached their peak, gives us this account,[268] which is considerably abridged here:

> WHAT is the truth about Turkey? This question is asked daily. I went to Turkey to ascertain the actual conditions there, and I have been bombarded with such questions since my return. Following are some of my answers:
>
> There are no prejudices against Christians in Turkey, let alone killings of Christians. Massacres of the past were enormously exaggerated by prejudiced writers and speakers. The harem has vanished out of Turkey, and there are fewer men with plural wives than there are married men with mistresses in the United States. There is more honesty to the square inch in Turkey than there is to the square yard in most other countries of the world. Turkey joined the Germans [in the First World War] with reluctance. After the United States became belligerent she would have joined the Allies if she could. In the first place, the wrong impression of the Turks was spread because their religious belief is different from ours. That and that alone lay at the bottom of the prejudice of America (and much of Europe) against the Turk...[269]
>
> [Talking about the supposed massacres by the Turks of Christians,] ... such as the so-called Adana massacre of 1909. That affair, however, was in no sense a massacre as the term is known to international law, for the

---

[267] A.J. Toynbee: *The Western Question*; op cit; p. 240.
[268] Rear Admiral Chester: Turkey Reinterpreted; *Current History* Vol XVI, No 6, Sep 1922, pp. 939-946.
[269] Ibid, p. 939.

Armenians (always in the majority in cities of Asia Minor, according to present-day accounts) fully armed, arose in their might and drove the Moslems from Adana, killing more of them than they lost by their own casualties. This fact was certified to before the Director of the Board of Foreign Missions in Boston, in my presence, by a woman missionary whose son had been accidentally killed in the fight. In spite of this admission, however, the Hymn of Hate, tuned to the key of the Adana massacres, is still being sung to Sunday school children in America.[270]

Since 1909 Turkey has been practically at war, due to machinations of the powers that be in Europe, and heinous offenses committed against anybody in Turkey have been "war atrocities," such as are common to all belligerents...[271]

I have visited Turkey a number of times. In the course of these visits, including the journey just completed, I studied the land from end to end.

Returning, I feel that I have come from the most wonderful country in the world...

The Turk, contrary to the general impression, is a tolerant man, not only willing but extremely anxious that others should do as they please in religion, as in other things. Naturally, however, he does not wish to have his own habits of religion or of daily life interfered with by outsiders. My religion differs from the Turk's, but I respect his great fidelity to his, and, no matter what may be declared to the contrary, he respects my own fidelity to mine and that of others to the faith they may espouse.

The Turk [the Admiral pursues] has been and is the most misrepresented person in the world. I know some of the falsehoods which have been and are being circulated in America. They amaze me. I was in Constantinople in 1911 when the first election was held. The Turks made a festival of it, and wagons, in every one of which were a certain number of pretty little girls in white, were driven around to take the ballots. On these wagons rode also the Christian missionaries who were there. In the meantime the people of America and European countries were being fed with tales of anti-Christian riots in Constantinople. These were supposed to be even then in progress. Learning of this, I was disgusted with the anti-Turkish propagandists. I know that what I say will be astonishing to most Americans. I myself should be astonished by such reports if I knew nothing about Turkey except such things as I have read in newspapers published in America and Europe, and inspired—although the newspapers have not understood this—by the enemies of Turkey. One reason why these misrepresentations persist is that Turkey never has felt it worth while to organize any agency to state her case abroad.

---

[270] Ibid, p. 941.
[271] Ibid.

> There have been riots, now and then, when local Turks have felt that their rights have been outraged by outsiders. It seems to me that once or twice I have read something about riots in America in circumstances of like sort, although of differing detail. Speaking generally, the Turks are far more patient than Americans would be.[272]
>
> ... It seems almost a pity to upset the good old myth of Turkish viciousness and terribleness, but in the interest of accuracy I find myself constrained to do so, although it makes me feel a bit like one who is compelled to tell a child that Jack the Giant Killer really found no monstrous men to slay... Today, although there are many ways in which falsehood can be circulated about Turkey, there is no way that I know of, save through the "word of mouth" of a few men who, like myself, have gone to Turkey and therefore know the facts, of getting the truth out of Turkey. The Turks ever have been curiously indifferent with regard to what the outside world has thought of them, or else have been unable to discover how to tell their story. Turkey's enemies are unwilling that the actual truth should become generally known.[273]

So, we can surmise that witnesses on the ground — it ought to be reminded, not the type predisposed to love the Turks, but all of them initially very hostile to the Turks, the last one, Admiral Chester, having even arrived in Turkey to blast the Turks with his fleet — tell us of Turkish humanity and others' bestiality. All these witnesses, without exception, tell us the same thing, that the image of the brutal mass-slaying Turk that prevailed (and that still prevails to this very day in 2017-18, in scholarship, media and in the Turks' 'friends and Allies' National Assemblies) was and remains wholly contradicted by what happened on the ground (the mass killing of Turks). Those who make claims from the distance, whether then, or today (scholarship and Turkey's 'friends and Allies' National Assemblies) tell the very opposite. Now this can only mean one thing:

- Either all the witnesses on the ground just cited and many others like them lie.
- Or the historians and politicians of the West and other opinion makers of the period dealt with here (and of today who speak of, or write of, or pass measures about, Turkish bestiality) are liars.

It is certain that the great shaper of opinion over the so-called Bulgarian massacres, Gladstone, was a liar. He says:

> I have carefully investigated this point; and am unable to find that the Bulgarians committed any outrages or atrocities, or any acts which deserve that name, have vainly tried to obtain from the Turkish officials a list of such outrages... No Turkish women or children were killed in cold blood.

---
[272] Ibid, p. 942-44.
[273] Ibid, p. 945.

> No Mussulmen women were violated. No Mussulmans were tortured. No purely Turkish village was attacked or burned. No Mussulman house was pillaged. No mosque was desecrated or destroyed.[274]

He was and will always remain a liar because his diplomats were telling him a different story. The newspapers he was receiving were also telling a different story. Tens, if not hundreds, of accounts were dispatched to the UK such as these:

(Telegram from Mr. Gay to "Daily Telegraph," London.)
Pera, July 14th, 1877:

> Yesterday I saw villages blazing near Vetova. I spoke with Circassian scouts, who told me that the Bulgarians were joining the enemy everywhere, that the Russian infantry and Cossacks were massacring Turkish villagers, all round, especially at Dikili-Tash, near Roustchouk. Cossacks marching towards Rasgrad are within three hours of that town. The railway probably is cut now. I now give the list of villages in which I know massacres absolutely to have happened. Beshpunar village, all the prisoners were killed and the women violated. Tchairly, in Rasgrad district, two hundred refugees from Sistowa all put to sword; at Kara-Tchoumak village, ten cartloads of refugees from Arnoutlou were killed.
>
> At Unt-Deitan, all the people of the village have been murdered. At Ostrantcha and Costova, four hours from Roustchouk, all the Mussulmans, among whom thirty five children, were butchered. At Kestan and Selvan, in Tirnova district, the Russians incited the Bulgarians to murder the Mussulman refugees from Selvi and Dobrudja and the miserable people were all killed near Khayn.

(Telegram from Mr. Englander to Reuter's Agency, London.)
Constantinople, July 22nd 1877:

> Consul Blunt telegraphs from Kezanlik to Mr. Layard that the Cossacks disarm the Mussulman inhabitants and the arms are given to the Bulgarians, who are outraging the women and children. Mr. Layard has sent a proof of the atrocities to Lord Derby. The Porte has received a telegram from Chumla, dated July 20th, bearing the signatures of 22 correspondents, of whom the correspondents of:
>
> *Débats, Post, Times, Telegraph, Manchester Guardian, Examiner, New York Herald,* and *Gazette de Cologne* have seen with their own eyes women and children wounded by lances and sabres. The Cossacks have committed many other terrible atrocities.'

Gladstone could have written or corrected his earlier stand, and showed sympathy to the Turks as his diplomats or war correspondents did; he died hating them to his guts, just like most.

Thus, the conclusion on this: the claim of Turkish barbarism is sufficient to justify anything done to Turks, and when Christian commit terrible deeds, their acts are

---

[274] W. E. Gladstone, *Bulgarian Horrors*; op cit; p. 16:

noble. As McCullagh, who was witness to the mass killing of Muslims in Libya in 1911, expresses it so well,

> There are Catholics who object to any criticism of the Italian soldier because many of the expeditionary troops went to the Sacraments before they embarked at Naples, and because the army in Tripolitania is well provided with Franciscan chaplains. Again, there are people in England who believe that the Turk is fair prey, that there is no harm in driving him out of Europe and Africa, and that, in the course of driving him out, no atrocity can possibly be committed.[275]

We come to Western historical narrative, followed by inept or corrupt non-Western narrative, with the rare exceptions already cited. Today's authors, instead of using contemporary sources or people who witnessed things, do the opposite: they disappear them entirely from knowledge. Any perusing through their reading lists shows this systematic suppression of contemporary sources except those that reinforce their crooked views, including Gladstone's and zealous Christian writing. You cannot write a correct history if you set aside the contemporaries and witnesses of events, and only rely on, or refer to, fellow scholars or opinion makers who hold the same crooked views as yours. This is overwhelmingly the case, though, today.

This distorted historical narrative could have been dealt with by a counter-narrative that is coherent, credible, and above all direct and robust, based on historical facts, backed by original sources. Four remarks need to be made here, though:

Firstly: Turks, just as all Muslims, can complain as much as they like about their sullied image. This is the price of intellectual ineptness. Nobody is going to do for them what they should do themselves, and weaknesses of all sorts have never been, are not, and will never be an option. The unavoidable fact, though, is: Muslim/Turkish scholarship excels at everything except scholarship. As a rule, whether as historians, intellectuals, media people, film producers, television producers, or whoever is in charge of knowledge, entertainment, culture, and with rare exceptions, they are just bunches of sold out, coward, crooked, inept beings. They care more for their careers and status, ever eager to please those they deem their superiors, incapable of mounting a robust telling of the real stories of the tragedies their peoples and nations have suffered at the hands of their tormentors in the past.

Secondly, if Turks, just as other Muslims, believe that truth, fairness, justice, integrity, and similar qualities rule the institutions of today — scholarly, media, or any international institution for that matter (including so-called human right organisations)— they ought to be qualified, to be kind to them and not use other expressions (which should apply,) as cretins.

---

[275] F. McCullagh: *Italy's War for a Desert*; op cit; preface xxxv.

Thirdly, the present narrative of history tarnishes the memory and history of Turks and Turkey, and it whitens other criminals of history.

Fourthly, and more importantly, each whitening of the mass-slayers of the Turks and each darkening of the Turks has led to another mass-culling of the Turks, or those deemed to be Turks, or called Turks. And here the call for vengeance is well stated by Gladstone:

> There is not a criminal in an European gaol, there is not a cannibal in the South Sea Islands, whose indignation would not rise and overboil at the recital of that which has been done, which has too late been examined, but which remains unavenged; which has left behind all the foul and all the fierce passions that produced it, and which may again spring up, in another murderous harvest, from the soil soaked and reeking with blood, and in the air tainted with every imaginable deed of crime and shame. That such things should be done once, is a damning disgrace to the portion of our race which did them; that a door should be left open for their ever-so-barely possible repetition would spread that shame over the whole.[276]

Which leads us to the final point:

What Happened to the Turks?

What happened to the Turks, i.e. their massacres and mass-expulsions between 1806-1922, has been dealt with by very few Turks, the likes of Salahi Sonyel,[277] by far the most able modern Turkish scholar of recent times; and to a much lesser extent by the likes of Pinar Üre,[278] or Fundagül Apak,[279] and of course the best works of all by McCarthy, Loti, and Jäckh, all already referred to. There are accounts by eyewitnesses who described these events much better than any author, and they should be consulted. This author has given countless references; it is up to others to use them or not to use them. There will, therefore, be no repeat here of the long list of gruesome facts. Only three concluding points need to be made:

1. No nation, no people on earth, throughout history, have had such an onslaught, in terms of literature and on the ground against them as much as the Turks.
2. No nation has had the real picture of its historical legacy, its exemplary humanity, tolerance and service to minorities so much tarnished and besmirched as much as the Turks.

---

[276] W. E. Gladstone, *Bulgarian Horrors*; op cit; p. 31:
[277] Whose web page is a must for any person seeking to know about recent Turkish history.
[278] Pinar Üre: Immediate Effects; op cit; pp. 153-170.
[279] Fundagül Apak: The Bleeding Wound of Turkish Independence Literature: The Balkans; available on the Internet.

3. Finally, and more importantly here, Turkey was, on the eve of the Long War, about to be inflicted upon yet another, or perhaps the mother of all wiping out. Had she lost the Long War, especially the final phase of it, i.e. the War of Independence, in view of the trend from previous history, there would be no Turkey today, and very few Turks to tell the tale.

Two

LIBYA, 1911-1912

Italy is the instrument of justice and of judgment against the high-piled iniquities of the Turk. The hour has struck for the exit of this barbaric people from the continent of Christian civilisation.[280]

1. The Italian Civilising Mission

On October 13, 1911, the Italian commander of the invading force of Libya issued a proclamation to the 'population of Tripolitania and Cyrenaica' announcing that the Italians had come
> Not to subdue and render [the inhabitants] slaves, now under the bondage to the Turks, but to restore to them their rights, to punish the usurpers, to render them free and masters of their fate, and to protect them from these same usurpers, the Turks.[281]

The Italians, like the French in Algeria, had invaded the country not just in order 'to remove the Turkish despot and liberate the Libyans (just as the French liberated the Algerians),' the Italians had also come 'to civilise the country.' In their ultimatum to the Turks to surrender Libya peacefully to them, the Italians particularly insisted on the necessity 'to bring Libya out of its backward state in which the Turks had plunged the country.'[282]

In Italian view, as expressed by one of their leading theorists,
> What the Turks have done for that country, since they took possession of it, nobody knows, or at least, everybody knows that they did nothing to improve it, but simply levied taxes on the poor Arab population, maintaining the commerce of slaves, as the principal trade of the country, while the Italian emigrants, especially those of Sicily, brought there the only industrial commercial and agricultural improvement and the only sign of modern civilization, so much needed in that country, the schools. Of course, with the wave of civilization, they also brought the war against slavery, and naturally at once encountered the hatred of the Turks, who saw in it the loss of their principal revenues, the loss of their power.[283]

---
[280] C. Lapworth: *Tripoli and Young Italy*; Swift and Co Ltd; London; 1912; p. 98.
[281] F. Malgeri: *La Guerra Libica 1911-1912*, Rome, 1970, pp. 396-407.
[282] W.C. Askew: *Europe and Italy's Acquisition of Libya, 1911-1912*, Durham, 1942, p. 32.
[283] Dr Paolo de Vecchi: *Italy's Civilising Mission in Africa*; Brentano's; New York; 1912; p. 8.

According to an Italian Nationalist leader, 'These two regions, Tripolitania and Cyrenaica, are all that remains to us as heirs of the empire which Rome established on the African coast. Only "Turkish barbarism" barred the way to a promised land.'[284]

Italian politicians, intellectuals and journalists also considered it to be a historical right and national obligation to impose Italian sovereignty in regions 'where the Roman Empire had ruled.'[285] The claims of Italy to the possession of Tripoli and Cyrenaica, the Italians insisted, were the same as those of France to the possession of her African Colonies, and Italy has, furthermore, the ancient rights which come to the heirs of the Roman conquest, to the more recent rights of the Genovese and the Venetian Republics.[286]

> We all know that Tripoli was first brought into civilisation by the Romans, but this civilisation was destroyed by the Arabs and by the Turks; the innumerable ruins of buildings, palaces, and aqueducts yet bear witness to this fact... To Italy the world owes to a great extent its present civilisation. Was it not the Italians at Lepanto who first checked the Turkish advance upon Europe? So little interest and responsibility did the Turks have in their Tripolitan subjects that the authorities never even caused a Census roll to be taken; and thus this country, in the heart of Mediterranean civilisation, was a region abandoned to ignorance and barbarity.[287]

At any rate, the Turks were just 'usurpers', who got Libya on the strength of 'a brutal force of arms, when nobody could contest it to them.'[288]

> The average imagination can hardly fail to be struck by Italy's resumption of territories that formed a part of Roman Africa [states McClure, a proponent of Italian colonisation of Libya.] It is the custom, in some critical quarters, to deny to modern Italy the proud descent from Imperial Rome which has been a natural inspiration to a reborn people; and, narrowly viewed, the denial has a sound enough basis. Ethnologically, no doubt, the modern Italians are far removed from the dominant people which founded and administered the greatest empire in history, and it may be the fact that of this race there are no true descendants. Yet, despite the admixture of foreign blood which gradually overwhelmed the original stock, the Roman tradition has inevitably persisted, and to admit the denial of Italian heirship would be to allow an unjustified predominance to the claims of strict heredity. In a sense, all nations have shared in the heritage of ancient Rome, but the legitimate heirs to its glories and traditions are those who,

---

[284] Quoted in F. Malgeri: *La Guerra Libica*, op cit, pp. 52-3. C.G. Segre: *Fourth Shore*, The University of Chicago Press, 1974, p. 25. E. Rossi: *Storia di Tripoli....* Rome, 1968.
[285] T. Barclay: *The Turco-Italian War and its Problems*, London, 1912, pp. 11-2.
[286] Dr Paolo de Vecchi: *Italy's Civilising Mission*; op cit; p. 8.
[287] Chevalier Tullio Irace: *With the Italians in Tripoli; the authentic history of the Turco-Italian War*; John Murray; London; 1912; p. preface ix.
[288] Dr Paolo de Vecchi: *Italy's Civilising Mission*; op cit; p. 8.

now weakened, now strengthened, by the infusion of alien blood, have occupied throughout the centuries the ancestral land. The Tripolitan provinces are rich in Roman remains, and history is full of allusions to the productivity of regions that are now desolate. In Roman times the Tripolitan coast strip and the Cyrenaican plateau must have been veritable gardens, and today the memorials of a vanished wealth are seen in the half-buried ruins of cities, and in the remnants of aqueducts and reservoirs.[289]

'Young Italy has dared to draw once more the sword of the Caesars in Northern Africa.
And the whole world is awaiting the issue.'
(By the Italian artist Cav. Edward Matania.)

Just as the French declared that they had only brought a once Christian land (Algeria) back into the Christian fold, the Italians were now only doing the same in Libya, restoring it back to its old Christian fold.[290] Just prior to the attack on Libya (in October 1911), a historical argument appeared in the Italian press, which recalled that the Spanish, assisted by the Sicilians, had occupied Tripolitania in 1510, and that the Emperor Charles V had in 1530 made a gift of it to the Knights of Malta on condition that they pay an annual tribute to the King of Sicily.[291] The Knights of Malta, the argument pursues, had in fact paid this tribute for many years, even after they lost Tripolitania to the Ottomans, and the reigning House of Savoy, as successor to the

---
[289] W.K. McClure: *Italy in North Africa*; Constable and Company; London; 1913; pp. 283-4.
[290] R. Simon: *Libya Between Ottomanism and Nationalism*, Verlag, Berlin, 1987, p. 47.
[291] T.W. Childs: *Italo-Turkish Diplomacy and the War Over Libya, 1911-1912*, E.J. Brill, Leiden, 1990, p. 59.

Sicilian throne, under its various names, had now inherited the ancient claim to Tripolitania. Many dailies picked up this theme to justify Italy's claim over Libya.[292]

It was the same argument elsewhere, Childs remarks, whereby Serbia, Bulgaria, and Greece, all of which in 1912 (in attacking the Turks) based their claims to Ottoman Macedonia, at least in part, on ancient and medieval history.[293]

Having put their colonisation on the moral high ground, the Italians, of course, needed practical justifications for their invasion — just as the French had used the fly whisk incident, when Hussein, Dey of Algiers, slapped the French consul with a whisk in order to justify their colonisation of Algeria. The Italians had many complaints in order to justify the invasion of Libya.[294] Premier Giovanni Giolitti listed them in a letter to the *Daily Express* of London:

> Dear Sir:
>
> I received your letter in which you request my statement in regard to the actual conflict between Italy and Turkey.
>
> After all that has been said and written on the subject it is very difficult to say anything new, especially as our enterprise evolved in such a frank and loyal way that it could not leave any misunderstanding with the old school of diplomacy, which had a chance to follow it step by step from the beginning.
>
> This conflict between Italy and Turkey is of an old standing. It has gone on for years, and often it has come to a crisis which have interested the outside world and compelled us, a few years ago, to mobilize our fleet on the verge of action.
>
> The reasons of this conflict are many, the principal one being, that Turkey would not admit the necessity of our expansion in Tripolitania, and the earnestness of our intentions.
>
> One needs only to look at a map, and will see at once the ethnic connection of Sicily with Tripoli.
>
> History tells us that Tripoli was Greek when Sicily was Greek also, and both became Roman under Roman domination. And in these last fifty years of our great evolution, with the growth of our population, and our prosperity and wealth, Tripoli could not but feel the effect of the old ethnic law, and be considered as an appendage of Italy.
>
> We cannot direct our emigration, but we are bound to protect our people especially where, on account of the condition of the country, our protection is most needed.
>
> We could not abandon our countrymen, their interests and their capitals, in a country so far backward in the progress of civilization, as Turkey, where

---

[292] P. Maltese: *La Terra Promessa*; Milan, Sugar Editore, 1978; p. 84.
[293] T.W. Childs: *Italo-Turkish Diplomacy*, op cit, p. 41.
[294] T. Barclay: *The Turco-Italian War and its Problems*, London, 1912, 114-119.

our countrymen are in constant need, not only of a moral but also of material protection, as are the citizens of other countries, who are compelled for that very reason to keep a legal constant watch over their subjects.

Being unable to prevent the emigration of our countrymen, Turkey resorted to a system of abuses, which compelled us to request her in a friendly way, to put a stop to the unjust prosecutions. But vainly, for Turkey took our patient protestations as a sign of weakness, and lately with an open impudent act of despotism violently carried away a young Italian girl in Adana, and for that barbarous act the Authorities refused to give any satisfaction.

The Turks have been abusing the Italians and their possessions without any regard and consideration that the Italians have always treated the Turkish subjects with just respect and humanity.

Things have gone so far, as to make it a question of National pride and honor, and we had but one way of settling it, to defend with arms, what we could not obtain in a peaceful way.

And now that we are engaged in this undertaking, with all respect toward the other nations, we shall settle with Turkey our difference, ready to enter in friendly intercourse with her, if we find her reasonable.

Everybody knows that Italy has taken active part in every just cause, and after these last fifty years of our unification, enjoying broad sentiment of liberty, our people feel entitled to the respect of other nations, and that it is their duty to step into the mission of civilization which is their calling.

Believe me, esteemed sir, yours

Giovanni Giolitti.[295]

There were further excuses such as the traditional view of the 'Turkish oppression of the local Arabs,' and the 'Arab hatred of the Turks.' According to the colonial apologist, de Vecchi:

The majority of the natives, well aware of the great advantages of the Italian immigration were favorable to our countrymen, but this did, only irritate more and more the brutal and prepotent soldiers, who saw in the spreading of education and liberal ideas among the native Arabs, a cause of anxiety and danger for the loss of their tyrannical power and supremacy.[296]

Of course these claims by the Italians had no real ground as will be seen gradually as this work progresses. With regard to the claim that the Turks had failed to develop Libya and were instead looting its wealth, the reality was quite the very reverse. The Ottoman Turks had ruled Tripoli since 1835, and the inhabitants regarded Turkish rule as a blessing; they enjoyed greater freedom and were

---

[295] Dr Paolo de Vecchi: *Italy's Civilising Mission*; op cit; pp. 5-7.
[296] Ibid; p. 1.

subjected to much less burdensome taxation than before.[297] The protectorate of Tripoli was an expense rather than a source of revenue for Turkey; expenses on the administrative running of the country much exceeding the revenue from harbor dues and agriculture.[298] Moreover, the claim that the Turks were doing nothing to advance the country was groundless, too, due to the many developments on the ground initiated by the Ottomans. These include vast improvements in education as well as in political involvement.[299] The local and Ottoman leadership had tried to reinvigorate the declining trans-Saharan trade, develop natural resources and local industry, and increase foreign trade, all the while ensuring that the revenues remained in Libya.[300] Internal and external security of the country was also improved thanks to the reorganisation of the security forces, local mobilisation, establishment of a reserve force, improvement of the gendarmerie, planning of armaments and partial demarcation of the borders.[301] The Ottomans, more importantly, had established very strong relations with the Libyan population, and especially with the Sanusiya Order, and all sides were actively working together for the advancement of the country.[302] Libya, Simon asserts, was in fact being changed from one of the most backward and marginal parts of the Empire into an advanced and developed region.[303]

The real reasons for the country's invasion by Italy lay elsewhere. These reasons should not be sought in all the usual complicated explanations found in most essays and academic works of today, which are, a few exceptions aside, just a pile of muck. The reasons for the invasion were far more simple and practical, including military. The Italians in the 19th century did not have the naval might that could have allowed them absolute command of the Mediterranean against the Ottomans.[304] Now, however, the command of sea enabled the Italians to ferry invading armies to Tripoli and Cyrenaica and subsequently to take islands in the Aegean Sea without any opposition by the Turkish navy.[305] Turkey had, in fact, agreed a contract with Britain for the construction of a powerful fleet, and had engaged a British Admiral for the reorganisation of her fleet.[306] To the Italians, should that happen, Turkey might be able to cause immense damage to Italian commerce in case of war.[307] So they had to act fast.

They had to act now for another principal reason: everybody was getting their morsel of the former Ottoman realm, and why should not Italy have hers, and now before all was gone. As the Italian apologist de Vecchi acknowledged:

---

[297] Commodore W.H. Beehler: *The History of the Italian Turkish War*; Annapolis; 1913; p. 6.
[298] Ibid.
[299] R. Simon: *Libya Between Ottomanism and Nationalism*, op cit, p. 64.
[300] Ibid.
[301] Ibid
[302] Ibid.
[303] Ibid.
[304] Commodore W.H. Beehler: *The History of the Italian Turkish War*; op cit; p. 107.
[305] Ibid.
[306] F. McCullagh: *Italy's War for a Desert;* Herbert and Daniel; London; 1912; p. 34.
[307] Ibid; p. 35.

But the political condition of Europe, which had made necessary the expansion of France in Africa, so far as to almost take possession of Tunis, which is under her protectorate, and which compelled England to practically capture Egypt, where her large interests demanded protection, woke up the political people of Italy to the realisation, that soon the Mediterranean Sea, that sea once her own, by right of conquest, was going to be entirely lost, for ever to her, if she did not dash to the remaining coast left to her.[308]

We must not be too preoccupied by the talk of taking away some territory from the Great Dying Man,' wrote Giustiano Rossi. 'After all, the pieces that have been taken away from the Ottoman Empire are now many, and nevertheless Europe does not fall into convulsions. First Bulgaria was subtracted and liberated from Ottoman servitude; next Greece, and afterwards Roumania, Serbia, and Montenegro enlarged themselves at the cost of the Turkish Empire. England added to her crown the diadem of Cyprus. Austria took Bosnia and Herzegovina. Tunis, under a pretext, was placed under the protectorate of France. Finally, Crete rebelled and was governed independently of Turkey by the mandate of several European Powers. Crete in some years' time will be quietly annexed by Greece. Next will come the turn of Albania; why not that of Macedonia? What share has Italy had today of this pulling to pieces of Turkey? Nothing. And we shall have nothing if we wait until others give it to us. Let us therefore go to Tripoli.[309]

On the eve of the invasion, during the Summer of 1911, the expansionist majority followed no particular party or sectional lines.[310] Left and Right, Republicans and Catholics, Nationalists and Socialists, North and South — all were part of the enthusiastic majority in favour of conquest.[311] From March 1911 onwards, the Turcophobe campaign in the Italian press became more intense and strident.[312] If *L'Idea Nazionale* took the lead, a number of the important daily newspapers were quick to stress the same. Guissepe Piazza in *La Tribuna,* Giussepe Bevione in *La Stampa*, not to mention the Catholic papers *Corrier d'Italia* and *Avvenire d'Italia*, that is all the great papers of the Peninsula, except the *Corriere Della Sera*, joined in.[313] From the Spring of 1911, Italian journalists in Libya agitated their home readership with reports on 'the failures of the Ottoman authorities, tensions among the local population, and the precarious situation of Italians in Libya.'[314] Such descriptions contradicted the reports of non-Italian consuls in Libya, which

---

[308] Dr Paolo de Vecchi: *Italy's Civilising Mission*; op cit; p. 9.
[309] In C. Lapworth: *Tripoli and Young Italy*; Swift and Co Ltd; London; 1912; pp. 99-100.
[310] C.G. Segre: *Fourth Shore*, The University of Chicago Press, 1974, p. 20.
[311] Ibid.
[312] N. Nelissen: Le Corriere della Sera et la Campagne de Presse a Propos de la Libye 1910-11; *Risorgimento* (1980-3): 295-316; p. 296.
[313] T.W. Childs: *Italo-Turkish Diplomacy and the War Over Libya*, op cit, p. 40.
[314] R. Simon: *Libya Between Ottomanism and Nationalism*, op cit, p. 52.

said that prior to the invasion, the region was generally calm and that Italian citizens were under no threat, let alone being harmed.[315]

The national mood for the colonial enterprise, however high, required yet another crucial element to be fulfilled: European acquiescence.[316] In a secret treaty in 1902, England and France had already recognised Italy's claims to Tripoli, and two years later France had definitely proclaimed Italy's priority to take possession of Tripoli 'under certain contingencies.'[317] Italy hesitated a little because of England's relations with the Young Turk government of 1908, but since England's sympathy cooled somewhat, Italy finally decided to act.[318] Sir Edward Grey, the British Foreign Secretary, when approached in July 1911, a few months prior to the invasion, assured Italy 'of Britain's sympathy in the crisis,' and in September when the crisis reached a high point, just prior to the invasion, he categorically refused a Turkish appeal to Britain to mediate.[319] That same year, France, too, reacted positively to Italian demands, stating on 12 September 1911 that Italy 'could rely on France unconditionally and that France's sympathy was on Italy's side.'[320] It was also promised that France would not float any more new Turkish loans until the Tripoli issue was resolved, in favour of Italy, of course.[321] From St Petersburg also came friendly words from Neratov, the Russian Foreign Minister.[322] Amidst Western generalised acquiescence, only the Germans tried to mediate, but Rome informed Berlin that mediation was useless; Italian 'patience was exhausted and the stability of the Mediterranean was about to be ensured.'[323] The Revolution of the Young Turks in 1908 was regarded with apprehension by some powers that 'wanted Turkey to remain weak in order that they might expand at its expense.'[324] The occupation of Libya by Italy would contribute to that.

In the third week of September, 1911, all was in place, and all that was needed were raw excuses to hurl the Italians onto Libya. By 24 September, days before the proclamation of war against the Turks, the Italian press had discovered 'a threat to the safety of Italian nationals in Libya.'[325] The Italian colony, it was alleged, was in a state of panic, and feared 'imminent massacre.'[326] Although the relatively unbiased *New York Herald* reported on 26 September that the Turkish

---

[315] P. Maltese: *La Terra Promessa*; Milan 1968, in W.C. Askew: *Europe and Italy*, op cit, pp. 24-39.
[316] R. Simon: *Libya Between Ottomanism and Nationalism*, op cit, p. 53.
[317] Commodore W.H. Beehler: *The History of the Italian Turkish War*; op cit; p. 6.
E. Rouard: *Accords Secrets Entre la France et l'Italy Concernant le Maroc et la Libye*, Paris, 1921, 21-22
[318] Commodore W.H. Beehler: *The History of the Italian Turkish War*; op cit; p. 6.
[319] J. Wright: *Libya*, op cit, p. 126.
[320] W.C. Askew: *Europe and Italy's Acquisition of Libya*, op cit, p. 52.
[321] Ibid.
[322] J. Wright: *Libya*, op cit, p. 126.
[323] Ibid; p. 126.
[324] M. Philips Price: *A History of Turkey: From Empire to Republic*; London, Allen and Unwin, 1956, p. 83.
[325] T.W. Childs: *Italo-Turkish Diplomacy and the War Over Libya*, op cit, p. 62.
[326] P. Maltese: *La Terra Promessa*; op cit, pp. 85-6.

authorities were maintaining order 'in an admirable manner' and that Tripoli and its surroundings were enjoying 'a perfect tranquillity,' *The Herald* continued that 'a mood of panic had set in among some of the European colony.'[327] San Giuliano, the Foreign Minister, claimed that the 'excitation against the Italians' was provoked by Turkish officials and supporters of the Committee of Union and Progress, which held power in Turkey at the time.[328] San Giuliano was particularly outraged by the supposed kidnapping of a 16-year old girl, who, the Italians insisted 'had been forcibly converted to Islam and violently married to a Muslim despite her parents' protests.'[329] Here, however barmy the justification, some people might give it credit. Where the problem lies is in the following: the girl was allegedly raped and converted to Islam in Adana, in Turkey, but this was used as an excuse to colonise Libya. Here is Lapworth, working as an apologist for the Italian government trying to make us see some logic in this:

> Quite recently a very serious case occurred, namely, the rape of the sixteen-year old minor, Giulia Franzoni, who was fraudulently kidnapped from her family, workers on the Ottoman railway in Adana, imprisoned, and forcibly converted to Islamism, and married to a Mussulman, despite the protests of her parents and foreigners of other nationalities, and despite the intervention of the Italian Consulate and the Embassy. This occurrence, which would be of grave importance to any nation, is still graver for Italy, who has to protect a large number of Italian emigrants occupied in the work of building railroads in Asia Minor. The very fact that this barbaric system of conversion by force, and this abduction of an innocent girl, remain unpunished, may lead to other similar actions against the whole working-class population, who are chiefly Italians, and who are obliged, owing to their work, to live in these regions.[330]

In words, because a crime took place in Turkey, in order to prevent its re-occurrence, Libya needed to be colonised.

Regardless, Italian patience seemed to have run out with all 'Turkish crimes.' Three days later, on 27 September 1911, Italy dispatched an ultimatum demanding that

> The Ottoman Empire agree within 24 hours to an Italian military occupation of Tripolitania and Cyrenaica, ostensibly justified by the state of neglect and disorder in which.... Turkey had left those regions and the dislike she had shown for Italian enterprise.[331]

The Hakki Pasha Ministry in Istanbul alarmed by the threatening language of the Italian press had already instructed Turkish ambassadors in Europe, on 20 September, to request the governments to which they were accredited to make

---
[327] Ibid; p. 92.
[328] T.W. Childs: *Italo-Turkish;* op cit, note 66; p. 63.
[329] Ibid, p. 34.
[330] C. Lapworth: *Tripoli and Young Italy*; op cit; pp. 55-6.
[331] L. Albertini: *The Origins of the War of 1914;* 3 vols; tr., by I.M. Massey; Oxford; 1952-57; vol 1; p. 343.

representations at Rome in favour of moderation. In most of Europe's chancelleries, however, all that the Turkish representatives received was a polite rebuff; the Germans alone tried to quell Italian threats.[332]

To the Italian ultimatum, the Turkish reply was delivered well within 24 hours, on 29 September, 1911. It was dignified and conciliatory in tone, and whilst accepting that Italy participate in the economic development of Libya, it also agreed that good relations with Italy were a priority, that peace and security for Italian subjects were guaranteed, and it made many conciliatory offers.[333] However, on 29 September, having received 'an unsatisfactory reply', Italy declared war, and Giolitti announced that the nation was about to fulfil *una fatalita storica* — a historic destiny — by invading Libya.[334]

2. The Invasion

If for the Italians it was a historical destiny, for the Turks it meant the start of the Long War; a war, which, except for a break of one year (September 1913 to November 1914), was to last until the conclusion of the Treaty of Lausanne in July 1923.

On 1 October 1911, a great iron battle-fleet sailed southwards across the Mediterranean, 'carrying the three-days-old war between the Italian kingdom and Turkey to the coast of North Africa.'[335] The fleet anchored on 2 October off the town of Tripoli, 'the only Mediterranean port that has preserved all its medieval originality,' said later a French observer.[336] The following day, at 15.15 the navy guns opened the bombardment of the three outlying Turkish forts, followed the next day by the landing of 1700 marines.[337] The Turkish commandant, who had few troops, decided to withdraw to save the town from destruction.[338]

Following their landing, the Italians, instead of attempting to destroy the Turkish forces of under 5,000 men, who retired inland and joined up with Libyan tribesmen, decided to wait for the arrival of their main expeditionary force, which only sailed in from Naples and Palermo seven full days after the first landing at Tripoli.[339]

---

[332] T.W. Childs: *Italo-Turkish Diplomacy*, op cit, p. 67.
[333] Sir Thomas Barclay: *The Turco-Italian War*; op cit, text of Ottoman reply in appendix One; pp. 111-2.
[334] J. Wright: *Libya*, op cit, p. 127.
[335] J. Wright: *Libya*, op cit, p. 118.
[336] F. Malgeri: *Guerra Libica (1911-1912)*; Rome, 1970, J. Wright: *Libya*, op cit, p. 118.
[337] T.W. Childs: *Italo-Turkish Diplomacy*, op cit, p. 74.
[338] J. Wright: *Libya*, op cit, p. 118.
[339] Ibid, p. 119.

Oddly, it would seem, the Turks now realised it was not just Libya that was threatened but the whole realm. Already the Italians had sent small naval forces to the Aegean Sea, chiefly scouting torpedo vessels, and on September 30 a panic was created in Smyrna, Salonica and Mityleni by the appearance of passing Italian warships, very likely the Vittorio-Emanuele, Roma and Pisa, searching for the Turkish practice squadron.[340] Turkish fears mounted over the safety of this squadron that had sailed from Beirut at 10 a.m., September 28, for the Dardanelles. It was composed of two battleships, two cruisers, nine destroyers and a torpedo-boat mothership; and the main problem was that they had no knowledge of war having been declared.[341] If this shows one thing, it shows the incompetence of the men in charge of Turkey then, as the Italians had given plenty of notice of their aggressive intentions. The same incompetence will be shown repeatedly through the Balkan Wars and the First World War as will be seen in the following chapters. Nonetheless, it took three days before the Squadron was informed of the state of war; then at great speed the fleet moved between Mityleni and the mainland, and safely anchored at Nagara in the Dardanelles that evening.[342]

Meanwhile, more landings had been made on the coasts of Tripolitania and Cyrenaica. The Italian navy had occupied Tobruk to the far east of the country on 4 October; Derna was taken on 18 October after heavy shelling, and troops went ashore at Homs the same day, although the town was not taken until the 21st.[343] On the 18th another fleet had anchored off Benghazi, and there met little resistance from the Turks, who only numbered 200 infantrymen, eighty horsemen, with eighteen small guns facing Italy's seven cruisers, and troops packed into twenty transports.[344] In total, the Turkish army stationed in Tripoli and Cyrenaica was composed of the 42nd Division, consisting of:

    4 regiments of infantry, of 4 battalions of 600 each
    1 battalion of chasseurs
    2 regiments of cavalry each of 10 squadrons of 80 to 120 horses
    1 regiment of field artillery each of 6 batteries of 4 to 6 field guns of 3-inch caliber.
    4 companies of engineers
    3 companies of fortress artillery.[345]

The complement was 12,000, but at the outbreak of the war the trained troops numbered altogether about 5000 infantry and 400 cavalry with about 2500 to 3000 raw recruits. The garrison of Tripoli consisted of:

---

[340] Commodore W.H. Beehler: *The History of the Italian Turkish War*; op cit; p. 23.
[341] Ibid.
[342] Ibid.
[343] J. Wright: *Libya*, op cit, p. 119. See also E.E. Evans Pritchard: *The Sanusi of Cyrenaica*, Oxford at the Clarendon Press, 1949.
[344] Ibid.
[345] Commodore W.H. Beehler: *The History of the Italian Turkish War*; op cit; p. 12.

> 6 battalions of infantry with two machine gun companies
> 1 battalion of chasseurs
> 6 field batteries
> 4 squadrons of cavalry
> 2 companies of fortress artillery

The garrisons in other parts of the province were distributed in small detachments. It is reported that just before the war Benghazi had 400, Derna 70, Tobruk 30, Solum 25, and Cyrene 10 men.

In addition to these regular troops, there were territorial units; organised in 30 battalions of infantry and 60 squadrons of cavalry with a total strength of 20,000. These combined gave a total strength of the Turkish forces at 28,000 men.[346]

The Italians, on the other hand, had vast superiority in numbers and war material. Their total force in Libya would eventually reach, by 20 Nov 1911, 85,000 men, before rising by the end of the year to 120,000.[347] They also had at their disposal automobiles, auto trucks, motor wagons, motorcycles, and a huge park of artillery, whose effects will be gradually seen. More importantly, they had a navy which was one the strongest of the time, including: 39 battleships, cruisers and gunboats, 30 auxiliary vessels of all kinds, 23 torpedo boat destroyers, 35 high sea torpedo boats, 16 coast torpedo boats, two hospital ships, one ammunition transport and one Vulcan repair ship; on top of 88 transports which were used to carry troops, and which had each a small detachment of officers and men of the navy.[348] Of course, to this should be added an essential factor that was obvious in Libya and subsequently in Gallipoli: the navy's guns playing a central role in land warfare. The Italian navy literally blasted the Turks from the sea, and the Turks who fought in Libya, Mustafa Kemal in particular, learnt precious lessons that were to serve them in Gallipoli.

The Italians also brought that new engine of war, the aeroplane. They thought, or hoped, McCulagh remarks, that the aeroplanes

> Would have on the Arabs the same effect as Pizarro's cavalry had on the Incas, that mollah, dervish, sheikh, and marabout would unanimously fall down and worship. Consequently one always found the intensely self-conscious Italians putting themselves mentally in the benighted native's place and marveling at the power of the god-like stranger.[349]

The Turks had none such armament, far from it. A Turkish transport, the Derm, sent from Istanbul, had managed just before the Italian landing to bring much needed war material, including 12,000 rifles, some Krupp guns, and a large quantity of ammunition, all of which was dispatched into the interior on camels.[350]

---

[346] Ibid.
[347] Ibid; p. 35.
[348] Ibid; p. 98.
[349] F. McCullagh: *Italy's War for a Desert;* Herbert and Daniel; London; 1912; p. 123.
[350] G.F. Abbott: *The Holy War in Tripoli*; Edward Arnold; London; 1912; p. 43.

In view of the large discrepancy in forces, fire power, and also in order to spare the cities and their populations — Muslims, but also Christians —the Turks elected to vacate all major places of Italian landing. By the time the Italians had established themselves, the bulk of the Turkish forces in Tripolitania and Cyrenaica, under the overall command of Neset (Neschat) Bey, had made no attempt to resist the landings and had been able to avoid capture, withdrawing into the interior and joining with armed Arab irregulars.[351] The Turkish garrison of Tripoli withdrew to Ain Zara, about five miles south of Tripoli, with their main body at Zanzur, 12 miles southwest of the city, whilst their outposts were close to the Italian lines.[352] In Cyrenaica the Turkish commander of Benghazi had withdrawn his troops to a camp at Benina, twelve kilometres away.[353] As a Turkish officer expressed it clearly:

> It would be madness with the force we dispose of, to wait for the Italians under the walls of Tripoli and immediately offer them battle in open country. One of the prime qualities of the Turks is to be tenacious and patient, and we will try to be both. Despite what the Italians think, we can rely on the collaboration of the Arabs.
> The important thing for us is to organise these auxiliary troops sufficiently... Within a few weeks we will thus have gathered 10,000 regular troops and twenty or thirty thousand well armed Arabs. Only then will the real struggle begin.
> We will fight in retreat at first, but soon we will be able to go energetically over to the offensive... in small actions incessantly giving the enemy no rest.[354]

Through intensive work, the Turkish commander, Colonel Neschat Bey, organised an effective force recruited from amongst the Libyan volunteers, whose numbers reached 20,000 men by 1 November; Aziziah, Kasr Gharian, and Kasr Yeffren, from 40 to 75 miles south of Tripoli, being the chief bases for recruits.[355] These volunteers were good riflemen and marksmen, courageous as few men anywhere were, but discipline had to be enforced all the time with them.

To the Italians, however, the easy landing with hardly if any casualties seemed to indicate that victory was total.
A song sung by the Italians in Libya went:
> The boats await us
> To land on the Bosphorous.
> And when we land,

---
[351] L. Albertini: *The Origins of the War of 1914*; op cit, vol 1; p. 343.
[352] Commodore W.H. Beehler: *The History of the Italian Turkish War*; op cit; p. 34.
[353] L. Anderson: *The State and Social Transformation in Tunisia and Libya*, Princeton University Press, 1986, p. 127.
[354] P. Maltese: *Terra Promessa*; op cit, pp. 123-4.
[355] Commodore W.H. Beehler: *The History of the Italian Turkish War*; op cit; p. 34.

> The Turks will run away,
> And we'll have for ourselves
> The ladies of the Sultan![356]

The Italian government propaganda machine was already at full speed. According to them, in the initial engagements, i.e. bombardments, the number of the Turks slain was between five hundred to five thousand; according to a local witness, Reginald Kahn, a well-known French war correspondent, the number was fifteen![357]

> The Italian Government [Mc Cullagh says] tried to make its own soldiers believe that the Tripoli adventure was a Crusade, that the mission of General Caneva was to plant the Cross in a heathen land. Instead of that he is busily planting brothels and grog-shops, gibbets and jails. And the triumphal music of the conquerors is the clank of chains, not the chains of prisoners captured in fair fight, but the chains of sick Turkish soldiers dragged from the Tripolitan hospitals and sent to Italy.[358]

3. Turkish-Libyan Resistance Oct-Dec 1911

According to the Italian General Staff:
> The political and military situation developed into something different from that which was at first expected. The population along the coast and the towns nearby became hostile. The efficacy of the Turkish propaganda, nourished by continuous assistance of arms, men, and money, renewed their hatred and revived hope in the success of the war. So that the Turkish Army became, little by little, transformed into what may be called a great square about the armed and turbulent Arabs. They profited by their admirable knowledge of the intricate and treacherous locality, and proved themselves adversaries capable of prolonging the conflict. Their religious fanaticism and savage instincts also fomented the rebellion in Tripoli, in the immediate vicinity of and adjacent to our lines of defense.[359]

The Italians had hoped that now that they had captured Libya, Turkey would have no choice but to agree a diplomatic settlement. But the Turks, in Libya at least, had no such intentions, with little if any desire to accept the occupation, and together with so many Libyans on their side, were now gearing to counter-attack.[360] The Turks made night attacks on Bu Meliana on October 15, 16 and 18,

---
[356] In P. Maltese: *Terra Promessa*; op cit, p. 168.
[357] F. McCullagh: *Italy's War for a Desert;* op cit; p. 110.
[358] Ibid; p. 150-1.
[359] Italian General Staff: *The Italo-Turkish War*; Engl. tr. by R. Tittoni, Franklin Hudson Publishing Company; 1914; p. 26.
[360] J. Wright: *Libya*, op cit, p. p. 119.

both sides suffering losses in killed and wounded.[361] Then there took place the main assault, which was going to have the greatest repercussions of all. On 23 October, a strong Turkish-Libyan attack was launched at Henni Sharia Shatt, a mile or two east of Tripoli, breaking through the strong Italian system of defence.[362] The assaults chiefly against the Italian center and left flank resulted in Italian losses of 382 killed and 1158 wounded.[363] It was a terrible shock to the Italians. Their reaction was extreme; so bloody the Turkish government had to appeal to the Hague Tribunal.[364] Besides the mass-killing of thousands, General Caneva, supreme commander in chief, sent 3000 of the citizens as prisoners of war to Gaeta and the Islands of Ustica and Tremiti.[365]

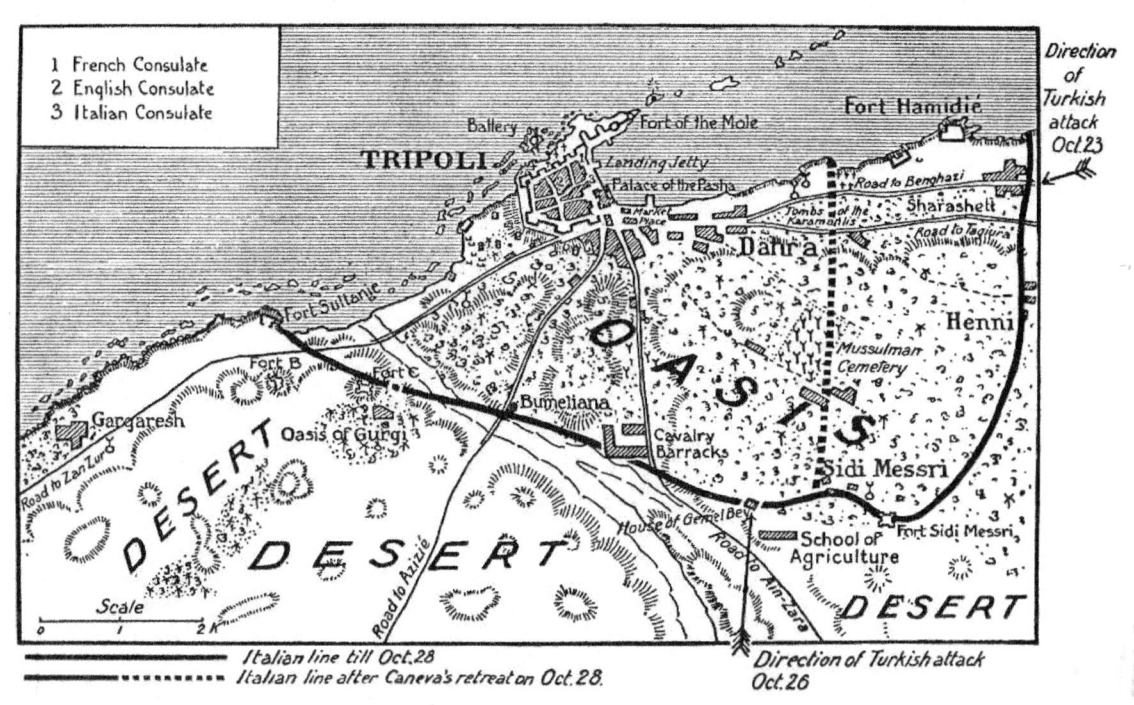

Map of operations of Oct-23-28

---

[361] Commodore W.H. Beehler: *The History of the Italian Turkish War*; op cit; p. 25.
[362] J. Wright: *Libya*, op cit, p. 119.
[363] Commodore W.H. Beehler: *The History of the Italian Turkish War*; op cit; pp. 34-5.
[364] Ibid; p. 35.
[365] Ibid.

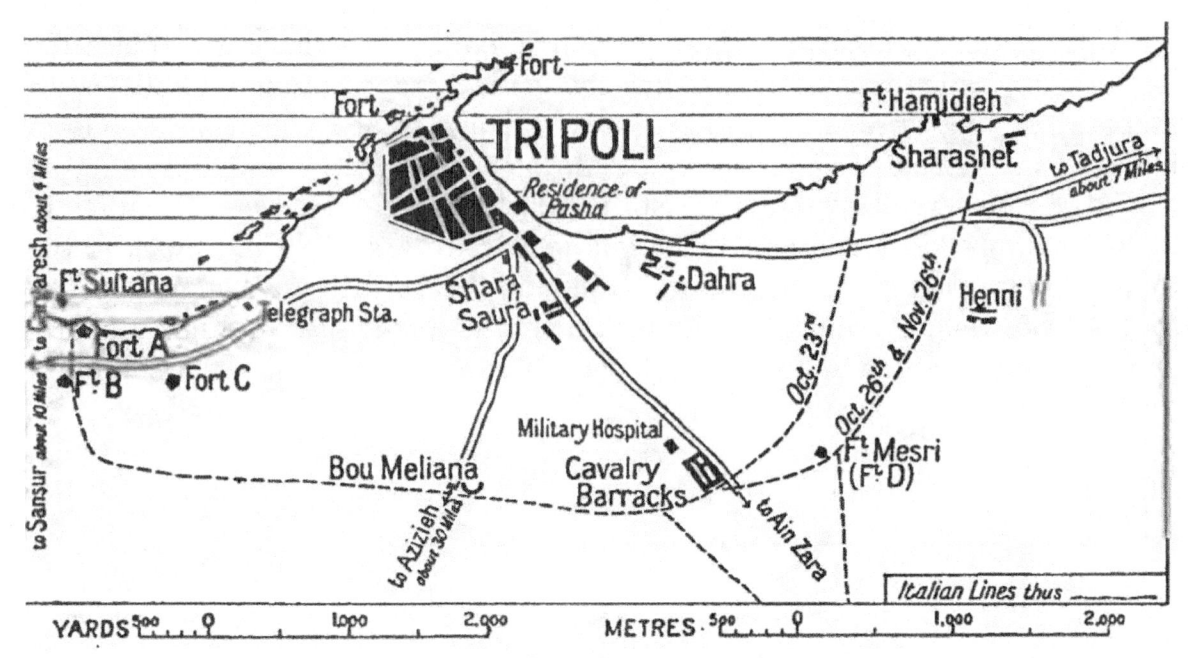

Tripoli and its environs

Libyans being led to be shot

On the way to execution

From the initial moment, the Italians threw everything at the Turkish-Libyan resistance. Bombardment by the navy was perhaps by this stage the most violent of the new century, Turkish positions, real or imagined, pounded without restraint. More importantly, airplanes were making their first battle trials. A dozen Farman and Blériot machines as well as two airships had been brought to Tripoli for reconnaissance purposes and before long the possibilities of airborne warfare were being exploited.[366] On 1 November 1911, an airplane was used as a weapon for the first time in war when Lieutenant Gavotti, flying over the Gefara Plain at 2,000 feet, tossed a hand-grenade at Libyan irregulars on the ground.[367]

The initiative on the ground, however, remained mainly with the Turkish-Libyan forces. On 15 November 1911, in the midst of violent storms over Tripoli, and under cover of darkness, Turkish and Libyan units, went through and encircled the Italian outpost outside Bou-Meliana; an action which enhanced the resistance morale, and highlighted the Italian fragile hold over the country.[368] It became obvious that the Italians could only march out of their strongly held coastal bases if they had vast numerical superiority and artillery cover from the sea. On 26 November, as an instance, some 5,000 men marched in two columns in order to face a Turkish force consisting of fifty regulars reinforced by between 150-200

---
[366] J. Wright: Libya; op cit; p. 119.
[367] Ibid.
[368] E.N. Bennett: *With the Turks in Tripoli*, Methuen & Co, Ltd.; London, 1912; p. 88.

Libyans (all under one Lieutenant), about thirty cavalry, plus a battery of three old guns and one machine-gun.[369]

For nearly two months, the Italians, with an army over 40,000 strong (not to mention their other armies at Khoms, Benghazi, Derna, and Tobruk), an enormous force of artillery, captive balloons, aeroplanes, and all modern equipment already cited, remained practically where they had landed, not gaining one single square meter, under constant protection of their naval guns; while the Turks and Arabs beyond that area, 'destitute of everything save valour, amused themselves with night and day attacks on the enemy's trenches.'[370]

Back in Turkey, although the country's naval inferiority as well as other factors made it impossible to send any sizeable reinforcements to Libya, a number of patriotic officers tried to make their way there incognito.[371] These officers were insistent not only on joining the fighting in Libya, they were even ready to disobey their superiors, whom they tried to convince of the necessity of supporting the population of Libya.[372] Most of them, either from various parts of the realm or from Europe, where they had been sent either as attachés or for studies, gathered in Istanbul, and from there made their way to Libya.[373] Enver Bey (later Minister of War) was among those who insisted on reinforcements to be sent to Libya, and he was joined by several young officers, including Mustafa Kemal (Atatürk), who discussed with him ways of joining the fighting in Libya.[374]

It was possible to penetrate Libya through Egypt and Tunisia by land, as well as by sea; there were numerous breaches of the Italian naval blockade.[375] Egypt, being in the hands of Great Britain, Turkish officers passing through it had to avoid identification. One day a shopkeeper with a Salonika accent asked Enver, 'You Enver Bey?'

To this, Enver replied nonchalantly, 'I wish I were,' and completed his purchases without further questions.[376]

Mustafa Kemal likewise had to be extremely inventive in order to cross into Libya. Writing to his friend Salih in Istanbul:

> I have no doubt that you are pleased by the fact that some of your brothers-in-arms have crossed the Mediterranean Sea, have covered distant deserts to confront an enemy based on his Fleet, and, after embracing their fellow-countrymen over here have managed to keep the enemy at bay at certain points on the coast... You know that what I like

---

[369] G.F. Abbott: *The Holy War in Tripoli*; Edward Arnold; London; 1912; p. 48.
[370] Ibid; p. 44.
[371] T.W. Childs: *Italo-Turkish Diplomacy*, op cit, p. 76.
[372] R. Simon: *Libya Between Ottomanism and Nationalism*, op cit, p. 112.
[373] Ibid.
[374] Ibid.
[375] *Militararchiv*, Freiburg (MA,) The Military Attache in Istanbul, 12 December 1911, RM 5/v 1570 reports on people who broke through the blockade.
[376] Lord Kinross: *Ataturk: The Rebirth of a Nation*; Weidenfeld and Nicolson; London; 1964; p. 49.

best in the soldier's profession is its craftsmanship. If we have here enough opportunity and enough time to carry out all the requirements of this craft, then we shall be able to perform services which will please the country. Oh Salih, God is my witness that up to now my only aspiration in life is to be a useful element within the army! I have for long been convinced that, to safeguard the country and give happiness to the people, it is necessary first of all to prove once more to the world that our army is still the old Turkish army.[377]

Many other officers came via different routes. A couple of Circassian cavalry officers, Major Isac and Major Sabi—'the one tall, blond, and broad-shouldered, with a face full of smiling good-nature; the other short, thick-set, and dark, with a strong, square forehead and a strong, square jaw,' arrived via the North African route.[378] They had left Istanbul 32 days before, and at Marseilles they disguised themselves in the manner that best suited their physique. Isac Bey passed himself off for a Russian nobleman, whilst Sabi Bey shaved his upper lip, wore a slouch hat slightly cocked, and adopted 'the swagger of a Yankee tourist.'[379] As they spoke foreign tongues, and had much native aplomb, they landed in Algiers without arousing any suspicion. From Algiers they travelled to Tunis by rail, and each time they found themselves in the carriage alone with some Muslims, they immediately revealed to them their identity and destination, not once doubting 'but that those True Believers would aid them. Nor were they disappointed.'[380] The Tunisians recognised in the Circassians

> Moslems brethren, harboured them in their homes at Tunis, disguised them as native merchants, engaged for them a motor-car driven by an Italian chauffeur, and saw them safely as far as Medenine.[381]

From there they hired camels, which took them in seven days to Nalut on the Jebel, then to Yefreen; and from Yefreen, leaving the mountains, they crossed the desert to Azizia, sleeping on the ground 'under the canopy of heaven,' with only a blanket between their bodies and the night cold, and subsisting on the little food they could pick up on their way.[382]

The group known as the *Teskilat-I mahsusa*, or special organisation, included in addition to Enver Bey and his brother Nuri, two other leading figures in the fighting: Sulayman (Sulaiman) al-Baruni and Ferhat Bey.[383] The latter two were the deputies who represented the province in the parliament that reopened after the 1908 Young Turk Revolution.[384] Sulaiman al-Baruni was a prominent man of letters; aged forty-two; and was an Ibadite Berber from the Jebel Nafusa. Bearded

---
[377] Ibid; p. 52.
[378] G.F. Abbott: *The Holy War in Tripoli*; op cit; p. 162.
[379] Ibid.
[380] Ibid.
[381] Ibid.
[382] Ibid.
[383] L. Anderson: *The State*; op cit; 128.
[384] Ibid, p. 126.

and well-groomed, he was a poet and a student of Arabic literature, and had sat for Tripolitania in the first Turkish parliament following the 1908 revolution.[385] When the war with Italy broke out, he immediately declared his support in the fight against the occupation, and appeared in the Turkish headquarters accompanied by 50 loyal sheikhs vowing both support and mobilisation of volunteers.[386] Very quickly he recruited about one thousand fighters who were involved in the first offensive against Italian positions near Tripoli (23 October 1911). Although he had no military training whatsoever, he still had great military skills, great capacity to lead men in combat, courage, and strong personality, and was sometimes referred to as the Commander of the Mountain Volunteers, and was even called 'the Minister of War of the Mountain District'.[387]

Ferhat Bey had spent his youth in Tunisia and France, had been a judge in his hometown, Zawiyah, and joined the ranks of the Young Turks, representing his native district in parliament.[388] Ferhat was offered by the Italians a large amount of money, many honours, including his nomination as Tripolitanian deputy in the Italian Parliament, but he refused, and remained throughout loyal to the Turks.[389]

Initially, Neschat Bey was the overall commander of Turkish forces. He is described as a brave and courteous gentleman of the old Turkish school; religious, dignified, leisurely in speech and in thought, and 'not much influenced by the European spirit.'[390] Ostler, one of the British war reporters, offers us a picture of this typical Turkish officer:

> Ordered from Constantinople to evacuate the town of Tripoli at the beginning of the war, and he did so. And if he had been ordered to hold the town in face of the Italian bombardment, Neshat Bey would be in Tripoli or under its ruins at this moment. Like most of his breed, he would suffer from a false impression of himself sooner than take the trouble to remove it; and consequently for some time relations between himself and some of the Arab leaders were strained. The Turk is in many respects like the traditional Briton — undemonstrative, slow-moving, and disdainful of self-justification; and Neshat Bey is essentially Turkish.[391]

Major Fethi Bey, formerly Turkish military attaché in Paris, was now in supreme command of the Turkish-Libyan forces.[392] Fethi Bey, an Albanian, tall, dark, had 'a grave, melancholy manner and a remarkably sweet voice.'[393] Almost alone of the Turkish officers, he seemed to have no illusion whatever as to the chance of any

---

[385] J. Wright: *Libya*, op cit, p. 131.
[386] R. Simon: *Libya Between Ottomanism and Nationalism*, op cit, p. 190.
[387] Ibid.
[388] L. Anderson: *The State*, op cit, p. 126.
[389] G.F. Abbott: *The Holy War in Tripoli*, pp. 116-7.
[390] A. Ostler: *Arabs in Tripoli*; John Murray; London; 1912; p. 64.
[391] Ibid; p. 65.
[392] Commodore W.H. Beehler: *The History of the Italian Turkish War*; op cit; p. 78.
[393] A. Ostler: *Arabs in Tripoli*; op cit; p. 67.

European intervention favourable to Turkey.[394] In the east, we have the future Minister of War, Enver, who like many, including Mustafa Kemal, had acquired his first war experience in Libya. These officers promptly took over organisation of the military resistance to the Italians. At the camps, they established procedures for arming, clothing, and paying the Libyan fighters.[395] Some of the Libyan fighters returned for a time to their farms, but the vast majority placed patriotism before pocket and remained at their posts even at the risk of subsequent starvation for themselves and their families.[396] Volunteers were paid in cash and daily rations of food and were organised in units by tribe, each company commanded by one Turk and two local Libyan officers.[397] The Turkish officers, who brought money and material from Istanbul, forbade every form of confiscation of local animals and insisted on paying for all they needed.[398]

The Sanusi religious order from the start gave its support to the Turks in its defence of Tripoli against the invader, and had already given assistance to Enver Bey in Cyrenaica.[399] Enver's letters, a selection of which is published in the *Lokal-Anzeiger* tell us a lot about the early campaign in Libya and much of the armament and its source:

> 'For January 28th,' he tells us, 'he travelled for nine hours at a stretch on a camel, partly through a district which the Italians thought to be favourable to them. "But they soon greeted me," says Enver Bey, "as the son-in-law of the Khalifa. They accompanied me, and told me how they also had fought against the Infidel. They spoke of the timid soldiers of the enemy, and I could not help laughing at the delusion under which the Italians laboured that they had these people on their side. If I had money I could do much, but it is my boast that I am forming an army without having a farthing in my pocket." And he succeeded in forming an army, for in a subsequent letter he says: "I found 900 desert warriors when I came here, and now I have under me 16,000 trained soldiers."
>
> On one occasion we took "2 machine-guns, 250 rifles, 2 cannon, 30,000 cartridges, 25 chests of shrapnel, which will be useful to us, and 10 mules which I have harnessed to my guns. Among the dead whom the enemy was unable to remove were 1 major, 1 captain, 5 lieutenants, and 200 men. We wanted to let one soldier whom we had captured run away again, but he seemed to be very pleased at having been captured, and now makes himself useful by cleaning the guns."[400]

---

[394] Ibid.
[395] L. Anderson: *The State and Social Transformation in Tunisia and Libya*, op cit, p. 128.
[396] E.N. Bennett: *With the Turks in Tripoli*, op cit; p. 23.
[397] L. Anderson: *The State*; op cit; 128.
[398] P.H. Stoddard: *The Ottoman Government and the Arabs, 1911 to 1918;* a Phd dissertation, Princeton University, 1963; p. 87
[399] E.N. Bennett: *With the Turks in Tripoli*; op cit; p. 27.
[400] F. McCullagh: *Italy's War for a Desert*; op cit; p. 56.

On 4 December 1911, the Italians undertook a more ambitious advance against the main Turkish base at Ain Zara. Before dawn on that day the Turkish camp and the positions held by themselves and Libyans round the town were subjected to a violent and concentrated bombardment by navy artillery. Then, after the ground had been prepared, three Italian columns issued from their camps and took part in the action, which was fought in the midst of heavy rain.[401] We have many accounts of this episode, and if by far the drawings by Seppings Wright capture the intensity of the operation, it is the description by Bennett which is far more interesting than the rest. At the launch of the operation, one Italian column remained in reserve at Sidi Mesri, whilst a second went into action, and not before long found itself fiercely engaged all day with the Libyans, who delivered a series of violent attacks from their positions east of the Turkish camp. By nightfall the Libyans had practically compelled the Italians to fall back on their lines.[402]

Here, once more, there was a great discrepancy between what happened and Italian propaganda. The Italians stated that after assaults on Ain Zara, they defeated an 8,000 strong enemy and captured field-guns. What happened, Bennett notes, was simply this: when the Turkish commander, whose forces numbered just a few hundreds, realised that this overwhelming Italian force, around 15,000, was moving past his left, and would soon be actually in his rear, he ordered a retreat. At 4 p.m. the Turks retired in 'a leisurely' way to their present lines.[403] What is of great interest here was the vast difference between Turkish and Libyan ways of operating. To the Turks, if a larger enemy force was about to cut your lines, the realistic thing to do would be to retreat before this happened. Not to the Libyans, who when receiving the order to retire, refused, protested, courageously, though recklessly, too, favouring frontal attacks, which left them exposed to intense Italian fire. This was not going to be the sole case of disagreement in similar situations; the only area where Turks and Libyans had a disagreement, for on everything else, in all accounts, the solidarity between the two sides was without equal. Eventually, at Ain Zara, both Libyans and Turks managed to extricate themselves from the encircling operation, the Italians, however, Bennett notes:

> Are always great at the capture of abandoned guns: there were some guns left behind at Tripoli which they kept on capturing and photographing for weeks. In the present action the Turks abandoned eight field-guns for the simple reason that they had no more ammunition for them, but the Italians made of the fact as if it was a major blow to the resistance.[404]

---

[401] E.N. Bennett: *With the Turks in Tripoli* op cit; p. 101.
[402] Ibid; p. 102.
[403] Ibid.
[404] Ibid; p. 103.

With the evacuation of Ain Zara, the Turkish-Libyan centre of resistance in the west had therefore moved further inland, but only a few miles, further away from the lethal effect of naval bombardment.[405]

The only way the Turks and Libyans could prevail was by draining Italian superior firepower, refusing direct challenge and pouncing at the right opportunity in the fastness of the great desert. Soon the opportunity to strike came on 19 December. Just around 2 in the morning, an Italian column of about 3,000 troops, led or misled by a group of local Libyans, for this was never asserted as they were subsequently slain by the Italians, marched inland in the direction of the oasis of Bir Tobras to destroy the local Turco-Libyan band there.[406] The Italian force made of three battalions of infantry, a squadron of cavalry and a good number of guns had left the entrenchment at Ain Zara to seek out the enemy.[407] There were in the area about 50 Turkish irregulars and under 500 Arab volunteers, including 60 Fezzanis (men from Fezzan); and 40 so-called Tunisians (men of Tunisian ancestry).[408] In the dark, the Italian column tired itself seeking to find its bearings, allowing the Turks and Libyans to organise their attack. Just before sunrise the assailants began to harass the Italians, the nimble Arabs attacking the column and disappearing as fast as they had appeared, 'leaping from one dune to another.'[409] By sunrise, the Italian column had already suffered much from the incessant attacks, and heavy losses had been incurred. Fatigue and sleeplessness caused the Italian column to gradually become disoriented and bogged down in the middle of sand. An operation that should have been over by now and the Italians resting in their camp had just begun. The Turkish commander tactics was to send batches of nimble Libyans to attack the flanks and rear of the Italians, which unsettled them further and deprived them from using their superior fire-power, especially the vast artillery at their disposal.[410] There were three groups of attackers: one attacking the Italians from the west, another from the east and another from the south.[411] And these three bodies of men, although few in numbers covered a huge area, fighting in scattered small groups, five here, three there, at times the distance between each group being 500 meters; the strongest of the groups being that made up of between 150 and 200 men, commanded by a Turkish lieutenant, attacking from the east.[412] Yet, the Italians were pinned down, heavily bled with fast mounting losses; in front of them, a deadly foe, springing from all directions, dangerous and brazen at once.

> I always thought, [said Hadj Mohammed, a Libyan fighter,] we Arabs were the bravest fighters in the world, but now I think the Albanians beat us!

---

[405] Ibid; p. 104.
[406] The best accounts of the battle are found in Abbot pp. 137- ff; and in Bennett pp. 108 ff.
[407] E.N. Bennett: *With the Turks in Tripoli* op cit; p. 109.
[408] G.F. Abbott: *The Holy War in Tripoli*, p. 138.
[409] E.N. Bennett: *With the Turks in Tripoli* op cit; p. 110.
[410] Ibid; 110-11.
[411] G.F. Abbott: *The Holy War in Tripoli*, p 143.
[412] Ibid 141.

> Drawing within twenty-five metres of the Italian cannon and shouting as they charged 'Ya hanzir! Ya Italiana!'[413]

All the Italians could do was to entrench themselves, and thus the day went and another draining night caught them in the vast desert, incapable of making any move that would expose their ranks. Harassed without respite, by the middle of the night, they were all but entirely encircled. They kept firing in every direction, including in the air to attract reinforcements from their base at Ain Zara, to no effect. Losses were rising, and were it not for the fact that their attackers were too few in numbers, the whole column would have been annihilated already.

Bewildered, exhausted, unaware, of course, of the true size of the enemy, springing from every angle, all the while shouting the Muslim war cry, Allah Akbar! the Italians, now began to give way.[414]

> 'I stood up,' said Hadj Mohammed, 'and fired! Then I saw all the Italians running away — the officers first, the men following helter-skelter. They had found themselves attacked on all sides, and were trying to escape back to Ain Zara. Ismail Effendi shouted to me: "After them, after them! Courage!"'[415]

Himself contemptuous of death, Ismail Effendi thrust forward, and for his daring received a wound; his fifth of the campaign, 'but being a Turk he gave Allah thanks, and made no boast of it.'[416]

In the midst of darkness, the Italians were in full retreat, still under attack. It was only at daybreak that the remnants of the column were met by reinforcements marching from Ain Zara.[417] It had been one of the early costliest operations for the Italians with several hundred killed amongst the troops and gunners.[418]

> Lucky indeed were the Italians [notes Bennett] who in the darkness of that dreadful night escaped the bullets and knives of the beleaguering Arabs and found themselves once more within the cover of their trenches and naval guns. No nation has ever failed more thoroughly than Italy to observe the Biblical injunction that those who think of engaging in warfare should first sit down and count the cost thereof![419]

> They (the Libyan fighters) came back [says Abbott who was in the Turkish-Libyan camp] loaded with spoils of war — infantry rifles and cavalry carbines, together with quantities of cartridges, officers' capes, men's plumed hats, sappers' shovels, tunics, shirts, breeches, haversacks, water-flasks, and a miscellaneous assortment of odds and ends, including lanterns, purses, cheap silver-plated little medals bearing the image of the Madonna, American one-dollar notes, Italian five-lire notes, fragments of

---

[413] Ibid 139.
[414] E.N. Bennett: *With the Turks in Tripoli* op cit; p. 111.
[415] G.F. Abbott: *The Holy War in Tripoli*, p 140.
[416] Ibid 146.
[417] E.N. Bennett: *With the Turks in Tripoli* op cit; p. 114.
[418] Ibid; 115.
[419] Ibid; 118.

Catholic Prayer-Books, and a whole collection of postcards and letters, which I was asked to read and translate. Some of these were found on a dead sergeant's body; they were letters from a mother to her son. Others were addressed to a corporal by his sisters, and others came to a hapless private from his sweetheart.[420]

*****
The Massacre of Libyans and Historical Narrative

On 23 October 1911, the Libyans and Turks launched a combined attack against the Italians in Tripoli. The attack was very costly to the Italians. In retaliation, the Italian army caused a bloodbath. McCullagh, the best-known war correspondent of the era, who just happened to be there, is the primary source of what happened.[421] Many other correspondents, mainly British and Germans, also wrote extensive accounts of the incident. The impact of this episode is extremely interesting, for the indifference of the Great Powers to the mass killing of Libyans led to the same reoccurring in other fields of war, including in the Balkans; and the ferocity and bitterness of the Balkan Wars itself led directly to the First World War. In fact all that happened in Libya served as trigger to what happened subsequently, including in how to shape information regarding events on the ground.

In regard to the incident narrated here, it is interesting to read first the following account by Lieutenant H.G. Montagu, of the 5th Battalion Royal Fusiliers, cabled to the *Central News*. His letter (with few omissions) dated November 4, 1911, is as follows:

> I feel it my duty to send you the following telegram, and I beg you, in the name of Christianity, to publish it throughout England. I am an English officer, and am now voluntarily serving in the Turkish army here. As you know already about the ferocious resistance which the Turks and Arabs are offering to the Italians, I will only just express my admiration for their bravery and fortitude, which would warm the heart of any Englishman and of any true soldier of the world.
>
> Imagine, then, my feelings when, on entering and driving the Italians out of the Arab houses which they had fortified and were holding, we discovered the bodies of some hundred and twenty women and children, with their hands and feet bound, mutilated, pierced, and torn. Later on at (?) we found a mosque filled with the bodies of women and children, mutilated almost beyond recognition. I could not count them, but there must have been three or four hundred.

---
[420] G.F. Abbott: *The Holy War in Tripoli*, p 143.
[421] F. McCullagh: *Italy's War for a Desert;* op cit; 1912.

> Sir, is this European war? Are such crimes to be permitted? Cannot England do something to stop such horrors. In our civilisation and times you can hardly believe it, but it is nevertheless true. I myself have seen it, and so I know. Even now we are getting news of further massacres of women and children discovered in different farms (?) lately occupied by the Italians.
>
> The idea of the Italians when they slaughtered these innocent was obviously one of revenge, from the way the bodies were mutilated, revenge for their heavy losses in battle.
>
> We are at this moment under a heavy shrapnel fire.
>
> You must excuse me if these sentences are somewhat disjointed. There is also an aeroplane circling over our position, directing the enemy's gunfire on us. Hoping you will do all you can to bring the barbarous atrocities I have mentioned before the British public and authorities.
>
> I am, Sir, yours truly,
> Herbert G. Montagu.
> Soukel Yohma, Tripoli.
> 5th Royal Fusiliers.
> Nov. 2, 1911.[422]

Lieutenant Montagu's letter was received with some caution. He was young, unknown, and a volunteer in Turkish ranks. His evidence was therefore considered suspect, and was disregarded. But soon there arrived evidence from all quarters.[423]

Francis McCullagh, who had been through the Russo-Japanese War, campaigning in Morocco, and few other places, wrote from Tripoli as the representative of *The New York World* and *The Westminster Gazette*.[424] Everyone at the Foreign Office was stunned by his communication of Monday, 6 November, for The Westminster Gazette. It said:

> As a protest against the murders of innocent Arab women, children and men last week, I returned my official papers as a war correspondent to General Caneva. About 400 women and children have been shot, and 4,000 men... Cripple and blind beggars have been deliberately shot; sick people, whose houses were burned, were left on the ground and refused even a drop of water.
>
> I personally witnessed scenes of horror, and photographed them. There has not been the faintest pretence of justice. The Arab quarter was overrun by crazy soldiers armed with revolvers, who were shooting every Arab man and woman they met. The officers were worse than the men, and the army is demoralised...

---
[422] W.T. Stead: *Tripoli and the Treaties or Britain's Duty in this War;* London; 1911; pp. 63-4.
[423] Ibid; p. 64.
[424] Ibid.

> The Arabs did mutilate corpses, but not till after the Italians began the massacres. The Arabs were at first most courteous opponents, bringing in the Italian wounded under a flag of truce.[425]

Bennet Burleigh, the veteran doyen of British war correspondents, a man of vast experience, tells the same story. Writing in Tripoli on 29 October, he reported:

> The oasis of palms is being ruthlessly cleared of its population of villagers, small farmers, and peasants. Very many have been killed, and their corpses bestrew the fields and roads. The scent of war's scythe poisons the air... Many have unquestionably been wantonly murdered. That is not always preventable in war, but in the twentieth century and in civilised warfare, it is quite without the pale to shoot men and lads wholesale on sight without trial, and because of their skin and dress.
>
> I have seen a crippled beggar — a man whose limbs were so deformed that he had to move by pushing along the ground in a sitting position — deliberately shot at near the Austrian Consulate. Dozens of other natives I have seen herded and corralled, and others fired upon in broad daylight. But there are half a dozen colleagues — English. French, and German — who assert that they have seen Arabs fusilladed in groups, and have even "snap-shotted" instances where soldiers and officers indiscriminately fired upon these unfortunate natives.[426]

Three correspondents rode out of the town into the oasis. It was four days after the fight. They thus record what they saw:

> On leaving the town, the first object which met our eyes was a group of from fifty to seventy men and boys who had been caught in the town on the previous day, or on October 25, and shot without trial of any sort. The majority of them were caught without arms, and were executed under a general order issued by the Governor, General Carlo Caneva, to exterminate all Arabs found in Tripoli or in the oasis. They had been led to this spot with their hands tied behind their backs and shot down indiscriminately. This mass of corpses lying in all attitudes in a solid mass piled on one another could not have covered a space greater than fifteen yards wide by five deep...[427]
>
> During our whole progress over a distance of two miles we never saw a single living Arab — man, woman or child.
>
> Lying just outside the outpost line was another group of about fifty men and boys who had evidently been taken out there on the previous day and shot en masse.[428]

---

[425] Ibid; pp. 64-5.
[426] Ibid; p. 72.
[427] Ibid; p. 73.
[428] Ibid.

Now, we have the pro-Italian narrative of the same event by McClure, who, like C. Lapworth, was brought to Libya in order to counter opinion unfavourable to the Italians:

> 'I will give, as an example of what may well have happened on other occasions,' begins McClure: 'one case recounted to me by an officer of the 82nd Regiment. His company was one of those sent to the relief of the eastern front, and as he and his men made their way through the oasis, they were continually fired upon by unseen enemies. At a bend of the road they sighted a group of Arabs in baracans. Some had rifles, and opened a scattered fire. The Italians fired back and several of the Arabs dropped. On arriving at the dead bodies, the officer found that one of them was that of a woman.[429] Is there any reasonable human being who can blame the officer or his men for the death of that woman, or of any others who may have been killed in like circumstances? Several women were killed (I have heard of half a dozen, and probably there were more), some by mistake, some because they were actually taking an active part in the fighting; the demands of self-defence made it necessary that these should be treated as combatants, not as women. The case already recounted, of the twelve-year old boy who attacked the Bersaglieri officer, may explain how some "children" were found among the dead, in addition to those who were killed by mistake, in the confusion of bush-fighting.
>
> These are cases of error, or of sheer necessity. I come now to cases of excess, where soldiers lost their heads, and failed to distinguish, where they might have distinguished, between innocent and guilty. For a reason which will be explained later, these cases must have been limited in number; and it can be shown conclusively that the Italian soldiers had received provocation enough to cause a loss of control, provocation which has caused other soldiers, of other nations, to see red. Putting aside all natural anger at the treachery of the Arab revolt, at the perfidy which turned against them those to whom they had showed kindness, with whom they had shared their food;[430] putting aside the desperate feeling that comes from a desperate situation; one fact stands out naked and horrible in all that it connotes:
>
> By the night of October 23 it was known only too well what had happened to some of the wounded and dead (Italians) who had fallen into the hands of the Arabs. An English correspondent has committed himself to the statement that the Arabs did mutilate corpses, but only after the massacres (sic). In the first place such a statement shows a blank ignorance of the A B

---

[429] Both men and women wear the baracan—a reputed descendant of the Roman toga—with one fold draped over the head. At a distance of twenty-five yards it is difficult for a newcomer to distinguish the sexes; at a hundred yards any one might be deceived. One correspondent has asserted that the dress of the women is totally different from that of the men. This is true of nomad Bedouins and Jews, but not of the Arabs who inhabit the Tripoli oasis. Note by W.K. McClure: *Italy in North Africa*; Constable and Company; London; 1913; p. 78.

[430] W.K. McClure: *Italy in North Africa*; p. 78.

C of Arab warfare. One may go farther, and say of Mussulman warfare. On the Indian frontier, in the Sudan and elsewhere, times without number, the same unprintable obscenities have been perpetrated upon the bodies of our dead. There are some who will never forget the field of Baker's El Teb, where many hundreds of corpses bore mute witness to the savage and insulting ferocity of the Arab warrior and his women.

And the few European witnesses of atrocities perpetrated by Turks, under the new regime as well as the old, will hesitate to suggest that the Arabs were left to themselves when they exercised their ingenuity upon the dead and living Italians who fell into their hands. The statement of the correspondent in question not only shows a general ignorance of what happens in war against Moslems, but a complete disregard of irrefutable evidence which was available to him as well as to other people, if he had chosen to try and see both sides of the question. Definite evidence of the discovery of mutilated bodies on the night of the 23rd and morning of the 24th has been put on record by (the Italian) Colonel Fara (now Major-General Fara), Captain Sereno, and other officers of the 11th Bersaglieri. Some of the few surviving soldiers of the 4th and 5th Companies report hideous scenes of cruelty and mutilation, outrages committed upon the dead and wounded when the fight was still raging, before there was any question of repression, when it was still doubtful whether the Italian left was going to be completely overwhelmed. One soldier, who escaped death by hiding in a well, declares that he saw his wounded comrades fall victims to the fury of Arab women, who dashed out their brains with large stones, stripped the dead bodies and proceeded to mutilate them. On the 24th, 25, 26, and 27th and at different times throughout the next six weeks, mutilated bodies were found in various parts of the oasis, but for purposes of evidence I have thought it well to limit myself to those cases which from their date cannot be considered, even by the most prejudiced critics, as being acts of revenge for Italian cruelty.[431] In the circumstances, is it surprising or extraordinary, is it really a matter for clamour, on the part of a friendly nation, that individual Italian soldiers should have lost control and been guilty of cruelty, or of undiscriminating slaughter? Such acts are ugly, and worse; they give just cause for keen regret; they may be fairly quoted as an argument against war; but they may not with justice be used as the ground of an indictment against an army and a nation, unless it can be conclusively shown that they were committed wholesale by a soldiery which gave itself up to massacre, whether deliberately or with an insensate desire to kill. Charges of wholesale massacre have been definitely laid at

---

[431] A special interest attaches to the fact that the earliest report of the fight of October 23 which reached Scutari (Albania) from Turkish sources, stated that the Turks had crucified fifty Christians. The news gave great satisfaction to the local Mohammedans, who taunted their Christian neighbours with this fresh proof of Turkish power. The report said nothing of Italian atrocities. Note in W.K. McClure; Italy; p. 80.

the door of the Italian army, yet these charges have not been supported by reasoned evidence, and seem, in fact, capable of disproof.'[432]

Why this account is fascinating is not in the denial itself, but in justifying the Italian action; and far more interestingly even, it shows that it is the men (and the women) of the pen who can reshape events, and plunge the truth of war into the darkest of meanders. In the end, what happened in Libya, just as on any ground of conflict, whether then or after, or today, becomes no longer what truly happened or is happening, but how ably any one side can present such an event. Likewise, morality, bestiality, human rights, barbarism, and similar definitions, are in truth relative associations with one group, or entity, or another, and have nothing to do with reality, depending essentially on who has power over, and control of, opinion, whether then or today.

4. The Myth of Arab Hatred for the Turk

> Between the Turk and the true Arab [McClure (the apologist for Italian occupation of Libya) reminds us] there is a deep antagonism that centuries of association have not bridged, and in the subject races of Tripolitania hostility to the Turk is firmly rooted. Everywhere it may be found, and though in the year of their brave and hopeless struggle the Turks attached the Arabs to them as never before, there are no regrets for their going.
> Some twenty years ago, a Turkish officer stationed in Tripoli took to wife an Arab girl of unusual beauty. The marriage was far from being a success, and their domestic unhappiness culminated in an appeal by the woman for the protection of the authorities. She alleged that she feared the violence of her husband, and prayed for a divorce. In reality the cause of the trouble was sheer incompatibility, and in support of her claim for protection she gave a striking illustration of the truth. Apparently the unfriendly atmosphere of his home had roused the Turk to exasperation and to the conviction that any improvement was hopeless. He had seized his wife, and, baring her thigh and his own, had grimly declared: "If I should cut flesh there from your body and here from mine, and put the two pieces in a pot and boil them together, even then they could not mix. For Turk and Arab must always be separate."
> The woman feared that he might one day make the test, and the Cadi recognised that their matrimonial differences were essentially incurable. A divorce was granted forthwith; the woman married one of her own people, and lives in Tripoli to-day.[433]

---

[432] W.K. McClure: *Italy in North Africa*; pp. 77-81.
[433] W.K. McClure: *Italy in North Africa*; p. 265.

This is the anecdote. The fact is, in the vast Western literature on North Africa's history, if one theme predominates, it is the alleged hatred between Turks and Arabs, just as amongst Arabs and Berbers. With hardly if any exception, amongst French historians, in particular, whether Brignon,[434] Fleury,[435] Julien,[436] and all the others, one constantly comes across the supposed atrocities inflicted by Arabs, Berbers, Turks, and Kuluglis on each other — a visceral hatred, it seems the region's history was a perpetual bloodbath, tens of times worse than the wars between Catholics and Protestants, French and Germans, French and English, or Germans and English.

This is precisely the view which drives the meddlers in North African or Middle Eastern affairs to always activate the sectarian button. These meddlers are the politicians, media people, and scholarship. These meddlers are at work today just as they have been for nearly two centuries, present in all Muslim fields of conflict, always keen to bring forth and exacerbate the sectarian element. And to be fair, they do find amongst Arabs, Turks, Berbers, Kurds, Sunnis, and Shias, some who are inhabited by the genes of gullibility and betrayal, and who are happy to be misled, ready to sell out, and eager to tear their own land and faith by the gun and by the pen.

In regard to scholarship, including historians, the clear aim is always to exacerbate the sectarian element (and hatred) in relation to Muslims, but hardly, if ever, when referring to Christians, who, it would seem, are all united today, just as they always have been, under the same fatherly or motherly ideology. This author himself had to fight off Western reviewers and editors of some of his articles pressurising him, that he should add words such as Berber, Arab, Sunni, and so on, when such additions were meant to exacerbate the sectarian element.

'The Turkish-Libyan hatred for each other' was a major reason in Italian view or claim to colonise Libya. The Italians, as noted, had come 'to free Libyans of the Turkish yoke.' The first armed encounters, however, had proved everything but that. War correspondent after war correspondent noted the same vast support given to the Turks not just by Libyans, but also by people from all around the region. Towards the end of 1911, we are informed:

> Arabs arrived almost daily. A war-drum would be heard in the distance and gradually a column would appear over the gentle undulations of the desert The Arabs, "chattering like cranes," advanced in ragged fours, the result of the elementary drill provided by perhaps a couple of silent Turkish regulars marching with them. At the head of the column rode the sheikhs, splendidly mounted, and Crescent flags embroidered with Koran texts waved in the air. Amid loud shouts of welcome and the trilling notes of

---
[434] J. Brignon et al: *Histoire du Maroc*; Hatier; Paris; 1967; p. 208.
[435] G. Fleury: *Comment l'Algerie Devint Francaise*; Perrin, Paris, 2004, p. 121.
[436] C.A. Julien: *History of North Africa*; tr., from French by J. Petrie; Routledge & Kegan Paul; London; 1970.

feminine joy the new arrivals would march round the camp, and then, taking up a bivouac ground, settle down in coloured masses "like garden beds," according to the picturesque wording of the gospel narrative. Splendid reinforcements came from Tibou and distant Fezzan, as well as from nearer regions in the east, south, and west. The Fezzani had actually taken forty-six days to cover their tremendous march across the desert, and a large contingent from the fierce Tuaregs of the Sahara was daily expected. One evening a caravan of five hundred camels arrived laden with dates, a present sent in advance by tribesmen in the far interior.[437]

'I remember,' says Ostler, 'the arrival of the vanguard of those from Fezzan, men who had been a month upon the road. They came in chanting to a savage roll of desert drums and the squealing of a goatskin bagpipe. There were negroes with them, with shocks of fuzzy hair outstanding from their temples; and their corded legs, coated with dust, were grey and silver in the sunlight.
At their head a huge Arab sheikh sat a white stallion, singing as he rode, and brandishing a little lance. He threw his hood back from a savage, war-scarred countenance, broad-nosed, full-lipped and with a sparse and curling grizzled beard; and gazed from under heavy lids with an incomparable haughtiness. A minstrel in the ranks broke into quavering song, and the men, shaking their weapons in the air and stamping till the earth shook, broke into a mighty chorus.
"Oulad bu zin!" they shouted, "Oulad bu zin!"
And the cry, meaning, roughly, "We are sons of mighty fathers!" — ["Chips of the old block" would be a sound equivalent in English of this desert slang] — ran through the camp like fire, and became the catch-word of the army.'[438]

Even the religious fraternities, which we read were in constant enmity with the Turks proved rather the very reverse. About the middle of January 1912, came the support of the Sheikh es-Senussi, who issued to the inhabitants of Tripolitania a manifesto inscribed on a silk banner urging them to continue the struggle, indicating that he himself would soon join in at the head of a large force; such a 'fervid' proclamation that Libyan tribesmen joined in ever greater numbers.[439]

They were not alone, among those who joined the Turks were Berbers, 'with broad cheek-bones and narrow, pointed chins, and cold, pale eyes with an intolerable glitter in them,' besides, Shamba Arabs, and Kabyles from the Algerian mountains.[440] There were volunteers from the Algerian oases, who came from Wargla, men 'of substance and consequence in their distant country,' who owned

---
[437] E.N. Bennett: *With the Turks in Tripoli*, op cit; p. 173.
[438] A. Ostler: *Arabs in Tripoli*; op cit; p. 90.
[439] G.F. Abbott: *The Holy War in Tripoli*; op cit; p. 269.
[440] A. Ostler: *Arabs in Tripoli*; op cit; 1912; p. 91.

large herds, the herd behind them 'a gift which they had brought for the army—their contribution to the holy cause.'[441] From even further came Hoggar Tuaregs — 'forbidding giants, swathed in black, and veiled till only their long cruel eyes were seen.' Many, at first, looking weak and ill-nourished, their lips and gums pale amber colour from lack of food, and their feet torn by the sharp stones of the mountain paths, but two days of rest and good feeding had restored them again to their full strength.[442] Their arrival was absolutely unexpected, for no emissaries had been sent to the Tuaregs, and no news of their coming had been received, as they crossed the desert by paths unknown to the telegraph. 'Could a better proof be adduced of the spontaneity and the sincerity of the spirit which animates the children of Islam?'[443]

Women also joined the fight, some of them 'of slightly negroid face, and of a richer hue of brown than the northern desert folk.' Some wore the skins of leopards, and had collars of panther's teeth. Afterwards, many went into battle with the men. One led the first attack at Gargaresh on 18-20 January 1912.[444]

Seppings Wright who was also in the Turkish camp, notes:

> Amazons accompanied them too in great numbers. There is a story told of a league composed entirely of women, in all about forty of them, banded together in spite of all objections, who vowed to take the sword and gun, and help their men-folk to drive the infidel out of the country. Let me picture one, Selima, as I remember her, a stocky pock-marked damsel, not beautiful, but possessing a perfect manner and the sweetest of voices. Squatting at the entrance to my tent, she had just arrived from the trenches, armed with Italian rifle and bandolier, a scimitar, and a long lance, once the arm of some unfortunate Italian picket whom she had surprised. She sat there talking of battle and fighting as if she were reading me out some choice menu. The fires of enthusiasm gleamed in her dark eyes as she told of how she had been shooting at the enemy for two or three months. The rifle that she held, as the lance, represented the spoils of war.[445]

Ostler, the correspondent of many fields of war narrates this quirky story:

> "How came you so far from Afghanistan to a fight which is none of your people's?" he asked the man sat in front of his tent.
> "God's battles are the battles of all Moslems," said he, "and I am a Moslem. It was at Mecca, as I told thee, that I heard about the war; and Mecca is half way here from my place. So I came on. After passing the border of Egypt, I fell in with a caravan for Benghazi. We had good fighting there, but the Italians would not come out against us; so I came here."

---

[441] G.F. Abbott: *The Holy War in Tripoli*; op cit; p. 165.
[442] A. Ostler: *Arabs in Tripoli*; op cit; p. 91.
[443] G.F. Abbott: *The Holy War in Tripoli*; p. 166.
[444] A. Ostler: *Arabs in Tripoli*; p. 96.
[445] H.C. Seppings Wright: *Two Years Under the Crescent*; Small, Maynard & Company; Boston; 1913; p. 89.

I asked him whether he knew of any others who had come as far as he to join in the war.

"No," he answered, "but there are men already here from Fezzan, down to Bornu and even Tibesti; and there are others on the road."

I asked him did he always go afoot.

"Mostly," said he, "but I'm a clever thief; and, who knows, I may steal a good beast some dark night. There's a fine bay stallion out there, now. Perhaps, when the Turkish soldier's eyes are off him"

"My horse." I said.

"Eh, well" — he rose and stretched himself — "guard him well at night, sahib. Now I shall go on to the Arab camp."

He swung out of the hut, and swaggered off down the road with a gait which marked him out from desert men. I never saw him again, but afterwards I heard that he had risen to some eminence amongst the Arabs.[446]

The Pan-Islamic solidarity that seems to fade away at times of peace, seems indeed to regenerate itself under a multiplicity of forms in times of conflict. A leader of the resistance thus put it:

> We owe our great prosperity nowadays partly to the generous and enthusiastic children of Islam, who have been raising funds for the holy war in every corner of the Moslem world—from Natal in the South to Stambul in the North, and from Morocco in the west to India in the east—funds which, collected in silver, reach us in gold—packing-cases full of glittering Turkish Liras, French Louis, English Sovereigns, and German twenty-Mark pieces.[447]

In fact it was at the time noted that one of the difficulties encountered at Tunis arose from the scarcity of gold coinage in the city. A subscription list organised by some Turkish officers in Tunis had yielded the vast sum of 70,000, and the banks had almost run out of Napoleons (gold coins), for paper money was useless in Tripoli; proof of the support to the Turkish cause by 'France's Moslem subjects.'[448]

There was also a health mission from England, formed under the auspices of the All-India Moslem League.[449] It was headed by Dr. Bernard Haigh and seconded by Dr. C.E.H. Smith; and Captain Dickson-Johnson as manager.[450] They were accompanied by nurses, and their aim was to set up a hospital on the hills beyond Gharien.[451]

---

[446] A. Ostler: *Arabs in Tripoli*; op cit; p. 292.
[447] G.F. Abbott: *The Holy War in Tripoli*; op cit; p. 229.
[448] E.N. Bennett: *With the Turks in Tripoli*, op cit p. 34.
[449] A. Ostler: *Arabs in Tripoli*; op cit; p. 303.
[450] Ibid.
[451] Ibid.

More interesting was the Yemeni stand, which provided the warmest support for the Turks.[452] The Yemen that had, until the Italian invasion, been the constant sore on the Ottoman side, now instantly changed from foe to friend, even more, in fact.[453] The Sultan received a letter from the rebel chiefs, who stated that, 'In face of the common outrage on Islam, all true followers of the Prophet must stand shoulder to shoulder.'[454]

And, at least symbolically, 'they offered the services of 100,000 Arabs for service in Tripoli.'[455]

As a result of the co-operation of Said Idriss with the Italians, the ruler Imam Yahia proclaimed a 'holy war,' and called upon all the inhabitants of Yemen to lay aside their grievances against the Turks and rally to their support instead, and to destroy Said Idriss.[456]

In Libya itself, by far the most charismatic of all Ottoman officers was a man of the Yemen. The Commandant at Zwara was a distinguished Arab, Bimbashi (Major) Mohammed Musa Bey. He was a relative of Imam Yahia. Musa Bey was trained in the Military College in Istanbul, and has shown incomparable ability during his command of the Zwara coast-line, his influence on, and respect from, the Arabs 'amazing.'[457] Musa Bey is described as having all the physical characteristics of a pure-blooded Arab — slender in form and small of stature; he had a lean, swarthy face, with a large forehead, an aquiline nose, a drooping moustache, and a short, curly beard under a firm chin. His hair, like his beard, was jet black.[458] This 'delicate little man' was entrusted with the task of defending an unfortified coast more than eighty miles long against the fleets and armies of a great European Power; and at first sight

> 'No one could have seemed less qualified for the task or less conscious of it. With his tunic and shirt unbuttoned, a grey overcoat thrown casually over his shoulders, a pair of yellow slippers imperfectly adjusted on his feet, and a conical white cap carelessly perched on his black curls, the Bimbashi was to be seen at all times sauntering about like one in a state of perpetual somnambulation. His words were few — perhaps twenty a day — and he had cut down even the short Arab inquiry "Keif el hal" (How are you?) into the shorter still "Keif." He never raised his voice above a soft whisper, and a curiously wistful smile always accompanied his monosyllabic speech. Nothing seemed capable of rousing Musa Bey from his apathy — not even the advent of the enemy.[459]'

---

[452] E.N. Bennett: *With the Turks in Tripoli*, op cit; p. 184.
[453] Ibid; p. 185.
[454] Ibid.
[455] Ibid.
[456] Commodore W.H. Beehler: *The History of the Italian Turkish War*; op cit; p. 60.
[457] E.N. Bennett: *With the Turks in Tripoli*, op cit; p. 60.
[458] G.F. Abbott: *The Holy War in Tripoli*; op cit; p. 23.
[459] Ibid.

Musa's staff included four distinct races — a fair Albanian, a black Fezzani Arab, a European Turk, and an Anatolian Turk. With them was a grey-bearded Lieutenant. Under their command was a battalion of khaki-clad regulars, made up of the above races, and 'some pure negroes.'[460] This force, and all the Libyan irregulars along the coast, were under Musa's command. The Turks under his command had long known him for being a just but very stern commander, who would not tolerate the slightest breach of discipline, and that any man who neglected his duty was immediately sent up to headquarters to be chastised by the Bimbashi himself, who even administered corporal punishment to a Captain.[461] The Arab volunteers soon got to know him, too. In matters of discipline, Bimbashi Musa Bey made no distinction between regulars and volunteers, between Turks and Arabs; all alike were soldiers and should have the same single-minded devotion to duty.[462] When following some rainfall, rare in the region, some of the tribesmen sought to return home to till their lands, the Bimbashi quietly told them that the penalty for desertion was death.[463] They straight gave up the thought. Some weeks before a tribesman had stolen arms from the Turkish camp at Suk el Juma, near Tripoli; he was caught and Musa Bey himself shot him.[464] When the Italians first bombed Zwara the townspeople panicked, and started fleeing, thus leaving Zwara at the mercy of an Italian landing-party. When Musa Bey's orders to "be steady" were disregarded, he drew his revolver and, without further ado, shot the two chief panic-mongers dead.[465] Order was restored. Briefly, 'this man, in appearance never awake, was in reality never asleep,' controlling silently and surely all around him.[466] 'The pickets that watched the sea on the north and the patrols that scoured the desert on the south were alike answerable to him; the caravans that passed to and from the Turkish camp were under his protection; his spirit was felt in every spot and by every man within the region entrusted to his care.'[467]

> But until I met this officer [says Ostler] I could not have believed the Arab nature so capable of self-discipline and steady application to the drudgery of military routine. Seeing the Bimbashi at work organising drilled troops from the raw Arabs of the countryside; receiving the reports of his scouts from every quarter of the area under his control (he had so perfect a network of pickets and patrols that not a stray camel could cross the frontier without his knowing it); deciding upon the affairs of the refuge camp; organising a constant supply of provisions for the headquarter camp; and keeping an unfailing outlook for Italian cruisers along eighty miles of coast-line — seeing all this, I should have thought Musa Mehmet

---

[460] Ibid.
[461] Ibid; p. 24.
[462] Ibid.
[463] Ibid.
[464] Ibid.
[465] E.N. Bennett: *With the Turks in Tripoli*, op cit; p. 61.
[466] G.F. Abbott: *The Holy War in Tripoli*; op cit; p. 24.
[467] Ibid; pp. 23-5.

an exception to the rule of Arab intolerance of routine: but that afterwards I met others like him.[468]

*****
The German Hospital

Seppings Wright unveils for us a German institution, a hospital, with typical German sense of order even in the middle of the desert.

> The camp was laid out with German thoroughness. There were six large marquees, each of which accommodated from thirty to forty patients. Cooking and scavenging were most scrupulously attended to, and the water, the cause of so much sickness in that country, was always filtered and boiled. At a short distance from the camp a squad of washerwomen were employed all day in keeping the linen scrupulously clean. The officers' quarters occupied about a third of the compound. The mess-room was in the open air, two long tables being fixed to the ground and shaded all day by the foliage of a big olive-tree.
> The staff consisted of two German and two Turkish doctors. The routine was carried out with the greatest regularity, and at five o'clock every day one or the other of the doctors spent two hours in attending to the medical needs of the whole district, which was no easy task. I have noticed as many as fifty or sixty patients crowding into the room for advice and treatment.
> Originally built by the Turks for a schoolhouse, the hospital contained a room that had been fitted up for operations. Another had been arranged for the Rontgeu rays with as much care and attention to detail as any of the great European institutions.
> Whilst we were there, one of the German nurses—the third victim of duty and Christianity—died, and that evening, as the sun sank, his remains were lowered into a vault. The ceremony was simple and impressive. Carried to his last resting-place by his German colleagues, followed by the grateful Turks and Arabs, the funeral cortege wound its short way to a shady corner in a peaceful clump of olives.
> After the ceremony, during which Christians and Mahomedans stood there hand in hand—East and West thus being united in the sacred bonds of brotherhood—one could not help condemning the craft and statecraft which brought so much misery upon the country. No one could have listened to the fervent address of the Bey without having responsive

---
[468] A. Ostler: *Arabs in Tripoli*; op cit; p. 30

feelings with regard to the duties of man to man, of nation to nation. There is but one God the Father of All.[469]

Our friends the Germans left shortly afterwards, and the whole district turned out to give them a good send-off, while women wailed as the little company disappeared at a turn of the winding road. With magnificent generosity they presented the whole outfit—tent, baggage, medicine, to the Turkish doctors. This splendid gift was estimated at a monetary value of ten thousand pounds. But beyond mere material value, this present was a record of brotherly love which was highly valued.[470]

5. From January 1912 till the end of War (Oct 1912)

From the beginning of the new year, there occurred a further tightening of the frontiers somehow to starve the Turkish-Libyan resistance. The French government earnestly endeavoured 'to stop all contraband trade,' and although seemingly seeking to stop the smuggle of arms, the measure was in truth to stop every form of basic supplies, including food. There were the odd and highly publicised seizures of arms such as on 17 January, when the Russian steamer Odessa arrived at Sfax from Prevesa and a large consignment of arms and ammunition concealed in the coal bunkers was found and seized by the French.[471]

Meanwhile the military campaign was still proceeding with even greater intensity and ferocity. The Italians made repeated attempts during January and early in February to capture Zanzur but failed with heavy loss of life.[472] A further attack on the place, weeks later on 22 February with four battalions of infantry and three field batteries was repulsed.[473] In their attacks against Zanzur the Italians used two dirigible balloons arranged for throwing various kinds of bombs and hand grenades, but the Turks and Libyans were in force, were strongly fortified and equipped with artillery and machine guns.[474]
Seeking to adapt to local warfare, the Italians collected 3000 burden-bearing camels and 300 riding camels for the camel corps in Tripoli. Without much success. A battalion of Askaris and a camel riding detachment that arrived from Eritrea late in February was routed by the Libyans on 4 March in Bir-el-Turki, the

---

[469] H.C. Seppings Wright: *Two Years Under the Crescent*; Small, Maynard & Company; Boston; 1913; pp. 134-5.
[470] Ibid; p. 137.
[471] Commodore W.H. Beehler: *The History of the Italian Turkish War*; op cit; p. 56.
[472] Ibid; p. 52.
[473] Ibid; p. 53.
[474] Ibid; p. 62.

Askaris only managing to escape into Tripoli under cover of darkness with heavy losses.[475]

The Libyans and Turks did not confine themselves to defensive action or to attacking marching units, but also directed operations against fortified positions. On the night of 10 March, a body of 500 tribesmen, divided into two columns, under the command of two Turkish Lieutenants and several Arab sheikhs from the Sahel, marched north towards the coast.[476] The object was Ain Zara where thousands of Italians had entrenched themselves. Both columns crept up close to the Italian trenches undetected until reaching a minefield where the explosion of two mines gave the enemy the alarm. Nonetheless the Libyans launched a fierce attack against the barbed wire, as ever crying, 'Allah Akbar!'[477] Before long, the first Italian line of defence was breached by the first column, and heavy loss was caused to the Italians.[478] The second column was less successful suffering great loss to heavy machine gun fire and artillery coming to the rescue.[479] The net result of the operation was the push back of the Italian defensive system even closer to the coastline, their elaborate network, the fruit of months of labour and sophisticated engineering, having been largely destroyed in one battle.[480]

To the east, where the group of Enver and Mustafa Kemal was based, likewise, attacks by the Turks at Derna on 3 March and at Mirsa Tobruk on 11 March were repulsed with difficulty, but the most serious fighting took place at Suani el Rani or "Due Palme" "Two Palms" (near Benghazi), on 12 March 1912.[481] The enemy, according to the Italian General Staff,

> Showed considerable force and started a general attack upon the city, but hesitated, owing to our immediate and energetic counter-attack. They attempted to withstand the attack, but in vain; our valorous troops surrounded them with a ring of fire and steel and annihilated them.[482]

In these engagements in Cyrenaica during the month ending 15 March 1912, the Italians lost 193 killed and 350 wounded.[483]

Neither side was able to register the decisive blow, though. The Italians could not venture inland, whilst the Turks and Libyans could not capture the Italian main strongholds despite their repeated attacks and mounting Italian losses. Tobruk did not yield, and neither did other fortresses along the coast.[484] The Italians

---

[475] Ibid; p. 63.
[476] G.F. Abbott: *The Holy War in Tripoli*; op cit; p. 294.
[477] Ibid.
[478] Ibid.
[479] Ibid; p. 295.
[480] Ibid; p. 295.
[481] Italian General Staff: *The Italo-Turkish War*; English tr., R. Tittoni, Franklin Hudson Publishing Company; 1914; p. 44.
[482] Ibid.
[483] Commodore W.H. Beehler: *The History of the Italian Turkish War*; op cit; p. 64.
[484] Lord Kinross: *Ataturk*; op cit; p. 51.

were constantly receiving reinforcements by sea, and naval artillery fire was a powerful arm in deciding encounters on the ground.[485]

The Italians, of course, could not be ejected, but could not advance either. They were restricted to the towns and their adjacent oases, and limited themselves to sorties and small operations, with little permanent effectiveness.[486] The situation reached a stalemate. And somehow this might have opened the way to activities on the diplomatic front. On 9 March, 1912, the representatives of Germany, Austria, England, France, and Russia took a united step for this purpose with the Italian government in Rome.[487] They asked confidentially upon what terms Italy would agree to suspend hostilities. The Italians demanded

> That Turkey shall recognize Italy's absolute sovereignty over the African provinces and withdraw all Turkish officers and troops from Africa, strictly forbidding Turkish officers to lead the Arabs in opposing the Italians; and Italy will then cease hostilities in all parts of the Turkish empire and reduce the imposts on Turkish goods to the former rates. Italy will, on the other hand, recognize the religious Caliphate and give amnesty to all natives. Italy will assume that part of the Turkish debt apportioned to Tripoli, and will purchase the Turkish government property situated in Tripoli from the Turkish government. Italy further promises to agree, with other powers, to preserve the integrity of the Turkish empire.[488]

Turkey replied to Italy's claim by

> Reasserting her claim to full sovereignty over her African provinces, and [stating that] the Arabians were determined to continue their resistance to the Italian conquest under all conditions.[489]

Libyan representatives in Istanbul declared that they would continue the war even if Turkey accepted the annexation of these provinces to Italy, and firmly stated that the Italian proclamation of annexation of Libyan provinces to Italy was null and void.[490]

This was the signal for the conflict to resume afresh. On 19 May, a strong Italian force of five battalions with mountain artillery and machine guns, marched towards El Atel, on the Tunisian caravan road southwest of Sidi Ali. Their advance was cut short, but it was during the Italian retreat that the Turkish-Libyan cavalry inflicted terrible losses on the party.[491]

The Italians started another expedition on the same route on 31 May and, after gaining some success, were compelled to return to Sidi Ali.[492]

---
[485] Ibid; p. 51.
[486] G. Volpe: *L'Impressa di Tripoli, 1911-1912*, Rome, 1946, pp. 66-8.
[487] Commodore W.H. Beehler: *The History of the Italian Turkish War*; op cit; p. 61.
[488] Ibid; pp. 61-62.
[489] Ibid; p. 62.
[490] Ibid.
[491] Ibid; p. 83.
[492] Ibid.

Zanzour, only 15 kilometres west of Tripoli, had remained a major objective of Italian attacks, and on 8 June, they marched from Tripoli in order to capture the oasis. The advancing army was composed of 14 battalions of infantry, one brigade of cavalry and a mountain battery, a total of 12,000 men under the command of General Camerana.[493] The Turks and Libyans had, however, occupied the heights of Abd-el-Gilil and the eastern border of the oasis, and were able to sustain the heavy firing by long-range artillery from the Italian ships off the coast.[494] After a hard-fought engagement, the Italians entrenched themselves and secured a position for a while before retreating back to Tripoli leaving the Turco-Libyan forces still in possession of the oasis.[495]

The early summer season was marked by fierce fighting along the front. One engagement at Sidi Said in the Zwara region, which lasted from the 26 until 28 June 1912, was particularly costly in loss of life.[496] Some of the spots were fought over recurrently, captured, lost, recaptured again, before being lost again. Lebda in the Homs region was fiercely contested; hard fought over in May before more fighting in June, and the contest still remaining undecided.[497] Misrata, east of Tripoli, was even more fiercely contested; the main fighting taking place on 8 July 1912, when it was at last captured by the Italians but at great cost; just as Gheran on 20 July 1912, where the Italians suffered heavily.[498] The Italian capture of Sidi Said and Sidi Ali (28 June and 15 July) was also dearly obtained, in both instances, once more, heavy naval bombardment of Turkish-Libyan positions deciding the final outcome.[499] The major problem the Italians found was that these successes meant defending new positions when they were struggling to hold on to others, with multiplication of garrisons and an extension of their trench system, lengthening their lines of communications, exposing themselves to ambushes in the desert, which in turn meant more troops, more guns, more money, and more deadlocks.[500] Then, further aggravation was caused by the onset of the summer season, which opened with intense heat and violent sandstorms.[501]

In what had become an un-winnable war, Italian morale threatened to flounder any moment. To counter the effects, throughout the conflict, the Italians kept a strict lid on reports of their losses in particular, and generally recast military failures into successes. The Battle of Kasr Ras el Leben in the Derna region (September 17, 1912) is thus described by the Italians:

---

[493] Ibid.
[494] Ibid.
[495] Ibid.
[496] Italian General Staff: *The Italo-Turkish War*; op cit; p. 82.
[497] Ibid.
[498] Ibid.
[499] G.F. Abbott: *The Holy War in Tripoli*; op cit; Note p. 326.
[500] Ibid.
[501] Commodore W.H. Beehler: *The History of the Italian Turkish War*; op cit; p. 78.

> On the 15th and 16th of September the enemy made tentative and weak attacks here and there on our front. The 17th was the day of battle. This engagement was not preordained on our part, but it was a direct consequence of our advance and the location assumed and maintained from the night of the 14th.
>
> The battle was composed of three distinct actions: a weak one early in the morning on our extreme left, in which the enemy was easily repulsed; the other two respectively heavy, at the head of the Bent in the morning, and again on our extreme left in the afternoon; but in the evening the enemy was defeated and left the field covered with dead and wounded.
>
> On that memorable day the Arab-Turk forces, several thousand strong, with plenty of well-commanded artillery, conducted by Enver Bey, arrayed themselves against the solidity, calmness, and vigor of the counter-attacks of our troops, white and native, conducted by the conspicuous ability of our officers and guided by a clear conception of tactics, with harmonious and effectual opportune dispositions of troops.
>
> Our losses of 10 officers and 174 men, dead and wounded, were small compared with those of the enemy, of whom 1,135 were found dead near our lines.[502]

In truth, Commodore W.H. Beehler, who was then following the conflict and compiled the most proficient military study of it (in fact in order to serve American war effectiveness for future conflicts), put the Turkish Libyan losses on this particular occasion at 111 killed.[503]

G.F. Abbott was also reporting on the conflict, and had already concluded that many if not most Italian war reports were just exaggerated fiction, Italian General Staff and media making all sorts of claims such as when Italian journals wrote:

> It shows that the Italian soldier, even after a long march in the Tripolitan summer, is more than a match for his foe. The long march in question was just about five miles, and a good many of the men who took that stroll were Abyssinians.[504]

On 20 September, at last, the Italian troops in Tripoli, under the command of Lieutenant General Ragni, succeeded in capturing the Oasis of Zanzur. Again the account by the Italians differs from independent sources. The Italian General Staff declared:

> The occupation of the heights of Sidi Abdul-Gehl gave us the control of the oasis of Zanzur. With a view, however, to further operations, it was necessary to materially secure the possession of the oasis and to push on towards the hills that skirted it on the south, to the valley of Hira; and

---
[502] Italian General Staff: *The Italo-Turkish War*; op cit; pp. 75-76.
[503] Commodore W.H. Beehler: *The History of the Italian Turkish War*; op cit; p. 93.
[504] G.F. Abbott: *The Holy War in Tripoli*; op cit; note p. 306.

exactly on the height of Sidi Bilal. On September 20, 1912, three days after the bloody defeat of Enver Bey's troops at Derna, the enemy left 2,000 more dead on the field of battle, and their resistance around Tripoli was definitely weakened. Our losses were heavy, but, compared with those of the enemy, small: 10 officers dead and 22 wounded; 105 men dead and 411 wounded. The troops had to fight and maneuver on ground difficult to march and deploy upon. The temperature at certain hours was 90 degrees in the shade. Led by officers who set a splendid example, our soldiers of all the arms, of all the corps, and those of the Colonial troops, gave admirable proof of endurance and elevated spirit during the twelve hours of combat.[505]

Commodore Beehler, again, had a different take of the story, not mentioning the heavy Turkish-Libyan losses stated by the Italians:

> After a desperate battle that lasted ten hours and in which the Italians lost 200 killed, the Turkish-Arabian forces retreated to Zawia, a place not far from the coast, and about 24 miles west of Tripoli.[506]

All in all, in the year's war, Italian casualties were about 4000 killed and 6000 wounded.[507]

The Italians put their losses in the main battles at 236 officers and 4,076 men (including dead and wounded).[508] Then they added:

> Besides the above, the following were lost in minor engagements at the various garrisons during the year of war, up to and including January 16, 1912: Officers and men, 5,652; of whom 1,432 died. Due to illness and disease, 1,948 died.[509]

Missing from the Italian figures are casualties from 16 January 1912 until October 1912.

Despite their losses, by September 1912, eleven months after the first landings in October 1911, the Italians had not linked up a single bridgehead.[510] Now events unfolding on other arenas were about to bring both sides, in the month of October 1912, to agree a peace treaty.

*****

The Burial of Fighters

During two days, December 10th and 11th, besides, Captain Ifket Bey, six Arabs were buried on the hill-top 50 yards above my tent. Most of these

---

[505] Italian General Staff: *The Italo-Turkish War*; op cit; p. 81.
[506] Commodore W.H. Beehler: *The History of the Italian Turkish War*; op cit; pp. 93-4.
[507] Ibid; p. 96.
[508] Italian General Staff: *The Italo-Turkish War*; op cit; p. 82.
[509] Ibid.
[510] J. Wright: *Libya*, op cit, p. 129.

deaths were due to wounds received in the last battle. The amount of battering these water-drinking Arabs and Turks will stand, before they succumb, is astonishing. One Arab walked 28 miles to Azizieh from the firing line with seven bullet wounds in him, and, after treatment, refusing to be sent to the big base hospital at Gharian, insisted on returning to the front!

These simple burials in the desert camp have none of the impressive accompaniments which surround a military interment in our army, even when on active service. There is no formation among the little group who follow the body of their comrade, no firing over the grave, no bugle-notes of farewell. Nevertheless, there was a certain grandeur about the funeral of the dead officer. No Imam was to be found in the camp, but an Arab recited the simple, rugged verses from the Koran used for the burial of the dead. He had died far away from home and family, in the service of the Padishah and the defence of Islam against the unjust assaults of the infidel; surely for such men as these were reserved the joys of Paradise.[511]

6. The End and Aftermaths of the War

From the start, the Italians had sought to bring the Turks to surrender by applying pressure not just in Libya, but anywhere possible. They had a major asset in their favour: their superior navy; and Turkey, due to its geography and territorial extent with immense coastlines, was vulnerable. A particularly weak spot of the empire was the Arab coastline. The Italians stirred a revolt in the Asir (now a province of Saudi Arabia) headed by Sheikh Idriss, via the Italian Red Sea colony of Eritrea.[512] This drained the Turkish defence system in terms of men and resources which had to be despatched there even if needed elsewhere.[513] Throughout 1912, the Italian navy patrolled the Red Sea, especially threatening Jeddah, the port used by Muslim pilgrims.[514] The purpose of these operations was to force the Turks to come to terms over Libya.[515] Then, on 24 February 1912, the Italians hit at Beirut, sinking two small Turkish warships and inflicting damage to buildings on shore, besides causing civilian casualties.[516]

The Italians also pressed the Turks elsewhere, in the Aegean region in particular. Their main attack was against the Island of Rhodes. This island, about ten miles from the coast of Asia Minor, had 26,000 inhabitants, including 17,000 Greeks

---

[511] E.N. Bennett: *With the Turks in Tripoli*, op cit; pp. 139-140.
[512] T.W. Childs: *Italo-Turkish Diplomacy*, op cit; p. 111.
[513] Commodore W.H. Beehler: *The History of the Italian Turkish War*; op cit; p. 71.
[514] DHE 644/EHE/2, No 19, *Asim Bey to Ottoman Embassies*, 17 January 1912.
[515] T.W. Childs: *Italo-Turkish Diplomacy*, op cit, p. 120.
[516] DHE 644/EHE/2, Cypher Bureau No 269, Asim Bey to all Ottoman ambassadors, 24 February 1912. G. Casoni: *La Guerra Italo-Turca*; Florence: R. Bemporad & Figli, Editori, 1914, p. 88.

and a Turkish garrison consisting of about 1000 infantry and artillery.[517] Despite stiff Turkish opposition, the island fell on 16 May to the Italians.[518] This was compounded by the loss of other islands at more or less the same time. In just two weeks, by 20 May 1912, the Italians took possession of the small islands of the Aegean Archipelago between Crete, Rhodes and Samos, capturing all their small garrisons.[519] The loss of Kaltria, Carpantos, Kasos, Episcopi, Nysiros, Kalimnos, Leros, Patmos, Kos, and Smyni was a disaster for the Turks, especially as the Greeks profited from Italian occupation to declare the Islands independence from Turkey. The two small islands about six miles west of Samos, Nicaria and Furni, with about 15,000 inhabitants, succeeded in overpowering the Turkish garrisons, declared their independence, sent delegates to Athens, and submitted a memorial to the European powers for recognition of their independence.[520] Following this, Crete sent an armed expedition of 600 men to Samos to lend assistance against the Turks there, thus further diverting Turkish military effort.[521]

Just then, it became clear that things were evolving dangerously in the Balkans. Balkan powers: Greece, Serbia, Bulgaria and Montenegro had designs on the Turkish territories in Europe.[522] In the spring of 1912, for the first and last time in their history, the Balkan peoples, temporarily, at least, resolved their differences to unite against the Turks.[523] Serbia and Bulgaria, the first aiming to reach the Adriatic and the other to reach the Mediterranean, signed a treaty in March 1912, which included a military convention. Two months later Greece joined the alliance.

> The iron ring around Constantinople was at last complete. The moment had come for the coup de grâce to the Ottoman Empire in Europe.[524]
>
> There is the opportunity of solving that Oriental problem which would be a great step toward civilization, a return to the just conditions of racial rights, the driving of the Asiatics to their own home, and free Europe from a shame which, to her disgrace, has lasted more than four hundred and fifty years.[525]

The King of Montenegro jumped on the opportunity by declaring war against Turkey on 8 October 1912. Serbia, Bulgaria and Greece joined in a few days later.[526]

---

[517] Commodore W.H. Beehler: *The History of the Italian Turkish War*; op cit; p. 73.
[518] Ibid; p. 74.
[519] Ibid; p. 76.
[520] Ibid; p. 93.
[521] Ibid.
[522] T.W. Childs: *Italo-Turkish Diplomacy*, op cit; p. 16.
[523] Lord Kinross: *Ataturk*; op cit; p. 53.
[524] Ibid.
[525] Dr Paolo de Vecchi: *Italy's Civilising Mission in Africa*; Brentano's; New York; 1912; p. 42.
[526] Lord Kinross: *Ataturk*; op cit; p. 53.

The Italians meanwhile had addressed yet another ultimatum to the Turks, that should they fail to reply to their demands for an armistice, European Turkey was under threat of attack as the Italians were now organising an expeditionary force against it.[527] As the onslaught became generalised, it threatened the survival of Turkey itself; now the Turks bent to the inevitable, and agreed a treaty of peace.[528]

Following their peace accords with the Italians, the Turks recalled most of their officers from Libya, and Enver Pasha and Mustafa Kemal among others reluctantly obeyed those orders.[529] In Cyrenaica, when Enver Pasha left in December 1912, he passed his command of some 800 Ottoman troops to Aziz Bey, who remained there until June 1913 continuing to fight and to organise resistance.[530] The Turks also left arms behind, and it would appear that some commanders were prevented from leaving Libya by the people themselves.[531] The Turks also sent thousands of gold coins to finance the resistance; the money coming from the Sultan in his capacity as Caliph of all the Muslims 'to aid those in need within the framework of his religious obligations.'[532] This assistance was essential in helping the resistance to organise without the Turks.[533]

The Turks did not cede sovereignty of Libya to Italy; rather, the Sultan issued a declaration to his Libyan subjects, granting them full and complete autonomy.[534]

Despite the Peace of Lausanne between the Turks and Italians, most Libyans still considered the Sultan 'their rightful ruler and the Italians as unlawful invaders to be driven back to the sea,' and so were determined to continue the fight.[535] As for the Turks, they were still deeply motivated by the feeling that they had fought a Holy War in Libya which they had been forced to abandon, and therefore sought to continue their support even if it was only by providing the resistance with arms.[536] The *Teskilat i-Mahsusa* officers who reluctantly had to leave for the Balkans still left several of their numbers, including Aziz Bey al-Masri, to advise the local fighters.[537] The Sanusiyya, in particular, with their well-integrated socio-political system, managed to mobilise and keep the Italian armies locked in their strongholds inside the coastal towns of Cyrenaica. There, Sayyid Ahmad al-Sharif had met with Enver before the latter left Libya, who gave him arms and supplies.[538]

---

[527] Commodore W.H. Beehler: *The History of the Italian Turkish War*; op cit; p. 95.
[528] L. Anderson: *The State and Social Transformation*, op cit, p. 130.
[529] T.W. Childs: *Italo-Turkish Diplomacy*, op cit, p. 237.
[530] Ibid.
[531] F. Malgeri: *La Guerra Libica*; op cit, p. 373.7
[532] R. Simon: *Libya*, op cit, p. 105.
[533] See *Mudhakarat Anwar Pasha* [Memoirs of Anwar Pasha], edited by Orkhan Quluglo and translated into Arabic by A. El-Horeir (Tripoli: Libyan Studies Center, 1979); and *Mudhakarat al-Zubat al-Atrak* [Memoirs of Turkish officers], translated into Arabic by Wajdi Kadak, and edited by 'Imad Hatim (Tripoli: Libyan Studies Center, 1979).
[534] L. Anderson: *The State*; op cit; p. 130.
[535] J. Wright: *Libya*, op cit, p. 131.
[536] R. Simon: *Libya*, op cit, p. 101.
[537] L. Anderson: *The State*, op cit, p. 130.
[538] A.A. Ahmida: *The Making of Modern Libya*; op cit, p. 118.

Outwardly, the Turkish authorities attempted to absolve themselves from responsibility for the continuous resistance in Libya. They claimed that the war had been renewed by the Libyans who had been unified during the struggle and who now led the campaign independently.[539] It was true that the fighting was done by the Libyans, and their military successes owed in large measure to their customary fighting spirit and bravery, but Turkish support, however, continued in covert ways. The most common method was for the Turkish Government to transfer through the Sultan's representative a monthly grant of 60,000 Ottoman pounds to the families of the fallen, to pensioners and their families.[540] The closeness of the population to the fighters made it easy to transfer such financial aid.[541]

During the First World War, Turkey was an ally of Germany fighting France and Britain, and so the secret Turkish organisation, *Teskilat—i Mahsusa*, endeavoured to stir Muslims to rise against them.[542] In this conflict, Italy was an ally of both France and Britain. German submarines brought in great supplies of men and goods through the port of Gasar Hamad near Misrata.[543] Steamboats travelling from the south-western Anatolian coast also brought in men and equipment in eastern Cyrenaica near the Egyptian border.[544] Only a few boats were sent to Tripolitania as it was harder to land there. Turkish aid was also smuggled overland across Egyptian and Tunisian borders. The local resistance movement received military advisors, arms, and money in this manner.[545] In 1915, more officers came in, some of whom were Arabic speakers or had participated in the first Turkish-Italian War.[546] Large amounts of money and gold also flowed in.[547] Exiled leaders of Libya, such as Suleyman al-Baruni, and Arab volunteers remained active and were now returning to the country.[548] They joined with Abd al-Rahman Azzam, an Egyptian Arab nationalist, and Nuri Pasha (brother of Enver Pasha, by then the Defence Minister in the Young Turk government) in Cyrenaica.[549] Al-Baruni won the support of the local resistance leaders, and from this alliance was formed an independent republic with its capital at Misrata.[550]

The struggle of the Libyans intensified during and after the First World War, and continued until 1932, when nearly the whole of the resistance was wiped out,

---

[539] *Tanin*, 21 February 1913.
[540] *Basbakanlik Arsivi*, Istanbul (BBA), file 1027/67/6 includes many references on this issue.
[541] R. Simon: *Libya*, op cit, p. 105.
[542] Ibid; p. 128.
[543] A.A. Ahmida: *The Making of Modern Libya*; op cit, p. 121.
[544] R. Simon: *Libya*, op cit, p. 129.
[545] A.A. Ahmida: *The Making of Modern Libya*; op cit, p. 121
[546] R. Simon: *Libya*; op cit; p. 129
[547] PRO (Public Record Office), Foreign Office 371/1969, FO 371/2356
[548] A.A. Ahmida: *The Making of Modern Libya*; op cit, p. 121.
[549] Ibid. 122
[550] J. Wright: *Libya*, op cit, p. 137.

together with nearly half the population of the country, and the capture of the great Libyan hero, Omar al Mukhtar.[551] Omar was taken to Suluq Camp still suffering from his wound, and after a summary court martial, the old fighter was hanged on 16 September 1931 before a silent crowd of 20,000 brought there from confinement to witness his end.[552]

*****

The Libyan War impacted on Turkey in three fundamental ways:
Firstly, this conflict signalled a major shift in warfare. Now new means meant the killing machine had become more sophisticated. The Italians, for the first time put into effect many such new means, including aeroplanes, wireless telegraphy, torpedoes, heavy naval bombardment against fortified or fixed positions, and so on.

Secondly, and more importantly, on a more positive effect for the Turks, all these developments also introduced the Turks to new methods of warfare, which served them afterwards. Search-lights would play a most important role in guarding the passage of the Dardanelles and at the Catalja Line.[553] The Turks also learnt from their deficiencies; the Italian navy suffered no losses during the war because the Turks were not trained in target practice. As Commodore Beehler noted at the time, modern weapons were instruments of precision and it was absolutely necessary to have skilled gunners to operate these scientific instruments of precision.[554] It cost over one thousand dollars to fire one projectile from the large modern guns of 12-inch caliber, which made it a criminal extravagance to waste a single shot from these guns. Thus training to fire these guns with perfect accuracy became an absolute necessity.[555] At Gallipoli, in 1915, Turkish firing was exceptionally accurate.

Another lesson the Turks learnt was in how to protect their waterways, especially the Dardanelles, more efficiently. Indeed, an Italian reconnaissance of the Straits on 18 July 1912 by Captain Millo and his flotilla of five torpedo boats, under the fire of over one hundred Turkish guns at close range for two hours, did not sustain any serious damage. This taught the Turks a great deal, which came handy at Gallipoli three years later.[556]

Soon after these incidents the Turks began to strengthen the defences of the western approaches to the Dardanelles at Kumkale and Sedd el-Bahr. The mine fields were reinforced and improved; 350 guns were added to the fortifications; the troops were drilled daily at target practice, and 40,000 infantry and cavalry

---

[551] See K. Holmboe: *Desert Encounter*, London, 1936.
[552] E.E. Evans Pritchard: *The Sanusi of Cyrenaica*, op cit, p. 190.
[553] Commodore W.H. Beehler: *The History of the Italian Turkish War*; op cit; p. 105.
[554] Ibid; p. 106.
[555] Ibid.
[556] Ibid.

were mobilised in the Dardanelles district.[557] The Turks also narrowed the open spaces through the barricades and mine fields, without interfering with the passage of merchant ships through the Straits.[558] Mines would play a decisive role in the early phase of the Gallipoli campaign; they might have even saved Turkey on that occasion.

The Italian campaign was a masterpiece of co-operation of army and navy, and Commodore Beehler was quite sanguine about raising this issue with the National Council of Defence for the United States Army and Navy to secure the harmonious co-operation of the two services.[559]

Thirdly, the main impact was this, well summed up by the British anti-war campaigner Stead, who kept condemning the war and its atrocities more passionately than any other, not because he loved the Turks, but because he understood what most could not. He said:

> The war which the Italian Government is waging against Turkey for the purpose of seizing Tripoli is a crime which ought not to be tolerated by a world which calls itself civilised. It ought to have been prevented by the other Powers. But as they failed in doing their duty, this atrocious crime has been committed, is being committed, and will continue to be committed until it is stopped. It ought to be stopped and stopped at once. If it is not stopped, it will breed more crimes. More plunder-wars will be waged, not only against Turkey, but against other nations, until at last this wicked war for Tripoli may involve the whole world in the catastrophe of a general war, in which civilisation itself may disappear.[560]

People of Stead's calibre, with great souls and brains, are never wrong; and so the war in Libya opened the way to the Balkan Wars, which, in turn, would lead to the First World War.

---

[557] Ibid; p. 59.
[558] Ibid; p. 90.
[559] Ibid; p. 106.
[560] W.T. Stead: *Tripoli and the Treaties or Britain's Duty in this War;* London; 1911; p. 56.

Three

THE BALKANS, 1912-1913

There is great glory in this crusade of the Allies against the heavy obstacle to progress which centres in Constantinople. Great glory for Western civilization by which these young kingdoms were informed when they set their house in order and united their forces to bold endeavour. Great glory to the faith they profess, which makes union possible and thus leads to victory. Greater glory still to those of all the other European nations who, seeing the plight of Christianity's old enemy, hastened to assist him. Here in Constantinople they are at work, these bearers of Western culture, under Red Cross or Red Crescent, helping where the Turkish authorities have proved helpless, saving thousands from death by wound or disease while their own stand by and let the mosques, built to commemorate the victories of Islam, overflow with untended sufferers.

Yes, it is a great and glorious victory this last crusade begun by the young kingdoms of the Balkans, informed with high purpose, trained by Western thought and action, completed by those soldiers of the Cross who risked their lives in fighting dread diseases, seeking no reward, moved by that mainspring of their faith, Charity.[561]

1. Crusade, Church Ideology, Literature, and the Turkish Fiend

Should anyone try to write a history of violence towards Turkey without the elements in this heading taken into account, and what they always lead to, i.e. the mass-carving of both populations and territory from the Turks, would mean that they have set aside the vast majority of facts and sources; that they have instead chosen to concentrate on some bland, meaningless, worthless stuff or ideas, their own that is, besides referring to their usual chums, and proceeded to complicate life for everyone.

Indeed, if someone is not prepared to take into account the crusading element, or put in a different manner, the long war between the Cross and the Crescent, then, there is no chance this person can explain the fundamental reason of enmity towards the Turks, whether in 1912, or 2020. Also, should one set aside the eternal conflict between the Eastern and Western Churches, then, nothing of

---

[561] B. Granville Baker: *The Passing of the Turkish Empire in Europe*; London; 1913; p. 317.

much that happened for centuries would make any sense. Also, should anyone ignore the impact of the vast anti-Turkish literature that crams Western culture and that has shaped and still shapes the minds of Westerners towards the Turks, then, trying to explain the inborn hostility to the Turks by other ways is like trying to graft cactus onto Vine trees. Then finally, should one set aside that the principal motivation that has always driven the Christian to kill the Turk pitilessly has always been 'a revenge for his (the Turk) massacres of Christians,' (which everybody is sure about although none has seen them,) then one can never understand why the Christians did to the Turks what they did, a frenzy of killing and cruelty, which in this case had been amply witnessed.[562]

So, here, we try to explain these four elements in relation to the Balkan Wars, this way it makes sense at last of why what happened happened, and the way it happened. Reliance in this chapter, as in most, is mainly on contemporary Western sources, by those who witnessed events on the ground and reported them, not the lamentable crooks of today disguised as scholars or intellectuals (one or two exceptions aside), for those who saw and wrote reflect how it truly was. Again, it does not matter whether these sources do not like Turkey or the Turks. Facts alone matter.

a. The Ever Undying Crusading Spirit

> In the cathedral of Sofia itself [says Gibbs, the war correspondent who was that year, 1912, on the Bulgarian side] the scene was solemn and beautiful, and even foreigners like myself were uplifted and stirred by the emotion of a service in which the help of God was invoked for Christian nations who once more declared a crusade against the Turk. There was but a twilight in the church, in spite of the bright sun outside, but shafts of light struck between the massive pillars and played about the enormous candelabra of cut glass suspended from the roof, and glinted upon the gold leaf of the ikons and holy pictures on the screen which hides the altar. The Queen knelt down before the sanctuary steps, and all around her were kneeling men and women of the highest and lowest classes of Bulgaria, Ministers of State, public officials, generals and staff-officers, peasants of the poorest kind, all mingled without distinction of rank, all deeply moved, even to tears, when from the Metropolitan and his priests there came words of appeal to God for those who were fighting under the Cross against the Crescent, and, for the first time in the history of Bulgaria, prayers for the rulers of the four Balkan Powers who had put aside all jealousies and enmities to join in a general advance against the powers of the Turk in

---

[562] In regard to cruelties inflicted on the Turks during the Balkan wars, see P. Loti: *Turquie Agonisante*; Calman Levy; Paris; 1913. Ernst Jäckh; *Deutschland im Orient nach dem Balkan-Krieg;* Chapter 7: Deutsche und französische Augenzeugen von christlichen Massakern. (Die Balkangreuel des 30 jährigen Krieges); Martin Mörikes Verlag, Munich, 1913; pp. 83-98.

Europe. From the west end of the church the music of the choir throbbed under the roof, so softly at first that it seemed very far away, as faint as angelic voices heard in dreams, but swelling and rising into a great volume of beautiful sound, and wailing at times plaintively in Oriental half-tones which have a strange and haunting effect upon the senses. The sermon was spoken by a young priest from the high pulpit outside the sanctuary, and his voice was very clear and strong, as in the Bulgarian tongue he called to the patriotism of the people and to the spirit of their faith.

"We have done," he said, "all we could to obtain justice for our Christian brothers, and yet to obtain Peace. Peaceful methods have failed, and now we must obtain justice and peace with the sword. God calls us to help our brethren, and He will aid us now that we answer the call. It is the Cross against the Crescent. The great Christian Powers have failed to obtain justice, and so to us falls this mission to wipe out from Europe the last remnants of the stain of barbarism and oppression."

Once again the Christian Church blessed her soldiers, spoke no word of anger against those who went out to kill, inflamed the ardour of men who needed no spur when the smell of blood was in their nostrils. Oh that this tragedy of war, so bloody and so damnable, should still be mocking at the spirit of love and peace preached by the ministers of the Christian Church, always trying to console themselves that the cause is just, that God is on their side! But who knows?

Those who have been working behind the scenes for interests which may only be whispered? The peasants, who know no politics and are but dimly aware why war has been declared, but rely just upon the simplicity of their hatred for the Turk? Such thoughts came to me, foolishly perhaps, for after all I think this war was justified, if any war is just. No such doubts, I think, crept into the mind of those who knelt in the old Cathedral of Sofia and who crossed themselves when the Metropolitan in his high-domed cap, in his robes of cloth of gold, a dazzling figure enframed in the glitter of the ikons, raised his great cross and held it up before the people.[563]

Everywhere, as the men were about to set off to kill the Turks, crowds gathered in the market squares round village orators who poured forth fiery eloquence, praising the men 'as heroes and Christian champions.'[564]

It was precisely the same scene as over a thousand years ago, in 1095 and in subsequent crusades, when similar crowds gathered around the Crusade preachers, telling them then also about Turkish atrocities towards the Christians and the need to free Christian land and people, and avenge all the woes inflicted on the faith and its followers by these same Turks.[565]

---

[563] P. Gibbs and B Grant: *The Balkan War*; Small, Maynard, and Company; Boston; 1913, p. 38-9.
[564] Ibid, p. 19.
[565] See S. Runciman: *A History of the Crusades*; see Ibn al Athir: *Kamil*; Thornberg ed.

Of course, just as in 1095 and after, Crusading had other earthly complementary motivations. In this case, the Balkan leaders easily realised that the Italian invasion of Libya and Italian attacks elsewhere had weakened the Turks considerably, and that this was the best chance they would ever have to patch up their differences, and deal the mortal blow to the Turk for the benefit of their nations, faith, and themselves.[566] There were only gains to make from war, and all these could now be fulfilled. Serbia had long set her heart upon an "open window" on the shores of the Adriatic, Montenegro sought the Sanjak of Novi Bazar, Bulgaria coveted Thrace and even beyond, seeking to thrust the Turk back into Asia Minor, Greece sought a lot from Crete to Macedonia, and all these allies in the Balkan confederation 'had old scores which they were eager to wipe out in Turkish blood.'[567]

There were also, we are reminded, 'financial gentlemen behind the scenes' who had invested a great deal of money for the purchase of war material, and they were not keen to be kept waiting indefinitely for repayment.[568] So, they forced the pace, and all rulers of Serbia, Bulgaria, Montenegro and Greece were financially indebted to them 'to the hilt.'[569] They had also drained their coffers dry, and had collected all the wealth of their kingdoms to the last ounce of gold; in the end 'War was the only way out, and a successful war.'[570]

b. Ideology: or the East/West Conundrum and the Fate of 'Constantinople'

The conflict between the Eastern and Western Churches, its history and effects from the Crusades (1095-1291) till our modern day has been dealt with by a great number of Western scholars for this author to bring his less competent take on the subject. So, everyone should seek clarifications from scholars such as Runciman, Godfrey, Durant, and a few others.[571] In regard to the effects of this conflict and its impact on Turkish history, this has also been dealt with by this author in chapter one and other works. So, just briefly here reflect on one issue in particular: the status of Istanbul. Westerners dreaded Russia's taking of the city. Russia's capture of Istanbul would place her in a too powerful geo-strategic position at the expense of Western powers. On the eve of the Balkan Wars, this was still the greatest fear, and as a result, each and everybody had their options open, and watching from close up, fear and trepidation high in equal measure.

---

[566] S.J. Shaw and E.K. Shaw: *History of the Ottoman Empire and Modern Turkey*; vol 2; Cambridge University Press; 1977; p. 292.
[567] P. Gibbs and B Grant: *The Balkan War*; op cit, pp. 9-10.
[568] Ibid; p. 11.
[569] Ibid.
[570] Ibid.
[571] J. Godfrey: *1204 The Unholy Crusade*; Oxford University Press; 1980. S. Runciman: *The Fall of Constantinople 1453*; Cambridge University Press; 1965, pp. 7-8.

'Beware England, beware Europe,' warned the war apologist, de Vecchi, citing the usual reasons. 'Don't let the opportunity of to day be lost forever, tomorrow might be too late.

Leave the old quarrels for a while, join hands for a good and noble cause, and with a formidable army of four big powers, invite Turkey to leave Europe, to return to Asia where she belongs.

Her 450 years experience of Asiatic civilization in Europe has failed, and has cost too much to be worth trying any longer. Europe is a Christian country, and as a Christian country has been striving to foster a civilization, which is her own, which is just the opposite of that of Islam. Europe's aim is peace, and following the dictates of Christ is struggling to settle with arbitrations the future troubles which may arise among civilized Nations.

A Nation like Turkey, whose power is based on a religion, which does not recognise science as the man liberal guide to the research of Truth, as the human mean toward perfection, but relies only in the fatal decrees of Allah, besides the brutal force of his gun, could never arbitrate with a civilized country.

There is not one point of contact between the two religions, between the two civilizations, there is nothing in common, nothing that socially could ever bring them together.

Nothing can be expected from the Turkish domination in Europe, even by the New Turks, for there is nothing they can give her now, nothing they will be able to give her in the future which will be congenial, acceptable to her way of almost uniform progress and advancement.

The place she holds in Europe as conqueror, she will have to relinquish some day in the future, and this is the historical evolution of Nationalities which will settle the great Balkan question with the force of arms later on, when again it will cost human lives by thousand, and untold fortunes.

Beware Europe, beware England.

The time has come that with an armed arbitration, Macedonia could be set free and Constantinople made the head city of an Hanseatic League, removing for ever the threatening cause of Russian interference.

A joint garrison of the almighty powers of Europe, would guarantee to that country that peace, which would set her soon on the road of a stupendous progress, and the city of Constantinople would be in a few years the pearl of Orient, the center of Christianity, the seat of civilization, the home of Peace.'[572]

And so, in great fear of the wrong places falling to the wrong people (i.e Istanbul and its surrounding areas falling to Russia), soon the Allied fleets would move into Constantinople, as usual 'to prevent massacres of Christians by the Turks,' but in reality to carve up Othman's realm under the shadow of the guns, hence contributing to tilt Europe even closer to the First World War catastrophe.

---

[572] Dr Paolo de Vecchi: *Italy's Civilising Mission in Africa*; Brentano's; New York; 1912; pp. 77-9.

c. Literature About the Turk: A Learning in Hatred

> The men who had been called [in Serbia] gathered in groups outside the village inns and were surrounded by excited women. It was the women who seemed to be urging their men on and firing them with enthusiasm. Every Servian sweetheart was eager for her lad to join in the war against the Turk, the Terrible Turk, whom they had been taught to hate in their nurseries and in their churches, and in tales of old barbarities round the winter hearthsides.[573]

Amongst the Bulgarians:

> "I heard the call," the Bulgarian volunteer said, "and was ready to take my place in the firing line. I shall be glad to give Hell to the Turks."[574]
>
> 'As the days passed,' says Gibbs, 'I met many queer types of Bulgarian reservists who had heard the call and answered it, because in their blood there was the same hatred of the Turks.'[575]

With the Greeks, on a ship on its way to Greece, was another War correspondent: Bernard Grant:

> There I first came in touch with the war-spirit. On board there were a good many Greeks returning from Egypt in response to the call of the army. They were all very excited, very enthusiastic at the idea of attacking the hated Turk. They seemed confident of victory, and appeared to me rather hysterical, as though their condition had got the upper hand. I could not help thinking that some of them would not be so cheerful when they came face to face with the Turkish forces, of whom, at that time, I thought a good deal as fighting men.
>
> Everywhere I went I was reminded of the undying and inherited hatred of the Greek for the Turk. It seemed an obsession with them, so that even the ancient monuments of Greece served as texts for my guide in his denunciation of Turkish rule.[576]

A few months later, in February 1913, after the war had begun, whilst the fighting was still raging, and after tens of thousands of Turks had been massacred by Serbs, Montenegrins, Bulgarians, and Greeks, the British writer, M. Pickthall, who eventually converted to Islam, travelled to Turkey, and stayed in a small Turkish village. There, he met three female Greek dressmakers from amongst the Greeks still living with the Turks despite the fact that many Turkish families had heard and been affected, too, by the slaughter of their relatives by Christians. Still the Greeks went on with their lives as ordinary, unmolested and treated fairly well by

---

[573] P. Gibbs and B Grant: *The Balkan War*; op cit, p. 18.
[574] Ibid. p. 28.
[575] Ibid; p. 29.
[576] B. Grant in P. Gibbs and B Grant: *The Balkan War*; op cit; 3, pp. 138-9.

the Turkish majority. This Turkish excessive kindness would surprise anyone, indeed, and yet it was not the main aspect of the story. The really interesting thing was this, as narrated by Pickthall himself, who was at the time a devout Christian:

> These Greek dressmakers, therefore, gave it out, at seasons when they were employed in Turkish houses, that they were working for a European, Misket Hanum, who thus acquired a reputation for extravagance and love of finery. They gave her house as their address in case of letters, and generally came to stay there in the intervals of work; Misket Hanum, like the Turkish ladies, keeping open house for women. Yet, though they owned to being much indebted to the Turks for kindness, they hated them, as I discovered presently; and did not see how any Muslim could really be regarded by a Christian as a fellow-creature. Seeing me in a fez, they took me for a Turk at first, and were going to withdraw when Misket Hanum introduced me, with a touch of malice, as an Englishman who much preferred the Turks to "Greeks, etcetera." At that they all broke out:
>
> "It was impossible! A European could not really like the Turks! What was there in them to inspire a liking? They were good-natured, truly; so were many animals. But were they not barbarians, and cruelly fanatical? Did they not keep their women in seclusion? In a word, they were not Christians. How could anyone prefer them?"
>
> As a return for Misket Hanum's little thrust, all three declared their firm belief that if I wore that hateful head-dress and pretended to love Turks, it was simply from terror of my hostess, who might otherwise have turned me out of doors.
>
> "Why, what have you against the Turks?" cried Misket Hanum. "Is it not true that when your father's house was burnt one night, the Turks, and not your precious Christian brethren, took you in, and got up a subscription for you?"
>
> That was true, the girls admitted: 'The Muslims often did kind actions, which, however, could not blind a Christian to their utter and essential wickedness, the product of a false religion. It was known that they esteemed it holiness to kill a Christian when they got the chance. As for this poor, wandering Englishman, how should he know anything about them, having just arrived! It was evident that he took his cue from present company, for peace.'
>
> 'I cannot honestly,' concludes Pickthall, 'endorse that judgment, in so far as it concerns the poorer peasant Christians, whom I know and like. It may be true of the rich Levantines; I cannot say. But the poorer Christians are not wicked; only they have been misled, and schooled to great intolerance, at a time when Muslim education tends the other way.'[577]

---

[577] M. Pickthall: *With the Turk in Wartime*; J.M. Dent &Sons; London; 1914; pp. 82-88.

Indeed, with few exceptions, the vast literature, just as scholarship, the media, or culture in general, in the past, or today, has remained over the centuries a huge fountain spurting with venom as far as the Turks are concerned. (For that matter, as this author discovered, scholars of Turkey today, who are adored in Turkey itself, and have a huge following, and when invited to Turkey given royal treatment, are, one or two exceptions aside, the greatest haters of anything Turkish, a bewildering, visceral, hatred of Turks. Turks, still to this moment, in 2020, have no idea whatsoever of the scope and effects of such hatred, and how deeply ingrained it is, and how it has shaped and still shapes opinion and narrative, and knowing them (Turks) now, they will never fathom it.)

It was not just the Eastern Christians who were gorged to satiation with the image of the blood-thirsty Turk, but anywhere Christian literature reached, including French Algeria where this author was taught to loathe the Turks by very beautiful French history books. In those books just as any others where they were portrayed, the Turks were always caricatured as messy, uncouth, destructive, always yelling and disorderly, and ready to tear their innocent, imploring, victims apart. So huge was (and certainly still is the impact of this literature (in view of what is being written and taught about Turks and Turkey today), Western correspondents with the Turks in 1912 could not believe some of their experiences. B. Grant and one of his fellow war correspondent were at the front in Thrace, isolated, lost amidst a mass of defeated, starved, retreating Turks:

> That seemed to me remarkable. Here were we, two men of a foreign race, in the midst of a starving army, while we had stores, yet there was no serious attack upon us, and our property remained as safely in our hands as if we had placed our cart in the middle of Hyde Park under police protection. The Terrible Turk, as he has so often been called, and as I had often imagined him, turned out to be a man of law, a respecter of property, and an honest fellow, even when he was gnawed by hunger and supported by enormous numbers of hungry comrades, who in one moment or two could have killed us and taken possession of all we had.[578]

The same was noted by E. Ashmead Bartlett:

> The aspect of the erstwhile prosperous little town of Chorlou [Çorlu] had completely changed. All the shops were now closed and barred, and the streets deserted by the inhabitants. Scores of hungry wolfish [Turkish] soldiers were wandering round the desolate town in search of a scrap of bread to eat, but everywhere they found the doors shut and bolted in their faces. Several soldiers came to the door of our inn, which had been left temporarily open. Inside were a number of Greeks and a few Turkish officers smoking in front of a warm fire, and drinking coffee or rakki. The men stood for a few minutes at the door, looking with envious eyes at the warm room and at the food and drink. Then the Greek proprietor came

---
[578] B. Grant in P. Gibbs and B Grant: *The Balkan War*; op cit, p. 192-3.

forward and asked if they had money, and when they shook their heads, he slammed the door in their faces and bolted it. I expected to see them storm and pillage the inn, but instead they just slouched off in the rain, shivering as they went. Poor wretches, all the spirit had been starved out of them, and I shall never forget the look of patient suffering in their faces.[579]

War correspondent after war correspondent, as one reads through their accounts, was indeed stunned by the humane behaviour of the Turk when they only expected the beast to leap out. What they discovered in reality contradicted fundamentally what they had been told or taught about the Turk.

On the eve of the Balkan Wars the generalised view of the Turks and Turkish rule was, indeed, as here summed up for us by the influential American, William E. Curtiss:

> Human life and property have been held as worthless by the Turkish officials and military garrisons. No woman has been safe from their lust. No man has been allowed to accumulate property or to improve his condition without exciting the avarice of the tax-gatherer and the military commandant. It has been useless for the inhabitants to save money or to produce more than enough to supply their own wants, for the slightest surplus would attract attention and be stolen from the owner. The Christian population has had no standing in the courts and is often prohibited from practising its religion. The number of lives wantonly taken, the number of women ravished and the number of children butchered in the Turkish provinces of Europe, particularly in Rumelia, where the population is almost entirely Christian, would shock the world if the truth were known. Macedonia is simply a replica of Armenia, so far as her grievances are concerned; but, being under the eye of the European powers, slaughter and pillage have not been permitted to continue indefinitely unrebuked.[580]

It is very easy to dismiss the impact of this sort of rhetoric that always depicts an entity in the manner the Turks (just as Muslims) have been to this day. Only somebody who has experienced the impact of such rhetoric (like this author) can tell: It simply makes one look at that entity in the same manner one looks at pests. The Turks were seen even worse than pests because of the next element.

d. Fiend/Massacrer in Chief

The issue of mass killing of Muslims is generally avoided by the overwhelming majority of Muslim authors, whether Arabs or Turks. One of the reasons is that

---
[579] E. Ashmead Bartlett: *With the Turks in Thrace*; op cit; p. 211.
[580] W.E. Leroy Curtiss: *The Turk and his Lost Provinces*; Fleming H. Revell Company; Chicago; 1903, in W.S. Monroe: *Turkey and the Turks*; L.C. Page and Company; Boston; 1907; pp. 52-3.

they see no need in disturbing awful events of the past which might upset the relations with others now and in the future. Another reason is that because many or most, in fact, are intellectually inept and know nothing of what happened on the ground, they just quickly pick information from the internet and Western sources, sources which obviously disappear such massacres from knowledge. Our 'scholars' then hurriedly compile some trashy paper for a conference or something, and quickly add this 'accomplishment' to their cv, which now extends to 60 pages. Another reason for many Muslim 'intellectuals' not informing about what had been done to their people is their inner perception of themselves as inferior, seeking not to offend their Western masters; but only in appearance, for they hate anything Western in their guts.

Western opinion-making agencies in all their forms, with a few exceptions, also ignore massacres of Muslims whether Turks or Arabs, because the rule today is to burnish Christian/Western history. Also the rule, whether in media or historical narrative, or any narrative, is to present any crime by the West/Christianity as an oddity, and any vile Muslim deed as a normality, a fruit of the Islamic faith.

One speaks a lot about this massacre issue and might sound a bit excessive, yet the reason this author raises this issue is that it is central for understanding the history of Turkey and Turks, including this Balkan War episode.

Firstly, the massacres of Turks:

Any defeat by the Turks, unique in the history of humanity, has ended in their massacres, their mass-expulsion, the ruining of their economic and social structure and condition, and above all in the reduction of their territory. At the rate this was happening by 1912, the whole of Turkey was about to fizzle away altogether. Had Turkey been defeated at Gallipoli in 1915, and during the War of Independence (1919-1922), there would be no Turkey today, for its territory and population would have been cut down by over 80%.[581]

Secondly, the massacres by Turks:

You will never hear or read anything about the Turks without being reminded of their massacres of others. You can type Turkish or Turkey on the internet, and there come zooming at you tens of references to massacres committed by Turks. You type kebab, or baklawa, or Turkish Dancing, and still the 'massacres committed by Turks' would hit your eyes. Of course, one knows the reason for this: the perennial hostility to Turks, and the Turks failure to deal with the way they are depicted and condemned in their 'friends and allies' parliaments for their 'crimes.' Of course, as an individual, one is dumfounded by such a systemic and systematic bombardment of the minds about Turkish sanguinary deeds. Yet,

---
[581] *Current History*, vol 12; Apr-Sep 1920; Dismemberment of the Turkish Empire. Terms of the Final Peace Treaty of the World War — Effects on the Map of Asia Minor p. 446.

the historian who knows a little about the Crusades, Colonialism, the World Wars, the Christian religious wars, and one or two other subjects, also knows that it is the best way for greater criminals in history to put what burdens their conscience and history onto somebody else's shoulders, especially if that somebody, the Turk, does not have the will, the guts, or the intellectual/media capacity to counter bombard them with the same filth.

More importantly, and in regard to our subject, Turkish massacres of others which fill literature, but hardly the ground, are the best way to fill such a ground with Turkish corpses, and gain a few rewards on earth and in the hereafter. Let's explain this from a historical perspective, for history always repeats itself. If any element has been used throughout the centuries as the Weapon against the Turks, it is "their atrocities committed against Christians." It has been, possibly, the most sharpened, most perfected, most polished, weapon from 1095 until today in 2020. Somebody like Robert Fisk (that great voice of humanity,) for instance, even saw the 2016 coup against 'Erdogan' (never mind if hundreds of thousands of Turks would have been slain had the coup succeeded) as justified, amongst other, by his failure to accept 'the Turkish genocide of Armenians.'[582]

So, back to the Crusades (1095-1291), as many might not know, they were not launched against the Arabs but against the Turks. In his call to the Crusades, Pope Urban II dwelt on Turkish atrocities, the Turks, according to him, devising the cruelest means of killing Christians.[583] This had the impact of stirring the masses into frenzied action, and once the crusading hordes arrived in the East, they descended on the Turks, just as on all Muslims, with a ferocity unequalled in history. It was the same in all subsequent history, 'Turkish massacres of Christians' the key to their retribution, i.e. wiping them out, regardless if all such massacres by Turks were mere isolated incidents, vastly exaggerated, or never took place at all.

During the Balkan Wars precisely the same occurred. As the Serbs, Greeks, Bulgarians, and Montenegrins were inflicting the worst deeds on the Turks, some of which will be seen further down, they were still using 'atrocities by the Turks' not just to justify their killings of Turks, but also to draw sympathy and support. One of the British war correspondents at the scene, Seppings Wright, could see the suffering of the Turks on the ground and at the same time could also hear reports of massacres by Turks widely circulated in various countries for the obvious purpose of creating prejudice against the Turks and also influencing the people and the Governments in favour of their foes.[584] Likewise, Ellis Ashmead Bartlett makes the parallel with what happened in 1876-1878, when

---

[582] Who wrote, amongst other: 'Recep Erdogan had it coming. The Turkish army was never going to remain compliant while the man who would recreate the Ottoman Empire turned his neighbours into enemies and his country into a mockery of itself... The real question will be the degree to which is his momentary success will embolden Erdogan to undertake more trials, imprison more journalists, close down more newspapers, kill more Kurds, and, for that matter, go on denying the 1915 Armenian genocide." R. Fisk, *The Independent*, UK, 16 July 2016.

[583] In D. C. Munro, "Urban and the Crusaders", Translations and Reprints from the *Original Sources of European History*, Vol 1:2, 1895, pp. 5-8.

[584] H.C. Seppings Wright: *Two Years Under the Crescent*; op cit; p. 154.

Gladstone had allowed himself to be hoodwinked by the Russians into believing that the Turkish troops possessed a monopoly of the atrocities committed in the Balkans, whereupon he started his Turkish atrocity cry and turned away the sympathies of Europe from the Ottoman army.[585]

If there is one image that has dominated world attention throughout the centuries, it is the following:

Above left: The Turk at work. Although everyone is aware this is a propagandist picture dating from the 15-16th century, modern authors (including today) still repeat the same story of Turkish empaling of babies.

Right: The Turk having just finished his task with great relish. And he does not have one sword only...
(Source: Punch; the Unspeakable Turk 1914)

---

[585] E. Ashmead Bartlett: *With the Turks in Thrace*; op cit; p. 38.

The Turk and his Algerian chums tormenting Christians by all means of cruelty

Nothing is more revolting than rape and impaling humans, especially babies and infants, and these practices have been associated with the Turks for centuries to this day, found in more or less every Western history book. We can see drawings of the Turks impaling Christians in Turkey proper, in Bulgaria, on the road to Vienna, on the road out of Vienna, in Algiers, in Palestine, wherever there was a Turk, in fact.[586] No matter if all contemporaries whether in Algiers, or in Turkey, or during the Balkan Wars, or anywhere, saw no such impaling of babies at the end of Turkish lances, or bayonets, depending on the time of history, Popes,

---

[586] See works which highlight this issue of misrepresentation of the Turks by A. Cirakman: *From the Terror of the World to the Sick man of Europe;* Peter Lang Publishing; New York; 2002. D.R. Blanks, and M. Frassetto ed: *Western Views of Islam in Medieval and Early Modern Europe;* St. Martin's Press; New York; 1999.

Churchmen, and Christian scholars, artists, novelists, and historians to this day, relate the same stories. Now what do you do with a mass-rapist and an empaler of babies? The answer is obvious: eradicate him and his progeny. And this is precisely what happened from 1095 till 1922, including in places where people are called Turks, i.e. Bosnia, until 1995. And should any time military events turn sour wherever there are Turks or people thought to be Turks, it will happen again, for history is a very logical beast — it simply repeats itself stupidly.

So, in regard to the Balkan Wars, as every war correspondent could see, on and on, there were vast rumours and news that Turks had been mass-raping and slaughtering Christians everywhere, and the war correspondents amongst the Turks, in their tens, were looking for the sites of such vile acts. Various officials were also earnestly searching for them in order to take Turkey to account. All Western fleets and their armies, also in Turkey then, were also searching for such massacres and their perpetrators. And yet, they were nowhere to be found or seen. Thus Seppings Wright, who was in Istanbul, reporting on the Balkan War, could not fail to notice this incongruous situation:

> 'M. Tokatlian, a Greek, owns the hotel, and I found myself at home at once. Everyone was most obliging; the terms were most reasonable; and the chef was acknowledged to be the best in the city. I wish to lay particular stress on the fact that the hotel is Greek, and that the attendants are nearly all of the same nationality. While I was there all sorts of rumours of atrocities committed by Mahomedans against Christians were circulated. The Tokatlian pursued the even tenor of its way, serving Mussulman, Christian, and Jew with equal impartiality. I saw nothing of the objectionable demonstrations which were freely reported in European journals, a fact which speaks volumes for the tolerance of the Turk.'[587]

Ashmead Bartlett, the famed war correspondent of those days:

> 'In common with almost everyone else in Constantinople, I expected to see a mass of starving, disbanded soldiery back in Stamboul, and possibly an uprising against the Christian section of the inhabitants.'[588]

Instead, all that could be seen was:

> The prospect of the taking of Constantinople and the possible looting of the town attracted art dealers from all over the world. They hoped that the priceless heirlooms contained in the Museum, the mythical hordes of gold and silver ware, and heaps of unknown but suspected jewels, including the famous Persian throne, would fall into the hands of the looters, who, in turn, would be only too pleased to part with them for a tenth of their value for cash down. As day by day went by and only a comparatively small number of fugitives, who were easily kept in hand, returned to Constantinople from the front, the disappointment was keen, and these

---

[587] H.C. Seppings Wright: *Two Years Under the Crescent*; op cit; p. 152.
[588] E. Ashmead Bartlett: *With the Turks in Thrace*; op cit; p. 229.

gentry, who had come so far to fill Bond Street, the Rue de la Paix, and Fifth Avenue with the spoils of Byzantium, went away very disappointed.[589]

And whilst the Western fleets, the ambassadors, war correspondents, travellers, anybody really, could not see any massacres by the Turks, and whilst authors like Pierre Loti, the Frenchman, back in 1912, warned that the Christian armies were using false reports of massacres by the Turks to hide or justify their own and cause even more opprobrium of the Turks,[590] modern historians today are repeating not just the same stories of massacres and mass-rape by the Turks, they are even emphasising that same story of Turkish soldiers impaling of children at the end of their bayonets. Here is one of the most influential scholars of today (also very influential at the BBC): Misha Glenny. He writes:

> As the Bulgarian army moved forwards the retreating (Turkish) army retaliated against the Christian population. The Carnegie Commission confirmed one incident in which a woman of Haskovo described how 'her little child was thrown up into the air by a Turkish soldier who caught it on the point of his bayonet.' Other women told how three young girls threw themselves into a well after their fiancés were shot. At Varna about twenty women living together confirmed this story, and added that the Turkish soldiers went down into the well and dragged the girls out. Two of them were dead; the third had a broken leg; despite her agony she was outraged by two Turks. Other women of Varna saw the soldier who had transfixed the baby on his bayonet carrying it in triumph across the village.[591]

Having cited these Turkish atrocities, Glenny straight adds:

> 'Turks who were unable to escape the oncoming army were subject to similar Bulgarian retribution.'[592]

Briefly here, Glenny makes the Turkish misdeeds the cause of what was inflicted on them in retribution, which contradicts reality as will be seen below. He also emphasises the one instance of alleged Turkish atrocities, reported by Bulgarian Christian women to the Carnegie Enquiry which arrived on the scene in the wake of the Second Balkan War, that is nearly two years after the Turkish soldiers' misdeeds supposedly happened. Glenny's account, furthermore, contradicts what every single witness who was on the ground saw: that it was the Turks who were victims, and not a single witness spoke of crimes by Turks. Finally, Glenny en par with modern Western historians (with few exceptions) does not refer at all to Loti, Jaeckh, or the war correspondents who were either on the ground, or received specific and detailed accounts and photographs from those on the ground; nor does he refer to Justin McCarthy and his tens of contemporary sources. Like most scholars of today, Glenny does not even cite them in his

---

[589] Ibid; p. 231.
[590] P. Loti: *Turquie Agonisante*; Calman Levy; Paris; 1913.
[591] *Report of the International Commission to Inquire into the Causes and Conduct of the Balkan Wars*, Carnegie Endowment of International Peace, Washington, DC, 1914, p. 131.
[592] M. Glenny: *The Balkans*; Granta Publications; London; 2012; 2nd paragraph under heading The First Balkan War: Thrace.

lengthy bibliography. This is bound to distort history whether done on purpose or not.

So, if modern historians, with all the sources at their disposal and with plenty of time to reflect, still depict and/or believe in the Turk as the mass-raping, mass-slaughtering, infant impaler, what could be expected of nations and their armed hordes, then already gorged with hate of the Turk, on a crusading mission, and seeking revenge?

2. The First Balkan War: Fighting Against the Odds

In late 1398, Timur the Lame launched a vast military campaign against Muslim India. Facing him was an army strongly equipped and with numerous warriors, headed by a great number of elephants to lead the charge. Timur the Lame resorted to a stratagem here narrated for us by a contemporary and former prisoner of the Ottomans from the Battle of Nicopolis (1396), the German Shiltberger:

> Camels should be taken and wood fastened on them, and when the elephants advanced, the wood should be ignited, and the camels driven up against the elephants; thus would they be subdued by the fire and the cries of the camels, because the elephants are afraid of fire. Then Tamerlin (Timur) took twenty thousand camels and prepared them as above described, and the king came with his elephants in front. Tamerlin went to meet him, and drove the camels up against the elephants, the wood on them being on fire. The camels cried out, and when the elephants saw the fire and heard the great cries, they took to flight, so that none could hold them. When Tamerlin saw this, he pursued them with all his force.[593]

Timur won the battle, captured Delhi, slaughtered its Muslim inhabitants, pillaged it, then set the city on fire, and then left.

This story highlights Mongol tactics of throwing confusion and chaos in enemy ranks including by using whole populations related to the enemy: pushing them in front so as to spread chaos and cripple the enemy's capacity for fighting.

The Bulgarians in 1912 did absolutely the same. They so much massacred the Turkish population from the first day of the war, and with such ferocity, that ahead of them fled tens of thousands of civilians, maybe even hundreds of thousands, who rushed forth precisely in the direction where the Turkish army and its supplies was coming from, or from where its wounded and retreating soldiers were trekking back. As a result, the mass of refugees with their carts, their distress, and their terror, coming together with retreating wounded soldiers and an army marching the opposite way to the front, created the utmost chaos in Turkish ranks. To make matters worse, the most atrocious weather conditions

---
[593] Johann Shiltberger: *The Bondage and Travels of Johann Shiltberger*; tr. from German b Commander J. Buchan Telfer; Printed for Hakluyt Society, London; 1879; pp. 25-6.

seen for generations were hampering movement, as carts, trains, heavy guns, and horses could hardly move, glued as they were to the ground by mud. All war correspondents, tens of them, caught and described the same scene of mayhem. E. Ashmead Bartlett, for instance:

> The four other trains which were waiting their turn to steam off down the single line of railway to Constantinople, were packed as I have never seen trains packed before. Women and children were piled into cattle trucks one above another, together with their household goods, in such a manner that numbers must have perished from suffocation. Other women with young children strapped to their backs were running about like frightened sheep, looking in vain for places in the already overcrowded trains. Wounded men were being thrown pell-mell into second-class carriages, to fall hopelessly on the floor or seats.[594]

> It was the same weary spiritless tramp to the rear, save that now most of the sick and wounded had dropped out and perished. There was not a vestige of order. Some of the men were riding on donkeys, others on broken-down horses. The majority having thrown away their boots, to which they were not accustomed in everyday life, were trudging along in blood-stained socks or bare feet. There was no complaining; only a vast silence as of the grave, until I felt that I was marching in the midst of an army of corpses without souls. A field gun was being drawn by two horses and two white oxen. Mingled with the rabble of soldiery, were thousands of bullock-wagons, in which the mussulmans, inhabitants of the country, were driving off all their worldly goods towards Stamboul.[595]

B. Grant:

> I shall not soon forget the sensation of pity that overwhelmed me at that moment. It was a horrible thing to see in the pale glamour of the moonlight a huddled mass of men, women and children exposed to the biting wind. Many of them were crying with cold and hunger. Now that the sun had gone, and the coldness of night had fallen upon them, the little ones were no longer merry. The sunlight had gone out of their eyes, too. It was no longer a gay adventure. They were crying out for food and shelter.

> And the hundreds of poor peasants who had brought their worldly goods in the bullock waggons, over the rough ways and through the mud and ruts, were now ready to abandon their waggons and their goods as well, so that they might get a place of safety on our train.[596]

Seppings Wright:

> I was greatly impressed by the stoical patience displayed by some of the refugees. A sharp cry of pain occasionally penetrated the sobbing gasps of people in torment, tired to death yet kept mechanically moving, and urged

---

[594] E. Ashmead Bartlett: *With the Turks in Thrace*; op cit; p. 214.
[595] Ibid; p. 217.
[596] B. Grant in P. Gibbs and B Grant: *The Balkan War*; op cit, p. 161.

ever onwards by the press from behind. I saw one soldier supported by two comrades on either side, who did not discover until afterwards that they had been carrying a corpse. Hastily excavating a grave by the wayside they placed him therein and resumed their flight. It is impossible to give more than a slight idea of the awful scenes witnessed on this retreat.[597]

Wearied children slept peacefully in the arms of rough soldiers. On that terrible march there were many good Samaritan soldiers assisting the old and helpless. I pitied the women more than the men, for the majority of them were unveiled, which added humiliation and shame to the torture of their terrible flight.[598]

If there is one illustration, better than any photograph or any description in any work, published or unpublished, that captures the situation then, it is this illustration by Seppings Wright — possibly one of the most powerful scenes of human distress ever caught and conveyed:

---

[597] H.C. Seppings Wright: *Two Years Under the Crescent*; op cit; p. 194.
[598] Ibid; p. 195.

Stuck in the mud: Turkish civilians fleeing the scene of war.

If Western correspondents were distraught by the plight of the refugees, one imagines the effects on the Turkish troops. Also, how to feed these people? How to feed the army and let the people starve, for there was not enough for all? And in respect to the so necessary logistics of war: how to convey food, ammunitions, supplies, reinforcements, and bring back the wounded when trains, carriages, roads, bridges, and paths were chocked with people, animals, carts, and all sorts of impedimenta coming from the other direction? Moreover, how to move anything when bridges were swept by swollen waters, streams turned into roaring rivers, and the ground made into the biggest quagmire of mud ever seen. Relying on contemporary sources, Uyar and Erickson sum up this situation perfectly:

> The deliberate attacks against civilians by regular or irregular enemy combatants uprooted thousands immediately after the start of hostilities.[599] Thousands tried to get away and endless convoys with makeshift ox-carts or wagons flooded the roads. It was horrible and demoralizing for soldiers to see their families or fellow Muslim citizens suffering from cold, hunger, and epidemics. Also, the convoys placed a huge burden on the military corridors that were supposed to support expeditionary forces. The limited food sources on hand were quickly exhausted, and the already poorly maintained roads turned into quagmires. Epidemics followed the refugees wherever they went and thousands of civilians and soldiers perished. The ever-problematic medical services rapidly broke down under this strain.[600]

---

[599] B. Grant in P. Gibbs and B Grant: *The Balkan War*; op cit, 74–81, 84–85.
[600] Ibid, 78–79, 82–85, 154–156, 159–162, 212–219; M. Uyar and E.J. Erickson: *A Military History of the Ottomans from Osman to Ataturk*; op cit; p. 232.

Quite importantly, the train line was only served by a single track. In normal times that meant hours and hours of delay each time. In times of war and chaos, train journeys were utter mayhem. Then, because of carts, or heavily loaded carriages with refugees, trains constantly fell to the side, and once that happened it was yet more hours, if not days of delay, and all that this entailed.

And not just that, as Seppings Wright notes, whilst it was a matter of vital importance for the Turks to keep this line open for communications, and for the transport of troops, material, and commissariat, the single lane, instead collapsed, thus breaking all forms of communications, and this, precisely when their enemies were pushing forward in their direction very quickly.[601]

The inevitable yet another derailed train

Turkish refugees seeking room on an overcrowded train

---

[601] H.C. Seppings Wright: *Two Years Under the Crescent*; op cit; p. 155.

In their presentation of the Balkan Wars, modern historians completely set aside these important elements; instead, they contrast Christian armies' efficiency with Turkish 'natural chaotic character or disposition, besides their flight in front of the brave Christian armies' as the cause of the Turks defeat. M. Glenny, for instance, states:

> Three days later, following a disastrous misunderstanding between two Turkish military commanders, Lozengrad fell to the Bulgarians. The Turkish army began a shambolic retreat, during which it suffered huge losses in the battles of Lüle Burgas and Babaeski. These defeats highlighted the damage which Abdülhamid had inflicted on Turkey's military readiness.[602]

Of course Glenny is talking nonsense, and unfortunately throughout his book. Abdülhamid, of course, remains the most maligned ruler in history, as if he had ever been given any chance to carry out his military reforms. Turkey had been ruined financially to be able to rebuild anything, and the endless wars forced on her never gave the necessary respite and stability needed. Glenny also talks about something he does not know, for the decapitation of the old officers corps was done by Abdülhamid's successors, the CUP. E.Ashmead Bartlett who knows his history better does indeed correctly note how amongst the radical changes which the Young Turks hoped to bring about was the complete reform of the army, which ended up destroying that very army. He explains: 'The old type of Turkish soldier who existed up to the end of the Hamidian regime possessed many excellent qualities which rendered him individually a stubborn and formidable opponent for the best of troops...' Ashmead Bartlett emphasises the trust the men had in one another, resembling 'a large, united, and happy family...,' the old officers being 'the backbone of the old Turkish Army. They knew their men and were respected and loved by them. On a campaign the men had the most implicit confidence in them, and would follow them anywhere... The Young Turks, on the other hand, brought changes in the character of the army, 'which have had the most disastrous results during the present campaign...' Most particularly their dealings with the old type of regimental officer whereby the Young Turks made the most fatal mistake of all. Trying to copy European armies with young regimental officers who enjoyed steady promotion, they said, "We must get rid of all these old subalterns and captains who were promoted from the ranks, and who are old enough to be colonels and generals, and replace them by young officers." Therefore, with a stroke of the pen they placed all the regimental officers over a certain age in retirement before they had enough young officers to replace them. Thus for the last three years the Turkish Army has been woefully short of officers, and when the war broke out it was short of two thousand such officers.[603]

---

[602] M. Glenny: *The Balkans*; op cit.
[603] E. Ashmead Bartlett: *With the Turks in Thrace*; pp. 49-55.

One has to admit that the principal error made by Turkish General Staff, to which it will be returned, was the same error they would keep committing on and on and on until the end of the First World War, which is their mad over-optimism over Turkey's system of logistics. High Turkish Command during the Balkan Wars and the First World War, especially the incompetent trio in power during the First World War: Enver, Tala'at, and Cemal, repeated the same mistakes over and over, and never learnt anything. They relied on systems and deliveries, which Turkey could never provide or fulfil. They sought to put into application plans that were in theory magnificent, but in their application bound to fail. The end result, as will be seen, was an endless series of disasters.

This aside, there is, however, a fundamental exaggeration of the other defect which foreign correspondents at war or at peace have kept throwing at the Turks: that somehow Turkish society and Turks are chaos personified, which led to defeat. The war correspondents' books on the Turks in Libya, or during the Balkan Wars, or when they visit Turkey as travellers, or diplomats, and all of them, whether friends or foes of the Turks, all these Western-minded people do insist on Turkish chaos and uncouthness. In fact they only marvel when they find order and neatness amongst Turks, such as Abbot coming across this Prussian looking Turkish officer who, in the Libyan desert was so neat, without a shred of uncouthness, that Abbott thought of him to be of Prussian origin or upbringing at least, until finding that the man, from Bursa, had never left Turkey.[604]

True, one must admit, any person used to Western order visiting Turkey today would find difficult to bear sights which can be seen in every town or city, and in every beach, in every wooded or rural area, such as waste dumped everywhere; messy pavements, slippery, deadly, narrow, crammed with objects; noisy, recklessly driven, loud banging, vehicles zooming at great speed through the streets (ready to cut you in case you found the pavement impassable); quarrying disfiguring the landscape everywhere (thus worsening the impression of hostility to harmony), and a few other failings, such as people smoking under the sign Smoking Forbidden, or coach drivers driving, smoking, texting with their mobiles, and talking to the friend sitting next to them, all at once, which give to the stranger a view of a society in utter chaos. These failings are real, witnessed by this author everywhere he went in Turkey, and are due to the excessive laxity of both society and the law. They are not synonymous with innate Turkish love for chaos, although they strike the senses. Like many awful developments in Turkish society in recent times, they are contrary to Turkish tradition and history. The historian knows that the Ottoman Turks had the best-organised society, and also the best organised army throughout the centuries as witnessed by foreigners

---

[604] His name was Nasmi Bey; in G.F. Abbott: *The Holy War in Tripoli*; Edward Arnold; London; 1912; p. 135.

themselves.[605] Khayr Eddin Barbarossa, when he more or less took charge of the French navy, could not stop from lambasting French carelessness and lack of adequate preparations on many occasions.[606] The army of the Sultan was a majestic sight of order and discipline, and the logistics when one reads of the campaigns of the Ottoman sultans in von Hammer were beyond impressive.[607] One only needs to look at the reception of Sultan, Selim III, to see perfection in order as here:

Order, harmony, and neatness as Ottoman Turkey alone could produce.

Moreover, whilst Turkish society to this day shows outwardly signs of neglect and disregard for basic rules of the law, order, and basic rules of life, inwardly, Turkish society is fundamentally orderly and extremely strong. It is this fundamental inner orderliness and strength which allowed it to recover from its wars, disasters, and traumatic experiences as will be shown throughout this

---

[605] According to the Austrian Ambassador in Istanbul in and around times of Selim I and Suleiman; *The Life and Letters of Ogier Ghiselin de Busbecq,* eds. C.T. Forster and F.H.B. Daniell, London, 1881.
[606] According to Ottoman chroniclers, the French requested the assistance. Hezarfen Huseyn b. Cafer: *Tenkih-I tevarikh-I muluk;* TKS Library, R.. 1180, fol. 131r; for the campaign see Kâtib Celebi: *Tuhfet ul Kibar fi Esfar ul Bihar;* Istanbul; 1911; 2, p. 68; Jean Deny and Jane Laroche, "L'expédition en Provence de l'armée de mer du Sultan Suleyman sous le commandement de l'amiral Hayreddin Pacha, dit Barberousse (1543-1544)," *Turcica* 1(1969): 161-211. G. Fisher: *Barbary Legend;* op cit; p. 67.
[607] J. Von Hammer: *The Campaigns of the Ottoman Sultans*, in 2 vols, tr., into English by T.A. Dale, London, 1835.

work. It is Turkish strength, unique, and admirable, which alone in human history caused a nation to rise against a coup in 2016, and defeat it. That is true social strength. And it is precisely the strength of Turkish society in its substance, which allowed it to recover extremely quickly from disaster at the beginning of the Balkan Wars and face the armies leagued against it. No nation would have performed as the Turks did during the Balkan Wars if attacked from four fronts at once by superiorly armed foes. Any other country put under the same strains would have totally disintegrated. Instead, only after a few weeks, the Turks were all geared for powerful counter-attacking, and fight-back. And not just that, whilst the initial chaos had its reasons as explained above (the Bulgarians pushing the refugees ahead of them), only a matter of weeks later, the whole chaos was brought under control by the Turks. And this was seen and acknowledged by every single war correspondent once more:

> It was nearly a month ago that I had last been here [says Baldwin] and what a different air the place now wore! All was order and directed activity where had been disorder and disorganization. The undisciplined soldiery who had been in occupation of the village when (Alain) Ostler and I rode in from Chorlu on that night in early November had been replaced by first-class fighting Redifs, who were to be seen busily digging fresh lines of entrenchment, and who were manifestly in excellent physical condition and spirits. Here were troops to be reckoned with; a glance was sufficient to show that the change in the army was a real one, and that the activities of the Commander-in-Chief and the War Office in Constantinople had been turned into the right channel.[608]

> This spectacle of a large army [admits Ashmead Bartlett] which had been fighting three days previously, being drilled and taught to shoot, with the enemy only a few miles away, is surely almost unique in the annals of war. I was amazed at all I saw. It was almost impossible to believe I was in the presence of the same army, which a fortnight before had been streaming back to Constantinople without officers, without discipline, the men starving and hopelessly demoralised. Certainly Nazim Pasha and his fellow workers deserve every credit for the remarkable transformation they worked in a short time. This recovery shows clearly of what the Turkish Army is capable, if only it is properly handled and given anything like a chance. I have already mentioned the vast improvement in the moral of the Army, which followed the arrival of the picked battalions from Erzeroum [Erzurum], Trebizond [Trabzon], and Smyrna [İzmir]. These men had not suffered defeat or privation. They were being fairly well fed and kept clear of cholera as far as possible, and in consequence, having successfully resisted the Bulgarian attack and having suffered but very few casualties, they were spoiling for another brush with the enemy. Of the original army

---

[608] H.F. Baldwin: *War Photographer in Thrace; An Account of Personal Experiences During the Turco-Balkan War 1912*; Fisher and Unwin, London, 1913; p. 266. J.B. Wolf: *The Barbary Coast*; W.W. Norton & Company; New York, p. 32.

which was defeated at Lule Burgas, most of the weaklings were now under the soil and the old and useless reservists had been sent back to their homes. Thus there was now concentrated along the lines of Chataldja [Çatalca] a powerful army, the organisation of which was improving every day. Trains were regularly bringing up food and medical stores from Constantinople, and already a reserve supply of five days' provisions had been collected at the front.[609]

Finally on this matter, subsequent battles, such as that of Dumlupınar, in August 1922, as we will see in the final chapter, were most certainly some of the best devised and best implemented military operations in world military history. Thus, the problem with the Turks is not intrinsic chaos, part of the Turkish gene as most scholarship seeks to convey, it is, instead, the result of rushed, unrealistic, targeting, and carelessness on the part of those with command or authority, just as carelessness and generalised laxity of the law in relation to the scenes of chaos we see today.

In regard to the Turkish military performance during the Balkan Wars, we are constantly deceived by modern Western scholarship which makes it look that the Turks were just about smashed everywhere, that they retreated in chaos, saved only by the fact that their victorious foes, for whatever reason (annoyed at their easy victory, it would seem according to some authors,) stopped their advance. No picture is as wrong. Even on the Bulgarian front, as soon as the Turks recovered from the disastrous first days, and even in the wake of the battle of Lule Burgas (late October 1912), they started battering the Bulgarian army to pieces. How do we know about this? Here, once more, we avoid wasting time with lousy academics dealing with Turkey today (including in this Turkish academics crawling in front of their Western colleagues), and rely, instead, on another war correspondent, Gibbs, perhaps the most anti-Turkish of the lot. He was present on the side of the Bulgarians and could see the effects of Turkish fighting. He witnessed the huge numbers of Bulgarian casualties being ferried to the back in their thousands, possibly even tens of thousands.[610] It was the Turkish retribution which, indeed, broke the Bulgarian advance. And so unbearable to the Bulgarians had this become, the war correspondents were forbidden from straying anywhere on their own, unlike the correspondents on the Turkish side who were left more or less entirely free to venture and act as they wished; many foreign correspondents were even thrown out of Bulgaria.[611] And what comes out of the correspondents on the Turkish side could only be true for the simple reason that the so important post of Censor was occupied at once by a Turk and

---

[609] E. Ashmead Bartlett: *With the Turks in Thrace*; op cit; p. 283.
[610] P. Gibbs and B Grant: *The Balkan War*; op cit, 129 ff.
[611] See Gibbs; chapter vii: battle with the Censors; p. 112 ff.

seconded by a British, E. Bennet, previously a Member of Parliament and subsequently Minister.[612]

Returning to the fundamental causes of the Turkish defeat, other than those cited already, a principal and obvious one was that the Balkan Allies attacked Turkey somehow treacherously. There was no preliminary build up; rather, the Turks were, as usual, counting on existing treaties to safeguard their frontiers, and they did that until the last minute. Thus, the suddenness of the attack caught them in a state of unpreparedness, which in some measure explains the early confusion described above. More importantly, the Turks were vastly outnumbered with no more than 580,000 troops against a combined strength of 912,000 troops of the Balkan Allies.[613] The army's seasoned recruits had just demobilised (more than 70,000 soldiers) and, moreover, many top officers were still in Libya or on the way from there.[614] Other armies were still in the Yemen, too far away to return to the war zone on time.[615] The Balkan Allies, on the other hand, had had time to prepare, mobilise, and equip their armies plentifully. They were now ready to blast the Turks from all sides at once.[616] It is, indeed, a challenge for any country to be able to put up with attacks coming from all directions at once. If Turkey had superior armament, then, after an initial phase of chaos, it could regroup. But Turkey did not have that; rather the opposite. Reading through accounts of the various fronts shows the same fact, that the Balkan Allies had much superior artillery and other modern means of warfare, including aircraft and navy. Also, as Uyar and Erickson explain, the Berlin Treaty of 1878 had shaped the borders of the Ottoman Balkans in such a way that it made it nearly impossible to defend against different enemies striking all at once.[617] General Staff also made many strategic and planning errors, which Uyar and Erickson, by far the best military historians of all things Turkish, explain at great length.[618] One serious error, as already noted, being the excessive reliance on logistics which did not exist, the eternal false optimism, the same delusional feeling one sees even today. In this Balkan situation Turkish army planners expected 30 days enough to complete mobilisation, when by the end of that, army units from Anatolia were still not in place, the single-track railway system had collapsed under the sheer volume of traffic, and the Greek navy had effectively blocked any use of the sea lanes.[619] Uyar and Erickson most certainly put the finger on the even more serious problem, whereby the much-hoped-for reform of recruitment of non-Muslims 'embarrassed its avid supporters' as a large percentage of them evaded the

---

[612] H.C. Seppings Wright: *Two Years Under the Crescent*; op cit; p. 158.
[613] Quoted by Erikan, Celâl, Komutan Atatürk (Atatürk as a Commander), T. İş Bankası, Ankara 1972; 106.
[614] M. Uyar and E.J. Erickson: *A Military History of the Ottomans*; op cit; p. 224.
[615] Ibid.
[616] S.J. Shaw and E.K. Shaw: *History*; op cit; p. 294.
[617] M. Uyar and E.J. Erickson: *A Military History of the Ottomans*; op cit; p. 225.
[618] Ibid; p. 225 ff.
[619] Ibid; p. 226.

service.[620] On this particular point countless contemporaries, war correspondents, and others could see how, no sooner the war started, local Christians, and Christians supposed to be serving the Turkish army, switched to the side of their coreligionists not in their hundreds but in their tens of thousands.[621] Many local Christians, who were Turkish subjects, no sooner the Christian armies entered their towns and cities, turned into the most vicious creatures, helping hound Turks in towns and cities, in fact being the most ferocious in the atrocities inflicted on the latter.[622] Other local Christians were left behind by the Turks in the empty villages waiting to greet and welcome the pursuing Christian armies, which caused the bewilderment of the foreign war correspondents.[623]

> We [says Seppings Wright] succeeded only, however, in reaching Tchorlu [Çorlu], which was now deserted by soldiers and left entirely in the hands of the Greek element and two correspondents—yourself and Sir Bryan Leighton. The Greeks of course were waiting to greet the Allies, and it was strongly suspected that these people had been sending money to the enemy.[624]

It was a whole fifth column now acting in various ways against the Turks.

On the side of the Christian armies, on the other hand, it was not just extremely motivated armies marching against the Turks, but rather, fanaticised hordes hurling themselves forth,

> They marched by with a long and swinging stride, old men who remembered many a massacre of their brethren by the Turks and many orgies of wild and terrible revenge, with young lads who had inherited the tradition of hate against the Moslems, who had made Macedonia a place of terror.[625]

> "This will be a cruel war," said a Bulgarian officer, as he sat at my [Gibbs] table in one of the cafes at Sofia. "There will be no non-combatants and no quarter."[626]

---

[620] Ibid; p. 233.
[621] As an example more than 45,000 Ottoman Macedonians volunteered for the Bulgarian army and militia. Bozhilov and Panayatov, Macedonia, 625–627, 631–633.
[622] P. Loti, *Turquie Agonisante;* op cit; i,e pp. 88-9. 208; 209.
[623] H.C. Seppings Wright: *Two Years Under the Crescent*; op cit; p. 209; see also Ashmead Bartlett, and M. Pickthall on Christian celebrations and jeering of Turks in Istanbul itself (see chapter one for all this).
[624] H.C. Seppings Wright: *Two Years Under the Crescent*; op cit; p. 234.
[625] P. Gibbs and B Grant: *The Balkan War*; op cit, p. 30.
[626] Ibid, p. 35.

3. The Military Campaign: October-December 1912

Montenegro started the war by moving into northern Albania as well as the *sancak* of Novipazar on 8 October 1912.[627] Soon after, its allies sent ultimatums to the Turks including among others demand for the autonomy of the remaining European provinces; redrawing the boundaries on ethnic lines, with Christian governors, native militias and gendarmes; new reforms under Christian supervision; and the immediate demobilisation of the entire Turkish army.[628] The Turks could not accept these demands, of course, and so war began.

The battles were spread out over an area of almost 170,000 square kilometres, stretching from the Albanian coast in the west to a mere 32 kilometres from Istanbul in the east; from the most northerly border of Macedonia down to Thessaly in central Greece.[629] The Turkish forces were obliged to fight four different wars: against the Bulgarians in Thrace; against the Bulgarians, Serbs and Greeks in Macedonia; against the Serbs and Montenegrins in northern Albania and Kosovo; and against the Greeks in southern Albania.[630] The main fighting took place in Eastern Thrace between the Bulgarians and the Turkish Eastern Army.[631] The fighting involved trench warfare and merciless sieges; intensive use of artillery on infantry and civilians inside cities, Edirne, primarily; aeroplanes were used for observation and at times bombing raids, and for the first time, technology enabled commanders to fight twenty-four hours a day as huge searchlights illuminated the killing fields.[632]

*****

Initial Turkish Disaster in Thrace

'The Bulgarian soldiers, urged to regard themselves as avengers and as strivers after a great Christian ideal, moved forward, in the words of King Ferdinand's proclamation, 'from victory to victory.''[633]

> I stood on this bridge as the soldiers passed on their way to the front [says Gibbs.] They had wound flowers round their bayonets, and had put garlands about their caps. A priest of the Bulgarian Church, in a long black gown and high black cap, cheered them and waved his arms as battalion after battalion marched past him. He was delirious with enthusiasm for the war against the Crescent, and they answered his wild and exultant cries by

---

[627] S.J. Shaw and E.K. Shaw: *History of the Ottoman Empire*; op cit; p. 294.
[628] Ibid.
[629] M. Glenny: *The Balkans*; op cit; Chap 3.
[630] Ibid.
[631] M. Uyar and E.J. Erickson: *A Military History of the Ottomans*; op cit; p. 226.
[632] M. Glenny: *The Balkans*; op cit.
[633] H.F. Baldwin: *War Photographer in Thrace*; op cit; p. 53.

> waving their caps on their bayonets and bursting out into some religious chant.[634]

The Bulgarians wanted to move immediately into Macedonia, but fearful of a Turkish offensive from Istanbul, they decided to send most of their forces toward the Turkish capital, thus allowing the Greeks and Serbs to conquer and divide Macedonia before they could get there.[635] This would eventually lead to the second Balkan War when the three countries squabbled over the spoils.

The Turkish plan was to fix an important portion of the Bulgarian army in front of the Edirne fortress, pulling the remaining units towards Kırkkilise and thereby giving the Eastern Army an opportunity to envelop them from the north (III Corps) and south (IV Corps and Edirne garrison).[636] The Turks were right in their assessment that a success against Bulgaria in Thrace would take Bulgaria out of the war, and once she did, the whole coalition would collapse like a pack of cards.[637] Therefore, from the start they sought to mobilise a powerful army for the invasion of Bulgaria under cover of the fortress of Edirne.[638] On paper the idea was great, but on the ground, it was an altogether different matter. The Grand Army of Thrace, which should have been already at the attack stage at the outbreak of hostilities, was now hopelessly scattered, some units still far in Asia Minor, with no chance whatsoever to even participate in the battle of Lule Burgas (29 Oct).[639] Kırkkilise was already fought over and lost before even the Turkish armies assembled as planned, thus foiling the plan from the very beginning.[640] The attacks by Mahmud Pasha, commander of III Corps, and his encirclement manoeuvres on October 22 at the Battle of Kırkkilise, were doomed to fail even if they initially achieved success. The reasons for failure for these as all other operations of similar nature, and on all fronts, in fact, owed to simple, military basics: The Turks were not only numerically much inferior they were simply blasted by much more intense artillery fire from their foes. The Turks simply did not have enough fire power to conduct operations that relied on heavy firepower. It was simply madness on the part of the Turkish General Command to order such operations. These fundamental reasons for failure were amply obvious to E. Ashmead Bartlett at Lule Burgas, where the Turks did not even have enough shells to fire at the thickly advancing Bulgarian infantry. Thus, by 24 October, the Battle of Kırkkilise was not just over, surviving units were retreating in the midst of crowds of refugees in the confusion cited above.

---

[634] P. Gibbs and B Grant: *The Balkan War*; op cit, p. 11.
[635] S.J. Shaw and E.K. Shaw: *History of the Ottoman*; op cit; p. 294.
[636] M. Uyar and E.J. Erickson: *A Military History of the Ottomans*; op cit; p. 226.
[637] E. Ashmead Bartlett: *With the Turks in Thrace*; op cit; p. 80.
[638] Ibid.
[639] Ibid.
[640] M. Uyar and E.J. Erickson: *A Military History of the Ottomans*; op cit; p. 226.

Only a few miles on the other (Bulgarian) side, the troops were pushing on the heels of the Turks. And maybe at this stage had they not busied themselves with massacring, burning, and pillaging, they could have caught huge chunks of the retreating Turkish Eastern Army. As it was, Gibbs, who was amongst them (the Bulgarians) could see where all the refugees now cramming the movements of the Turkish army came from:

> The spectacle around me was grim and terrible, and when the sun began to sink into a great blaze of bloodred light overspreading the western sky above the sombre line of hills, it assumed an awful grandeur and beauty. Four, five and then six villages a little way across the river began to burn with a fierce and swift destruction. The Bulgarian troops had fired them, not I believe out of mere blind hatred of the Turk, but strictly for military purposes. They burned like flaming torches, great tongues of fire licking from roof to roof until the villages were burning furnaces of red light, intense and vivid as molten metal, with black patches breaking through the glare where houses had once stood, and with trees in the foreground silhouetted as black as ink.[641]

Then with the Bulgarian troops, he reached a place called Pashachivlik [Paşaçiftlik], once a place of Turkish homesteads, with neat little wooden houses and big farms enclosed by a circle of great haystacks.

> Turkish peasant farmers had gone home to this place after their long day's work in the fields, glad to see the lights twinkling in their windows; women had brought children into the world in those old cottages; from generation to generation small black-eyed boys and girls had played in the barns and in the gardens. Now it was all just a black, blazing ruin. The peasants had fled with their children, and the only living things left were lean dogs, who howled around the relics of their old homes, and one miserable donkey with singed hair and burnt feet, as black as the cinders upon which it lay.
>
> I wandered about the small streets, half suffocated by the poisonous smoke which rolled out of the gaping windows and shattered roofs, scorched by the intense heat of this horrible bonfire. Now and again there would be a clatter and rumble, and down would fall a pile of bricks, or a great beam, scattering sparks as it hit the earth. At some hazard I went into one or two of the ruined houses, and picked up the pages of Turkish books, and scraps of letters written in Turkish script.[642]

It was at this stage that the Western correspondents on the Turkish side reached the scene, desperately trying to catch the battle of Kırkilise, not knowing it was already over. They were moving in counter-flow with both refugees and retreating soldiers. And then the disaster became apparent. E. Ashmead Bartlett, on a train with some of his colleagues, was now stopped at a station, where they

---

[641] P. Gibbs and B Grant: *The Balkan War*; op cit, p. 89.
[642] Ibid, pp. 90-91.

were told to wait three hours until trainloads of wounded, coming from the front passed towards Istanbul. All around, the whole area was chocked with fleeing people, a chaotic mass of women, children, and old men, with their carts and last belongings struggling under the heavy rain and mud, one old man telling him that Kırkkilise was on fire

> Then he shook his fist towards the north and swore a vengeance that he could never hope to take. We were told that we should be taken back to Chorlou at once, but a train became derailed behind us and we were compelled to wait until the line could be repaired. All day long an endless line of refugees wound across the plain, and towards evening a train arrived from Burgas with women and children clinging to the front of the engine and the tops of the railway carriages.[643]

Kırkkilise was lost; onto the next battle scene: Lule Burgaz.

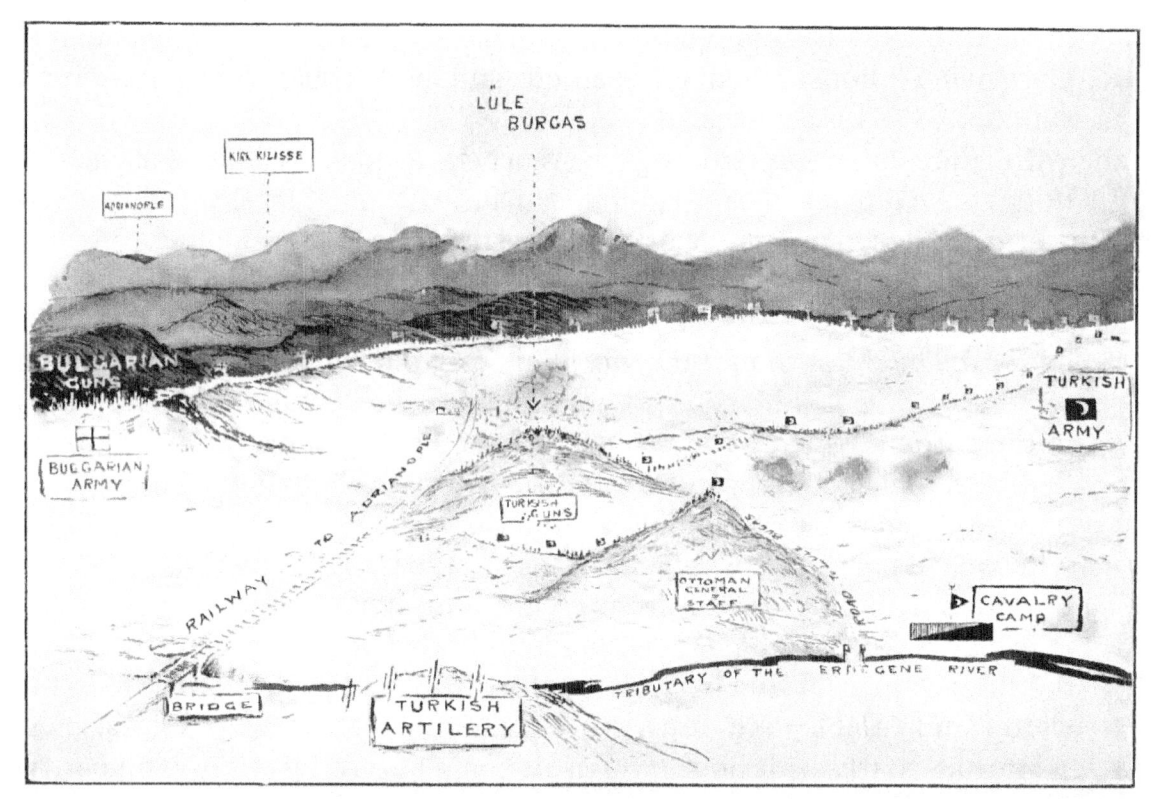

A sketch of Lule Burgaz front-line (by Seppings Wright)

---

[643] E. Ashmead Bartlett: *With the Turks in Thrace*; op cit; p. 96-7.

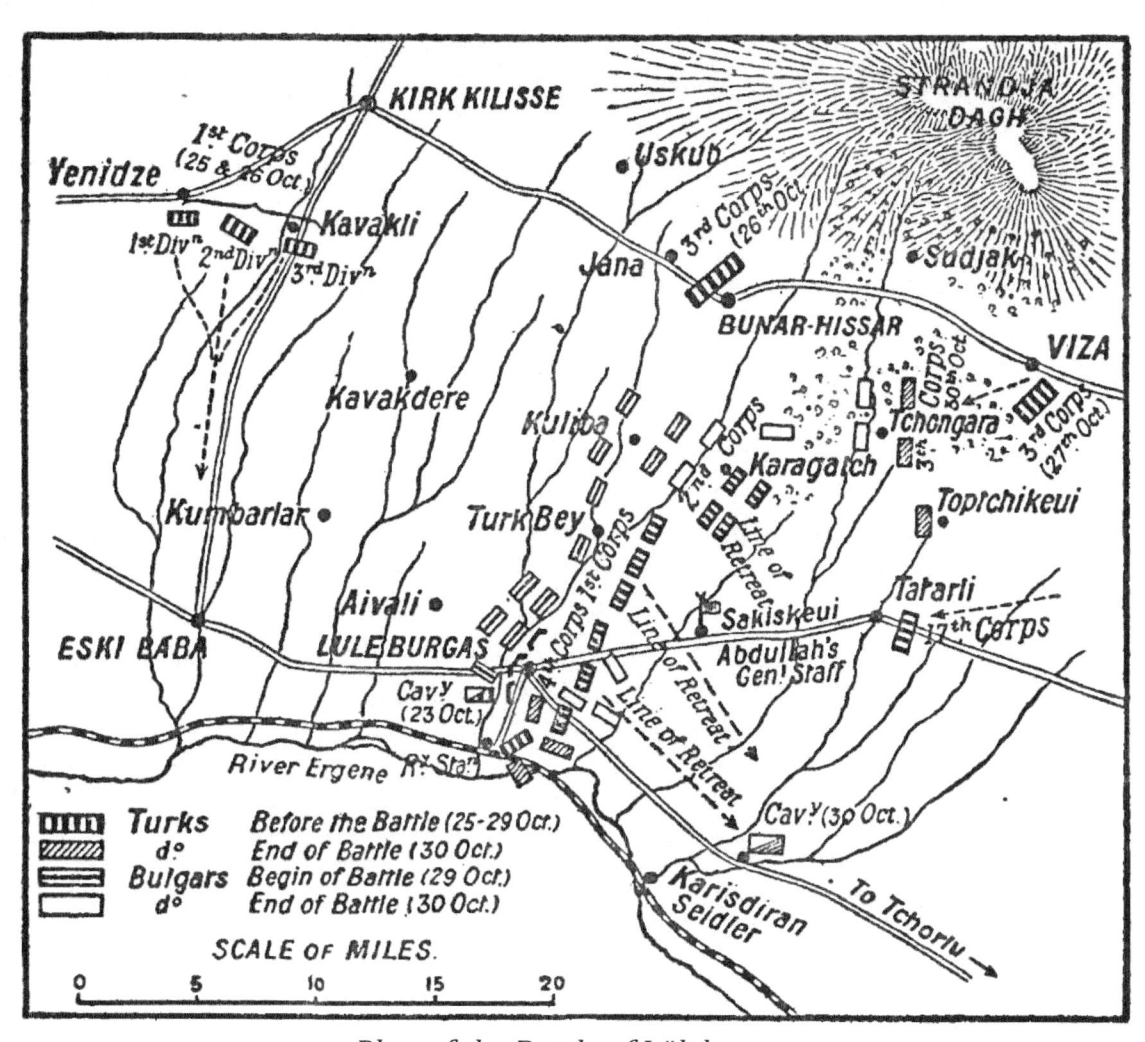

Plan of the Battle of Lüleburgaz

The five-day long (29 October–2 November) battle fought around the Lule Burgaz-Pınarhisar line became the largest and costliest battle of the war.[644] Here, indeed, the Turks put on a more tenacious fight, and although they ultimately lost, it is perhaps safe to say that it was at Lule Burgas that Turkey was saved at the cost of terrible sacrifices. The toll the Turks took of the Bulgarians literally broke their impetus. Here we have E. Ashmead Bartlett on the Turkish side, whilst on the Bulgarian side, we have Gibbs, and both of them give us the right picture of what happened a Lule Burgaz.

E. Ashmead Bartlett's account:

> Ismet [A Turkish colleague] and I [E. Ashmead Bartlett] then made our way slowly to the rear, but were dragged into a vortex of men, women, children, carts, stray soldiers, unarmed men and wounded, all hastening to escape from the enemy's shrapnel, which had commenced to burst over the town

---
[644] M. Uyar and E.J. Erickson: *A Military History of the Ottomans*; op cit; p. 227.

itself. The confusion was awful. A complete panic had seized the flying mob, and every minute we expected to have the enemy's shells burst in our midst...

Two separate engagements were now taking place in this portion of the field, for part of the Bulgarian infantry had right-wheeled, and were making a desperate attack on Salih's dismounted cavalry, who were nobly trying to check the advance on the railway station, the capture of which would mean the cutting of the line and the isolation of Adrianople. The fighting in this quarter was of the fiercest character, and the Turkish cavalry, only about 800 strong, lost 150 men before being obliged to retire. Turks in the town inflicted very heavy losses on the invaders, who were quite devoid of any cover. But now the Bulgarian artillery had been brought up to the crest of the ridge, and commenced to shell the town and the Turkish entrenchments on the higher ground where we stood. Their fire was wonderfully accurate, but the Turks stood their ground well and refused to leave the town. For more than two hours this rear-guard held out heroically. About two o'clock fresh masses of Bulgarian infantry debouched from the hills and rushed down into the firing line, and the whole line dashed forward with magnificent elan. The fire from the Turkish entrenchments now rose into a sullen roar. It was independent, and as rapid as each man could load and fire. The Bulgarians fell in scores, and the advance came to an end only a few hundred yards away from the entrenchments. Along the whole of this front the battle raged furiously throughout Tuesday, October 29th. All along the line the Bulgarians were on the offensive, and, to gauge from the severity of the artillery fire, their evident object was to break through between the right of the 1st Corps and the left of the 2nd Corps, between Turk Bey and Karagach. The whole of the battle front for twenty miles was clearly shown by the masses of bursting shrapnel shells. Never before have I seen such an artillery fire. For every battery the Turks seemed to have in action, the Bulgarians were able to produce half a dozen.

Here again, the Turkish defence was crushed by the immense superiority of the enemy's artillery fire. Here again, the old story was repeated of Turkish batteries unable to play any part in the battle from lack of ammunition. Here again, a half-starved and worn-out infantry were expected to fight like men.

By two o'clock in the afternoon (30th October) the position of Abdullah's army was critical, almost desperate, and the glasses of the staff were all turned towards the north-east in the direction of Viza, from which point Mahmoud Mukhtar with the 3rd Corps was making tremendous efforts to come up.

An engagement of a desultory character had been taking place in that direction throughout the morning, but the smoke of the bursting shells showed that up to the present the 3rd Corps had been making steady progress. About three o'clock in the afternoon, it became obvious that Mahmoud Mukhtar's advance had been completely checked.

I will interrupt a further description of the day's fighting to present to the reader the hopeless position of the Commander-in-Chief of the Turkish army, directing as he was, or as he should have been directing, the movements of four army corps, ranged over a front of twenty-five miles.

Abdullah remained throughout the entire day, except for one brief interval, on the mound of which I have already spoken. His sole companions were his staff and his personal escort, and his sole means of obtaining any information as to what was happening elsewhere were his pair of field glasses. Not a line of telegraph or telephone had been brought to the front, and not a single wireless installation, although the Turkish army on paper possesses twelve complete outfits for its army corps; and not an effort had been made even to establish a line of messengers by relays to connect headquarters with the various army corps. I need hardly add that not a single aeroplane was anywhere within 100 miles of the front, and if any exist there was no one to fly them. Thus the battle, instead of being directed by one master-mind, practically resolved itself into four isolated engagements with four separate commanders, each completely ignorant of his comrade's movements, and each having the same difficulty as his Commander-in-Chief in communicating with his divisional and brigade commanders. Again, as in the morning, had the Turkish general had but a fresh corps in hand and a few batteries of artillery the day might have been saved.[645]

---

[645] E. Ashmead Bartlett: *With the Turks in Thrace*; op cit; pp. 142-164.

The Turkish army in full retreat from Lüleburgaz

The Turkish retreat was yet another disastrous sight, again, civilians with their carts, mud and rain, wounded and dying soldiers, everyone starved, all the officer corps annihilated in the fighting, abandoned equipment spread all over the muddy fields, so much so, the possibility of the Turks ever recovering being utterly beyond any imagination.[646] Everyone was waiting, in fact, for the Bulgarian cavalry and artillery to just spring forth and finish the whole Turkish army and reach Istanbul.

> I think [admits Ashmed Bartlett] almost every European and certainly every war correspondent hoped to see the triumphal entry of King Ferdinand, at the head of his legions, into Constantinople.
>
> This was needed to give a grand dramatic finale to the campaign. There were many who wished to be present at the solemn ceremony of substituting the Cross for the Crescent on the dome of Saint Sofia. Many well-known writers commenced their accounts of the march of Ferdinand's legions through the Golden Gate, and the exit of the Turks into Asia Minor after an occupation of six hundred years. It seemed to us, who had come straight from the battle-field, that the Bulgarians could perform any miracle or feat of arms they chose. They appeared now as a mythical monster, who had only to open his jaws and swallow up whole tracts of

---
[646] Grant in Gibbs and Grant: *Adventures of War with Cross and Crescent*, 172–175; E. Ashmead Bartlett: *With the Turks in Thrace*, 166 ff.

country and whole armies. It seemed incredible that the beaten Turk, worn-out, starving, and hopelessly mismanaged, could ever again rally or offer any resistance in the field. For a few days it was continuously rumoured that the Bulgarians had swept past Chataldja and were hammering at the gates of the city.[647]

However, two major developments prevented that:

First, Gibbs who was on the Bulgarian side could see that although the Turks were defeated, their spirited fight at Lule Burgaz (which Ashmed Bartlett had just described) had its toll on the Bulgarians:

FOR two weeks I watched the first men back from the quickest war in history.

They came back, not with medals on their breasts and with bands playing them into the towns, but with bandages round their heads and limbs through which the blood had oozed with horrible stains, and with the jolting of trains and the shrieking of whistles for their music.

I do not know how many thousands of wounded men I saw, but they numbered many great battalions, and the roads of Turkey and Bulgaria were rutted deep by the wheels of league-long convoys bringing back these victims of war.

The Bulgarians issued no lists of their casualties. With that amazing and almost inhuman secrecy; with which they veiled all but the barest facts of the war, they steadily refused to give the names and numbers of the dead and wounded, so that few peasant women in Bulgaria knew whether their men would ever come back again. But they were not able to conceal the wounded men. The bright sun of autumn in the Near East shone down upon those winding caravans of Red Cross waggons jolting down the hill-tracks and over roads axle-deep in mud; the rain which swept the sunshine out of the sky at times poured down upon men lying in misery and in sodden straw, and peasants standing by the roadside with great flocks around them, which they kept driving forward to the front as food for men who were food for powder, saw their comrades passing, passing, passing, day after day, towards hospitals in Turkish villages and Bulgarian towns. The agony of that long journey from the front must have been terrible. The men who fought at Kirk Kilisse and Lule Burgas had sixty leagues and more to cover in haycarts and bullock-waggons before they reached the railways. Many of them never reached the railways; the last flicker of life was shaken out of them before they came to the trains; the drivers called:

"Haide! Hai-de!" not knowing that a corpse lay in the straw behind them. The faces of some of those wounded men were terrible as they passed me. They were the faces of dead men with living eyes, of an earthen colour already, splashed by blood, and stamped with the sharp imprint of pain. Some of them had their tongues lolling out, parched with thirst, and others

---

[647] E. Ashmead Bartlett: *With the Turks in Thrace*; op cit; pp. 231-232.

were terribly smashed so that never again will they be able to follow the plough in the field. At the railway stations all ordinary trains were held up while the ambulance trains poured through in one long traffic of human freight. For hours, and sometimes for two days at a stretch, while I waited for a passenger train to take me fifty miles or so further to the front, I stared at the convoys of wounded and became weary of all their woe. Poor devils! These heroes of the war against the Turk knew the meaning of heroism to the last bitter drop of the cup.[648]

Here the second factor that held off the Bulgarians is explained for us by Seppings Wright, who, too, was there.

> Refugees were stimulated by the roar of artillery to extra exertions, only to fall exhausted in the mire. Had it not been for the heavy rains the insignificant streams, several of which had to be crossed, could have been easily forded. Now the waters roared like a mountain torrent and surged against the bridge, which acted like a dam, flooding the country for miles on either side.
> I marvelled that the frail bridge stood against the flood. As the human torrent flowed onward I watched a horse and rider struggling in the water, while attempting to cross to the other side. Nothing could prevail against such a flood. Carried away by the crowd of refugees it was some little time before I succeeded in extricating myself and returning to Tchorlu [Çorlu]. I arrived there wet and wearied, only too glad to rest.
> All that night a ceaseless stream of fugitives poured into the town. Every house was filled to overflowing, and the streets and square were crowded with soaking people.
> The morning brought no relief. The rain came down like a deluge, blown by a hurricane of wind, whirling about flocks of scolding jackdaws.
> The Bulgarians were expected to follow on the heels of the Turkish army, and we looked for their arrival every moment. Neither friend nor foe would willingly have faced the havoc of such a storm, otherwise the correspondents as well as the fugitives might have been captured by the victors without much difficulty.[649]

Seppings Wright, possibly throughout the conflict, was the correspondent with the keenest sense of observation (he by profession being in fact a war illustrator) thus, alone, he was able to see that that same factor that had made life a misery for the Turks, i.e. the awful weather, had contributed in the first place to saving the whole army, very possibly also saving tens of thousands of civilians, and very certainly Turkey as well. The Bulgarians, especially with their heavy equipment, could not advance on Turkey because of the raging streams and floods, and the land now an utter quagmire; the muddy ground that had hampered the Turks so

---
[648] P. Gibbs and B Grant: *The Balkan War*; op cit, pp. 129-130.
[649] H.C. Seppings Wright: *Two Years Under the Crescent*; op cit; pp. 195-6.

much had been made much worse by the Turkish masses preceding the Bulgarians, thus making it un-passable.

*****

The Walls of Çatalca and Edirne

Tchatalja [Çatalca] lines, even without the formidable fortifications, looked unassailable due to the terrain. A deep valley, watered by the river and a wide shallow lake, forbids the approach of an enemy from that direction. There is only one road running by way of a long narrow bridge which connects the mainland with the village of Büyükçekmece; but to make sure even this narrow pass is secure, the bridge is mined.[650]
The centre of the position is a powerful system of defence. Its climbing hills provide a good position for both artillery and rifle trenches. It is across the low-lying plain, between these heights and the hills opposite, that an invading enemy had to advance under a barrage of artillery shells and heavy machine gunfire.[651]
At the Derekoi [Dereköy] end of the line, shallow lagoons and morasses protect the right flank. The flanks are further reinforced by trenches and fortresses, and also navy guns which guard land and sea approaches. Then, on top of all this, is a network of barbed wire, which thus makes the line nearly impossible to cross.[652]

Whilst it would seem to some that Çatalca was about impossible to pass, others, including here Baldwin who likewise was present as a war photographer, relying on the views of military experts who were there, still saw that it could be breached and captured at enormous sacrifice. En par with other war correspondents, except Seppings Wright, he could not understand either why the Bulgarians had failed to continue their offensive and allowed the Turks to reinforce there.[653]

---

[650] Ibid; p. 180.
[651] Ibid.
[652] Ibid.
[653] H.F. Baldwin: *War Photographer in Thrace;* op cit; p. 221.

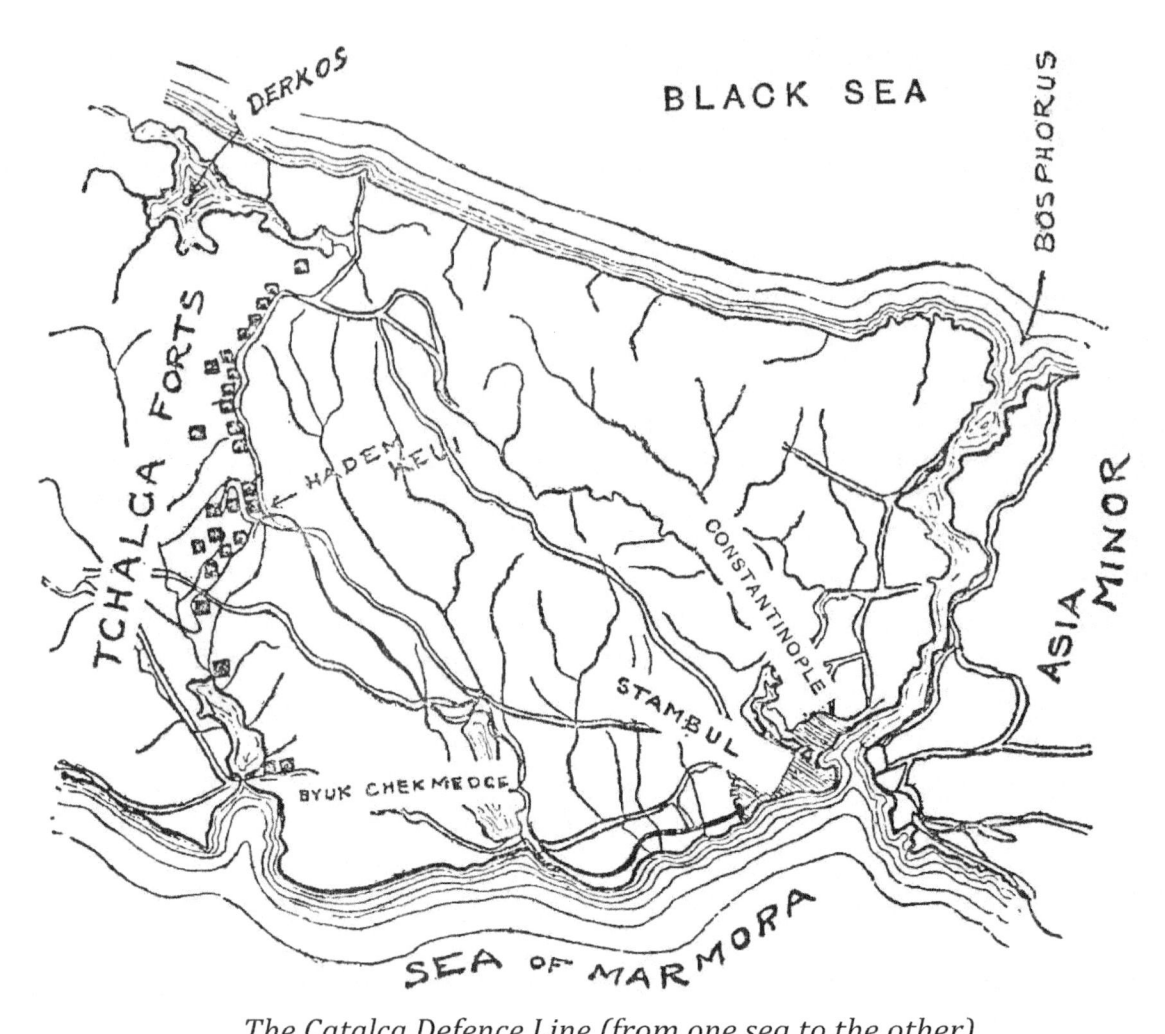

The Catalca Defence Line (from one sea to the other)

The assault on Çatalca began in the early morning of 17 November, 900 Bulgarian guns submitting the Turkish defences to the most intense bombardment to date. The Bombardment was so violent it caused a dense fog of smoke and explosions on a front of about 50 kilometres, from the Derkos forest on the Black Sea down to Çatalca.[654] Some people who lived through it compared it to the most formidable of earthquakes; so much so, panic seized the inhabitants of Istanbul.[655]

Just as Bulgarian fire, Turkish defence seemed to be on a mammoth scale. Each Bulgarian concentration or push was met by a wall of Turkish firing.

> The Turkish soldiers [B. Grant says] seemed to be firing almost continuously, reloading as fast as they could and sweeping the enemy's line with a perfect hurricane of lead. Only now and then did the fire drop and languish away. In a few moments it would break out again fiercely, with that kind of screaming song of death which cannot be described in words,

---
[654] M. Glenny: *The Balkans*; op cit.
[655] Ibid.

but which leaves an ineffaceable sensation in the minds of those who have once heard it.[656]

The air, [likewise,] was alive with those flying shells which burst high up and scattered the missiles of death as they fell. They had a strange and deadly beauty. I was fascinated with those sudden flashes of flame, those white puffballs, those bursting clouds. One knows the terror that falls with them.[657]

The Bulgarians had made the village of Çatalca their headquarters, and now 'it seemed to be vomiting fire.' There was a huge concentration of artillery there, and from that direction there came an immense number of shells, which burst well over the Turkish lines.[658]

The Turks were deeply entrenched, and were also determined to hold their lines at all cost, and soon it became obvious that as the battle progressed, the Bulgarian quick sweep forward was over.

Here, Grant also agrees with Baldwin and others as against those who have overestimated the strength of the defensive structures. To him if Çatalca did not and would not fall, the main reason should be attributed to the defenders rather than the defences.[659] Grant draws attention to the fact that the Bulgarians had lost in front of Çatalca many more men than their official statics show, and it was this major factor, which made them recoil at risking more.[660]

Edirne proved to be as tough as Çatalca. It was the strongest fortified position on the main line to Istanbul from Bulgaria, and its strategic position was of immense significance to both Turks and Bulgarians.[661] Syed Tanvir Wasti wrote a remarkable essay on its siege, relying on the accounts of many of those who were involved in it from within.[662] Gibbs was on the besieging Bulgarian side and provides very interesting complementary information. The fortress of Edirne was under the command of Mehmet Şükrü Pasha,[663] who had been ordered to ensure that in the event of a siege the fortress would not surrender for a period of 50 days.[664] Instead, with the defenders, he held out in the face of falling food supplies, intense artillery bombardment, regular infantry assaults, and bitter winter conditions for 5 months and 5 days, surrendering, on Wednesday, 26 March 1913, only because he feared that further bombardment would destroy the historic structures such as the famous Selimiye Mosque in the former Ottoman capital.[665]

---

[656] B. Grant in P. Gibbs and B Grant: *The Balkan War*; op cit, p. 232.
[657] Ibid.
[658] Ibid, p. 233.
[659] Ibid, p. 234.
[660] Ibid.
[661] Ibid, p. 97.
[662] Syed Tanvir Wasti: The 1912-1913 Balkan war and the Siege of Edirne; *Middle Eastern Studies;* vol 4; 2004; pp. 59-78.
[663] Mehmet Sukru Pasha was born in Erzurum in 1857 as the only child of an army officer. He was marked out for a military career and became a Lieutenant in the Artillery in 1879.
[664] This was the period envisaged in the mobilization plan for the fortress of Edirne
[665] Syed Tanvir Wasti: The 1912-1913 Balkan war and the Siege of Edirne; op cit; p. 61.

The first battle which the Bulgarians had to deliver in their attempt to capture the advanced positions on the way to Edirne was at Kadikoi [Kadıköy], on the right bank of the Maritza. The battle took place on 22 October, and despite fierce Turkish resistance, the Bulgarians were victorious.[666] Then, following their advance, the Bulgarians swept away in front of them any Turkish resistance, burning all villages around the city, and soon began their siege, followed by intense bombardment. The position of the city and its inhabitants in the last days of October and throughout November gradually worsened as the Turkish defeat at Kırkkilise had completely isolated the city, leaving it without any means for receiving supplies.[667]

On 15 November 1912, a Bulgarian plane flew over the Edirne skies, showering leaflets below containing the following message:

> We have surrounded Edirne with a thousand guns. Come and surrender. O people of Edirne, we shall save you from your despotic officials. The Bulgarian armies are victorious everywhere.[668]

The offer was rejected and the siege and bombardment intensified in succeeding days and weeks, bringing to the ground houses, shops and structures, causing a high human toll.[669] The more the bombardment lasted, the more constructions were flattened, the more the survivors became squeezed in an ever shrinking liveable space.[670] Now that the Turks had lost the battles of Kırkkilise and Lule Burgaz, the troops within the city walls relied on their initiative, and effected regular sorties, hoping to dislodge the Bulgarians out of their entrenched positions and break a way through to the main army. Some of these sorties, even when repulsed, left a heavy toll amongst the Bulgarians.[671] A Bulgarian priest, who used to drive repeatedly to the area of fighting, told Gibbs that on one day alone the Bulgarians had lost 800 men.[672] A Bulgarian officer also reported that the Turks had improved their position after the first Bulgarian successes, and had recaptured some of their forts, driving out the Bulgarians 'by a fury of shell fire which they were unable to sustain.'[673] On another occasion two battalions of Bulgarian infantry went forth, and stumbled upon a Turkish mine, which blew up suddenly and caused 'a frightful slaughter.'[674]

To the besieged, the bombardment soon developed into some sort of routine, and people somehow learned to live with the siege despite their worsening situation.[675] 'Fires broke out, soldiers and civilians were wounded, and those who

---

[666] P. Gibbs and B Grant: *The Balkan War*; op cit, p. 100.
[667] Ibid, p. 101.
[668] The text of the leaflets is given in greater detail by Yigitgiuden, q.v., pp.122-3 and by Kestelli, q.v., p.48.
[669] Syed Tanvir Wasti: The 1912-1913 Balkan war; op cit; p. 65.
[670] Gustav Cirilli: *Journal du siege d'Adrianople*; Paris, 1913; p. 142.
[671] P. Gibbs and B Grant: *The Balkan War*; op cit, p. 102.
[672] Ibid, p. 103.
[673] Ibid.
[674] Ibid.
[675] Syed Tanvir Wasti: The 1912-1913 Balkan war; op cit; p. 65.

died, whether from the shelling or from natural causes, were carried to their graves.'[676] All sounding like normal times, indeed.

On 2 December, the Bulgarians asked for the surrender of the fortress again. A Major was asked to deliver an envelope to Şükrü Pasha, but he refused scornfully, saying:

> We have not yet given battle for the control of the fortress, and will defend it till the last man. We have not sought this meeting. We would like to face either a real friend or a serious enemy.[677]

The besiegers' position was not to be envied either. The Bulgarians were not only exposed to Turkish shellfire, they were also exposed to the terrible wintry conditions which made their trench life virtually impossible. They having burnt Turkish villages had by that action removed means that could have given them support now. In fact, at times, they were themselves threatened with starvation when supplies failed to reach them in the wake of heavy fighting or artillery fire.[678]

Militarily the situation was deadlocked, and in December an armistice was concluded. However the Bulgarian had not given up. They were only disheartened by the failure to capture a city which, Gibbs says

> Had seemed like a ripe pear ready to fall into their hands, and they were angered by the great losses which they sustained from the surprise attacks and the continued shell fire. They also made vows of vengeance, and kept their bayonets very sharp and covered them with grease.[679]

The Greek Grand Idea, the 1912 Step

> It is quite impossible for Greeks and Turks to look at the First Balkan War from the same angle of vision [wrote Toynbee back in 1922.] For the Greeks it was a war of liberation against a tyranny, incompletely successful in so far as a single Greek was left under Turkish sovereignty at the conclusion of peace. Any Turks ruling over Greeks were felt to be oppressors, even if they were in a local majority, for here the romantic element came in. If the Turks had secured a majority, that, in the eyes of the Greeks, was only one robbery the more. Wherever they were and whatever their numbers, they were intruders, and pretensions based on the present could be put out of count by a monument, an inscription, a legend, or a name. In any war with Turkey, Greece could not feel herself the aggressor. In invading Ottoman territory she was simply recovering what she regarded as her own. A war of liberation always seems to those who

---
[676] Ibid.
[677] Ibid.
[678] P. Gibbs and B Grant: *The Balkan War*; op cit, p. 103.
[679] Ibid, p. 107.

> make it to be morally a war of defence, even when they take the offensive.[680]

Indeed, for the Greeks the matter was simple: there was a Grand Idea, the recovery of the whole Byzantium Empire, i.e. Greece was not just like the others happy to expel the Turks to Asia. What Greece wanted, and maybe still wants today in 2020: Asia Minor without the Turks. Back in 1912, the matter was at least in appearance a united Christian Crusade as stated in the declaration of war, when King George I published a proclamation summoning his people 'to fight for the liberation of oppressed Christians.'[681]

On the very day the war began, the Greeks captured Elassona, followed three days later by their successful landing at Lemnos; Veria 5 days later, on 28 October; Thosos two days later, on 30 October; then Prevesa on 3 November, and then, the biggest prize of all, Salonika, on 9 November.[682] The Turkish VIII Corps which was to defend the Greek border suffered precisely from the same deficiencies as other armies elsewhere: caught unprepared, its ranks incomplete, overwhelmed by huge Greek superiority in numbers, arms, and logistics, and Turkish courage matched by Greek hatred and fanaticism. Therefore, the Greeks had all the ingredients for winning and for doing what they did next.

The fall of Salonika had already become unavoidable and obvious, when days earlier tens of thousands of refugees began to stream into the city, seeking refuge in mosques.[683] Soon, in their wake, arrived the debris of the Turkish army, fleeing in front of the rampaging Serbs, Greeks, and Bulgarians, pushing in from every direction, all of them after the same great prize, Salonika. The Greeks beat the Bulgarians to it by a matter of hours. Crown Prince Constantine made his ceremonial entrance drenched by a cold winter rain.[684] The enthusiasm on his part and the local Greeks was too great to mind the inconvenience of the weather, the city at last captured from the Turks, the greatest prize to date. As the King marched on, the Greek inhabitants adorned the city in blue and white colours[685] and showered its Great Liberating Army with roses, the fanatical mob yelling 'Zeto! Zeto!'

As the blue-and-white Greek flag waved from the roofs and the windows, the Turkish flags were disposed off, vanishing for ever.

Beaten to the city, surely not happy, the Bulgarians soon made their entry, took over houses, certainly Muslim, and churches, and occupied a sector of the city.[686]

---

[680] A.J. Toynbee: *The Western Question in Greece and Turkey*; Constable; 1922; p. 137.
[681] Ali Fuad Türkgeldi: *Görüp İşittiklerim* (What I Saw and Heard), 2nd edn, TTK, Ankara 1951, 57ff.; K. Paparrigopoulos: *Istoria tou Ellinikou Ethnous* (History of the Greek Nation), Eleftheroudakis, Athens 1932, VII, 137–8.
[682] Clyde Sinclair Ford: *The Balkan Wars, a Series of Lectures;* Press of the Army Service Schools; Fort Leavenworth; Kansas; 1915: Chronological Table of the Principal Events of the Balkan Wars 1912.
[683] M. Glenny: *The Balkans*; op cit.
[684] S.J. Shaw and E.K. Shaw: *History of the Ottoman Empire*; op cit; p. 294.
[685] Lord Kinross: *Ataturk*; op cit; p. 54.
[686] Ibid.

Meanwhile, the Greeks were quick to celebrate their success. The Patriarch of Athens joined the King and the Metropolitan of Salonika, Gennadios, in celebrating a special Mass in the Church of St Minas.[687]

> 'Glory to the triumph of the Hellenes and the venerated diadoque [the Crown Prince]', proclaimed Gennadios. 'Hosannah to the glorious sons of the warriors of Marathon and Salamina, the valiant liberators of our fatherland!'[688]

Once the celebrations were over, there came the next matter of importance: settling scores with the Turks. Those amongst the latter who had no illusion in Christian charity, and could flee, did. In their tens of thousands they fled along with the wounded soldiers, but huge numbers amongst them would never reach Istanbul alive.[689]

> When the Turkish refugees flocked in panic to Constantinople to escape from massacre, when cholera broke out among the immigrants and in the army, when one saw an entire population dying in the mosque yards in the icy grip of winter, the sight of the misery in Constantinople seemed too grim to be true.[690]

Mustafa Kemal, a native of Salonika, looking for his own family, found thousands of its Muslim inhabitants massed together in the courtyards of the mosques, ragged and destitute and dying in the cruel winter weather.[691] Eventually he found his mother and sister; his mother, suddenly looking aged and broken by the loss of her home. Mustafa Kemal found them a house and then turned to his duties on the General Staff.[692]

These were the refugees; some more fortunate than others. As for those who stayed behind and hoped for Christian benevolence, they experienced what hundreds of eye witnesses saw, that is what the Greeks, Bulgarians, and Serbs did to them.[693] Briefly here, all the Christian allies engaged in large-scale massacres of Muslims. For example, in the region of Avret-Hissar and Doyran, Bulgarians carried out extensive massacres: in Rajanova, 'scarcely a male Muslim has been left alive.'[694] All of the males of the village of Kurkut, along with many of the women and children, were collected in the mosque and in barns and were burned to death.[695] Serbian komitajis flogged the Muslim villagers of Drenova to death.[696] Western observers estimated that approximately 5,000 Albanian Muslims were killed 'between Kumanova and Uskiib' and 5,000 in the Pristina area.[697]

---

[687] M. Glenny: *The Balkans*; op cit.
[688] Bernard Lory, '1912, Les Hellènes entrent dans la ville,' in Veinstein, op. cit., pp. 247–8.
[689] Lord Kinross: *Ataturk*; op cit; p. 54.
[690] Halide Edib, Memoirs of Halide Edib (London: John Murray, 1926), p.334.
[691] Lord Kinross: *Ataturk*; op cit; p. 54.
[692] Ibid; p. 55.
[693] See accounts in P. Loti: *Turquie Agonisante;* op cit.
[694] F.O. 195-2438, no 6650; Lamb to Lowther, Salonica 3 December 1912.
[695] Ibid.
[696] FO. 371-1762, no 55161; Greig to Crackanthrope, Monastir, 19 November 1913.
[697] Reports of Austro-Hungarian consuls given by the correspondents of the Daily Telegraph: Les Atrocites des coalises Balkaniques; No 1, Constantinople, 1913; pp. 14-18.

Witnesses on the ground, French gendarmes, including Colonel Foulon and Colonel Malfey, in Salonika, Austrians, Germans, functionaries from all nationalities, health personal, chaplains, doctor Ernst Jäckh, General Baumann, Colonel Veit, Captain Rein, Professor Duhring, all provided written accounts backed by photographs of all sorts of cruelties that were inflicted on Turks, including blinding them in their thousands; and how the local Christians, once neighbours of the Turks, guided the killers to the Turkish houses, which had most wealth and young women in the household.[698] Young women being led to the Christian soldiers smeared themselves in mud along the way in hope of putting off their tormentors.[699] Regarding what had been inflicted on the women, and countless other crimes with precise location, and who carried them out, Dr Ernst Jäckh, was witness and also received hundreds of accounts and photographs, all of which he summed up in a chapter of his book.[700] Of course, we are not going to recount what the witnesses saw done to the Turks. It is up to the Turks themselves to do it if they want their people to know.

Back to the Greek front, Turkish disaster was only partly salvaged thanks to initiatives of some independent-minded junior officers, the best example being the defence of Grebene (a small town at the Ottoman-Greek border).[701] A provincial gendarmerie officer, Captain Bekir Fikri (a veteran of the Macedonian and Yemen Campaigns), gathered under his command all the available border guards, Redifs, and gendarmeries (approximately 800 strong), besides some civilian volunteers.[702] He waged a relentless guerrilla campaign against Greek regular units and irregular gangs, which started immediately after the defeat and withdrawal of the VIII Corps.[703] At the peak of his campaign, Bekir Fikri covered a 100-kilometer-long strip of mountainous region between Kozana and Yanya and held between 10–15 regular Greek battalions and various irregular gangs.[704] His six-month-long guerrilla campaign was proof that had High Command employed guerrilla warfare, perhaps even in conjunction of conventional warfare, the fate of the Greek and Montenegrin Campaigns would have ended differently.[705]

On sea, the Greek fleet was able not only to capture some Aegean Islands but also to block Turkish movements, most essentially the transport of freight and troops from Anatolia through the Aegean to the garrisons in Rumelia.[706] But it was the

---

[698] In P. Loti: *Turquie;* op cit; pp. 155-7.
[699] Ibid.
[700] Reports by persons of all ranks, all of Christian denomination, in E. Jaeckh; op cit; pp.83-98.
[701] M. Uyar and E.J. Erickson: *A Military History of the Ottomans;* op cit; p. 229.
[702] Ibid.
[703] Ibid.
[704] Ibid.
[705] Bekir Fikri, Balkanlarda Tedhis, ve Gerilla, supra 42; Yasar and Kabasakal, Balkan Harbi (1912–1913), 330–358; Fuat Balkan, Ilk Turk Komitacısı Fuat Balkan'ın Hatıraları, (ed.) Metin Martı, (Istanbul: Arma Yayınları, 1998), 8–9.
[706] S.J. Shaw and E.K. Shaw: *History of the Ottoman Empire;* op cit; p. 294.

vessel, Hamidiye, and her exploits, Kinross says, that gave a real lift to the morale of the Turkish people. Although receiving shells that partly crippled her while bombarding Varna at the outset of the war, the 'phantom' cruiser had 'limped home' to the Golden Horn, brought in safely by Rauf Bey (subsequently a hero of the War of Independence), not expected to see service again.[707] Then the news came that she had slipped out through the Dardanelles, evading the Greek fleet, navigating through the Aegean and up the Adriatic, and throughout her course making the Greeks taste some of their medicine, before eventually in January and March 1913 sinking Greek transports, but in chivalrous style (a non-existent feature amongst the others in reality but vastly abundant in fiction and crooked historical narrative) saving the lives of passengers and crew to put them ashore on some deserted coast.[708]

Serbs at Work

> Every Servian sweetheart had already made her boy a hero, however stolid he seemed in his sheep-skin coat, however dazed he looked at this sudden call from the familiar things of daily toil. She put a medal about his neck, blessed by the priest, and a proof against bullets. As additional safeguard she gave him a charm which he wore in a little bag next to his heart. It was to be a Holy War, a new Crusade against the Crescent, and so these fighting men went to the front, strengthened by the prayers of the Church, by the blessing of the priests or popes, as they are called by whispered words of old mothers who pulled their boys' heads to their breasts, and said:
> "God is with you, little one. He will shield you from all harm. He will give power to His own side."[709]
>
> I sat with Servian officers in a café and found them gay fellows, but it seemed to me, perhaps unjustly, that, in those days before the war, when they laughed and raised their glasses, and said: "To our first dinner in Constantinople."[710]

Four large Serb armies swept south. The main force under the command of Crown Prince Aleksandar aimed at the largest concentration of Turkish troops at Kumanovo in northern Macedonia; the second army crossed into Bulgaria and from there into eastern Macedonia to harass the main Turkish army from the rear; Kosovo was the target of the third army, while the fourth was tasked to capture Novi Pazar and to link Montenegro and Serbia.[711]

---

[707] Lord Kinross: *Ataturk*; op cit; p. 55.
[708] Ibid.
[709] P. Gibbs and B Grant: *The Balkan War*; op cit, p. 18.
[710] Ibid, p. 20.
[711] M. Glenny: The Balkans; op cit.

The Serbs, just like other members of the Alliance, quickly registered great successes at the expense of the outnumbered and outgunned Turks. They took much of northern Macedonia, joined the Montenegrins in taking Pristina and Novi Pazar (22-23 October), occupied much of northern Albania and put Iskodra under siege.[712]

The main Turkish disaster was at Kumanova (Koumanovo). The commanding general, Halepli Zeki Pasha, employed offensive tactics while some of his divisions were still incomplete,[713] i.e. more or less the same error made elsewhere, and to be repeated on and on, during the Balkan Wars and in the First World War. The error consists in this: The Turks seeking to encircle and destroy their enemies according to plan excellently devised on paper, but all suffering from the same flaws, i.e.:

- Lack of awareness of logistical necessities or constraints, most particularly transport; including the foolish reliance on the most decrepit train transport system.
- Utter disregard for the time factor, i.e either mistiming the movements and synchronisation in action of various units, or regiments, or arms; or grossly miscalculating and misestimating the timeframe it takes to complete some operations.
- Failure to take into account enemy's superiority in numbers or its capacity to reinforce quickly.
- Discounting enemy's vast superiority in artillery.
- Lack of awareness of weather constraints.
- Utter carelessness about basics such as feeding the army, providing decent Winter vestments, footwear, and so on.

These errors are historically unforgivable for the simple reason that they were made not once, but repeatedly: in the Balkans from the Bulgarian through the Greek to the Serb fronts. They were going to be made again at Bulayir in February 1913, when the Turkish army was nearly wiped out; at Sarıkamış in December 1914; and in Cemal's Egyptian campaign in 1915; and repeated in the Summer Campaign of 1916. Absolutely the same costly error, which left hundreds of thousands of Turkish soldiers at the mercy of the enemy's artillery, cold, hunger, and disease. In fact, Turkish High Command from 1912 until 1918 was an entire disaster. It is the great fortune of Turkey that High Command between 1919 and 1922 was of an entirely different sort, i.e. at the other extreme: one of the best in the history of warfare.

Back to Zeki Pasha, who attacked the Serbian 1st Army on the morning of 23 October. At first he was successful, but he failed, of course, to realise, that the Serbs had an army which was at least double his and an artillery park that could be at least five times superior to his. And so, on 24 October, Serb artillery was

---
[712] S.J. Shaw and E.K. Shaw: *History of the Ottoman Empire;* op cit; p. 294.
[713] M. Uyar and E.J. Erickson: *A Military History of the Ottomans*; op cit; p. 228.

ready to act, and the effects on the Turks were disastrous: the ill-trained, ill-equipped, and poorly led Redif divisions, under fierce Serb pounding, began to retreat in great chaos.[714] Zeki Pasha made things worse, first by ordering already outgunned, outnumbered and demoralised troops into quick defensive positions, before ordering an even more chaotic retreat with terrible consequences.[715]

The impact was, indeed, and once more, a tragedy for the Turks, not just in losing considerable numbers of men and territory, their towns and cities falling quickly to the Serbs, but in what always follows Turkish defeat. The atrocities the Serbs inflicted on the Muslims of Albania far surpassed those already atrocious ones committed by the Greeks and the Bulgarians. Trotsky who was present writes:
> The horrors actually began as soon as we crossed the old frontier. By five p.m. we were approaching Kumanovo. The sun had set; it was starting to get dark. But the darker the sky became, the more brightly the fearful illumination of the fires stood out against it. Burning was going on all around us. Entire Albanian villages had been turned into pillars of fire... In all its fiery monotony this picture was repeated the whole way to Skopje... For two days before my arrival in Skopje the inhabitants had woken up in the morning to the sight, under the principal bridge over the Vardar – that is, in the very centre of the town – of heaps of Albanian corpses with severed heads. Some said that these were local Albanians, killed by the komitadjis [četniks], others that the corpses had been brought down to the bridge by the waters of the Vardar. What was clear was that these headless men had not been killed in battle.[716]

At Prizren in Kosovo, following its capture on 31 October, some 12,000 local Muslims were massacred according to contemporary press reports.[717] The same scenes repeated themselves all over European Turkey under all Christian allies.[718] Again, we will say nothing on the details of what happened.

Now, we have the same defining matter of the whole First Balkan War:
Why did the Serbs, just like the Greeks, and Bulgarians, fail to make the most of it, and wipe out both Turks and Turkey as they had always wished, and as no opportunity might ever present itself to them as this one?
Here, we ought let someone like R.C. Hall, the modern expert of the Balkan Wars explain this to us:
> The Serbian 1st Army entered Skopje without opposition on 26 October. Three days later the Morava Brigade, which had been attached to the 3rd

---

[714] Aleksandar M.Stojichevich, *Istorija nashih ratova za oslobodjenje i ujedinjenje od 1912–1918 god* (Belgrade, 1932) 164.
[715] Hallı, Balkan Harbi (1912–1913), 64–81, 105–110, 122–130, 154–211; K. Kocaman, 'Kumanova Muharebesinde Sırp Ordusu,'' Askeri Mecmua, vol. 10, no. 114, September 1939, 674–678; E.J. Erickson, Defeat in Detail, 171–181.
[716] L. Trotsky: *The Balkan Wars, 1912–1913,* New York, 1980; pp. 267-8.
[717] For a Turkish account of Bulgarian atrocities, see İlker Alp, Belge ve Fotoğraflarla Bulgar Mezalimi (1878–1989) (Bulgarian Atrocities in Documents and Photographs (1878–1989)), Trakya Üniversitesi Yayınları, Ankara 1990
[718] A. Mango: *Ataturk;* John Murray; London; 1999; p. 115.

> Army, arrived from Prishtina. Vojvoda Putnik and his staff failed to appreciate the extent of their victory. They continued to adhere to their plan to concentrate their forces at Ovche Polje. The main part of the 1st Army, strengthened with a division from the 3rd Army, pursued the Ottomans toward Bitola. Another part followed disorganized Ottoman units toward Veles. Because they did not realize the extent of their victory at Kumanovo, the Serbs did not closely follow the fleeing Ottomans. Had they pressed their victory, they might have destroyed the main force of the Vardar Army in central Macedonia and ended their campaign two weeks after it had begun. The failure to pursue the defeated enemy was the same mistake that the Bulgarians had made after their big victories at Lozengrad and Lyule Burgas-Buni Hisar.[719]

Then, just after this, he says:
> Bad weather and difficult roads hampered the 1st Army's pursuit of the Ottomans after Kumanovo. Road conditions forced the Morava Division to move ahead of the Drina Division.[720]

One at times truly despairs at the dire standards of modern Western scholarship, for Hall is not alone in saying one thing and then its opposite a paragraph or two below. Indeed, it was the bad weather, which delayed all armies in the region from advancing against the Turks. As noted above, the war correspondent Seppings Wright could see the awful weather causing havoc amongst fleeing Turkish refugees and retreating troops, forcing the former to abandon their carts and the latter their cannons. It was the same problem that hindered the Bulgarians, Serbs and everyone else, and together with the resolute fight of Turkish units especially at Catalca, it stopped the Christian Allies from annihilating the Turks in the space of two weeks.

In the meantime the ever deluded/foolish Turkish General Command planned to concentrate the broken Vardar Army around the centrally located town of Manastır (Bitola) in order to face both the Serbians from the north and the Greeks from the south.[721] The Vardar Army reached Manastır on 7 November, but it lost most of its limited artillery and baggage on the way, and the Serbs had vast numerical superiority once more.[722] Zeki Pasha nonetheless tried to encircle the Serbs by launching a surprise attack with his demoralised units, under heavy Serb artillery fire. Of course, there was no chance of success.[723] It was the Vardar Army's second disastrous defeat, and only, and once more, the same factor that rescued Turkey, i.e. the courage of the men and the officers, preventing total

---

[719] R.C. Hall: *The Balkan Wars 1912-1913*; Routledge London, 2000; p. 49.
[720] Ibid.
[721] M. Uyar and E.J. Erickson: *A Military History of the Ottomans from Osman*; op cit; p. 228.
[722] M. Glenny: *The Balkans*; op cit. M. Uyar –Erickson: *A Military History*; op cit; 228.
[723] M. Uyar and E.J. Erickson: *A Military History*; op cit; p. 228.

annihilation.[724] The fighting cost the Turks 17,000 dead; 45,000 prisoners, and another 30,000 escaping to the mountains of the Macedonian-Albanian border.[725]

End and Outcomes of the First Balkan War

'I talked to one old peasant, and he said: "We are going to seek in Asia the peace that we have never found in the land of the Giaours."[726]

'The obvious intention of those who murdered Muslims and forced their exodus,' McCarthy notes, 'was to "de-Turkify" the Balkans. Inspired by partially assimilated ideas of nationalism on the one hand and by the desire to take Muslim lands and belongings on the other, Balkan Christians pursued policies that would insure that Muslim refugees would not return and that those who had not left would do so.'[727]

Indeed, Jacob Gould Shurman, who writing straight in the wake of the Balkan Wars, towards late 1913-early 1914, hailed the Christian achievements:

> Great and momentous results have been achieved. Although seated again in his ancient capital of Adrianople, the Moslem has been expelled from Europe, or at any rate is no longer a European Power. For the first time in more than five centuries, therefore, conditions of stable equilibrium are now possible for the Christian nations of the Balkans.[728]

In two months, therefore, apart from the four besieged cities, the Turks had lost all their remaining territories in Europe. The impact of the defeats, food shortages, and the government's inability to pay official salaries led to a series of violent demonstrations, which soon spread from Istanbul to the other major cities.[729] Not only had Turkey been immensely bled by the conflict, those who had long had property and prosperity in European Ottoman Turkey were now left utterly destitute.[730] They suffered much worse, even:

> Refugees kept arriving in enormous numbers and in the most deplorable state [notes Grant who was there.] They camped out in open places round the city and in the graveyards, and many of them died every day from exhaustion and hunger. The condition of the little children was especially terrible. Cholera continued to ravage these armies of unfortunates, and the Turkish authorities, realising the immensity of the danger, bestirred

---
[724] M. Uyar and E.J. Erickson: *A Military History*; p. 228 express the same view but in a different manner as this: 'the iron will of its (Vardar Army) subordinate commanding officers saved the day.'
[725] M. Glenny: *The Balkans*; op cit.
[726] E. Ashmead Bartlett: *With the Turks in Thrace*; op cit; pp. 250-1.
[727] Justin McCarthy: *Death and Exile*; The Darwin Press Inc; Princeton; New Jersey; p. 148.
[728] Jacob Gould Shurman: *The Balkan Wars, 1912-1913*; 1914. Available on the internet.
[729] S.J. Shaw and E.K. Shaw: *History of the Ottoman Empire*; op cit; p. 294.
[730] Ibid.

themselves, and with the help of medical authorities from other countries organized an isolation system and took sanitary precautions.[731]

Whilst the Turks were under the shock of defeat and the atrocities they had just suffered from, and doing their best to heal the woes of their people, it was, as per usual, other news that were circulating. B. Grant again:

> I was convinced, however, that all fears of an attempted massacre of Christians were unfounded and fantastic. The starving people who invaded Constantinople were too broken in spirit and too weak in body to attempt any acts of violence, while the soldiers who had escaped from the Bulgarian guns and from the cholera had only one desire to hide themselves, so that they should not be sent back to the fighting lines.[732]

Instead of busying itself with massacring Christians, the Turkish Government was 'calm and dignified in the face of its appalling disasters,' strengthening the lines of defence at Catalca, besides bringing reinforcements from Asia Minor.[733] Fresh troops came from all parts of the east, and were drafted quickly behind the defensive lines. The men were in excellent spirits; and 'at the last ditch, as it were, the Turks regained hope and put themselves in a position to retrieve some of their great disasters.'[734]

Indeed, at Adrianople and at the Çatalaca Line, the Bulgarians were stuck in the winter quagmire, unable to progress through the now better defended Turkish trenches.[735] They had lost great many men, for even in disaster, Turkish courage maimed its foe enough to hinder his advance; disease was also rampaging through Bulgarian ranks, and their lines of communication were difficult to maintain.[736] Political and financial necessities also favoured a halt, and the time was ripe for negotiations, and so as they stalled in front of Çatalca, the Bulgarians came to an agreement with the Turks for a truce (December 3).[737]

*****

Turning Things Upside Down and the Power of Opinion Making

> 'The Turks are massacring!' in large capital letters these words are filling the pages of the media together with accounts of their bloody defeats. Of course a couple of Bulgarian atrocities are cited but only printed in very small characters at the end of paragraphs. The Turks are massacring. This is taken for granted "The poor Turks."[738]

---

[731] B. Grant in P. Gibbs and B Grant: *The Balkan War*; op cit, p. 240.
[732] Ibid.
[733] Ibid.
[734] Ibid.
[735] Ibid.
[736] Ibid.
[737] S.J. Shaw and E.K. Shaw: *History of the Ottoman Empire*; op cit; p. 295.
[738] Pierre Loti: *Turquie Agonisante*; Calman Levy; Paris; 1913; p. 39.

Thus wrote Pierre Loti at the time, as he was disgusted by the gigantic scale of the tragi-comedy, whereby the massacred Turks were being instead turned into the perpetrators of the crimes by the manipulations of all sorts of opinion makers. Loti devotes the major part of his book to details of atrocities committed upon the Turks relying on ordinary witnesses, foreign army officers present in the places of conflict, Western officials exerting under various guises, including as diplomats or in the sectors of health and other institutions, foreign correspondents, nuns, engineers, travellers, and many others. These witnesses were French, Germans, Austrians, British, Swiss, Jews of all nationalities, who all, without one single exception, only spoke of massacres, in fact horrendous atrocities, committed on the Turks, supporting their accounts with photographs, and precise details of day, time, and locality of outrages, and who were directly responsible, including the names of Bulgarian, Greek, and Serb officers. How the Turks were slaughtered in specific places were provided in meticulous detail.[739] Many more details were sent to the various news agencies. And yet, as Loti noted, it was the very reverse that was printed in the news in large headlines, i.e. that it was the Turks who were massacring.[740] When Loti at last got some major newspapers to acknowledge the fact that it was indeed the Turks who were being mass-killed, not the other way round, this is what happened:

> How can it be accepted that even the newspapers that now recognise at last the massacres of the Turks now justify this on the ground that it was only a reaction to five centuries of frightful Turkish rule in Thrace and Macedonia, always the same fable of ferocious Turks, but ferocious against whom I beseech you! Was it against the Jews, to whom they had given the best hospitality for four centuries? Was it against ourselves, French, whom they have welcomed since the Renaissance? Was it against the Orthodox to whom Mohammed II had left their church, their schools, their language...[741]

Ellis Ashmead Bartlett, the leading British war correspondent of the conflict highlighted the same problem, that is the vast difference between what really was happening on the ground and what was conveyed or known:

> The following despatch from Lieutenant Wagner appeared in the Reichspost, of Thursday, November 7th:
> "It had already been seen in Turkish military circles that the defence of the Chataldja line was untenable and useless. The Turkish troops fled in breakneck style to Constantinople, without paying regard to the cries of their officers. The situation at Constantinople is desperate. The city is full of refugee soldiers, who, half-starved, take revenge upon the defenceless Christians. The left wing of the Bulgarian army, after a determined struggle, reached the heights east of Strandja, driving the right Turkish wing into the

---
[739] Pierre Loti: *Turquie Agonisante*; Calman Levy; Paris; 1913.
[740] Ibid.
[741] Ibid; p. 143.

forest district west of Derkos Lake. The Bulgarians are strongly reinforced at Strandja and Yenikoei to give a final blow to the Chataldja positions south of the Derkos Lake. The centre and right Bulgarian wing forced the conquered Turkish rearguard along the railway line and through Cauta, and will continue the attack upon the Turkish positions on both sides of the village of Chataldja. The immediate fall of all the Turkish positions is now a dead certainty. The Turkish artillery has very insufficiently supported the infantry thus far, and has seldom remained till the last moment. Insufficient action with the too early retreat of the Turkish artillery left the retreating Turkish infantry defenceless against the attacks of the onstorming Bulgarians and firing of the Bulgarian batteries so that the retreat almost resembled a flight."[742]

'Lieutenant Wagner,' Ashmead Bartlett points out, 'heads his despatch "Bulgarian Army Headquarters," but he does not say where the headquarters were, neither does he date his despatch. The despatch appeared in the Vienna Reichspost of November 7th, and must, therefore, have been sent off at the latest on the previous day, which brings us to Wednesday, November 6th. The battle which it describes, therefore, must have taken place on Tuesday, November 5th, at the latest. Now on Monday, November 4th, Seabury Ashmead-Bartlett [Elis Ashmead Bartlett's brother who was also in the Balkans] was at Cherkeskeuy, 80 miles north-east of Chataldja, and there was no sign of the Bulgarians; on Tuesday he was at Sinekli — still no sign of the Bulgarians, while the Turkish peasants and soldiers continued their retreat unmolested. On Wednesday, November 6th, he was actually at Chataldja and yet he saw no signs of an attack on the lines, no signs of the taking of Derkos — which, incidentally, lies behind the Turkish position — while the Turkish headquarters were still in telegraphic communication with Cherkeskeuy. The remnants of Abdullah's army of Thrace only began to reach the lines on November 7th, whereas Lieutenant Wagner describes how, at least two days previously, they had abandoned their positions and "fled in breakneck style to Constantinople."[743]

Then he [Wagner] goes on to describe how Constantinople is "full of refugee soldiers, who, half-starved, take revenge upon the defenceless Christians."

Which is a pure calumny, for 'At the time,' Ashmead Bartlett who was there says:

There were no starving soldiers in Constantinople, and later on, when a certain number of sick and stragglers found their way to the city, they were segregated in the mosques under a strong guard, and at no time did they take revenge upon the Christians.[744]

---

[742] E. Ashmead Bartlett: *With the Turks in Thrace*; op cit; pp. 245-6.
[743] Ibid; p. 246.
[744] Ibid.

Wagner for his part adds:
> After four days of sanguinary fighting, the Bulgarian army has succeeded in breaking through the centre of the Turkish positions at Chataldja in the direction of Hademkeuy, and in completely rolling up the Turkish defences. The advance will be continued with the greatest energy, in order to force the Turkish troops as far as possible from Constantinople.

Yet, Elis Ashmead Bartlett who was there saw the very reverse:
> The course of events will show that the fighting at Chataldja was never of a sanguinary nature; that the battle only lasted two days, and that, far from rolling up the Turkish forces, the Bulgarians were themselves forced to retreat. But Lieutenant Wagner did not hesitate to state in the course of another despatch, that the gallant, but defeated Turkish troops behaved with shocking brutality:

"The atrocities committed by the retreating Turks are awful. All the villages were burned to ashes; all the Christians were massacred, and dozens of female corpses have been found with mutilated bodies. The Anatolian Redifs, especially, behaved like wild beasts."[745]

'Poor, gentle and kind-eyed, courteous Anatolian Redifs!' [Remarks Ashmead Bartlett, who, once more was at the scene described by Wagner] 'You were starving and disorganised, and yet we marched with you all the way from Lule Burgas to Chataldja, rather more than 140 miles, without a passport or any other paper to show who we were, and with a cartload of equipment and stores, and none of you ventured to molest us. We were Christians, and King Ferdinand had proclaimed a Holy War, and yet one of you offered to share his last crust of bread with us, because we gave him a drink of water. Nor did we see you massacre and ill-treat Christians or mutilate their women-folk, although, when you were starving, they used to shut their doors in your faces and refuse to give you of the food which they possessed in plenty. Their flocks also you left untouched in your extremity, and their chickens and their corn. Few European armies would have behaved in such a gentle and forbearing manner as you. Few races could show such a spirit of tolerance.'[746]

What Loti, Ashmead Bartlett, Seppings Wright and all those on the front line could see, i.e, the reshaping of reality, was also experienced by the writer M. Pickthall as soon as he arrived in Turkey early in 1913. Whilst on the boat, just off Istanbul, he was accosted by an Ottoman Christian, who, once learning he was an English writer, straight burst with the usual lines:
> "Ah, it is very fortunate that I have met you. I can tell you everything. Are there any questions you would like to ask me? I am well informed of

---
[745] Ibid; p. 248.
[746] Ibid.

everything in Turkey. I have secret information which I can procure for you."

'I,' says Pickthall, 'put a question as to the atrocities committed by the Bulgarians in Macedonia.[747]

This made him snigger: "That is all a fabrication. I have private information from a friend of mine at Dede-Aghach, where the Turks have slaughtered all the Christians."

'It so happened,' Pickthall pointed out, 'that Dede-Aghach was one of the very few places where we had respectable European evidence upon the horrors committed by Bulgarian troops and komitajis. I said as much.

At once my friend revoked, exclaiming: "I will tell you how it was. The Turks began to massacre, killing two or three; so the Bulgars said: You will either become Christians or leave the country, or else we will massacre you all. Were they not right? Ah, sir, you do not know all that we have to suffer, we Christians here in Turkey, from the fanaticism of the Mussulmans. I shall be happy to inform you fully. I am at your disposal."

I smoked in silence for a while before replying: "You talk nonsense. If it had not been for the Turks, not one Oriental Christian would have been alive today. The fanaticism of Latin Europe was in a fair way to destroy you when the Turkish conquest came and, with its toleration, preserved you in existence."

"Ah!" he veered round at once. "What you are saying now is very true. Formerly the Turks were not at all fanatical. And even now they are not half so bad as people think. I have heard gentlemen on board saying that there has been another revolution, and attacks on Christians in Constantinople. I, who am of the country, well acquainted with the Turkish character, find myself wondering how such false reports can be believed."

'I may be wronging my unknown interlocutor,' concluded Pickthall, 'but I cannot help suspecting that, but for the firm line I had taken with him, he would himself have told me those reports were true.'[748]

4. Interlude and Through till the End of the Second Balkan War

Peace negotiations began in London on 16 December, with British Foreign Secretary Sir Edward Grey acting as mediator. The Balkan states demanded full cession of all Ottoman European territories and the Aegean Islands, which the Turks refused to agree to, offering their counter-proposals.[749] As the conference threatened to break down, Sir Edward Grey proposed a compromise solution, including that Edirne ought to go to Bulgaria, and the powers would make a final

---

[747] M. Pickthall: *With the Turk in Wartime*; J.M. Dent &Sons; London; 1914; p. 5.
[748] Ibid; pp. 5-7.
[749] S.J. Shaw and E.K. Shaw: *History of the Ottoman*; op cit; p. 295.

decision on the Aegean Islands.[750] There were further Turkish counter-proposals, the Turks refusing to budge on Edirne, arguing that the city's population was mostly Muslim and that the area between it and the Dardanelles should be formed into a neutral and an independent principality that would constitute a buffer zone to protect the Straits from direct Bulgarian incursion.[751]

Meanwhile in Istanbul, the CUP, fearing that Kâmil Pasha was going to give away 'the sacred city of Edirne,' organised on 23 January 1913 the famous "Raid on the Sublime Porte". As the Cabinet deliberated on the peace terms, Enver, followed by Talat and others, hurried across the vast hall to the door of the chamber, and there one of them shot dead Nazim Pasha.[752] The Grand Vizier coolly remarked, 'You want the Imperial Seal, I suppose.' He handed it over and wrote out his letter of resignation, and Mahmud Shevket was appointed Grand Vizier.[753] Mahmut Sevket's task was to insist on retaining Edirne and eastern Thrace, and at the same time keep the London Conference going long enough for him to strengthen the army and appease the public at home.[754] And there, once more, took place the offers and counter-offers,[755] but in the end, the Bulgarians had enough, and the London Conference broke up.

The armistice ended on 2 February and the Bulgarians returned to business, slaughtering the Turks left to slaughter, and restarting the military onslaught.[756] Fighting continued in Edirne and along the Çatalca lines, even more bitterly than in the first phase, with intensive bombardment and infantry assaults.[757] Enver himself took part in the fighting at the head of volunteers from among revolutionary officers, who were to form his Special Organisation, and of cadets from the Istanbul War College.[758] Despite all sacrifices, the dim reality dawned on the government that simply they did not have the resources to both fund the war and restore the army at once. It had to be one or the other.[759] The Turkish war effort was simply doomed, and so was Edirne, but not without its defenders proving to be the most gallant of all fighters.

Collapse of Turkish Resistance and Turkey's Losses

Ertur's journal for 25 February reads:

---

[750] January 17, 1913; Yusuf Hikmet Bayur, *Turk Inkilabi Tarihi* (History of the Turkish Revolution), 3 vols in 10 parts, Ankara, 1940-1967. III, 954-970.
[751] F. Ahmad, *The Young Tutrks: The Committee of Union and Progress in Turkish Politics, 1908-1914*, Oxford, 1969, pp. 116-119.
[752] Lord Kinross: *Ataturk*; op cit; p. 55.
[753] Ibid.
[754] S.J. Shaw and E.K. Shaw: *History of the Ottoman*; op cit; p. 296.
[755] Bayur, IV, 1200-1202; Ahmad, pp. 123-124.
[756] S.J. Shaw and E.K. Shaw: *History of the Ottoman Empire*; op cit; p. 296.
[757] Orbay, Rauf, Cehennem Değirmeni (The Mill of Hell), I–II, Emre, Istanbul 1993.
[758] A. Mango: *Ataturk;* John Murray; London; 1999; p. 119.
[759] S.J. Shaw and E.K. Shaw: *History of the Ottoman Empire*; op cit; p. 296.

> In the eight or ten days before the fall of Edirne... bread for the soldiers had been reduced to 450 grams. The poor soldiers looked inhumanly emaciated. They had virtually no strength to walk and sat huddled under the snow. I don't think that any other nation would be able to bear such conditions. Of course, the enemy was not comfortable either. But a large part of their soldiery could rest in warm surroundings and eat well. With the freezing cold and pangs of hunger the complexions of our soldiers had turned unhealthily dark. After nightfall, some soldiers would knock at the doors of houses asking for a crust of bread, but to little avail. Very likely the people on whose doors they knocked had also gone hungry that night.[760]

After resisting weeks of shelling, intense fighting, under ceaseless snowfall, hunger and deprivation, finally, it was the explosion of the ammunition dump within the Turkish fortified command and the resultant fires which led to the surrender of Edirne on Wednesday, 26 March 1913, at 13.00 hours.[761] The fall was caused primarily from within the walls by a Fifth Column of 'well-fed Greeks and Bulgars, undermining the defence of the starving Turkish garrison.'[762]

The victorious Bulgarians gave the city over to three consecutive days of unrestricted pillage, rape and murder.[763] The remnants of the Turkish garrison were imprisoned in Sarayiçi, a small island separated from the city of Edirne by the river Tunca. There, among the ruins of an old Ottoman palace, some 20,000 prisoners of war are said to have perished from disease and starvation.[764] Gustav Cirilli, who had witnessed the entire siege of the city and its fall, describes the fate of the soldiers:

> Long lines of prisoners pass on the streets, their officers leading them. They are gaunt, dejected, emaciated from starvation. They are driven like vile beasts by blows from fists, boots, and rifle butts. These unfortunates are penned in a place known as Eski Saray, a wooded island on the Toundja [River], outside of the city, where they are left to die of cold and starvation, unless a bullet puts an end to their suffering.[765]

It soon turned into a hunt, whereby the guardians shot or executed Turks on any excuse; their bodies thrown in the streets, in the fields, in the rivers, anywhere.[766] On the island where the prisoners were kept, corpses were lying in heaps, men sleeping in the open in winter, bad weather and cholera sharing out the heavy toll of deaths. Two hundred were dying each day.[767] What seemed to cause the greatest impression upon Western Europeans, however, was the fact that all the trees on the island of detention had been stripped of their bark 'as far as a man

---

[760] Syed Tanvir Wasti: The 1912-1913 Balkan war and the Siege of Edirne; op cit; pp. 68-9.
[761] Ibid.
[762] Lord Kinross: *Ataturk*; op cit; p. 56.
[763] See Carnegie; 326-330.
[764] İlker Alp, 134; in Mango 119.
[765] Gustav Cirilli: Journal du siege; in J. McCarthy: *Death and Exile*; op cit; p. 144.
[766] G. Cirilli: Journal; p. 155; p. 156.
[767] Justin McCarthy: *Death and Exile*; op cit; p. 144. F.O. 371-1762; No 17618.

can reach.'[768] Out of hunger the prisoners had eaten all the tree bark throughout the Island. By April of 1913, only about half the prisoners had remained alive.[769]

In Çatalca, meanwhile, the Bulgarians stubbornly repeated the frontal assaults against the Line of defence between 24 March and 3 April 1913, with the same disastrous high casualties.[770] The Turks not only clung on strongly and unwavering, their stout fortifications and the intensity of their firepower hammered the Bulgarians.[771] The Bulgarians could never breach the line.

Elsewhere, on 6 March, Janina fell to the Greeks; Iskodra would fall on 22 April, thus finally ending Turkish rule in Europe with the exception of Istanbul.[772]

In the face of all the disasters, the new Turkish government at last agreed to the truce and full acceptance of the Powers' peace terms (March 31, 1913). The armistice was restored on 16 April, and negotiations resumed. On 30 May, the Treaty of London was signed, with the Midye-Enez line made as the new boundary and with Thrace and Edirne in enemy hands; Crete was ceded, and the settlement of the Aegean Islands and the Albanian boundaries were left to the pleasure of the Powers.[773]

It was yet another disaster for Turkey, but a source of jubilation elsewhere:

> It may be taken for granted [says Granville Baker] that the Ottoman Empire as a European Power is a thing of the past, that all those provinces carved out of Europe by the sword of Othman have been lost by the sword, and that of Turkey in Europe nothing remains but the strips of land which the Allies are pleased to leave to their old enemy. Constantinople will remain Turkish for some time yet — ten years, perhaps fifteen — but me thinks the Turk is tired of his stay in Europe, that he will soon pack up his small possessions and return to Asia Minor, whence he came.[774]
>
> The Turk was in the way, he proved inefficient and went under. Now that he is down it will be noticed how few friends he has.[775]

Yet, all the sudden, the situation for the Turks brightened up, for the same spirit that motivated the allied Christian nations to tear the Turks apart, drove them now to tear each other apart.

---

[768] Carnegie p. 111.
[769] F.O. 371-1762; No 17618.
[770] Mahmud Muhtar, 3ncü Kolordu ve Dogu Ordusunun Muharebeleri, 143–152; Belig˘, Bulgar Komitalarının Tarihi ve Balkan Harbinde Yaptıkları, 25–233; M. Kadri Alasya, TSK Tarihi Balkan Harbi (1912–1913): Sark Ordusu Birinci Catalca Muharebesi, vol. 2, book 1, 2nd printing, (Ankara: Genelkurmay Basımevi, 1993), 20–245; E.J. Erickson, Defeat in Detail, 122–137, 285–290.
[771] M. Uyar and E.J. Erickson: *A Military History of the Ottomans*; op cit; p. 230.
[772] S.J. Shaw and E.K. Shaw: *History of the Ottoman Empire*; op cit; p. 296.
[773] C. Bayar: *Ben de Yazdım* (So I Wrote Too), I–VIII, Baha, Istanbul 1968–72, IV, 1202-1222.
[774] B. Granville Baker: *The Passing of the Turkish Empire in Europe*; London; p. 323.
[775] Ibid; p. 328.

On 29 June 1913, King Ferdinand of Bulgaria ordered his troops to fire at the Greek and Serbian lines. Soon after, Rumania also joined the battle against Bulgaria.[776]

This second Balkan War is of no interest in this work as it did not involve the Turks, and one is not going to indulge in the business of depicting Christian armies tearing each other. Most of all, one is not going to engage in describing the horrors which they inflicted on each other, equal in tenor to those they inflicted on the Turks. The only point to raise is that suddenly, the whole world became aware of these atrocities 'unworthy of Christian people,' and speedily a commission of enquiry (for which the Turks, seconded by the Italians, had long been calling for before, but in vain) was sent to the site of war and began the gory task of unveiling who did what to the other, only to find out that there was nothing to choose between them.[777]

Now the Turks made the most of the situation. With the Bulgarians occupied on no less than three fronts, the Turks felt that a golden opportunity was presenting itself for the recovery of Edirne.[778] Despite doubts from some, the views of Talat and Enver prevailed.[779] Informed of the Turks intentions, Sir Edward Grey, the British Foreign Secretary, said in a speech in the House of Commons that if the Turks used Bulgarian difficulties to try to recover Adrianople, 'in defiance of the Treaty of London, they would be heavily punished for it afterwards, and would lose not only all their possessions in Europe, but even Constantinople itself.'[780] The French government likewise was fervently against the Turkish plan, the French Ambassador in Istanbul issuing a stern warning.[781] The Turks did not listen, and on 21 July, they were able to reoccupy all of eastern Thrace and move into Edirne without meeting any resistance, since the Bulgarians had withdrawn their army to fight their former allies.[782]

5. The Impacts of the Balkan War

Toynbee remarks:
> As for the distinction between technical and moral aggression, which seemed so obvious to the Balkan peoples and their Western sympathisers, it could not survive the spectacle of streams of Turkish refugees fleeing before the face of the Serbian, Greek, and Bulgarian armies. As the Turkish

---

[776] Syed Tanvir Wasti: The 1912-1913 Balkan war; op cit; p. 70.
[777] The Carnegie Enquiry; op cit.
[778] Syed Tanvir Wasti: The 1912-1913 Balkan war; op cit p. 70.
[779] S.J. Shaw and E.K. Shaw: *History of the Ottoman Empire*; p. 297.
[780] Cemal Pasha: *Memories*; op cit; p. 48.
[781] Ibid p. 49.
[782] S.J. Shaw and E.K. Shaw: *History of the Ottoman Empire*; p. 297.

forces fell back, the Christian population rose against the Moslem minority in the invaded provinces. Villages were looted and burnt wholesale; there was also murder and violation; and the reign of terror by no means ceased when the victorious states took over control. The hundreds of thousands of refugees who arrived at Constantinople, and kept on arriving after the conclusion of peace, were destitute and terror-stricken.[783]

First, the atrocities towards the Turks: Anyone seeking to know the details should peruse through the accounts by Germans, French, Austrians, Swiss, Jews; nuns, war correspondents, army officers, diplomats, health workers, and whoever witnessed them.[784]

Secondly, the Balkan Wars cost the Turks 83 percent of their land and 69 percent of their population in Europe.[785]

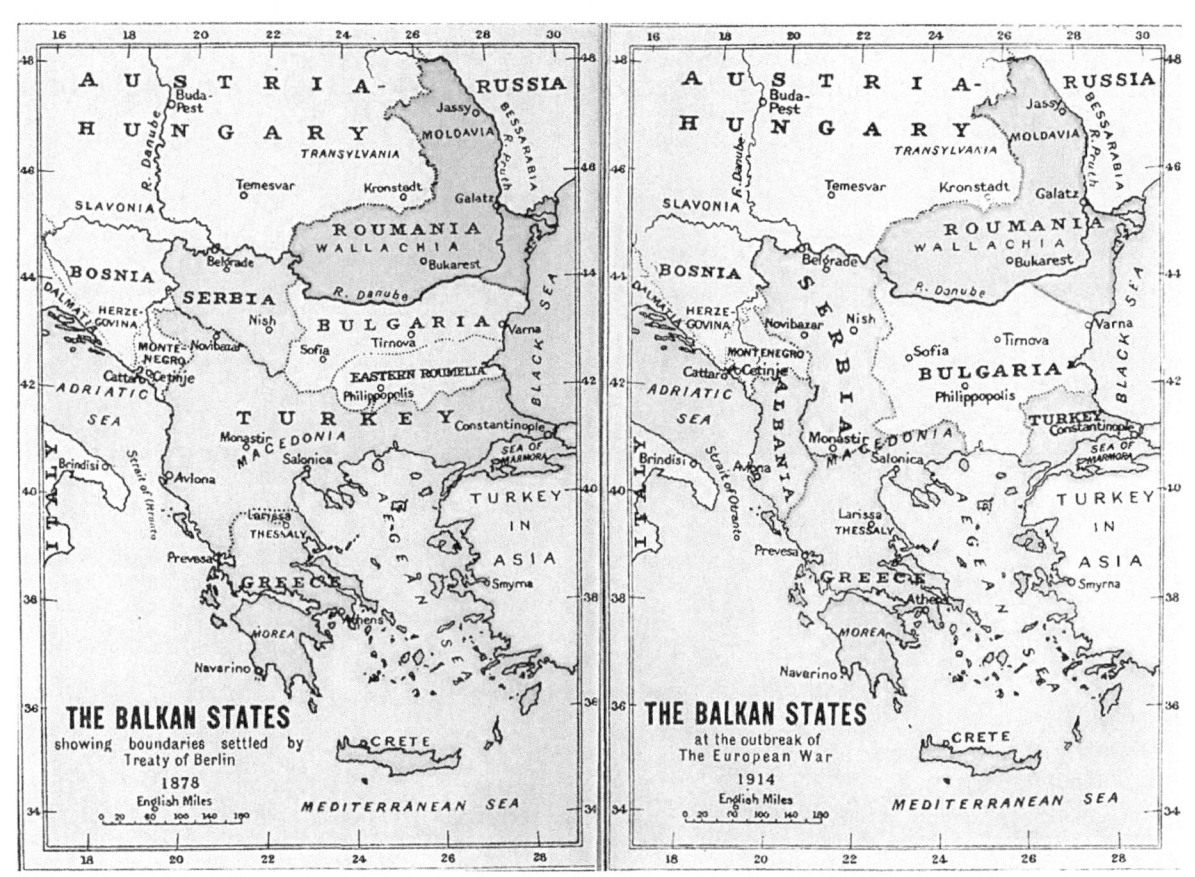

The great beneficiaries were Serbia and Greece, and also Bulgaria up to a point.

Thirdly, the First Balkan War was glorified by the leaders of the warring parties as a modern 'Crusade of the Balkan states against Asiatic barbarism.'[786]

---

[783] A.J. Toynbee: *The Western Question in Greece and Turkey*; Constable; 1922; p. 138.
[784] All in P. Loti; E. Jaeckh; J. McCarthy: all cited above.
[785] S.J. Shaw and E.K. Shaw: *History of the Ottoman Empire*; op cit; p. 298.

Fourthly, and more importantly, the victory over 'Asiatic Barbarism' had created its own demon. Here, just as we concluded with Stead in the previous chapter, we conclude with yet another genius of world history, Napoleon:

> Who could calculate [he wrote to the Senate] the duration of wars, the number of campaigns that it would be necessary to make some day in order to repair the misfortunes that would result from the loss of the Ottoman Empire, if the love of a disgraceful repose and the pleasures of a great city should prevail over the counsels of a wise foresight? We should leave to our nephews a long- heritage of wars and woes. The Greek tiara rising again and triumphant from the Baltic to the Mediterranean, we should see in our time our provinces attacked by swarms of fanatics and barbarians; and if, in that too dilatory struggle, civilized Europe ran risk of perishing, our culpable indifference would justly excite the censures of posterity and would be a brand of opprobrium in history.[787]

Indeed, out of the smouldering ruins of Ottoman Turkey, there was kindled the fire of the First World War.

---

[786] For example in the manifesto of the Bulgarian Tsar Ferdinand I (1861–1948) to the Bulgarian people on the occasion of the declaration of war; cf. Hemberger, Illustrierte Geschichte 1914, p. 43.
[787] Sutherland Menzies: *Turkey Old and New*, 2vols; Allen Lane; London; 1880; vol 2; p. 114.

Four

THE FIRST WORLD WAR, 1914-1918

This book is not about the First World War, it is about the Turkish Long War, and the First World War was only a part of this wider conflict. Therefore, this chapter is incapable of dealing with all events of this particular conflict. It will only focus on those of central importance, especially those that have been largely ignored by scholarship. These include how military campaigns were carried out on the Turkish side, their deficiencies and successes, the effects the war had on the Turkish populations, the reasons why Turkey went into the war in the first place, the impact of the Bolshevik Revolution on Turkey, the decisiveness of Turkish victories at Kut al Amara (Amarah) and Gallipoli, and similar issues of primary importance.

Furthermore, this work is not going to be a repeat of what can easily be found in hundreds of other works; this author abhors the idea of collecting material from the hundreds of other secondary sources and collating everything together. To him this is a waste of time and effort, for should people be interested to read the same stuff, there is no need for this author to convey it to them as they can easily find it elsewhere. It is all the more important that this author should avoid that, for without a doubt many existing works are much better quality than this author could ever contemplate of producing. So why produce something mediocre when better can be found elsewhere.

This chapter focuses, as already stated, on crucial issues, especially from the Turkish side, that have been set aside, but above all — as is this author's policy — by relying primarily on sources of the time, i.e. on people who either were directly involved in the fighting, or those who were present as war correspondents. It is of course extremely difficult to rely on primary sources in regard to very old historical events of say the Middle Ages or many centuries ago for a variety of reasons; access to them, their writing in old, defunct, languages, and a few other reasons explain the difficulty. However, when it comes to events of the 20th century, such as the World Wars, it is utter madness to rely on secondary material, when there is a wealth of primary sources. Like every historical subject, the crucial fact is: whilst one cannot totally avoid secondary sources and recent material, one has to avoid it as much as possible, especially the more recent material, i.e. of scholars of today, for the reasons so many times stated already: their incompetence; their distorting tendencies; their bland, boring, style, and much worse, even, they pour out stuff that makes no sense whatsoever but makes one sick at times.

Regarding primary sources, there are so many good such sources by army commanders on all sides who have left us a great deal of works: Mustafa Kemal, Kazim Karabekir, General Townshend, Sir Ian Hamilton, Cemal Pasha, Liman von Sanders, Falkenhayn, Allenby, and a few more, which are widely used here. War correspondents such as E. Ashmead Bartlett (already encountered during the Balkan Wars), and above all Philips Price of the *Manchester Guardian*, who was on the Caucasus front, are invaluable sources, and so are a few others who will be cited throughout. We also have the exceptional contemporary *Current History*, i.e. the New York Times Magazine.

One must insist, it does hardly matter if some of these sources do not like the Turks. *Current History*, for instance, is full of articles depicting the Turks in the most dire manner. Liking or disliking the Turks is of no interest to writing history at all. In fact, it is a great deal better when the source declares openly its hostility to the Turks and truly shows it, and gives us facts. What is indeed essential in writing any history are not opinions, refrained or expressed, but facts and sources of facts, which is the biggest flaw of today's scholarship, for it suppresses both of the latter.

What also harms historical knowledge is the current symptom continuously raised by this author in all his works which consists in modern scholars' reinterpreting contemporary sources, most often by stating the very opposite of what they say. It is highly crucial to let contemporary sources speak, and generously. It is the only way to have historical truth. It is, indeed, one of the most irritating experiences to generally come across a secondary source deciphering an old source, and one takes that secondary source at face value to only — some months, or years, later, once coming across the primary source — find out that one had been deceived, because the author of the secondary source had selectively chosen a little passage that runs 180 degrees the opposite to what the primary source says.

Because most of the sources used in this chapter are Western, it is highly important to balance them with Turkish accounts. Now, the problem with the Turks is this: They have great archives, and there are works by great Turkish generals such as Fewzi,[788] and Karabekir,[789] which any good historian would have loved to read and use. However, the Turks, that is their cultural institutions, incompetent as they are, possibly some of the world's most incompetent institutions, have not deemed it important to have them translated into other languages. This drives one to ask: But how on earth do they expect anyone to know about the Turkish side of the story if they keep the great works in Turkish, and if Turkish historians, with rare exceptions, keep writing for themselves or for each other in Turkish?

---

[788] M.F. Cakmak: *Buyuk Harpte Sark Cephesi Hareketleri, Sark Vilayetlerimizde, Kafkasyada ve Iranda* (Ankara, 1936,: Genelkurmay Matbaası).

[789] K. Karabekir 1937–38): *Cihan Harbine Neden Girdik, Nasıl Girdik, Nasıl Idare Ettik?*, vol. I–II (Istanbul:vTecelli Basımevi)

As a compensation for this, we have, fortunately, the works by E.J. Erickson and Mesut Uyar, as well as E.K. and S.J Shaw, who have extensively used Turkish archives, and thus provide us with plenty of good material from the Turkish side that somewhat balances the picture. But still, one would have dearly loved to read the memories of such great men of history such as Karabekir, Nurettin Pasha, Fevzi, İsmet, and many others.

Most certainly there must be a couple more great secondary sources and scholars of the older sort, dealing with this subject or others related to Turkey, but here, again, this author has his limits and cannot be expected to know all and about everything.

Finally, readers should not expect to find in this chapter some of the usual stuff they find in other works. If they want that stuff, they have already found it elsewhere, and if they have not, they should not look for it here.

1. How Turkey Entered the First World War

The First World War was the first in which not only new mass-killing machines were used: intense, continuous, heavy artillery fire; planes; gas; and the lethal machine gun blasting young men pinned against thick, barbed, wire. It was also the first war, especially on the Western Front, where armies entrenched themselves, and then slaughtered each other in turn or simultaneously by all the means just cited, thus wiping out a whole generation of Western men.

When one reads of the destruction of that war one thinks it must have been fought by people who simply hated one another to death, distant bloody hordes descending on people they were bound to wipe out, somehow like the Mongols descending on the World of Islam in the 13th century. In reality, that was not the case at all. The following extract is a note from a German intellectual to the British, written not long after the conflict began:

> It is with pain and with bitterness that I speak the word England. I am one of those barbarians on whom the English University of Oxford conferred the degree of Doctor Honoris Causa. I have friends in England who stand with one foot on the intellectual soil of Germany. Haldane, formerly English Minister of War, and with him countless other Englishmen, made regular pilgrimages to the little barbarous town of Weimar, where the barbarians Goethe, Schiller, Herder, Wieland, and others, have created another world for humanity. We have a poet, whose plays, more than those of any other German poet, have become national property; his name is Shakespeare. This Shakespeare is, at the same time, the prince of English poets. The mother of our Emperor is an English woman, the wife of the King of England a German, and yet this nation, so closely related by blood and choice, has declared war against us. Why? Heaven only knows. This much,

however, is certain, that the now beginning European concert, saturated with blood, as it is, has an English statesman for its impresario and its conductor. It is doubtful, however, whether the finale of this terrible music will find the same conductor at the stand. "My cousin, you did not mean well either with yourselves or with us when your tools threw the firebrand into our dwellings!"[790]

The First World War itself was not caused by the murder on 28 June 1914 of Archduke Franz Ferdinand, the heir to the throne of the Austro-Hungarian Empire. That murder was just the spark that caused the explosion. An even less grave incident, say, a gun fired by accident, a brawl in a casino or in a street could have caused the outburst of violence. The First World War simply was the most unavoidable conflict on earth. One can just compare the situation to stew brewing inside a pressure cooker with a tight lid, on slow, but permanent, fire; pressure mounting, and bound to explode sometime. And yet none it would seem was capable or willing to turn the fire off. It was in words the most incomprehensible war, where everyone was responsible and none was.

To go into all the issues regarding the reasons of the war is impossible in this work, and there are tens if not hundreds of books that have dealt with this matter. The best source, however, remains the New York Times *Current History* Magazine — not just a goldmine of information, but once one gives oneself to it, one is straight conveyed into that moment, that atmosphere of 1914, and it is as if one had become part of that setting, and all somehow becomes frighteningly real — and then, the sorry, but unavoidable fascinating, character of the war becomes all too gripping.

For the historian of today using *Current History*, the temptation is to cut and paste everything. The reason is simple, no author can ever be able to rephrase, sum up, express, or convey what the sources of the time did. The material is so good, the style so powerful, so true, so full of the emotions of the moment that no one writing a century later can imitate or reproduce. Things written in the rawness of the war, conveying the sense of loss, anger, waste, powerlessness, frustration at the incapacity of humans to avoid their unavoidable worst are not the same as things written under different emotions a century later.

Brief mention must be made here of Volume One of *Current History*, issue One. There we have expressed views of Western intellectuals about the conflict — the thoughts of Bernard Shaw, Arnold Bennett, H.G. Wells, John Galsworthy, H. Rider Haggard, Henry Bergson, and many others — one of the most extraordinary set of exchanges one would ever care to read.[791] Then we have the views of the political elites of the time, and the blame game, and countless other articles catching the conflict just as it began, without the element of hindsight, that element which is

---

[790] Gerhart Hauptmann: Are we Barbarians; in *The New York Times Magazine Current History*; Vol One, Number One; From the Beginning to March, 1915; pp. 178-179.
[791] The New York Times Magazine *Current History*; Vol One, Number One.

beneficial at times, but also a true foe to understanding correctly historical reality in many situations. *Current History* is in words a great legacy no historian should ignore.

More than any other actor, Turkey on the eve of the war was in an impossible situation. It had to be dragged into it even if possibly every Turk with a degree of power sought to avoid it as much as possible. First and foremost, for many decades already, as seen in chapter one, Turkey had become the playground for the Great Powers, primarily Britain, France, Russia, Italy, Austria, and now add Germany. At times one simply considers it the greatest miracle of all that no Sultan shot himself after shooting the ambassadors of such countries first. They acted according not just to the interests of their own countries, but according to their whims it would often seem. As one reads through their dealings with the Turkish Sultans, or Viziers, one truly believes they acted according to what happened to them right before the meeting. Moreover, the story of the Great Powers and Turkey was that of uninterrupted blackmail, threats, and meddling. The memoirs of Cemal Pasha are a wonderful window into such times preceding the war, where the Turks had to listen everyday to what the ambassador from one country or another had to warn or threaten about one decision or another taken by the Turks. Cemal here tells us:

> A few days after this incident [with an Italian envoy] the English Ambassador, Sir Lewis Mallet, came to me at the Ministry and told me he had heard that the Ottoman Government was about to grant the Italians a concession for the Adalia Railway, and that such action would be an encroachment upon the rights of the English Aidin [Aydın] Railway Company.[792]

Somehow, it was expected of Turkey to please the British, the French, the Germans, the Italians, the Russians, and all the Christian minorities, all at once, and all the time, and if not...

Turkey was very reluctant to join the war. If a conflict had to take place, and she could not avoid being involved, it would have been preferable if it took place not in late 1914 as the Western and Russian war-mongers were pushing for, but around 1920, if at all. As Cemal Pasha, one of the three leading persons in power in Turkey noted, the country, already bled and broken by earlier wars, especially the Balkans in 1912, would have first to strengthen its means of defence, and make the army stronger.[793]

> In case of a European war [he said] as long as the conflict was postponed for between five and ten years we should have brought up the fortifications of the Straits and our different coasts to such a standard, made our army so

---
[792] Djemal Pasha: *Memories of a Turkish Statesman*; Hutchinson & co; London; 1922, 79.
[793] Ibid, p. 114.

> strong, and developed our country to such a degree that we need not hesitate to take our part in such a war.[794]

That the country could not afford a war then was noted straight by Liman von Sanders, the head of the German mission in Turkey, when he arrived and he found that many infantry companies did not have more than 24 men, and that was in the Summer of 1914.[795]

The Turks were rebuilding their strength as much as their means would allow, and they were trying in earnest. Strengthening the navy was a major priority, knowing as they did, that with or without a world war, the Greeks would be onto them any time. The battleship *Fatih* was to be ready in twenty-two months, and the other units which had been ordered in England and France were to be constructed in approximately the same period.[796] The dreadnought *Osman* was to be delivered by the end of July, 1914, and the *Reschadich* by the beginning of 1915. By 1916, the Turks should be in possession of a new fleet of three dreadnoughts, two light cruisers, twelve destroyers and four submarines, as well as a second fleet consisting of the old units, thus enough vessels to dissuade the Greeks.[797]

Whilst the Turks were hurriedly preparing, the Allies were not wasting their time either, and once more were using the same tricks as before. The Istanbul correspondent of *The Daily Atlantis* of New York wrote on 17 September 1914, that is before Turkey entered the war:

> The Porte has learned that efforts are being made in the Balkans for common action against Turkey. It also became known that the Governments of London and Petrograd agreed to indemnify Bulgaria by giving her Adrianople and Thrace, while Greece was to have Smyrna, with a considerable hinterland.
>
> The President of the London Balkan Committee, Mr. Noel Buxton, went to Bulgaria and made certain promises to Mr. Radoslavoff, the Bulgarian Premier, in the name of Sir Edward Grey. He promised the restitution to Bulgaria of the Enos-Midia line, including Adrianople. The Bulgarians, however, are not to be fooled in this way by promises at the expense of third parties, and especially when the eventual cost of these gifts might be a heavy one. We must not forget that Bulgaria wants not Thrace, but Macedonia. If Great Britain had promised Bulgaria Macedonia, including Saloniki, and the Bulgarian Government was convinced beforehand of the fulfillment of the promise, then it is certain that the proposal would be accepted. But this is not in line with England's interests, because in that

---

[794] Ibid.
[795] Liman von Sanders: *Five Years in Turkey*; tr. from German by C. Reichmann, United States Naval Institute. 1927; p. 30.
[796] Djemal Pasha; op cit; 95.
[797] Ibid.

case she would lose her two other customers—Greece and Servia. And so there goes Mr. Buxton making offers out of our own pocket.[798]

Regardless, the Turks still wanted neutrality, and were the least keen on entering a conflict, which by the late Summer of 1914 was already weeks old. The Germans, in particular, were beginning to feel annoyed at the Turkish reluctance. Even the otherwise mild Liman von Sanders was beginning to lose his patience:

> The situation was most painful for the German officers as the war at home had begun. After a few days it was given out that Turkey would remain neutral. Then, on August 11, I sent an explicit telegram to H. M. the Emperor inviting attention to the provision of the contract referred to and requesting prompt recall of all German officers to the German Army. On August 22 a telegram brought the decision of the Emperor that for the present we were to remain in Turkey and that we should not suffer any disadvantage thereby as our service here would be counted as though we were in the field with the German Army. I at once called the German officers together and there was much gloom among them when informed of the decision. All believed that the war would not last long and would be fought without us. Hardly anyone in those days counted on Turkey entering the war, as it was known that the majority of Turkish Ministers were in favour of neutrality.[799]

Not just that, forced to choose, Turkey went first for the Allies, France and Britain.[800] Cemal himself made approaches to them early in 1914 to counter Enver's efforts,[801] who was courting, or being courted by Germany. Shortly before the beginning of the war, Cemal had attended the French naval manoeuvres as guest of the French government and had been shown warm feelings by the French.[802] As late as 9 August, on board of French vessels, he shared with them very friendly exchanges.[803] Britain and France, however, did not want Turkish offer of an alliance.[804] The reason was simple: They wanted Russia. They knew what Russia wanted: Constantinople. So they could not have Russia and Turkey at once; and when it came to choosing, there was not a shred of hesitation: Russia, of course, was the friend. Furthermore, Turkey, still quite weak, could be defeated easily, and because of her participation by the side of Germany, would easily be partitioned/carved up at will. So why have a feeble partner when you can have his or her inheritance easily.

---

[798] In *Current History*, The European War, Vol 1; March 1915. How Turkey Went to War; pp. 1025-1035; at p. 1030-1.
[799] Liman Von Sanders: *Five Years in Turkey*; p. 29.
[800] S.J. Shaw and E.K Shaw: *History*; op cit; vol 2; p. 310.
[801] Ibid.
[802] Liman von Sanders: *Five Years*; op cit; 38.
[803] Ibid.
[804] S.J. Shaw and E.K Shaw: *History*; op cit; vol 2; p. 310.

As for Turkey's alliance with Germany, negotiated by Enver primarily, all the members of the government, with the exception of two ministers, in the end, were convinced to go along. The reasons were: it was already a fact and also it did provide the realm with the protection against Russian ambitions, something neither Britain nor France would agree to.[805] Cemal, again, in his memoirs, admitted:

> Germany, whatever else might be said, was the only power which desired to see Turkey strong. Germany's interests could be secured by the strengthening of Turkey, and that alone. Germany could not lay hands on Turkey as if she were a colony, for neither the geographical position nor her resources made that possible. The result was that Germany regarded Turkey as a link in the commercial and trading chain, and thus became her stoutest champion against the Entente Governments which wanted to dismember her, particularly as the elimination of Turkey would mean the final "encirclement" of Germany. Her south-western front remained open thanks to Turkey alone. The only way in which she could escape the pressure of the iron ring was to prevent the dismemberment of Turkey.
>
> Thus we had two groups of Powers before us, the ideal of one of which was to get us in its power, while the aim of the other was to make friendly approaches to us in view of certain prospective advantages, and to conclude an alliance with us based on equal rights and obligations.
>
> Could this offer be rejected?
>
> In the first place, none of the small Balkan States would dare to assert itself with a view to intervening in the domestic affairs of a government which was a member of so powerful an alliance, so that we should, at any rate, be left in peace.
>
> In the second place, no member of the Entente group would venture to lay hands on us for fear of starting a general European war. Above all, Germany's savants, her art and commercial experts would place their services at the disposal of Turkey in the way she desired. Thus, within a short time we should be able to obtain our release from the bonds of the capitulations.
>
> A mighty Empire like Germany was offering us an alliance based on equality of status, we who five or six months before had tried to escape from our isolation and associate ourselves with a group of Powers by making an attempt — a vain attempt — to form an alliance with Bulgaria, from which we promised ourselves great profit.[806]

However, even after they had finally opted for the German side, the Turks still sought ways to avoid getting dragged into it by an excuse or another. The Allies, in fact more than the Germans, were pushing Turkey into the conflict. So, in the

---

[805] Cemal Pasha: Hatıralar (Memoirs), Selek, Istanbul 1959, pp. 124-129.
[806] Djemal Pasha: *Memories of a Turkish Statesman*; op cit, pp. 113-4 112.

Summer of 1914, the British Admiralty requisitioned two cruisers built for the Turkish Government by Armstrong Whitworth, which had been paid for and were ready for delivery.[807] Though a clause in the contract had allowed for its cancellation in the event of war, this roused indignation against Britain even among those who had favoured a pro-Allied policy. The women of Turkey had contributed their jewels and other valuables in a public subscription to help towards the purchase.[808] Then, on 27 September, a Turkish destroyer was stopped by a British destroyer outside the Dardanelles, to which the Turkish Government reacted by closing the Straits to all shipping.[809] Still the Turkish Government went to great lengths to justify in the official press of Istanbul that the measure was only undertaken after a Franco-British fleet had established an actual blockade of the Straits 'to the detriment of Turkish commerce and neutral navigation.'[810] The reasons the Allies wanted Turkey to fight was very simple: it, i.e. its territory, would be the bait for anyone to enter war against the Germans; it would be something like this:

'Fight Germany and get such and such plot of land in Turkey!'

Only Turkey was offered as a prize for participation 'on the right side'; only it could be carved up for the benefit of the participants, not Austria, not Germany; nobody else.

The Turks desperately, still, sought ways to escape their agreements with the Germans, hoping, maybe, for some miracle. But when something is unavoidable... On 27 October, a small part of the Turkish fleet was manoeuvring in the Black Sea, when the Russian fleet, which at first confined its activities to following and hindering 'every one of [our] movements, finally, on the 29th, unexpectedly began hostilities by attacking the Ottoman fleet.'[811]

> 'During the naval battle which ensued the Turkish fleet, with the help of the Almighty,' adds the Turkish official declaration, 'sank the mine-layer Pruth, displacing 5,000 tons and having a cargo of 700 mines; inflicted severe damage on one of the Russian torpedo boats, and captured a collier. A torpedo from the Turkish torpedo boat Gairet-i-Millet sank the Russian destroyer Koubanietz, and another from the Turkish torpedo boat Mouavenet-i-Millet inflicted serious damage on a Russian coastguard ship.'[812]
>
> 'The Ottoman imperial fleet, glory be given to the Almighty, escaped injury, and the battle is progressing favorably for us,' added the same source.[813]

---

[807] Lord Kinross: *Ataturk*; op cit; p. 66.
[808] Ibid.
[809] *Current History*, The European War, Vol 1; March 1915. How Turkey Went to War; pp. 1025-1035; at p. 1031.
[810] Ibid.
[811] War Declared in *Current History*, The European War, Vol 1; March 1915. How Turkey Went to War; pp. 1025-1035; at p. 1032.
[812] Ibid.
[813] Ibid.

The engagement, Liman von Sanders notes, had taken place under the Turkish flag, so most probably the Turkish Minister of Marine, Cemal Pasha, had given his consent to the departure of the ships.[814] He was, Liman von Sanders continues, most certainly the Turkish Minister who in those days made a decisive switch in attitude, for Enver was already in favour of Germany; Talat had favourable leaning; but Cemal was definitely pro Franco-British.[815] Not only was Cemal's shift in position important in itself, he also was one of the leading persons in Turkey, and his joining the pro-German Ministers was of great significance.[816]

What is remarkable is that even at this late stage after fighting had already occurred, the Turks were still trying to make the ultimate efforts to avoid conflict. The Turkish Government proposed a joint enquiry to ascertain which fleet had attacked first, so that the commander of that fleet could be made personally responsible, but the Russian Government rejected that proposal.[817] A few days later, on 2 November, Russia declared war, followed by Britain and France on 5 November. Turkey responded with its own declaration of war on 11 November.[818]

The Turkish headquarters when mobilised had given orders as early as August for the formation of several armies. Liman von Sanders says that he was given command of the First Army, which consisted of five army corps in and near Constantinople, Thrace, the Dardanelles, near Panderma and to the south of it.[819] Cemal was given command of the Second Army, with two army corps to be stationed on the Asiatic side.[820] A Third Army was to be formed west of the Caucasus, approximately in the vicinity of Erzurum; Enver would take charge of that front.

Whilst this division of the armies, Liman von Sanders remarks, was a sensible one, during the war, gradually, some rather wacky decisions began to be taken, whereby nine armies were set up, which, he correctly remarks was contrary to good sense, as these armies more or less existed on paper only and with hardly any troops.[821] He notes, for instance, how the First Army in 1917 hardly had any infantry regiment, whilst the Second Army in 1918 had an infantry which barely had seven effective battalions, whilst the three armies on the Palestine front in 1918, had the same numbers as a single Turkish infantry division had at the beginning of the war.[822]

---

[814] Liman von Sanders: *Five Years*; op cit; 37.
[815] Ibid.
[816] Ibid 38.
[817] Cemal; op cit; p. 131.
[818] Menteşe, Halil, Halil Menteşe'nin Anıları (The Memoirs of Halil Menteşe), Hürriyet, Istanbul 1988. 53.
[819] Liman von Sanders: *Five Years*; op cit; p. 31.
[820] Ibid.
[821] Ibid.
[822] Ibid.

2. First Blood (Late 1914-Early 1915)

When on 31 October 1914, the war between the Central Powers and the Allies spread further east into Asia, the Russian Caucasus army, which had been already mobilised, took the initiative at once.[823] The 2nd and 3rd Army Corps had been previously transferred to the European front, leaving only the 1st and the 4th Caucasian Army Corps, and some frontier guards, to hold the 3rd Turkish Army.[824] Early in November 1914, a Russian advance in the direction of Erzurum was checked by the Turkish 3rd Army just inside Turkey.[825]

In the meantime, whilst the Russians were probing on that front, a conference had taken place in Erzurum during October between the leaders of the Committee of Union and Progress and the Turkish Armenians in which an ambitious plan was being discussed for invading the Caucasus, driving the Russians back to the Cossack steppes, and forming three autonomous provinces under Turkish suzerainty between the Black Sea and the Caspian.[826] However, whilst the Turks were laying plans for a grand offensive, Russia already had promised the Armenians an autonomous state including not only the areas under Russian rule in the Caucasus but also great sways of territory in eastern Anatolia.[827] The Armenian leadership declared their neutrality, but already soon after the meeting several prominent Turkish subject Armenians joined the Russian side.[828] Meanwhile, Czar Nicholas II himself had journeyed to the Caucasus and put in place a practical plan of alliance with the Armenians. In reply, the president of the Armenian National Bureau in Tiflis declared:

> From all countries Armenians are hurrying to enter the ranks of the glorious Russian Army, with their blood to serve the victory of Russian arms.... Let the Russian flag wave freely over the Dardanelles and the Bosporus. Let, with Your will, great Majesty, the peoples remaining under the Turkish yoke receive freedom. Let the Armenian people of Turkey who have suffered for the faith of Christ receive resurrection for a new free life under the protection of Russia.[829]

It was not long before scores of Armenians joined the Russians, and the Czar, E.K. and S. Shaw note, returned to St.Petersburg 'confident that the day finally had come for him to reach Istanbul.'[830]

---

[823] M. Philips Price: *War and Revolution in Asiatic Russia*, George Allen & Unwin Ltd, London, 1917; p. 54.
[824] Ibid.
[825] S.J. Shaw and E.K Shaw: *History*; op cit; vol 2; p. 315.
[826] M. Philips Price: *War and Revolution in Asiatic Russia*, op cit; p. 55.
[827] S.J. Shaw and E.K Shaw: *History*; op cit; vol 2; p. 314.
[828] Ibid.
[829] *Horizon*, Tiflis, November 30, 1914, quoted by R. Hovannisian, *Road to Independence*, p. 45; FO 2485, 2484/46942, 22083.
[830] S.J. Shaw and E.K Shaw: *History*; op cit; vol 2; p. 315.

Enver, whether he knew of these plans or not, felt the Turks were strong enough for a Winter assault. He came to take charge of the campaign, assisted by a German officer, von Schellendorf, acting as Chief of his Staff.[831] He learnt that the Russians were not much effective on this front, and, more importantly, that there were some weak spots in the long line across the plateau, stretching from the Black Sea to northwest Persia, particularly in the Olti region, where only a regiment of frontier troops guarded the fortress of Kars and the supply base of Sarıkamış.[832] Some years before, a Georgian officer had warned his colleagues on the Russian General Staff for the Caucasian Army of the danger of a possible Turkish flanking movement on Kars via the Olti depression.[833] He was ignored on account that this was an impassable piece of land, especially in winter, but, Philips Price remarks, 'the Russians had not reckoned on the endurance of the Turkish soldier.'[834] Enver, on the other hand expected too much from the Turkish soldier. He aimed to launch an offensive, cut the Russian lines of communications from the Caucasus to their main base at Kars and to reoccupy it along with Ardahan and Batum as the first step toward an invasion of the Caucasus.[835] The key to success was the border town of Sarıkamış, which lay astride the main route from Kars to the north.[836] Enver was warned of the rashness of his plan by one of his Staff officers who clearly understood the risks and unfeasibility of the operation, of leading two Army Corps into a country without roads, in mid-winter with only horse and mule transport.[837] Liman von Sanders, himself notes:

> Map in hand Enver sketched to me the outline of intended operations by the Third Army. With one army corps, the Eleventh, he meant to hold the Russians in front on the main road, while two corps, the Ninth and Tenth, marching by their left were to cross the mountains by several marches and then fall on the Russian flank and rear in the vicinity of Sarikamisch. Later the Third Army was to take Kars.[838]
>
> 'I had heard of this intended march several days before from a German officer at headquarters and studied its feasibility,' adds Liman von Sanders. 'My conclusion was that the operation was difficult, if not wholly impracticable. According to the map and everything else I could learn of them, the roads in question were narrow mountain roads or trails over high ridges. At that time they were probably deep in snow. It would require a special study how to effect the supply of ammunition and food with the available Turkish means. I called Enver's attention to these grave objections as was my duty; he replied that they had already been considered and that all roads had been reconnoitered or were being

---

[831] M. Philips Price: *War and Revolution in Asiatic Russia*, op cit; p. 56.
[832] Ibid.
[833] Ibid.
[834] Ibid.
[835] S.J. Shaw and E.K Shaw: *History*; op cit; vol 2; p. 315.
[836] Ibid.
[837] M. Philips Price: *War and Revolution in Asiatic Russia*, op cit; p. 56.
[838] Liman von Sanders: *Five Years*; op cit; 42.

reconnoitered. At the conclusion of our conversation he gave utterance to fantastic, yet noteworthy ideas. He told me that he contemplated marching through Afghanistan to India. Then he went away. Soon after him appeared his chief of staff, General von Bronsart, to report his departure; he was to accompany Enver. I called his attention also to the great difficulties of the march as planned and to the responsibility that would rest upon him as a German chief of staff.'[839]

Now, of course, Liman von Sanders might be putting the blame on Enver, for the latter was dead by the time Liman van Sanders released his book, and could not defend himself. So, it is difficult here to blame Enver alone, but blame the whole General Command. And the main reason for the blame is not for this operation, for a blunder in war to happen is all too normal. Where the problem was, as noted in the previous chapter, was in repeating the same error and failing to take account of the factors also listed: poor logistics, mistiming of operations, lack of synchronisation of the different units, lack of equipment, including appropriate clothing and boots for the troops, and so on. And indeed, here, we see the same problem as at Kırkkilise, Lule Burgaz, and so on. Turkish General Command from 1912 till 1918 was perhaps the most dire the country ever had, so incompetent, so incapable of learning from mistakes, it only shows criminally deluded characters in control, men incapable of accepting error on their part, and hence incapable of correcting them or improving. Already before its launch, Enver's operation had already failed as the slowness of mobilisation, and the lack of railways and good roads in Turkey, caused a delay of at least six weeks in bringing the forces to the front.[840] Six weeks at the door of winter make the mother of all differences.

So, in the third week of December (according to Uyar and Erickson) (one week earlier according to Philips Price), after many delays, in the middle of a snowstorm blowing across the desolate highlands, the 9th and 10th Army Corps left all their heavy artillery and equipment behind and took only light mountain guns in order to move fast.[841] Initially the operation was successful, and on 15 December, the Turks entered Olti, easily beating the small Russian force, and then speedily moved onwards to reach, on 26 December a point of being within a few hours of Sarıkamış, the Russian supply base.[842] The Russian Caucasus army was literally surrounded, but the Turks had neither captured Kars nor Sarıkamış, and their main force was still on the wooded heights above Sarıkamış.[843] Just then, the initial six week delay began to have its effects: a huge snow-storm hampered the movements of the Turkish troops, and soon the Russian garrison in Sarıkamış began to add to the problem by a vigorous artillery fire at the Turkish army, whose men, poorly fed and poorly clothed (with summer clothes) began to freeze

---

[839] Ibid; 43.
[840] M. Philips Price: *War and Revolution in Asiatic Russia*, op cit; p. 55.
[841] M. Uyar and E.J. Erickson: *A Military History of the Ottomans*; op cit; p. 247.
[842] M. Philips Price: *War and Revolution in Asiatic Russia*; op cit; p. 57.
[843] Ibid.

to death.[844] Then, in the mayhem, the troops lost contact with each other, and became stuck in the mire of impassable dirt roads and tracks due to the heavy snowfall.[845] The Russian reinforcements arrived, and on 2 January, the left wing of the Russians, now facing north in the valley of Mezhingert, moved forth against the half-frozen Turks on the heights above Sarıkamış.[846] Again Turkish courage ruled supreme, but the desperate defence by the 9th Army Corps, which allowed the 10th to retreat was at a terrible cost; besides the huge toll of casualties — over 200 officers, including the 9th Army Corps commander, were captured.[847] The Turks might have lost up to 100,000 men between those killed, wounded, and captured; it literally destroyed the Turkish Caucasus army.[848] It definitely put an end to the grand plan of conquering Azerbaijan and inciting rebellion within the subject nations of Afghanistan, Central Asia, and India.[849]

Beside all the losses cited already, the moral and political effect of this disaster on the local Caucasus populations was considerable.[850] When the Turkish army moved in, rumours spread in the bazaars of Tiflis, Erivan and Kars, that a new Shamyl Beg would appear to welcome the Turks.[851] None of that now.

In the meantime, the same policy of mis-planning, or no planning at all, just throwing in courageous men forth, the same speed in devising operations, the same muddling through as ever before, the same lack of awareness of the poverty of Turkish logistics, the same narrow-mindedness in not looking at the big picture and not learning from previous disasters, and so onto another disaster: the Egyptian campaign launched by Cemal Pasha in February 1915. Accompanied by his German chief of staff, Kress von Kressenstein and by members of Enver's Special Organisation, Cemal led a force of 18,000 troops across the Sinai desert to the Suez Canal.[852]

> No one shared my views [says Liman van Sanders] and all were convinced of the great effect produced by a swift descent on Egypt. Neither then nor later could I understand how it could be thought possible to conquer Egypt with the limited means of the Turks and in view of the very poor communications?[853]

Again, as with Enver above, it is very difficult to prove the stand by Liman von Sanders as Cemal was dead before von Sanders completed his work. Regardless, it was yet another blunder. Indeed, the times when an army could conquer a country with less than a hundred thousand men were gone long ago. These days

---

[844] Ibid; p. 58.
[845] M. Uyar and E.J. Erickson: *A Military History of the Ottomans*; op cit; p. 248.
[846] M. Philips Price: *War and Revolution in Asiatic Russia*, op cit; p. 58.
[847] M. Uyar and E.J. Erickson: *A Military History of the Ottomans*; op cit; p. 248.
[848] S. Selısık: *Kafkas Cephesinde 10nuncu Kolordunun Birinci Dünya Savaşının Başlangıcından Sarıkamış, Muharebelerinin Sonuna Kadar Olan Harekatı*, 2nd edition. Ankara: Genelkurmay Basımevi, 2006; 188–194.
[849] M. Uyar and E.J. Erickson: *A Military History of the Ottomans*; op cit; p. 248.
[850] M. Philips Price: *War and Revolution in Asiatic Russia*, op cit; p. 58.
[851] Ibid.
[852] A. Mango: *Ataturk;* John Murray; London; 1999; p. 141.
[853] Liman Von Sanders: *Five Years*; op cit; 32.

belong to the 7th century, and only the likes of Muslim generals such as Khalid ibn al-Walid, or 'Amr ibn al-'As, the Arab conqueror of Egypt in 639-640, could do it with a force of just over ten thousand men.[854] Even then these hardy conquerors needed reinforcements at some point, and even more importantly they could move out into the desert and back in swiftly, which was then the necessary requirement in case the enemy counter-attacked massively.[855] And this is precisely what the British could do even if Cemal surprised them. They could either ship large forces to Egypt from India, from the colonies or from the mother country; or they could simply blast to pieces Cemal's tiny army thanks to their long-range artillery, either from land or from the sea. The British positions on the Suez Canal were, furthermore, extremely well defended, and were equipped with every kind of modern arms. Four railway tracks on both sides of the canal and ample rolling stock gave them the capacity to concentrate at threatened points very quickly.[856] The fire power of the British army could crush an army of even 100,000.

Yet, again, the rush to do things, and badly, was at the source of the Turkish disaster. Cemal could have read about the descent on Egypt by Selim I in 1516-1517 and could have derived many lessons on how to conduct such an operation — all the preparatory, careful work, the political and other actions on the way to Egypt, gaining support first from locals, weakening the enemy, organising the logistics and the march of the army, and so on.[857]

Liman von Sanders says that:

> Such an enterprise might come as a surprise and thus be crowned by temporary success, but it never could be of decisive character because any expeditionary force advancing across the canal, unless of great strength, would face destruction.[858]

This is completely untenable and quite barmy a view. Cemal's operation was utterly suicidal, even if he had invaded not with 18,000 but with 180,000, for British artillery would have blasted a fine Turkish army scattered in the sands. Also, how would have Cemal secured supplies for such a large army far from his initial base, that is even if he was successful at first? Every army needs to be supplied, whether by sea, or land, or even by air, as experienced by the French at Dien Bien Phu in 1954. Supposing Cemal had captured the whole Canal Zone, he would have just ended up being cornered there, and eventually had the Turkish army survived massive bombardment from the British navy, which ruled supreme, such Turkish army would have had to surrender eventually, for again: How and from where would supplies reach it? Through the sea controlled by the

---

[854] See A.J. Butler: *The Arab Conquest of Egypt*, Oxford 1902.
[855] See J. Glubb: *The Great Arab Conquests*; Hodder and Stoughton; 1963.
F.M. Donner: *The Early Islamic Conquests*, Princeton University Press, New Jersey, 1981.
[856] Liman Von Sanders: *Five Years;* op cit; 32.
[857] For Selim I operations in Egypt, see G. Casale: *The Ottoman Age of Exploration;* Oxford University Press; 2010.
[858] Liman Von Sanders: *Five Years*; op cit; 33.

British? Through air with a Turkish air force that did not exist? By land through an endless desert?

In the end, there was not even such an eventuality arising. As W.T. Massey, the official British war correspondent in Egypt could tell us, the defences of the Canal were formidable, as the British had performed some engineering works that made it virtually impregnable.[859] So, on 2/3 February 1915, the Turks reached the Canal and succeeded in getting 600 men across, but these were beaten back and the Turks in the end suffered some 3,000 casualties.[860] As Massey, notes, the British were fully aware of the arrival of the Turkish troops, they had enough troops, and the fighting never went beyond a fairly simple task for the British; a truly lamentable operation despite, as usual, the great courage of the Turkish troopers and their officers.[861]

Only General Falkenhayn seems to have seen something useful out of this operation, stating:

> Even if the Chief of the General Staff did not expect any decisive influence upon the war from such operations, he yet hoped to cut the Suez Canal, one of Great Britain's most important arteries, for a time, or at least to keep strong English forces away from the main theatre of war, whilst Germany's resources were not involved to any harmful extent by enterprises in Asia.[862]

As for Cemal Pasha, his excuse for the disaster was rather lame. He said:

> If perhaps I did not succeed in really driving the English out of Egypt, had it not been for the secret betrayal of Sherif Hussein, who thereby committed an unforgivable sin against the Mussulman world, I should, at any rate, as I shall show hereafter, have prevented the usurpers from attempting anything against Palestine and Syria, and in so doing have held the hundreds of men composing the English Army inactive in Egypt.
>
> It was the treachery of Sherif Hussein which made that desirable object unattainable for us. It divided the two (Mussulman) brother nations, Arabs and Turks; he made the former the slaves of the English and French and forced the latter to fight a hopeless fight against the most pitiless foe.[863]

Obviously Cemal Pasha is typical of the delusional leaders who never accept that they make errors and so keep repeating them. His operation achieved nothing except the death of thousands of troops and excellent officers. It diverted nothing. It would have never succeeded. Then he misleads his audience, or just simply an ignorant, he confuses dates and historical facts. He blames his failure on the betrayal of Shereef Hussein, which is utter nonsense. The Shereef's betrayal dates from late 1916 onwards. It, hence, comes nearly two years after Cemal's

---

[859] W.T. Massey: *The Desert campaigns*; G.P. Putnam's Sons; New York; 1918; pp. 6-7.
[860] Liman von Sanders: *Five Years*, 46.
[861] W.T. Massey: *The Desert campaigns*; op cit; pp. 10-15.
[862] General von Falkenhayn: *The German General Staff and its Decisions 1914-1916;* Dodd, Mead and Company; New York; 1920; p. 54.
[863] Cemal: *Memories*; op cit; p. 139.

operation (late 1914-early 1915). At the time Cemal was conducting his operation, the British had not even agreed anything with the Shereef (these agreements only occurring late in 1915).

As for the Egyptian rising, as Massey explains, the British did their groundwork as Cemal should have done. In Egypt as elsewhere, then as today, they had people in high positions who defined British policies. These people, great academics, know Muslims better than the latter know themselves. They study the Muslim world for decades, understand fully Muslim weaknesses, rivalries, and anything else, and so could, then, just as today, devise the appropriate policies of how to deal with them.[864]

Back to the first front, the Caucasus, other than the Sarıkamış disaster, the other operation of note was undertaken a month or so earlier, in November when a small Russian detachment, with a battalion of Armenian volunteers under Andranik, had advanced from Khoy, and in an engagement with the Turks west of Kotur had entered Turkish territory and occupied Serai.[865] During the fighting at Sarıkamış, this force had retreated to the Persian frontier at Djulfa, whence it advanced again to Khoy in January 1915.[866]

The Russians for their part were putting forth their terms prior to attacking the Turks with force. On 1 October 1914, a Russian high official stated:

> 'This war can be of no use to us if it does not bring us Constantinople and the Narrows. Constantinople must belong to us and to us alone.'[867]

It took some time of haggling between Britain and France on one side, and the Russians on the other. For Britain and France to give in to the Russian demand would be the decision of the century. Yet, they took it, reversing a policy, which had prevented the final carving up of Turkey for nearly a century (since 1807 in fact, when Tsar Alexander met with Napoleon at Tilsit).[868] Now, by late 1914, and definitely by February 1915, it was agreed that Russia could have what she always wanted.[869] The final agreement was reached early in March, that not just Istanbul, but also territories of the Gallipoli Peninsula and a strip along the European coast of the Marmara joining it to the Peninsula of Istanbul could be had by Russia.[870] Also agreed was a twin attack from the east by the Russian-Armenians, and from the west by the Allies through Gallipoli, such a joint attack to take place in the first months of 1915. The aim was simply to remove Turkey off the field of war, in fact removing it off the field/map altogether.

---

[864] W.T. Massey: *The Desert Campaigns*; op cit; p. 4.
[865] M. Philips Price: *War and Revolution in Asiatic Russia*, George Allen & Unwin Ltd, London, 1917; p. 59.
[866] Ibid.
[867] Lars Kannengiesser: *The Campaign in Gallipoli*; op cit; p. 34.
[868] W.E.D. Allen: *The Turks in Europe*; John Murray London, 1919, p. 103. Sutherland Menzies: *Turkey Old and New*, 2vols; Allen Lane; London; 1880; vol 2; p. 129; 135; 136.
[869] W.S. Churchill: *The World Crisis*; Thornton Butterworth, London; 1923; vol 2, pp. 197-200.
[870] A.J. Toynbee: *The Western Question in Greece and Turkey*; Constable; 1922; p. 47; see also E. Mead: *The Baghdad Railway; A Study in Imperialism*; MacMillan; New York; 1924; p. 293.

The two attacks were simultaneous indeed and were meant to stretch the Turkish front to breaking point. In the East, the joint Armenian-Russian offensive was in progress by late Winter-early Spring of 1915. From the very beginning, Armenian conscripts had deserted their Turkish units, and Russian forces now had four regiments of Armenian volunteers, besides agent provocateurs sent into Turkish territory well before the start of the hostilities.[871] The Armenians captured the city of Van on 14 April 1915.[872] The Turkish 3rd Army, or what was left of it after Sarıkamış, speedily deployed a mobile gendarmerie division, a few regulars and reserve cavalry regiments, to besiege the city, but the Armenians fought fiercely, and the Turks were unable to retake the city.[873] Whilst the Armenians were holding on, the Russians had begun an advance with a view to occupying the basin of Lake Van, and also seeking to protect their flanks from a possible Turkish counter-thrust.[874] They advanced in three columns

-From Khoy in Persia, approaching Van by way of Serai from the East.

-From the Alashgert, crossing the Aladağ range and approaching Van from the North.

-By the Eastern Euphrates Valley to Melashgert and to the Muş plain.[875]

The Russian advance was irresistible, and all the Turks could do was to retreat, raising the siege of Van, which was relieved by the Russians on 19 May.[876] Melashgert was also captured by the Russians, and their advance patrols had already reached the plain of Muş and were also in control of the eastern portion of the Van basin.[877]

Just as they were being beaten in the east, the Turkish situation in the west was not boding well at all. It had become evident, from intelligence reports of enemy naval and troop movements that Allied forces were assembling on the islands before the Dardanelles, and that an Anglo-French attack on Istanbul, through the Narrows and across the Sea of Marmara, was imminent.[878]

> The failure of the Caucasian and Egyptian campaigns [Kinross remarks] had lowered morale, and 'the people of Constantinople,' began to talk despondently of the capture of the city as though it had already occurred.[879]

---

[871] M. Uyar and E.J. Erickson: *A Military History of the Ottomans*; op cit; pp. 262-3.
[872] Ibid; p. 263.
[873] A.P. Hacobian: *Armenia and the War: An Armenian's Point of View with an Appeal to Britain and the Coming Peace Conference*, (London: Hodder and Stoughton, 1917), 70–80; Garegin Pasdermadjian: Why Armenia Should be Free: Armenia's Role in the Present War, (Boston: Hairenik Publishing, 1918), 17–23; McCarthy, Armenian Rebellion at Van, 180–221.
[874] M. Philips Price: *War and Revolution in Asiatic Russia*, op cit; p. 61.
[875] Ibid; pp. 61-2.
[876] Ibid; p. 62.
[877] Ibid.
[878] Lord P. Kinross: *Ataturk*; op cit; p. 71.
[879] Ibid.

Rumours had spread that the Germans, fearing the arrival of the Russians, began to talk of a separate peace, and Turkish families began to leave for Anatolia.[880] The Turkish Government had already prepared two special trains on the Asiatic side, ready to depart at an hour's notice, one for the Sultan and his suite and the other for the Diplomatic Corps.[881] The Government had also taken steps to move to Eskişehir, where both important Archives and the gold from the banks had already been despatched; whilst works of art were being hurriedly buried in the cellars of the museums.[882] Indeed, there were good reasons for all this; Istanbul, just as much of Turkey, would not be Turkish anymore. As the American Major, Edwin Dayton, wrote just a short time before the Gallipoli Campaign:

> In addition, and perhaps paramount to all other incentives for a campaign against Constantinople, was the fact that the ancient city on the Golden Horn was the one great prize in Europe that might enrich the spoils of the victors. Berlin and Vienna would remain German and Austrian, after the final treaty should be signed, but the Turk's capital might be expected to change hands and fly a new flag.[883]

3. Gallipoli (February-December 1915)

The decision to launch an operation 'to bombard and take the Gallipoli peninsula with Constantinople as its objective' was taken by the British War Council on 8 January 1915. Lt Colonel Douglas J. Scott of the American army notes:

> In 1915, a window of opportunity existed for the Royal Navy to seize the Dardanelles solely by the use of sea power. This would open up the sea line of communication to Constantinople thus allowing Allied forces to attack the German homeland from Constantinople through the Balkan states.[884]

The success of this operation would link both the Russian and Western fronts, leading to the fall of Istanbul, and taking Turkey out of the war, and most certainly its dismemberment right then. Bulgaria would be incapable of continuing to fight, thus opening the way for an attack on Austria-Hungary through the Balkan states, and thus bringing the war to a successful end for the Allies.[885]

When subsequently Sir Ian Hamilton was appointed head of the operation, Lord Kitchener, the British Secretary of State for War, stated to him:

---

[880] Ibid.
[881] Ibid.
[882] Ibid.
[883] Major Edwin W. Dayton: Military Operations of the War; *Current History*; Vol 6; p. 501.
[884] Lt Colonel Douglas J. Scott: *The Naval Campaign in Gallipoli*; Lessons Learned; Air War College Research Report; Maxwell Air Force Base, Alabama; March 1986; p. 1.
[885] Ibid; p. 5.

> Once the Fleet got through the Dardanelles, Constantinople could not hold out. Modern Constantinople could not last a week if blockaded by sea and land. That was a sure thing; a thing whereon he could speak with full confidence. The Fleet could lie off out of sight and range of the Turks and with their guns would dominate the railways and, if necessary, burn the place to ashes. The bulk of the people were not Osmanli or even Mahomedan and there would be a revolution at the mere sight of the smoke from the funnels of our warships. But if, for some cause at present non-apparent, we were forced to put troops ashore against organized Turkish opposition, then he advocated a landing on the Asiatic side of the Bosphorus to hold out a hand to the Russians, who would simultaneously land there from the Black Sea.[886]

Throughout the conference between Hamilton and Kitchener, reference was made repeatedly to the expectation that the Turks would not fight.[887] They would not be able to resist the Royal Navy, but if they did, the Army's services were required, and an army landing would surely cause them to capitulate.[888]

Before Sir Ian Hamilton came onto the scene, another plan was put to effect. On 3 January, the Admiralty telegraphed Admiral Carden, who was commanding the British fleet in the Mediterranean, asking him for an assessment of whether or not the Straits could be forced and if so, for his plan for forcing them.

A little later, Admiral Carden answered the request and stated his plan: four successive operations. First, the destruction of the outer forts at Helles and Kumkale; second and third, two operations consisting in removing the mine fields and destroying the forts between the entrance and the narrows; and the fourth phase, the passage of the narrows onto Constantinople.[889] There was no mention here of the landing.

Before 15 February, a powerful allied fleet was assembled in the Aegean Sea and the neutral Greek islands of Tenedos, Imroz, and Lemnos had already been occupied as a naval advance base.[890] The first of Carden's four operations started on 15 February, its object the destruction of the forts at the entrance of the Dardanelles, which was done by the navy without any trouble, as they remained at a range of 12,000 meters, which was beyond the reach of the Turkish guns.[891] Bad weather between 16 and 25 February prevented any further bombardment, but on the 26th, a detachment of marines was landed at the mouth of the Strait

---

[886] Ian Hamilton: *Gallipoli Diary* (London: Edward Arnold, 1920), vol 1; pp. 10-11.
[887] Major Gregory A. Thiele: Why Did Gallipoli Fail? Why Did Albion Succeed? A Comparative Analysis of Two World War I Amphibious Assaults, in *Baltic Security and Defence Review*, vol 13, issue 2, 2011, pp. 128-161; at p. 130.
[888] Ibid.
[889] G.S. Patton: *The Defence of Gallipoli*; Headquarters Hawaiian Department; August 1936; p. 4.
[890] Ibid; p. 5.
[891] Ibid; p. 6.

and blew up the old forts. Phases 2 and 3 consisted in minesweeping and in destroying further forts.[892] Minesweepers protected by battleships entered the Straits daily, the sweepers removing the mines and the battle ships bombarding the forts. By 4 March, the operation was successfully completed. At this point, many believed victory to be inevitable. In a dispatch from Athens, on 6 March, the reporter of *The London Daily Chronicle* stated:

> The bombardment of the Dardanelles forts, according to the latest news, proceeds with success and cautious thoroughness. It is now anticipated that before another two weeks are over, the allied fleet will be in the Sea of Marmora, and Constantinople will quickly fall to the victorious Allies.[893]

However, seven days earlier, under cover of rain and darkness, the Turkish steamer *Nusret* was able to lay a line of twenty mines parallel but offset to the right of the center of the channel.[894] These mines were laid after the Allied minesweepers had cleared this area in preparation for the ships which were to steam up this channel.[895] Just as the Ally fleet was on its way to blast Istanbul and force Turkey into surrender, disaster struck. *The London Times* naval correspond in its issue of 20 March:

> The further attack upon the inner forts at the Dardanelles, which was resumed by the allied squadrons on Thursday, has resulted, unfortunately, but not altogether unexpectedly, in some loss of ships and gallant lives.[896]

Three ships, the *Bouvet*, *Irresistible*, and *Ocean*, struck mines and were sunk with a heavy loss of life, nearly all the men on the *Bouvet* perished, whilst *Inflexible* and the *Gaulois* were damaged by gun fire.[897] Now the Allies were in a quandary: would they or would not they risk further heavy loss. In the end, it was decided to cancel the original plan of the naval-only campaign and replace it with a plan to wait for the ground forces and then proceed with a combined operation.

At this juncture, awaiting a huge Ally landing, the Turks made some changes. Von Sanders was put in charge of that front, and he and his small staff arrived, taking command of the Dardanelles Fortified Zone on 26 March.[898] The new army had six infantry divisions organised into two army corps, one of which was III Corps containing Mustafa Kemal's 19th Infantry Division, which was subsequently to play a vital role in the whole campaign.[899] Von Sanders identified the Bolayır (Bulair)-Saros region and Besika Bays as the probable main landing sites.[900] So he

---

[892] Ibid.
[893] *The London Daily Chronicle*, Saturday 6 March 1915, in *Current History*, vol 2; Apr-Sep, 1915; p. 170.
[894] Lt Colonel Douglas J. Scott: *The Naval Campaign in Gallipoli*; Lessons Learned; Air War College Research Report; Maxwell Air Force Base, Alabama; March 1986; p. 6.
[895] Ibid.
[896] *The London Times* naval correspond- March 20; in CH pp. 219-220.
[897] BRITISH OFFICIAL REPORT. [From *The London Times*, March 20, 1915.] Plus Chronology, CH; p. 396.
[898] See Liman von Sanders.
[899] E.J. Erickson: *Mustafa Kemal Ataturk*, Osprey, 2013, p. 15. L.V. Sanders, *Five Years in Turkey*, 57–59;
[900] L.V. Sanders: *Five Years in Turkey*, 59–61.

concentrated the defence in three areas: at the Bulair isthmus, the northern neck of the Peninsula between the sea of Marmara and the gulf of Saros in the Aegean; at the southern tip of the Peninsula; and on the Asian shore, at the entrance to the Straits.[901] Von Sanders had elected these sites against the view of the Turkish commanders, Mustafa Kemal, in particular, who were all convinced the Allies would land to the south.

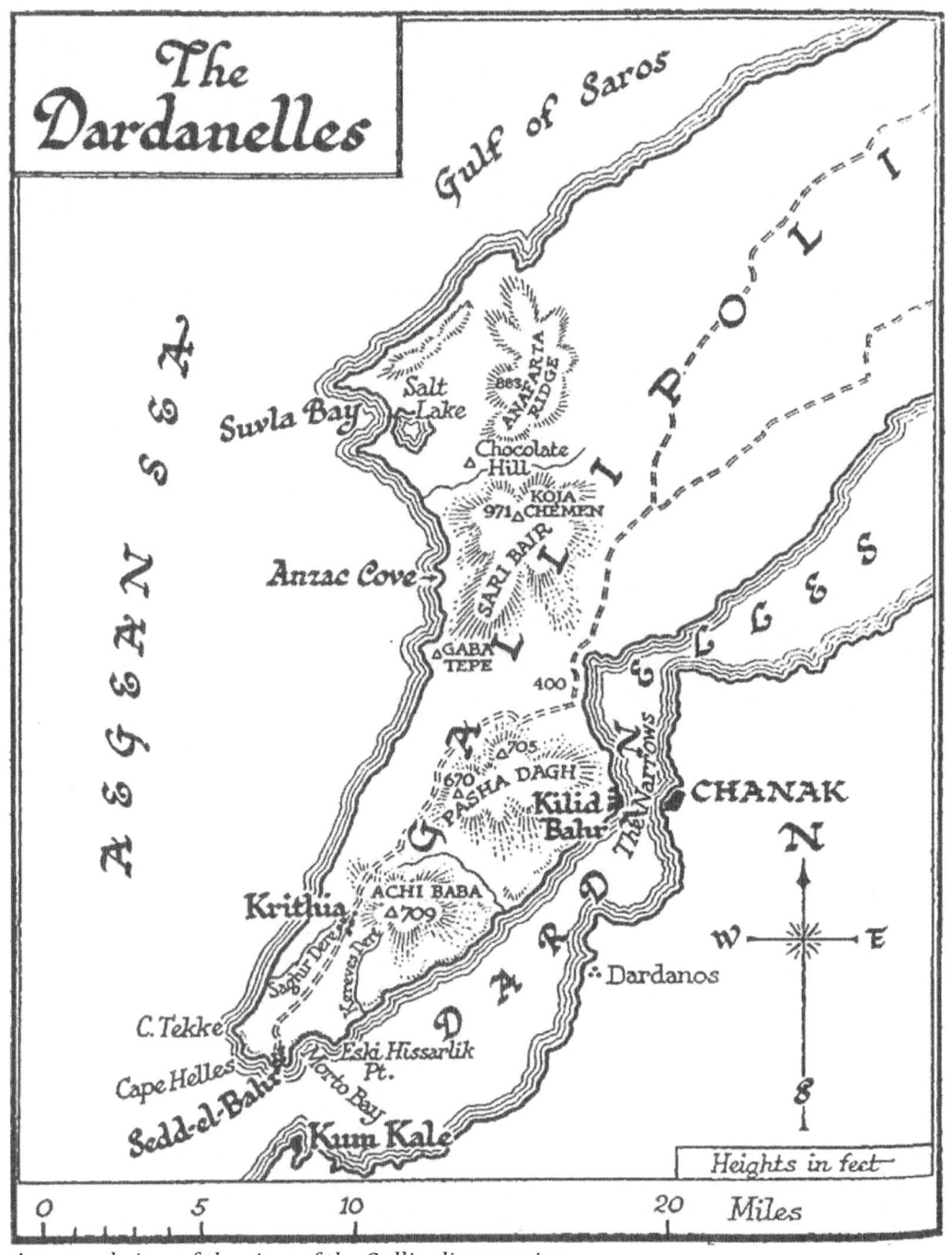

A general view of the sites of the Gallipoli campaign.

---

[901] A. Mango: *Ataturk;* John Murray; London; 1999; p. 144.

This was precisely what General Hamilton did; his detailed plan for the landing on 25 April was as follows:

> The ANZACs [Australian and New Zealand Army Corps] were to land on the west side of the Peninsula and approximately 20 kilometres north of the Gallipoli peninsula's southern tip; in the vicinity of the Gaba Tepe and, having secured their left flank by the capture of Hill 971, were to advance rapidly on Maidos with the object of severing the Turkish communications.[902]
>
> The British planned to land on several beaches at the southern end of the Gallipoli Peninsula; each beach given a letter to distinguish it from the others (S; V; W; X; Y). The landing parties at the toe of the peninsula, supported by navy guns, would advance and capture the commanding height of Achi Baba.[903]

The French were to land in Asia at Kumkale in order to prevent the Turks from bringing reinforcements over from Asia to the other side, at short notice and, even more importantly, to stop the Turks from shelling V Beach.[904]

The news of the landing reached General von Sanders at the town of Gallipoli shortly after 5 a.m. and is described by him in the following terms,

> From the many pale faces among the officers reporting in the early morning, it became apparent that, although a hostile landing had been expected with certainty, a landing in so many places surprised many and filled them with apprehension. My first feeling was that our arrangement needed no change; that was a great satisfaction.[905]

Towards 8 a.m., a report from the vicinity of Bulair arrived informing that a considerable number of transports and war vessels were approaching and shelling the shore in the higher part of the Gulf of Saros.[906] Von Sanders inspected the transports in action and decided, owing to the fact that they rode very high in the water, that they contained no troops and were simply engaged in a diversion.[907]

---

[902] G.S. Patton: *The Defence of Gallipoli*; op cit; p. 13.
[903] Ibid.
[904] Eleanor van Heyningen: *Helles; The French in Gallipoli;* The Joint Imperial War Museum / Australian War Memorial Battlefield Study; Tour to Gallipoli, September 2000; p. 3.
[905] L.V Sanders: *Five Years*; p. 63.
[906] G.S. Patton: *The Defence of Gallipoli*; op cit; p. 13.
[907] Ibid.

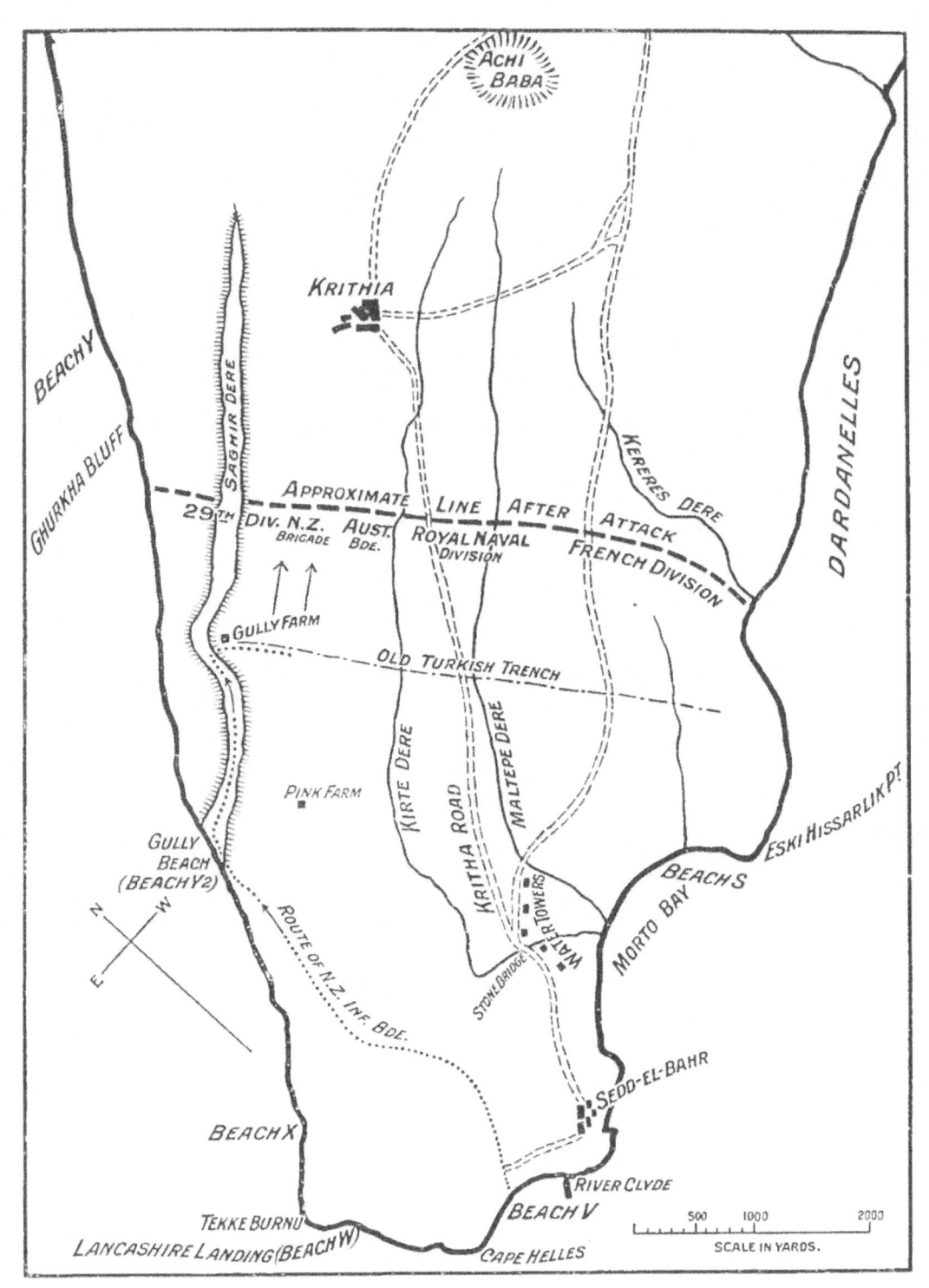

The Cape Helles area and the Landing Beaches. There was no landing at Beach Y2 (Gully Beach between X and Y Beaches). The Anzacs would land further north (see following map). The fighting involving Mustafa Kemal would take place in the latter site.

From the start, the Allies met stiff Turkish resistance. On some of the beaches the Turks inflicted so high casualties on the landing party that they threatened to annihilate them in their entirety. On the V Beach, where the troops, emerging one by one from the sally ports on the *River Clyde,* presented perfect targets to the machine guns in the Sedd-el-Bahr (literally, Sea Barrier) fort at the southern tip of the Gallipoli Peninsula. Out of the first 200 soldiers to disembark, only 21 men made it onto the beach.[908] In many of the boats, every man was killed or wounded before he had a chance to land. Those hit while yet in the water, if wounded, quickly drowned weighed down with more than 80 pounds of equipment.[909] The Turks claim that not a single boat of the first wave was able to return to the vessels for its second load.[910] In fact, on some of the landing boats, the average life of an Allied soldier was not more than three minutes.[911] On V Beach, more men tried to land, headed by Brigadier-General Napier, who was instantly killed with nearly all his men.[912] In all beaches, the Turks were inferior in numbers, and of course, armament. On X beach, by 11.30 a.m., seven British companies were engaged against a Turkish force of one and a half companies.[913] Despite that, the Allies could hardly move forward as their losses, especially of commanding officers, were too high.[914] At V beach the Munsters lost more than one-third, and the Dublins more than three fifths, of their total strength. The Lancashires at W beach were as badly hit as the Dublins.[915] At X beach, the Royals lost 487 out of 979. Further north, at Anzac (where Mustafa Kemal was positioned), one Australian battalion lost 422 out of 900. All these battalions had lost more than half their officers.[916]

It was at a considerable cost that the Allies established beachheads where they could progress from; two of them that could have resulted in Turkish disasters, instead, ending in Ally abysmal failure: i.e. Arıburnu point (Anzac Cove), and Y Beach. The Anzac Cove is notoriously famous, for there, it was that Mustafa Kemal saved the situation with his men. The confusion in this battle of sudden hand-to-hand encounters and shifting positions was indeed such that, with bullets raining from every direction, neither Turks nor Australians knew who was friend or foe.[917]

Elsewhere, the fighting was equally fierce and bloody, and the soldiers on both sides fighting to the bitter end. Captain R.W. Whigham, commanding 'D' Company of the 1st KOSB, recalled this:

> By this time one could see far better what was going on as the moon, which was nearly full, lit up the whole of our front and one could see line upon line of Turks advancing against our position. They fought with extraordinary bravery and as each line was swept away by our fire another one advanced

---

[908] "Irish battalions—major battles (Part III of XI) Helles Landings, Gallipoli, April 1915" *Royal Dublin Fusiliers: Remembering the Great War website*. 2005.
[909] G.S. Patton: *The Defence of Gallipoli*; op cit; p. 28.
[910] Ibid.
[911] J. Masefield: *Gallipoli*; S.B. Gundy; Toronto; 1916; p. 39.
[912] Ibid; p. 40.
[913] G.S. Patton: *The Defence of Gallipoli*; op cit; p. 23.
[914] J. Masefield: *Gallipoli*; op cit; p. 61.
[915] Ibid.
[916] Ibid.
[917] Lord Kinross: *Ataturk*; op cit; p. 76.

> against us... The attack worked up and down our whole front as if they were looking for some weak spot to break through our line. I saw one man, during one of these advances, continue to run towards us after all his companions had stopped. He ran at full speed towards us, dodging about all over the place. He got up to within about fifty yards of the trench and then I saw him drop. Four times during the night they got right up to my trench before they were shot and one Turk engaged one of my men over the parapet with his bayonet and was then shot.[918]

By the end of the first day, the Allies had successfully seized a precarious foothold, but at great cost.[919]

From that moment on, the two armies dug in, and there began a fight of attrition, with assaults and counter-assaults, which left the Gallipoli field strewn with the corpses of thousands of men, nearly always unburied, decomposing under the hot sun of late spring and early summer. Each square metre was fought over by both sides with such fierceness that it would seem a few hundred metres gained in the vast landscape corresponded to a major victory. At the Third Battle of Krithiya, on 4 June, the Allies launched a major offensive with men from various nationalities, reinforced by the newly arrived 42nd Division.[920] After a terrific artillery bombardment and after one of the most murderous fighting, an advance of 600 to 700 yards was made and the summit of Achi Baba almost taken.[921] And what was gained at immense cost was soon lost when the Turks counter-attacked equally fiercely, and in 'a brave' fight recaptured that same spot for which the French, in particular, had paid the heaviest price.[922] Then, from this position the Turks 'enfiladed the British lines' in such deadly fire, both the British Royal Naval Division and the Manchester Brigade were forced to abandon the lines which they had also won at terrible cost.[923]

Most certainly the greatest Turkish disadvantage lay in artillery fire, whether in respect to the range of the guns or the lethal power of the shells; they also had both in much lower numbers. Turkish field batteries were only able to fire approximately 18,000 artillery rounds between early May and the first week of June.[924] Which was utterly negligible in comparison to the Allies, who could fire that amount in just a few days. In fact when they landed, the Allies pounded Turkish positions with 345 naval guns, without any interruption for long stretches of time, meaning that if each of them fired only fifty rounds, which was

---

[918] Papers of General Sir Ian Hamilton, File 17/7/33 – ms transcription of a letter written by Captain R W Whigham, 25 April – 10 May 1915, pp.5-6.
[919] Major Gregory Thiele: Why did Gallipoli Fail? 136.
[920] Major Edwin W. Dayton: Military Operations of the War; CH Vol 6; p. 503.
[921] Ibid.
[922] Ibid.
[923] Ibid.
[924] E.J. Erickson: *Ordered to die;* op cit, p. 89.

certainly far exceeded, that would mean they equalled in one day what the Turks fired in one month.[925]

Whilst on land, the French 75-mm guns caused terrible havoc on the Turks, naval gunfire was most effective on many instances against the Turkish flanks, such as on 6-8 May, when Turkish front-line trenches on the left flank at Helles were destroyed.[926] The effects of Ally shells were utterly overwhelming. The war correspondent Ashmead Bartlett writes:

> Turkish infantry moved forward to the attack, they were met with every kind of shell which our warships carry, from 15-inch shrapnel from the *Queen Elizabeth*, each one of which contains 20,000 bullets, to 12-inch, 6-inch, and 12-pounders. The noise, smoke, and concussion produced were unlike anything the imagination can picture, or words can paint. The hills in front looked as if they had been transformed into smoking volcanoes; the common shell throwing up great chunks of ground and masses of black smoke, whilst the shrapnel formed a white canopy above. Sections of the ground were covered by each ship all round our front trenches, and, the ranges being accurately known, the shooting was excellent.[927]

Technically, in order to offset their inferior firepower, and avoid the pulverising effect of Ally shells, the Turks had to attack by night. This option, though, was also closed to them. Operating close to the beaches, the Ally destroyers were still able to provide quite adequate support. For example, for the assault on the Turkish right on 28 June, the only support provided was by the light cruiser *HMS Talbot* and four destroyers.[928] Even this limited support destroyed the Turkish front-line trenches nearest the sea, allowing them to be easily occupied and the second line quickly overrun. A Turkish counter-attack that night was detected by the searchlights of the destroyers *Scorpion* and *Wolverine* and "was swept away by their guns."[929]

The violence of the Gallipoli Campaign is best caught by the participants who left us their accounts. Here, we have the accounts of men of the Scottish Borderers who were amongst the many nationalities who fought on 12 and 13 July. The aim of the Allies on those two days was to overwhelm the Turkish centre and left system of trenches from the sea at the mouth of the Kereves Dere to the main Sedd-el-Bahr-Krithia road, along a front of some 2000 yards.[930]

> 'On getting the order to go,' said Corporal Richardson of the *4th Bn. King's Own of Scottish Borderers*, 'we all scrambled over the parapet, and on

---

[925] For the figure of 345 guns, G.S. Patton: the Defence of Gallipoli; op cit; 25.
[926] R. Pelvin: *Suvla: Sea power at Suvla, August 1915: Naval aspects of the Suvla Bay landings and the genesis of modern amphibious warfare;* The Joint Imperial War Museum / Australian War Memorial Battlefield Study Tour to Gallipoli, September 2000; pp. 1-10; p. 2.
[927] E. Ashmed Bartlett: *The Uncensored Dardanelles*; op cit; p. 52.
[928] R. Pelvin: *Suvla: Sea power at Suvla, August 1915*; p. 3.
[929] Ibid.
[930] S Brown Editor: *War Record, 4th Bn. King's Own of Scottish Borderers;* John McQueen and Son, Galashiels; 1920; p. 35.

running a few yards round ourselves in dead ground. We doubled forward, and on reaching the crest of the ridge, were met by very heavy artillery fire, and we had many casualties. It was here that Lieut. Henderson fell, shot through the head. We went on to the first enemy trench, and jumped over it and made for the second trench. By this time we had got so far to the right that we never saw the communication trench, and practically the whole of No. 14 Platoon went straight on, as well as a number of No. 13. On reaching the second trench, some jumped in, while others lay on the parapet and fired into the trench. A number of Turks were showing fight, and were firing their rifles through the loop-holes. I saw a great many dead and wounded Turks lying in this trench. To the right the trench ran in the direction of another wood. In both these woods a number of men were running about, but whether friend or foe I did not know...'[931]

An officer wrote:

About four o'clock in the afternoon an order came in from Divisional Headquarters ordering an officer and all available men from the Battalion Reserve to report at Brigade Headquarters. It took this party, consisting of 49 all ranks, over an hour to reach the Brigade Headquarters owing to the continuous cry, "Clear trench for stretchers." The scenes outside the dressing stations were beyond description. Around each station were rows upon rows of stretchers-each containing what had been or, rather, what remained of a human being. The slightly wounded were waiting in long queues for treatment. What impressed one was the absolute deathly silence which prevailed over each station-not a word or a groan to be heard.[932]

The following day

At 4 o'clock, just as the first streaks of dawn were appearing over the Narrows, we were once more startled by a heavy burst of firing and loud cries of "Allah! Allah!" from the advancing Turks. This proved to be a more formidable attack, and Lieut- Colonel Pollok McCall ordered our party, along with some Scots Fusiliers, to get over the parapet and make for a part of the trench to our left front, from which reinforce signals had been sent up. The intervening space was covered successfully without a casualty. After jumping into the trench we looked round to see if we had come in among our own men, and there saw one of our Machine Gun Sections under Sergeant Jardine. The trench was literally filled with dead and wounded from practically every unit in the 52nd Division.[933]

The total casualties of that operation as stated by Hamilton 'in the French Corps were not heavy, though it is with sorrow that I have to report the mortal wound

---

[931] Ibid; p. 24.
[932] Ibid; pp. 28-9.
[933] Ibid; p. 31.

of General Masnou, commanding the 1st Division. Our own casualties were a little over 3000.'[934]

As the situation reached stalemate, a major offensive was decided for 6 August. It was, Erickson explains, an attempt by the Allies 'to break the deadlock by a comprehensive series of battles that ranged from Cape Helles up the peninsula to Suvla Bay (five-six miles north-west of the base established by the Australian and New Zealand troops at Anzac Cove).'[935]

In Western narrative, this phase of the campaign is simply and most frequently referred to as 'Suvla Bay,' but Hamilton's principal objective was not Suvla Bay at all but was actually the high ground dominating the ANZAC perimeter known as Sari Bair [Sarıbayır] Ridge (from Koja Chemen Tepe or 'Hill 971' to Battleship Hill) (see preceding map), whose capture would render the Turkish defences at Anzac untenable.[936] Suvla Bay, although an important component of the operation, was merely a secondary attack designed to widen and deepen the beachhead.[937]

Norman Wilkinson, who was on his way to witness the landing at Suvla Bay, left us wonderful colour sketches of the campaign, and here he gives an idea of the scale of the operation on arrival at Mudros:

> A distant view of Mudros, one of the finest natural harbours in the eastern Mediterranean, showed a vast concourse of ships, which grew in interest and numbers as we approached. Eventually, we steamed between lines of warships to an anchorage given us by signal. I have seen many reviews and naval pageants, but nothing to compare, in interest, with the assemblage of ships that we now witnessed. British battleships, French battleships, cruisers of both nations; a Russian cruiser, the Askold, which had incidentally been badly hammered in the war with Japan); destroyers, torpedo boats of all ages, submarines (some fresh with the laurels of raids in the Sea of Marmora), North Sea trawlers, tramp-steamers, transports, food-ships, motor-boats, Greek sailing vessels, motor-barges for landing troops, private yachts taken over by the Admiralty (the Admiral conducting operations being himself in one of these), and endless other craft gathered from everywhere to assist in the enormous undertaking of supplying food and munitions and to guard the routes to the various other bases established in the islands around. Towering above all the vessels could be seen the Aquitania and the Mauretania, their immense bulk dwarfing every ship in the harbour.[938]

---

[934] Ibid; p. 38.
[935] E.J. Erickson: *Gallipoli, the Ottoman Campaign;* Pen & Sword, Military; Barnsley, UK, 2010; p. 139.
[936] Aspinall-Oglander, *Military Operations Gallipoli, Vol. 2*, p. 182.
[937] E.J. Erickson: *Gallipoli;* op cit; p. 139.
[938] N. Wilkinson: *The Dardanelles;* Longmans, Green & CO; London 1915; pp. 5-6.

This phase of the Gallipoli Campaign has been described by this author in great detail elsewhere,[939] so here, focus is on some interesting aspects of the operation not examined there, most particularly the first landings at Suvla Bay; far to the north than the earlier landings in April. Two cruisers, the *Theseus* and *Endymion*, carrying large numbers of men and specially fitted with gangways over their sterns to ease the troops walk over into motor-lighters, were dispatched with destroyers towing motor-lighters full of troops to be at the point of disembarkation at about 11.30 p.m.[940] The flagship, on board of which was Wilkinson, steered a slightly more northerly course, in order not to interfere with these vessels in the darkness, and arrived in Suvla Bay at about an hour after the first landings, at 12.30 a.m.[941]

The operation started with great hopes. Following the landing, the Turkish response was 'desultory' rifle-fire from the shore, but of very low intensity as von Sanders, again, had got it completely wrong in regard to where the enemy would land. The effect of surprise in some places was total. By dawn the picture became clearer: on some of the beaches, the troops had landed from the cruisers and destroyers during darkness with hardly any opposition.[942] The shore had proven so favourable that the troops just jumped off the motor lighters onto the ground, and dashed forward inland, decimating the few Turkish defenders in the trenches, before advancing towards the dry salt lake some considerable distance.[943] However, gradually, the Turks regained control, and then began the Ally disaster. On some of the beaches, where water was deep, the landing host was met with intense fire, and suffered heavy casualties.[944] Turkish artillery likewise met the host with dense fire with shrapnel and high explosives; even a Turkish aeroplane dropped four large bombs.[945] In the meantime, more men were landing, whilst the Ally vessels, the *Talbot* and *Chatham* were now busy with their 6-inch guns pounding Turkish defences, seeking to protect the large transports which were now arriving with more troops and stores.[946] The Turks were responding with all they could muster — whether with artillery, machine guns, or rifle fire; and so stubborn was the Turkish defence that the Allies' hopes of capturing the ridges in the first day of operation were abandoned.[947] Artillery fire had also set the dry undergrowth into fire, which the wind pushed towards Ally direction. Dense Turkish sniper fire — and here, Wilkinson mentions both men and women snipers— came not only from Turkish advanced posts but also from behind Ally firing line, and great numbers of Ally officers fell.[948]

---

[939] For great literature, see Asmead Bartlett: *Dardanelles*; see also Sir Ian Hamilton: *Gallipoli*; *Current History*.
[940] N. Wilkinson: *The Dardanelles*; op cit; p. 11.
[941] Ibid.
[942] Ibid.
[943] Ibid.
[944] Ibid; p. 12.
[945] Ibid.
[946] Ibid; p. 13.
[947] Ibid; p. 14.
[948] Ibid.

On the participation of women snipers, we have this particular story by an Ally soldier:

> On another part of the field — north of the bay — a pretty harem lady sniper was, after considerable effort, rounded up and brought into the British lines. She cried and struggled, pointing pitifully to another part of the bush from whence she had been brought. At length a detachment of men allowed her to lead the way to the spot indicated by her, and here they found her child in a dugout, tastefully furnished. In a corner was a pile of identification disks, probably taken systematically from the necks of dead soldiers, and an almost endless supply of ammunition. Carefully hidden away was her yashmak, (veil,) which the men allowed her to take away.[949]

Sir Ian Hamilton was following the fierce fighting from his vessel command:

> The ponderous mass of the enemy swept over the crest and down the slopes, turning his right flank and piercing his lines below, so that his troops were driven "clean down the hill". It was a series of struggles "in which generals fought in the ranks, and men dropped their scientific weapons and caught one another by the throat... The Turks came on again and again, fighting magnificently, calling upon the name of God. Our men stood to it and maintained, by many a deed of daring, the old traditions of their race. There was no flinching. They died in the ranks as they stood.[950]

Ally artillery pounded mercilessly at the Turks; and Chunuk Bair (Conk Bayır), as Mustafa Kemal wrote, was turned

> Into a kind of hell. From the sky came a downpour of shrapnel and iron. The heavy naval shells sank into the ground, then burst, opening huge cavities all about us. The whole of Chunuk Bair was enveloped in thick smoke and fire. Everyone waited resignedly for what fate would bring.[951]

Asked by Kemal where his troops were, a commander replied, 'Here are my troops. Those who lie dead.'[952]

The Turks showed both heroism and a great spirit of chivalry:

> No nation could possibly have conducted warfare in a more above-board and clean-handed manner than the Turks [says Norman Wilkinson.] The fact that such qualities could be attributed to the Turk was a surprise to me, though naval officers generally have long regarded him as the gentleman of the Eastern Mediterranean. This is further borne out by his reported refusal to use poisonous gas when attacking... So brutally, however, have many of the theoretical usages of war been violated that the action of the Turk stands out in bright contrast, and shows that this much-

---

[949] Sidney A. Moseley: Pictures From Gallipoli; *Current History;* vol 3; October 1915; March 1916; p. 957
[950] Sir Ian Hamilton: Gallipoli Diaries; in Lord Kinross: *Ataturk*; p. 91.
[951] Lord Kinross: *Ataturk*; p. 92.
[952] Ibid.

maligned race retains a sense of honour which seems to be lacking in others who claim the right to lead the world in this direction.[953]

On the morning of 8 August the British and Australian regiments renewed the battle north of Anzac and gained some initial successes, although at considerable cost.[954] The delayed advance on their left from Suvla cancelled these successes and made the battle a costly waste of life.[955] British regiments, especially led by the Ghurkas, which had won one of the most vital hill crests, were shelled and decimated by their own warships, after which a fierce Turkish counter-attack annihilated several British regiments.[956]

Strong British attacks followed on 12 August and again a few days later. The fighting on those days of August was most certainly one of the fiercest and bloodiest of the First World War. Describing it as 'the Most Ferocious "Soldiers' Battle"' since the Crimean War, Ellis Ashmead Bartlett, writing for The London Morning Post, stated:

> In this extraordinary struggle, which took place almost under ground, both sides fought with utter disregard of life. The wounded and dead choked the trenches almost to the top, but the survivors carried on the fight over heaps of bodies.[957]

Further Allied attempts to break out of the beachhead were made, the last large-scale British attack taking place on 27 August and, like the rest, failed to achieve any decisive results.[958]

By the beginning of September, both sides had thrown so much at each other not much was left to do to make the other yield. In early September, Hamilton requested 95,000 additional troops, most certainly to break the deadlock, once more. This time Kitchener refused the request. Fighting went into a stalemate, and the British losses by now had reached proportions no longer easy to bear. On October 15, it was officially announced that the British had lost 90,899 men up to October 9 at the Dardanelles.[959] Other Allied nations had been bled, too. That same month, there was growing demand in the British press and parliament for the evacuation of Gallipoli. The Suvla Bay offensive was in fact the last throw of the dice, and despite all the means and numbers used on that occasion, it had been a failure.[960] To make matters worse, in November, an unusual and violent blizzard raged for several days, causing temperatures to drop sharply, freezing to

---

[953] N. Wilkinson: *The Dardanelles*; Longmans, Green & CO; London 1915; pp. 21-2.
[954] Major Edwin W. Dayton: Military Operations of the War; CH Vol 6; p. 504.
[955] Ibid.
[956] Ibid; p. 505.
[957] Ellis Ashmead Bartlett: How the British Lost Sari Bari; dispatch sent to The London Morning Post, dated Eastern Mediterranean, Aug. 19, 1915, and published on Sept. 1. See *Current History*, vol 3; Oct 15-March 16; p. 48 ff.
[958] E. J Erickson: *Ordered to Die*; op cit; p. 91.
[959] *Current History* vol 3; oct 1915-March 1916; p. 612.
[960] Major Edwin W. Dayton: Military Operations of the War; p. 505.

death hundreds of British soldiers and disabling thousands more.[961] There was only one course left: evacuation.

In great secrecy, in December the Anzac and Suvla positions were evacuated, and early in January 1916, the last British soldiers were carried away from the Cape Helles sector.[962]

> Thus ended one of the most original strategic conceptions of the 1st World War with the Turks again in possession of the peninsula.[963]

> The British failure at the Dardanelles [Kinross says] gave a momentary psychological lift to the Turkish people. For the first time within living memory they had won a victory against a European power. Few Turks perhaps nourished the illusion that the tide of foreign pressure had been turned, that the Empire could look forward to a period of resurrection and recovery. But at least there had been a flicker of light and hope to illuminate the dark defeatist horizon. There was life in the old Turk yet. The national qualities of tenacity and courage and pride had vindicated themselves once again, as in the glorious past, here on the ridges of the Gallipoli Peninsula.[964]

The official British account of the campaign attributed two important factors in their failure to win in Gallipoli. These were the determined fighting qualities of the Turkish soldiers and the brilliant leadership in the fifth army.[965] The British lost 205,000 men; of the 79,000 French, 47,000 became casualties.[966] Drawing the curtains on this campaign, Major Edwin E. Dayton of the American army, then wrote:

> When the allied forces were withdrawn from the peninsula, practically all the veteran Turkish troops were freed for use in Rumania or Asia Minor. Throughout the terrific fighting in April, June, and August, the Turks fought with magnificent courage and proved themselves equally valiant in both attack and defence. They treated captured and wounded prisoners with real kindness. The British Twenty-ninth Division (regulars) and the Australian and New Zealand Corps won imperishable fame.[967]

---

[961] Ibid.
[962] Ibid.
[963] E. J Erickson: *Ordered to Die*; op cit; p. 92.
[964] Lord Kinross: *Ataturk*; op cit; p. 96.
[965] E. J Erickson: *Ordered to Die*; op cit; p. 94.
[966] Ibid.
[967] Major Edwin W. Dayton: *Military Operations of the War*; op cit; p. 505.

4. The Russian Front 1916-Early 1917: A Series of Blunders and Good Fortune

Following the Russian gains and entry into Van to relieve the besieged Armenians in May 1915, the main counter-thrust by the Turks was led by Halil Bey, who with a fresh force of two divisions, on 20 July, was advancing up the valley of the Eastern Euphrates into the Alashgert again.[968] The Russians briefly retreated before gathering forces and counter-attacked ten days later, thus bringing Halil Bey's advance to a standstill.[969] A Russian division soon threatened Halil Bey's rear, causing him to retire quickly to the Muş plain.[970] By the Autumn of 1915, the Turks had been entirely removed from much of far eastern modern Turkey.[971] Thus, the campaign which had begun badly for the Russians had, by the end of 1915, turned entirely in their favour.

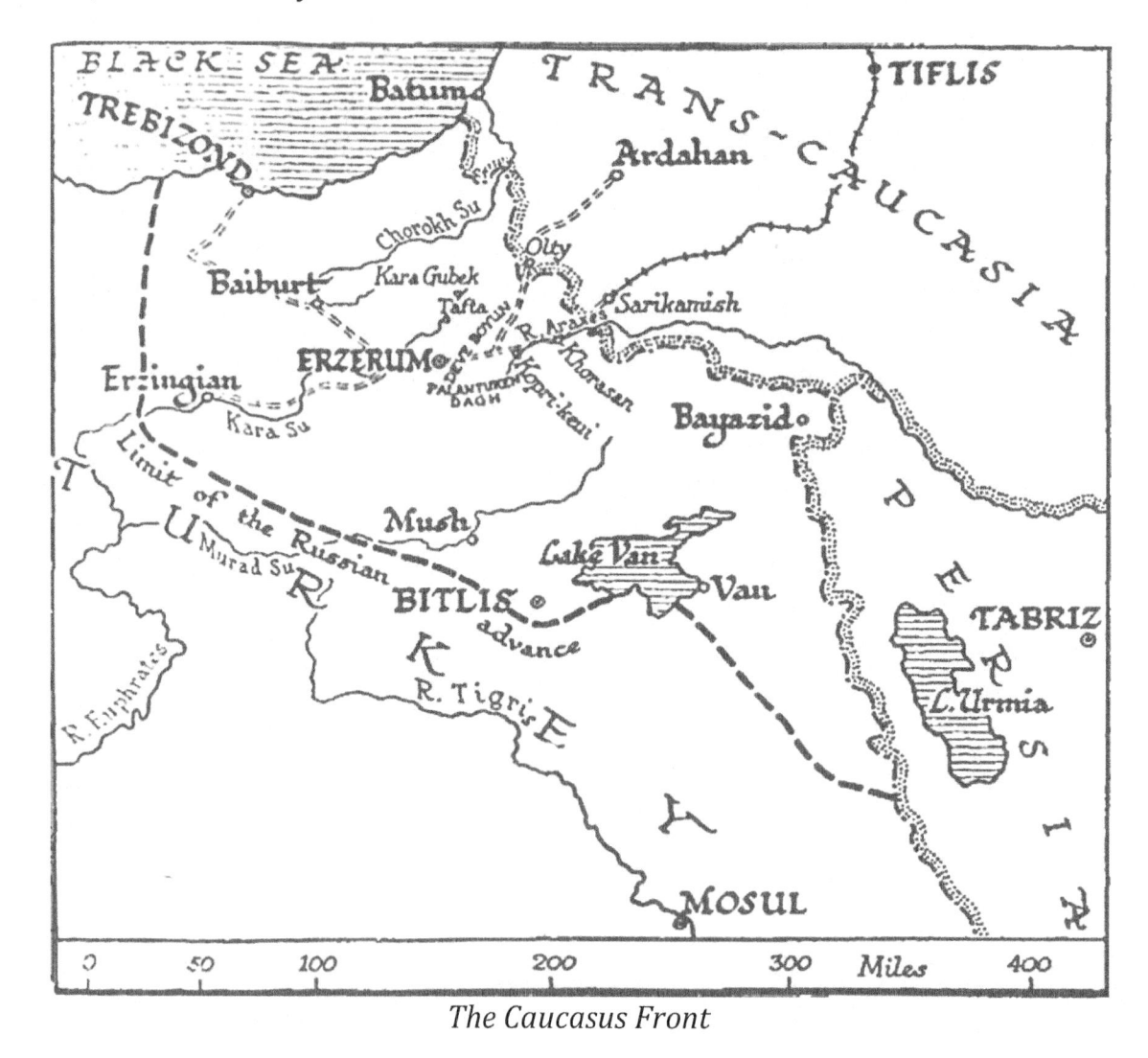

The Caucasus Front

---

[968] M. Philips Price: *War and Revolution in Asiatic Russia*, op cit; p. 62.
[969] Ibid.
[970] Ibid.
[971] Ibid; p. 63.

The exceptional mildness of the Winter of 1915-16 made it possible for the Russians to attack as early as January 1916. The weak Turkish 3rd Army, already thinned, suffering from lack of supplies, was everywhere pressed back.[972] Marching alongside the Russian-Armenian forces, Philips Price of the *Manchester Guardian* could see the effects of Turkish defeat:

> We saw many signs of the Turkish retreat, as we continued our way. Through the snow on the roadside protruded a number of objects, camels' humps, horses' legs, buffaloes' horns, and men's faces, with fezzes and little black beards, smiling at us the smile of death, their countenances frozen as hard as the snow around them. That was all that was left of the "Drang nach Osten"[973]

Following on their success, the Russians captured, on 16 February, Erzurum, which had to be evacuated by the Turks; then two months later, in the middle of April, the important port of Trabzon also fell to them.[974] The Turks managed to re-establish themselves on a line from Platana on the Black Sea through Zighana, north-west of Bayburt, and through Mamakhatun to Bitlis and along Lake Van.[975] However, they had suffered heavy losses, and their lines of communications were so bad, that further advance by the Russians was expected.[976]

Now, Enver, as Minister of War, once more, embarked onto another of those operations that had destroyed Turkish armies time after time since 1912: launching operations which on paper looked sublime, but in implementation repeating the same errors on and on again. Enver decided on possibly the most ambitious and most unrealistic pincer movement ever devised in the history of warfare. His plan was this:

While the 3rd Turkish Army would counter-attack from the west, the 2nd Army would be transferred from Thrace to the east, and attack the Russian left flank, south of lake Van, from the south.[977]

To see the madness of the operation has nothing to do with hindsight, but with a simple awareness of the logistics. How could an army be transferred such a long distance with hardly any adequate logistics, on land, in winter, and be ready for an offensive? Examples of past campaigns by early Ottoman sultans such as Mohammed II and Selim I in their campaigns east showed such realism, awareness of weather conditions and logistical constraints. For a proper understanding of the lines of communication, which are vital to this operation, it

---

[972] General von Falkenhayn: *The German General Staff and its Decisions 1914-1916;* Dodd, Mead and Company; New York; 1920; p. 295.
[973] M, Philips Price: *War and Revolution*; op cit; 168.
[974] General von Falkenhayn: *The German General Staff*; p. 295.
[975] Ibid; p. 296.
[976] Ibid.
[977] A. Mango: *Ataturk;* John Murray; London; 1999; p. 160.

is necessary to insert here a few words about the condition of Turkish railroads during the war as described by both Generals von Falkenhayn and von Sanders. All the railway sections which cut across the highlands of Asia Minor suffered from acute shortage of rolling-stock, building-materials, fuel, and both workmen and personnel.[978] Coal was supplied from Istanbul either not at all or in insufficient quantities, and even obtaining wood was near impossible in a country that is timber poor.[979]

For the troops to leave Thrace and reach the eastern front would take under the conditions a minimum of forty days.[980] After using the railroad to the Taurus and through the Amanus, would leave another 550 to 650 kilometers to be covered on foot.[981] The problem was in keeping this army supplied under terrible logistical strains. Not just that, bringing the army of Thrace and sending the Gallipoli survivors east meant that now there were about four armies (if the southern Mesopotamian/Arab front is also brought into the equation) competing for the meagre means and supplies.[982] Adding the usual delays to the difficulties, the transfer of the 2nd Army, which started in April, was not completed until August.[983] A vast movement of an army could not, of course, escape the attention of the Russians, and they were not going to wait until the two armies assembled. So they attacked the 3rd Army in June before the arrival of the 2nd; a counter-attack led by Fevzi Pasha on the heights south of Trabzon was successful, but without effect for lack of support.[984] Then, on 7 July, superior Russian forces launched a major offensive against the center, then the following day on the right of the 3rd Army.[985] The 3rd Army sought assistance from the 2nd, but the latter was still a long way too far, and only a weak detachment could assist; the result: Bayburt and Erzincan (Ersingyan) were lost.[986] Then for the following days in July the Russians focussed their attacks on the incoming 2nd Army, crippling it before it even got ready; whilst at the same time unleashing cavalry attacks against the 3rd until it was pushed down to the line Kighi-Ognot—south of Muş.[987]

The arriving 2nd Army became involved in some fighting, but with hardly any positive effect; only in few places was the front salvaged or prevented from entire collapse.[988]

Setting aside all the problems of logistics, mistiming, and the same errors already looked at (Kırkkilise, Luld Burgaz Sarıkamış, Egypt), there was a further flaw in

---

[978] General von Falkenhayn: *The German General Staff*; p. 56.
[979] Liman von Sanders: *Five Years*; op cit; p. 35.
[980] Ibid; 116.
[981] Ibid.
[982] Ibid.
[983] Ibid.
[984] Lord Kinross: *Ataturk*; op cit; p. 99; Liman von Sanders: *Five Years*; 117.
[985] Liman von Sanders: *Five Years*; op cit; p. 117.
[986] Ibid.
[987] Ibid.
[988] M. Uyar and E.J. Erickson: *A Military History of the Ottomans*; p. 261.

this latest Summer 1916 operation. Liman von Sanders captures the problem perfectly:

> The nature of the strategic flank attack implies a certain degree of surprise. But a surprise can hardly be expected, when the assembly of the army, as in this case, took three or four months. For a flank attack, moreover, a certain guaranty was needed that the enemy remained approximately in the same place where it was intended that the offensive should strike him on the completion of the long-winded approach.[989]

Von Sanders is absolutely spot on. The key to success in an enveloping operation, other than perfect synchronisation of different units/arms, is surprise. Without it, it is utter foolishness to risk an army as was done on this occasion. In great contrast with all this muddling-through which occurred from Kırkkilise through the First World War, and as a lesson of how it should be done, we have Dumlupınar in August 1922. On the latter occasion, the Turks moved a whole army from north to south so secretly, that the Greeks, who went dancing the night before in Afyon, awoke to find the Turks at their trenches.

To make things much worse, there was another huge factor which Enver and General Command completely set aside, and that had disastrous consequences for the Turks — a repeat of Sarıkamış in every single aspect. Enver had decided to bring the 2nd Army from Thrace to the Caucasus front to carry out a summer operation. This meant that two armies (at least, for one has to add the units from Gallipoli) were now concentrated in possibly the most devastated area on earth at the time. The conflict between Russians and Armenians on one side, against Turks and Kurds on the other, had simply ruined the whole eastern region of Turkey. Both sides simply devastated everything, burning all that stood; and in the ferocity of combat, no side showed any quarters; not just to the soldiers, but also to the civilians, who, in their hundreds of thousands either died, or fled, or were cleansed en masse. As he marched with the Armenians and Russians, Philips Price could see the destruction on a vast scale, difficult to imagine, and how all sections of the population, Muslims and Christians, paid the heaviest price,[990] even in times of peace, succumbing to famine, diseases, and extremes of weather:

> The scene changed, and we saw the charred ruins of a burnt village. The timber roofs of the half underground houses were all destroyed or fallen in. Under canvas sheets some Khurds with their families were trying to live, while they attempted to rebuild what had once been their homes. They were in rags, and their children naked. A few thin sheep were all that remained of their flocks. Yet there had been a prosperous village here before the war. Several of the inhabitants had owned 500 or 800 head of sheep and cattle. They used to wear gaudy dresses and ride on Arab horses, and their underground houses were little palaces of warmth and

---
[989] Liman von Sanders: *Five Years*; op cit; p. 119.
[990] M. Philips Price: *War and Revolution*; p. 168 ff.

> comfort. And all this disaster had befallen these people for no fault of their own. But it was only one example of the hundreds and thousands of villages, from Mesopotamia and Palestine to the Caucasus and Persia, where the same ruin and disaster had taken place. As I looked upon the scene I kept thinking of the work of restoration that will be required in all these countries, to say nothing of Europe, in the days after the war.[991]

In a land that had been scorched by both sides, men needed no enemy to kill them. With the extreme pressure of numbers, the utter inadequacies of supplies, thus the perfect Malthusian scenario, and the war ravaging the country, they would die by themselves. And this is precisely what happened. Mustafa Kemal perfectly captured this situation in his diary. Everywhere he looked people were starving to death:

> 7 November. Immediately after crossing Batman bridge, we saw a man lying on the road. He appeared dead from hunger. Another two, between the bridge and our bivouac. It seems they are refugees... After the bridge, two horses that have just died (men and horses are dying of hunger).
>
> 9 November. Saw many refugees on the road, going back to Bitlis. They are all hungry and wretched. A child, aged four or five years, abandoned by its parents and left to die, was dragging its feet 100 metres behind a man and a woman. I reproached them for not taking the child with them. "It's not ours," they said.[992]

Turkish troops starved or froze to death in their tens of thousands. Men were reduced to one third of their ration, whilst animals had no fodder whatsoever.[993] Poorly fed, poorly clothed, troops still in their summer uniforms, with foot rags for boots-High Command having learnt nothing whatsoever from Sarikamis or previous disasters-were caught by the harsh Eastern winter.[994] In the wake of blizzards, whole detachments perished in caves where they had sought shelter from hunger and freezing temperatures.[995] Then, to make things even worse, there came diseases, rampant in filthy military hospitals, defeating the efforts of Turkish and German medical staff.[996] Thus was destroyed the fine Eastern Turkish army.[997] And so were destroyed the armies that had come from Thrace and from Gallipoli. By early 1917, there simply was no Turkish army left to fend off any Russian offensive had this taken place in the Spring of 1917. But it did not. There was one major reason for this, and of course, modern and today's scholars are generally too cretin to understand it; one of them, Mango, says this:

> In the circumstances, Ottoman commanders did well to establish a front which held until the Russian Revolution led to the collapse of the Tsar's

---

[991] Ibid; p. 190.
[992] A. Mango: *Ataturk;* p. 163.
[993] Lord Kinross: *Ataturk*; op cit; p. 100.
[994] A. Mango: *Ataturk;* John Murray; London; 1999; p. 162.
[995] Lord Kinross: *Ataturk*; p. 100.
[996] Liman von Sanders: *Five Years*; op cit; p. 122-3.
[997] Ibid.

armies a year later. True, this defensive achievement fell well short of Enver's hopes: the Russians had realized their main objective of protecting the Caucasus, and had kept a large slice of Turkish territory. But, battered as they were, the Ottoman armies did not disintegrate, and, in the end, the morale of the Russians broke before that of the Turks.[998]

Of course it had nothing to do with what he says at all. It had nothing to do with collapse of Russian morale. Turkey, just as the Turkish survivors of the Caucasus, were saved by one fortuitous event, one of such events that no human can control, some might call it an act of providence, others might attribute it to chance: The Russian February-March Revolution of 1917 (or Petrograd Winter Revolution), the precursor to the Bolshevik Revolution. If it were not for this revolution that led to the Tsar's abdication (16 March, 1917) and infighting between Russians themselves, and had the Russians launched their Winter-Spring offensive in 1917, there would have been no Turkish defence to stand in front of them, and the way to Istanbul would have been open. It was this simple.

Here once more to understand things correctly, let's set aside the trash tellers of the likes of Mango and today's 'scholars,' and let's go back to contemporary sources.

Current History is by far the best depository of information on how the Petrograd Winter Revolution, and subsequently the Bolshevik revolution, unravelled and how this revolution impacted on the war and the gradual rising enmity between the West and Soviet Russia. The publication has possibly tens if not hundreds of articles written as events unfolded, most certainly the best source available to any historian. Volume 6 of the publication, dated, April 1917-Sep 1917, straight begins with a long outline on the early stages of the Revolution as in these extracts:

> RUSSIA IN REVOLUTION
>
> Abdication of Czar and Rise of a Republic in the Stronghold of Autocracy
>
> For weeks there had been protests and threats of a general strike, but it was the opinion of the liberal leaders in the Duma that, despite the wretched state of affairs, an open revolution was impossible, as the country realized that a revolution would seriously interrupt the work of the war and would be playing into the hands of those who had this very end in view... Demonstrations or cause disorders which might lead to interruption of the manufacture of munitions or paralyze the industrial activity of the city.
>
> Thursday, March 8. Strikes were declared in several big munitions factories as a protest against the shortage of bread.
>
> The troops exchanged good-natured raillery with the working men and women, and as they rode were cheered by the populace.
>
> Long lines of soldiers stationed in dramatic attitudes across the Nevsky Prospect, with their guns pointed at an imaginary foe, appeared to be

---

[998] A. Mango: *Ataturk;* p. 162.

taking part in a realistic tableau. Machine guns, firing rounds of blank cartridges.

Then came a clash between troops and police, which had fired at the people. The first serious outbreak came when the men of the Volynski Regiment shot their officers and revolted when they received an order to fire upon striking workingmen in one of the factory districts. Many more regiments went over, and many troops deserted, then began the fighting between troops on either side of the fence: pro or against the government. The troops did not know what to do, and their officers likewise hesitated which side to join in.

The revolt seemed to overspread all Russia simultaneously. Kronstadt, the great fortress and seaport at the head of the Gulf of Finland, joined the revolutionary movement without firing a gun.

Moscow joined in with enthusiasm, as did Odessa. Within twenty-four hours news came from all parts of Russia that city after city, fortress after fortress, provinces, towns, and villages were aflame with enthusiasm, and that the revolutionists were in control, with the soldiers and workingmen in fullest accord.

Czar Nicholas's abdication was announced on March 16. The document was signed at the town of Pskoff, where the train on which he was traveling toward Petrograd was halted early in the week.[999]

Following the revolution, the impact on the front was dramatic. There followed some fighting on the part of the Russians, but it was only brief, spasmodic, and without any effect. Everywhere Russian troops were seen dropping their arms or joining the revolution. The relations were no longer the same with the British and the French, and more importantly, the overall policy towards Turkey had changed. Possibly the most dramatic and most decisive shift of policy in human history was the following, again reported to us by *Current History* 6 (April 1917) just as it happened:

'NOT TO CLAIM CONSTANTINOPLE

That free Russia has no desire to annex Constantinople was the inference drawn from a statement made by the very influential Minister of Justice, Kerensky, that the Dardanelles should be "internationalized". This view was further strengthened in the declaration of Premier Lvoff on April 10, 1917:

"The new Government considers it its duty to make known to the world that the object of free Russia is not to dominate other nations and forcibly take away their territory. The object of independent Russia is a permanent peace and the rights of all nations to determine their own destiny."[1000]

So, now, Russia had abandoned the main reason for its war on Turkey!

---
[999] *Current History*, Volume 6; April 1917-Sep 1917; opening page, 10 and ff.
[1000] *Current History*; vol 6; p. 295.

The shift in policy was obvious on the Caucasus front as here caught by Philips Price, who was present at the scene as events were taking place:

> The (Russian) Staff of the Caucasus Army had decided in January (1917) that an offensive should be begun in the Spring, in conjunction with the British in Mesopotamia and Palestine, so as to complete the process of closing in on the Turkish Empire from three sides. The Expeditionary Force in Persia was to demonstrate before Kermanshah, and the Army Corps on the Armenian plateau was to do the same before Kharput and Erzinjan. An attacking force was to advance from the shores of Lake Urumiah, descend into the Mesopotamian plains, occupy Mosul and cut off the retreat of Halil Pasha, who would be at the same time pressed by the British from Bagdad. But the internal conditions of Asiatic Russia prevented the realization of this plan.
>
> When in the middle of February the Allied offensive against the eastern side of the Turkish Empire began, only a part of the programme was realized. Baghdad was occupied by General Maude, but the advance on Mosul had to be abandoned, and Halil Pasha's army was able to retire thither in safety. The news of the fall of Bagdad (to the British) reached Tiflis on March 12th (1917,) and created scarcely any interest whatever. People were thinking of other things. The Duma had just been dismissed, and news of disorders in Petrograd was secretly coming through. For the next two days there was the most intense suppressed excitement in the city. The Grand Duke Nicolas kept back all the telegrams from Petrograd, refusing to allow any to get out. Nevertheless the news was public property. One of the telegraph clerks knew the ciphers, and kept all the revolutionary societies informed.
>
> On the same day came the news that Tsar Nicolas the Second had abdicated; and then the flood was let loose. On the 16th and 17th March the whole fabric of the Russian imperial authority was in process of dissolution.
>
> Sunday March 18th was the great day in the Caucasus. The Revolution was then known to be secure in the Asiatic provinces; the old government had collapsed, and the hour for rejoicing had arrived. On the morning of that day I passed down the Golovinsky Street of Tiflis, and crossed the bridge over the Kura to the outskirts of the city. The streets were full of silent and serious people walking in the same direction. They were all going to a great mass meeting of the Caucasian people on the Nahalofsky square to welcome this great day in the history of Russia. In a large open space six raised platforms had been built, and round them was assembled a vast multitude composed of almost every element in the multiracial population of the Caucasus. There were wild mountain tribesmen, Lesgians, Avars, Chechens and Swanetians in their long black cloaks and sheepskin caps.

> The eddies of the wave of revolution had swept up into the recesses of the Caucasus, where they had lived sunk in patriarchal feudalism until yesterday. They had come across miles of mountain tracks out of curiosity to confirm the rumours they had heard, and in order to pay their humble tribute to the Russian Revolution.[1001]

Then, some pages down Philips Price adds:

> On March 20th, I left by the night train for Kars, as I hoped to see what effect the Revolution was having on the people of the Armenian plateau. When in the afternoon of the 21st, my train entered the Kars station, the platform was crowded with troops from the garrison, waving red flags and singing the Marseillaise. I recalled the days in February of the previous year, when I had been here and had seen the commencement of the great offensive against Erzerum. There was no talk then of anything but of war against the Turk, and every road was covered with troops marching to the slaughter. I also remembered how during the Summer I had talked to the soldiers on my way back from the Chorokh, and how I had despaired at their fatalism and helplessness in the clutches of the military machine, yet how I had felt their subconscious self trying to assert itself and speak for humanity. Now at last I saw the triumph of those hopes that had seemed so far off in the Summer. The grey-coated men who had marched like sheep to the slaughter were now raising the red banners of revolt against militarism and tyranny, and were sending a silent message to their Turkish brethren across the plateau to follow their example.[1002]

Obviously, the Turks could not and would not follow. They had to save their country from utter annihilation, which was not the case for Russia. More urgently, there was a foe tearing them further south, in Arabia.

*****

Starving Turkey

As E.K and S.J. Shaw remark, it is up to 6 million subjects of the Ottoman realm - Turks, Greeks, Arabs, Armenians, Jews, and others, who had been killed by a combination of revolts, bandit attacks, massacres and counter-massacres, famine and diseases, all made worse by devastating and brutal foreign invasions 'in which all the people of the empire, Muslim and non-Muslim alike, had their victims and criminals.'[1003]

Here, the focus is not on the direct killing or massacres; plenty of them having been cited already. Focus is on the starving of people. Let's set aside for a moment the destruction of hundreds of villages and devastation of the region by all sides:

[1001] M. Philips Price: *War and Revolution*; 278-282.
[1002] Ibid; 288.
[1003] S.J and E.K. Shaw: *History*; v2; 316.

Armenians, Turks, Russians and Kurds as described to us so well by Phillips Price. He was marching along the Russians and Armenians, and he could witness such a gigantic obliteration of towns, hamlets, farms, and the landscape in general.[1004] Let's look at the other two factors that contributed to the starving of hundreds of thousands, possibly millions.

1. The problem of food supplies in Turkey owed in large measure to the same problem already noted: the poor state of the means of transport.[1005]

Despite their great suffering, General Falkenhayn has words of praise for the Turkish allies:

> It is impossible to praise too highly the bearing of our allies; not even under these trying circumstances was there ever the slightest wavering. They steadfastly rejected the Entente's repeated attempts to reduce them, and saw to it that so far as was within their reach the Entente activities among the people should not develop into more serious mischief.[1006]

2. What the Allies were doing throughout the war, and this was the main reason for the Turks being starved, was the imposition of one of the worst blockades seen in the history of warfare. We have some instances here from contemporary sources

> Aug. 3, 1915; — It is reported from Petrograd that nearly 900 Turkish vessels have been burned or sunk in the Black Sea by Russian destroyers since the beginning of the war.[1007]
>
> Mid-late 1916, torpedo boat raids along the eastern coast of Turkish Anatolia are already known from the telegrams; more than 200 Turkish transports were sunk by us in that corner of the Black Sea, and about half of these ships carried freight.[1008]

Uyar and Erickson explain how, the British and Russian blockade ended the coastal shipping trade on which Turkey depended. This caused nearly twice more personnel and ten times more pack animals to be allocated to securing the poor lines of communication.[1009] The blockade caused millions of deaths through starvation, even if Turkey was an agricultural country.[1010]

[1004] M. Philips Price: *War and Revolution*; 168 ff.
[1005] General von Falkenhayn: *The German General Staff*; p. 298.
[1006] Ibid.
[1007] Chronology; *Current History*; vol 2; p. 1228.
[1008] Raiding on the Black Sea; By a Russian Marine; in *Current History*; Vol 4; Apr -Sep 1916; p. 136.
[1009] M. Uyar and E.J. Erickson: *A Military History of the Ottomans*; p. 273.
[1010] Ibid.

5. The Arab Front: From Initial Success to Final Disaster

Whilst 1917 brought the greatest relief from the east, to the south, on the contrary, the year was only a succession of disasters; the sources of all problems going back to the latter part of 1916. Initially the year 1916, began with a great success in the south, at Kut al-Amara, in modern day Iraq. This was one of the most crucial victories in Turkish warfare.

As already noted, early in 1916, the Russians had captured Erzurum, Trabzon and many other places, and were thrusting south, aiming to make junction with the British. The aim was for the two armies (the Russians and the British) to act in a simultaneous pincer movement, encircle and destroy the Turkish armies (the 3rd and 6th) and take Turkey out of the War. In more detail on this, the Russian capture of Trabzon was to serve them as a base for supply for another advance of at least fifty miles. South of Erzurum, in the Lake Van district, the advance had been equally rapid, and with the capture of Muş and Bitlis, the whole district was now under control, bringing the Russian centre within fifty miles of the Baghdad railroad.[1011] Whilst the Russian centre was advancing against Diyarbakır, the left was swinging rapidly around 'like the lash of a whip... pivoting on Bitlis and hurrying through Persia.'[1012] The objective of the Russian left was Baghdad, the point of junction agreed with the British, General Townshend's army, coming up from the opposite direction.[1013] Once the junction accomplished, at least two Turkish armies would be entirely destroyed, and the very survival of Turkey in question.[1014] There was only one problem: General Townshend was beaten and was now in great quandary at Kut al-Amara.

The campaign had begun well for him months earlier when he irresistibly swept north towards the Russians, initially defeating the Turks at Kut al-Amara in September, 1915, and was on his way up the Tigris Valley to Bagdad. By 22 November, he had victoriously fought his way nearly 100 miles northward to Ctesiphon, within eighteen miles of Baghdad.[1015] It was there that he was attacked and defeated by the Turks, suffered terrible casualties, and was forced to march back to Kut al-Amara, eighty miles to the southeast.[1016] His retreat, accomplished under extraordinary disadvantages, was hailed in England as a remarkable achievement, especially as he both escaped the Turks in pursuit and brought with him all his wounded.[1017] Still, this was such a severe defeat that the *Frankfurter Zeitung* wrote on 8 December that 'The Turkish victories in Mesopotamia had a speedy influence upon the attitude of the entire Persian Gulf

---

[1011] War Events from two viewpoints; in *Current History*; vol 4: Apr-Sep 1916; p. 47.
[1012] Ibid.
[1013] Ibid.
[1014] Ibid.
[1015] British Disaster at Kut-el-Amara; *Current History*, vol 4; p. 552.
[1016] British Defeat in Mesopotamia; Reports in *Current History* vol 3; Oct 1915-March 1916; p. 616.
[1017] British Disaster at Kut-el-Amara; *Current History*, vol 4; p. 552.

district.'[1018] The official Turkish communication of 2 December, speaking of the battle, was withheld from the public for two days by the British censor.[1019]

Townshend's defeat was all the more frustrating that the Russians were at the rendez-vous, waiting not far from Baghdad. General Townshend was blamed of rashness. On 8 December, J. Austen Chamberlain, Secretary of State for India, announced that reinforcements ordered to Mesopotamia before Townshend doomed advance to Ctesiphon began were already arriving at the front, and it was his move north before the army was complete that cost everything.[1020]

Now, this meant that the planned Russian-British rendez-vous had to be delayed, and the new plan for 1916 was this: Townshend would hold at Kut al-Amara where he was besieged by the Turks commanded by Nurettin, and once the British reinforcements broke through the Turkish lines and relieved him, with them, he would resume the same advance north, and this time meet with the Russians following their usual late Winter-Spring offensive (of 1916).[1021]

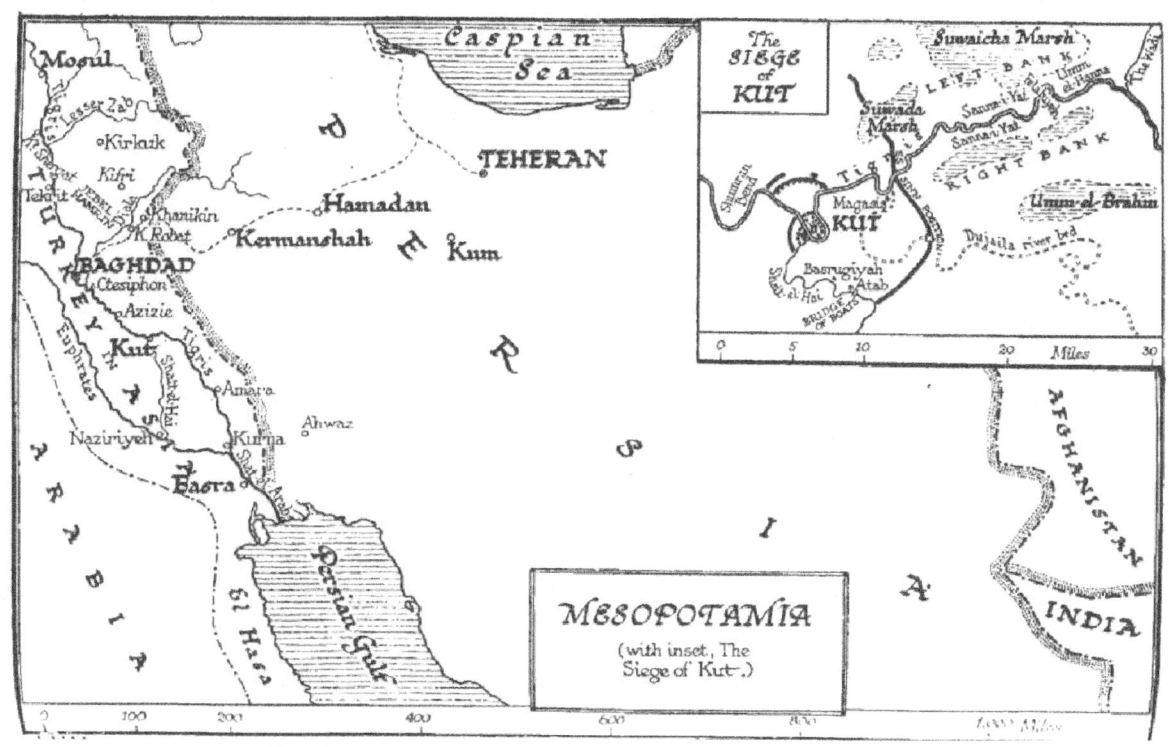

The 'Mesopotamian Front,' and the siege at Kut.

General Townshend, recognised that holding on to Kut al-Amara was of decisive importance; it commanded everything; besides offering possibilities for the

---
[1018] British Defeat in Mesopotamia; Reports in *Current History* vol 3; Oct 1915-March 1916; p. 616.
[1019] Ibid.
[1020] Ibid.
[1021] Significance of Events in Mesopotamia; in *Current History* vol 3; p. 877.

British to drive north, it blocked the advance of the 6th Turkish Army, which, like the British, depended on water transport.[1022] He expressed this thus:

> So long as his steamers and lighters could not pass under my guns, so long should I save the whole of Mesopotamia from being overrun, and from assuming the offensive and driving the British from Mesopotamia.[1023]

So, it was on the success or the failure of the siege that everything depended. As a result, General Townshend took the sternest measures to sustain the Turkish siege:

> It will have been seen in my defence orders that I had ordered all the inhabitants to be turned out of the town, but, on the intercession of Sir Percy Cox on behalf of the women and children, who, he declared, would perish in the desert from hunger and the bullet of the desert Arab, I changed my mind. When first Sir Percy came to me to ask me not to turn the inhabitants out I told him that it was my duty as the commander of a place about to be besieged to do so. "Very well," he replied, "but I must tell you that all the women and children will perish on the way." I considered that this would have a disastrous political effect in Mesopotamia amongst the Arab population. I always bitterly regretted my clemency.[1024]

Subsequently, it ought to be noted, Townshend would become a great friend of the Turks in gratitude for the way they treated him in captivity. But now, he was giving no quarters, indeed. Even though the Turks lacked adequate resources for a siege, Colonel Nurettin (Sakallı) Bey (who was subsequently replaced by Halil [Kut] Pasha (Enver's uncle) on January 10 in order to reap the laurels of the victory won by Nurettin) (yet another example of sickening Eastern nepotism) still blockaded the British quite efficiently.[1025] Nurettin, from the accounts of General Nixon who had dislodged him from Kut al Amara months earlier in September 1915, was a master at defensive strategy. General Nixon fell in awe with his defensive structures and organisation:

> Three or four months of preparation, had been converted into a formidable position. On the right bank the defenses extended for five miles southward along some mounds which commanded an extensive field of fire. The river was blocked by a boom composed of barges and wire cables commanded at close range by guns and fire trenches. On the left bank the intrenchments extended for seven miles, linking up the gaps between the river and three marshes which stretched away to the north. The defenses were well designed and concealed, commanding flat and open approaches. They were elaborately constructed with a thoroughness that missed no detail. In front of the trenches were barbed wire entanglements, military pits, and land

---

[1022] Major General Vere Ferrers Townshend: *My Campaign;* The James A. McCann Company; vol 2; 1920; p. 3.
[1023] Ibid.
[1024] Ibid; pp. 38-9.
[1025] M. Uyar and E.J. Erickson: *A Military History of the Ottomans*; p. 257.

mines. Behind were miles of communication trenches connecting the various works and providing covered outlets to the river, where ramps and landing stages had been made to facilitate the transfer of troops to or from ships, while pumping engines and water channels carried water from the river to the trenches.[1026]

So, Nurettin had not only very adequately besieged Kut, he had also made his position virtually impregnable against the troops coming to relieve Townshend and to advance with him north.[1027] Following that, he submitted the place to intense artillery fire. General Townshend tells us:

> The enemy's guns shelled the fort violently the whole afternoon of 7th December... On this date a letter was sent by Nureddin, asking me to avoid useless bloodshed by laying down my arms. He pointed out that my troops were enfeebled and weak in numbers, and it only needed a serious effort on the part of his numerically superior forces to overwhelm us. He complained also that the occupation of the town of Kut, thus exposing peaceful inhabitants to the horrors of war, was against the laws of civilised warfare. I sent a reply that I had no answer to give to such an absurd demand as the laying down of my arms. But I thanked him for his courtesy in conforming to the usual custom in war in summoning the commandant or governor of a town to surrender before starting bombardment of it. I observed that he was curiously and extraordinarily in error in imagining that the defence of a town was against the laws of civilised war; that there was no battle of any consequence in Europe and no siege which did not include the attack or defence of a town or village; and that his friends the Germans not only always occupied towns and villages, but did so in a manner peculiar to themselves.[1028]

In the meantime, the British relieving forces, led principally by General Aylmer sought to reach General Townshend. They stubbornly tried to break through the Turkish lines for much of the early Winter of 1915-1916, at heavy cost, losing 3000 men in one encounter on 11 January.[1029] It would seem from the accounts of General Townshend and the messages from the relieving forces that the weather caused havoc to the communication lines and the movement of the convoys and heavy artillery.[1030]

[1026] The Battle That Won Kut-el-Amara By General Sir John Nixon; *Current History*; vol 4; 554.
[1027] Major General Vere Ferrers Townshend: *My Campaign;* p. 25 M. Uyar and E.J. Erickson: *A Military History of the Ottomans*; p. 257.
[1028] Major General Vere Ferrers Townshend: *My Campaign*; p. 27.
[1029] Significance of Events, CH; 3; p. 877
[1030] Major General Vere Ferrers Townshend: *My Campaign*; p. 148.

Under tightening grip and bombardment, the defence of Kut was weakening daily despite Townshend's efforts and tenacity. The Turks benefited from the support of the local Arab population, whilst at the same time, Muslims amongst the Indian troops serving the British either deserted or blew off their trigger fingers in order to get themselves out of the fighting.[1031]

Doggedly, the British tried to break through Turkish lines and reach Townshend, only to pay heavy price. On 14 April 1916, it was admitted that the Tigris Army had lost 8,100 men up to that time.[1032] Then, more attempts to break through were made, and always at heavy cost.[1033] As a last resort, the British sought to bribe Turkish officers, which likewise failed; and so, in the end, Townshend was forced to surrender unconditionally on 29 April.[1034] The surrender of 13,309 British forces was received with dismay in Britain, it being the largest surrender of a British army between Yorktown in 1781 (during the American War of Independence) and Singapore in 1942 (to the Japanese in the Second World War).[1035] The Turkish official report states that in addition to General Townshend, were captured General Povna, Commander of the Sixth Infantry Division; General Dabmack, Commander of the Sixteenth Brigade; General Hamilton, Commander of the Seventeenth Brigade; Colonel Evans, Commander of the Eighteenth Brigade, and an officer named Smith, Commander of Artillery.[1036] Altogether 514 British officers were captured; and quite considerable at the time, $5,000,000 in cash was seized.[1037] But this was not the main accomplishment. Precisely at the time the British surrendered in April 1916, the Russians were obliterating the Turks further north, and had moved so much down south that they were just within eighty miles of Baghdad 'Sufficiently near for a detachment of Cossacks to make a detour and join hands with the British at Kut-el-Amara.'[1038] When news of the British surrender came, the Russians fell back.[1039] Never had final victory been so near. The following two maps show how close the Russians and British came to make junction if the British had won at Kut al-Amara.

The Turkish victory at Kut al-Amara once more delayed the great Ally scheme of taking Turkey out of the war and carving it up right then. Yet, the Allies were fully confident of that. Writing at the time, James B. McDonald held:

[1031] Ibid; pp. 55; 38-39.
[1032] British Disaster; CH vol 4; p. 553.
[1033] Ibid.
[1034] M. Uyar and E.J. Erickson: *A Military History of the Ottomans*; p. 257.
[1035] Ibid; p. 249.
[1036] British Disaster at Kut-el-Amara; in Current History vol 4; Apr Sep 1916; p. 551.
[1037] Ibid; p. 589.
[1038] James B. Macdonald: The Russian campaign in Turkey, *Current History;* vol 4; p. 1087; (see the full account of Russian progress) ibid pp. 1084-ff.
[1039] Ibid.

But when the Allies again get to business in this theatre of war we may look for dramatic happenings, and the early elimination of Turkey from the war need not surprise us.[1040]

MacDonald was right (as the French would say, it was only parti remise), but only up to a point. Indeed, as we would see below, the British would recapture Kut al-Amara, sweep aside the Turks, and begin marching north, once more in order to make junction with the Russians. With one major caveat, though: this time it was the British who were at the Rendez-vous and the Russians who were missing; the reason: The Petrograd Winter Revolution already looked at above and its effects. And this third delay would postpone Turkey's removal and carving up by more than another year.

How Turkey Nearly Got Squeezed out of the War Except for the Victory at Kut al Amara

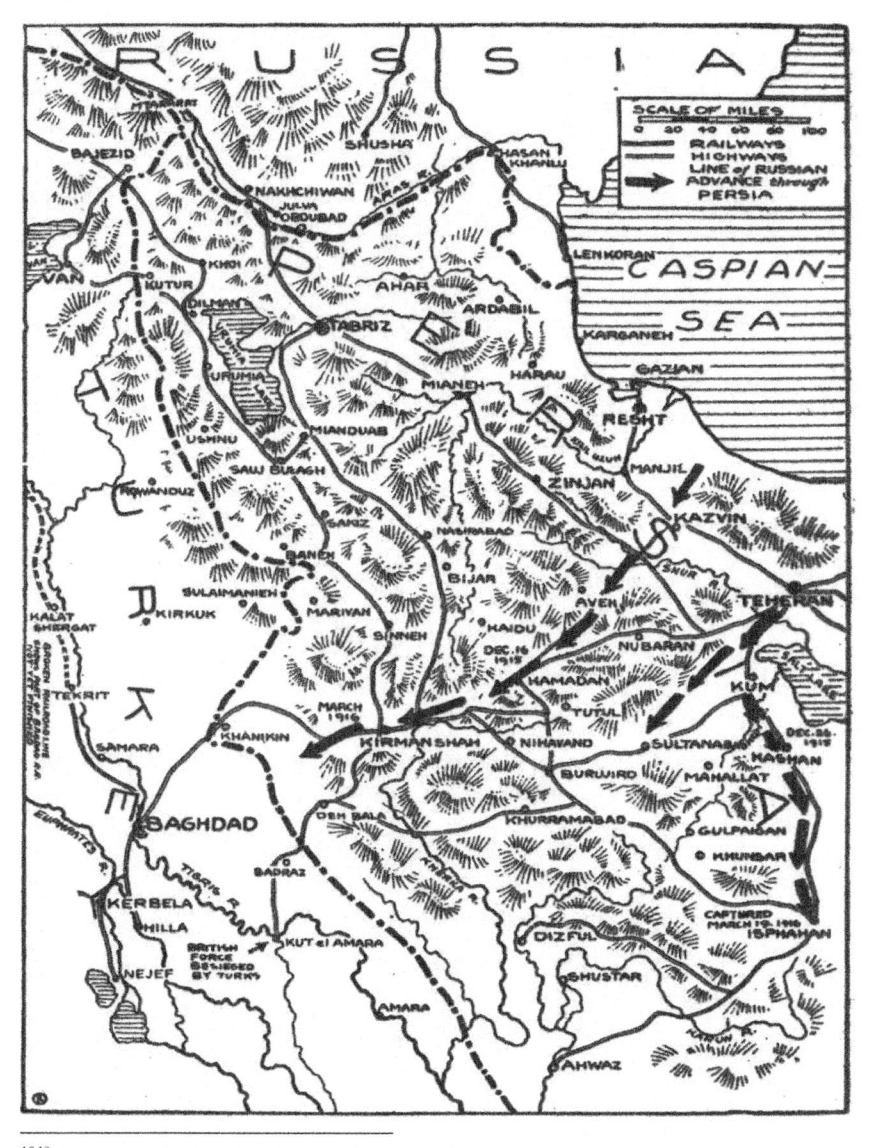

This map shows the early 1916 advance by the Russians, and how they came near Baghdad.

[1040] James B. Macdonald: The Russian campaign in Turkey, CH vol 4; p. 1088.

This Map shows how the British were trying to break through the siege, and move north to make junction with the Russians.

The Rising of the Shereef of Makkah

The rising of the Shereef of Makkah against the Turks began in October 1916. Here some three points first need to be made:

Firstly, the rising of the Shereef was the culmination of the concept of Arabism, a concept that had been cultivated by Arab Christians with support by Western countries, Britain and France primarily. Arab nationalists worked under Western umbrella from Paris and London and subsequent founded the Ba'ath parties. Amongst these early Nationalists can be cited the newspaper owner, Louis Sabunji; the writer Nagib Azoury; and Edmond Rabat, another 'intellectual.'[1041] It was Arab nationalism that sowed the anti-Ottoman seeds. So, the Shereef should

---
[1041] See: S. Lavan: Four Christian Arab Nationalists: A comparative Study; *The Muslim World*; vol 57; pp. 114-25; Caesar. E. Farah: Great Britain; Germany and the Ottoman Caliphate; in *Der Islam;* vol 66; pp. 264-88.
George Antonius: *The Arab Awakening,* New York, G.P. Putnam's Sons, 1946; pp. 101-11, and subsequently.

not be singled out and blamed for everything; the corroding spirit of Arab nationalism had already gained a lot of ground, including amongst Muslims, especially in Syria, Palestine, Egypt, and Iraq. The Ottoman decline and the mismanagement by local officials did not help either. This, combined with the works of various Western secret agencies, made the task of the Turks impossible. Mustafa Kemal, as brilliant as ever, and far ahead of everyone as ever, was able to read the situation very quickly when he arrived in Syria. In a letter he sent to his doctor in Istanbul, Rasim Ferit (Talay), he wrote:

> I have studied Syria thoroughly once again and visited the front line... My conclusion is that Syria is in a pitiable state. There is no [overall Turkish] civil governor or commander. Instead, there is an abundance of English propaganda. English secret agents are everywhere. The people hate the government and look forward to the arrival of the English as soon as possible. The enemy is stronger than we are in men and equipment. We are like a cotton thread drawn across his path.[1042]

Under this situation the best course of action the Turks could adopt was either to counter the corrosive spirit, or to withdraw north before it was too late and protect safer grounds or Turkey itself. The problem was: Enver, Cemal, Talaat, von Sanders, and everyone else involved at the top echelons, incompetent as they had been throughout the war, understood nothing of the situation. They adopted neither of the two solutions, and even when the cause was lost in the early autumn of 1918, they kept pouring men and defending lines and territory which could not be defended.

Secondly, true, there was a climate of corrosion working amongst Arabs, however, it is a great mistake to believe, as portrayed by Western propaganda, then or today, or as found in most Western history works,[1043] that the whole Arab nation betrayed the Turks. Far from it, in fact, as will be shown in detail under a separate heading to follow. Most of the Arabs, as any serious study with statistics, as done by Uyar in particular, shows that either they sided with the Turks, or at worst remained neutral.[1044] Had in fact leaders such as Cemal, rather than plunging headlong into wasteful, meaningless, military operations, stayed behind in Syria and prepared reliable alliances, just as Selim I did centuries earlier, Syria would have become the place where the Allies would have been broken, for the Syrian Muslims, years later, would prove a real hard nut to crack when they rose in rebellion against the French.

Thirdly, here, it is not that the Shereef was a traitor by nature. Far from it. Like nearly every true Arab, he was a man of honour who believed in agreements.

[1042] Bayur, Hikmet, *Atatürk Hayatı ve Eseri* (Atatürk's Life and Work), Vol. I (from his birth to his landing in Samsun), AKDTYK, Ankara 1990, 156.
[1043] See, for instance Andrew Mango, who in his book on Ataturk, only refers to Arabs as traitors, or at best, cowards.
[1044] M. Uyar: Ottoman Arab Officers between Nationalism and Loyalty during the First World War; in *War in History*; Sage Publishing; vol 20; No 4 (2013); pp. 526-44.

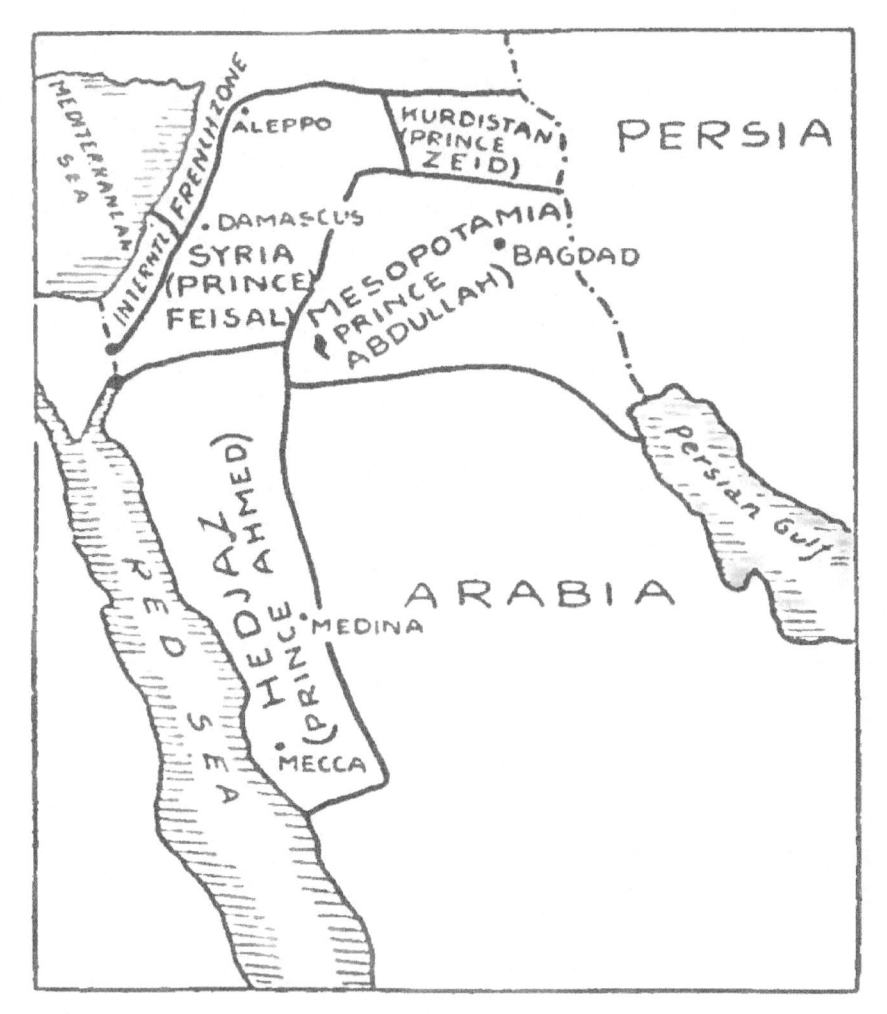

What the British offered the Shereef of Makkah

What the British offered him was quite attractive indeed: an independent Arab nation, which could arise stronger (in view of Ottoman decline), and the whole of it ruled by his four sons. His decision made good sense. His only mistake was in repeating the same Arab mistake since the Middle Ages, of always being fooled in the same manner, history seeming to teach them nothing.

British Victories at Kut al-Amara, Baghdad, and Jerusalem

The Shereef's rebellion cost the Turkish-German alliance very dearly. Led, misled, instructed, and duped, all at once, by captain T.E. Lawrence, the Bedouins indulged in raids and sabotage that crippled Turkish defence and supply lines.[1045] This coincided with the British launch of their new Iraq-Palestine campaign meant to take Turkey out of the war by early 1917. After considerable preparations, on 13 December 1916, General Maude, now in command, launched a new advance on Kut al-Amara along the right bank of the Tigris.[1046] The British had put together a powerful force of 120,000 men, besides a considerable fleet

---
[1045] M. Uyar and E.J. Erickson: *A Military History of the Ottomans*; p. 253.
[1046] Regarding General Maude's campaign, see E. F. Eagan: *The War in the Cradle of the World* (London, 1918); Kermit Roosevelt: *War in the Garden of Eden* (New York, 1919); Sir Charles Collwell: *Life of Sir Stanley Maude* (London, 1920); E. Betts: *The Bagging of Bagdad* (London, 1920); E. Candler: *The Long Road to Bagdad* (London, 1920); C. Cato (pseudonym): *The Navy in Mesopotamia* (London, 1917); F. Maurice, "The Mesopotamian Campaign," in *Asia*, Volume 18 (New York, 1918), pp. 933-936.

specially adapted for river work.[1047] General Maude registered considerable progress, smashing Turkish defences; the British establishing themselves on the Shatt-al-Hai, a canal which enters the Tigris above and below Kut from the south.[1048] After a spell of bad weather, early in January 1917, when conditions improved, the advance resumed, and on 9 and 10 January, Turkish positions northeast of Kut were captured after fierce fighting.[1049] The Turkish positions were commanded by yet another able officer, Colonel Kâzım Karabekir, who had earlier fought successfully on the southern sector in Gallipoli.[1050] He would play even greater roles subsequently. Against overwhelming power the Turks stood their ground, General Maude noting in his account of the campaign how 'the enemy lost heavily, both from our bombardment and in violent hand-to-hand encounters.'[1051] Only after two months of strenuous fighting, early in February did the British manage to drive the Turks from the right bank of the Tigris in the neighbourhood of Kut.[1052] The capture of the Sannaiyat position, in particular, was only accomplished at great cost, in which, the British infantry, closely supported by heavy artillery fire 'displayed great gallantry and endurance against a brave and determined enemy.'[1053]

It was a fight to the finish, and just as at Gallipoli, the trenches were choked with corpses, and the open ground, where attacks and counterattacks had taken place, was covered with them.[1054] At the end of the third week of February 1917 Kut al-Amara fell at last, and the remaining Turkish troops retreated further north.

Between 26 February, when Kut fell, and 8 March 1917, the British had advanced nearly a hundred miles.[1055] The previous day, on 7 March, a British cavalry unit found the Turks in position on the Diala River, eight miles outside Baghdad. As the river was unfordable, General Maude withdrew his cavalry and brought his infantry into action.[1056] Baghdad could not be effectively defended, and any defence of it would lead to its destruction, so the Turks withdrew north. On 11 March, British forces entered Baghdad, which was followed on the 19th by the capture of Feluja, thirty-five miles west of Bagdad.[1057] The occupation of Feluja, and with Nasariyeh already in British hands, gave them control over the middle Euphrates from both ends.[1058] During the remainder of the month, General Maude states, minor operations were undertaken on the Diala districts, 'pending the

---

[1047] The British Advance on Bagdad and Jerusalem; *Current History*; vol 6; p. 44.
[1048] Ibid.
[1049] Ibid.
[1050] A. Mango: *Ataturk*; John Murray; London; 1999; p. 166.
[1051] General Maude's Official Narrative of the Fighting From August, 1916, to March, 1917; *Current History*; vol 6; p. 544.
[1052] The British Advance on Bagdad and Jerusalem; CH vol 6; p. 44. General Maude's Official Narrative: p. 546.
[1053] General Maude's Official Narrative of the Fighting From August, 1916, to March, 1917; p. 548.
[1054] Ibid.
[1055] The British Advance on Bagdad and Jerusalem; CH; vol 6; p. 45.
[1056] Ibid; p. 44.
[1057] General Maude's Official Narrative; p. 550.
[1058] Ibid.

arrival of the Russian forces advancing from Persia.'[1059] He waited needlessly. The Russians were not advancing for the simple reason that precisely as the British were making their breakthrough northbound, the Russians had opted out of the war due to the beginning of the Bolshevik Revolution, and the Caucasus front, as noted above, had gone silent or more precisely passive. This was possibly one of the greatest fortunes of Turkish history, for precisely then, on 7 March, the news was received that the advance guards of the British forces marching through Palestine from Egypt were within fifteen miles of Jerusalem.[1060]

No sooner the Russians opted out, the Turks withdrew their remaining troops from the Caucasus and sent them south to oppose the British.[1061] This had the immediate effect of checking the progress of the latter until they too, could be reinforced, and the conflict reverted to trench warfare.[1062] As W.T. Massey, the London Times War correspondent who was with the Egyptian army, could describe in March 1917, the campaign developed into an atrocious, and costly war of attrition.[1063] The biggest battle in all Palestine's long history was fought at Gaza by bodies of troops on both sides much larger than any that had taken part in the countless campaigns of the Holy Land, with the use of the latest in modern weaponry, including even tanks.[1064]

The stalemate lasted for months until the autumn of 1917; then began the final act. General Allenby launched the attack with a terrific artillery bombardment, the worst since Gallipoli, it was said. General Allenby's official report said:
> Oct. 30 British and French naval forces commenced to co-operate by firing on the Gaza defenses, and on the road and railway bridges and the railway junction at Dir fe'ineid, [eight miles north of Gaza.][1065]

The capture of Gaza on Nov 7, on the coast and fifty miles southwest of Jerusalem, was made after a nine-mile "drive."[1066] Askalon was taken on Nov. 9. Six days later the British occupied the junction of the Beersheba-Damascus railway, from which ran a line to Jerusalem.[1067] The Turks evacuated Jaffa leaving the town in good order. When the Anzac troops entered on Nov 17, they were met by European residents there. They found convents and hospitals undamaged, and on the road to Ramleh came across a thriving Jewish farming colony.[1068]

[1059] Ibid.
[1060] The British Advance on Bagdad and Jerusalem; CH vol 6; p. 45.
[1061] *Current History*; Part two: vol 6: The War in Western Asia By James B. Macdonald; p. 160.
[1062] Ibid.
[1063] The British in the Promised Land. W. T. Massey, war correspondent with the Desert Column in Egypt, wrote to *The London Times* under date of March 20, 1917.
[1064] Ibid.
[1065] In *Current History*, vol 7; part two; p. 100.
[1066] The Taking of Jerusalem in *Current History*; Vol VII Oct 1917-march 18; Part two; p. 94.
[1067] H. Pirie-Gordon: *A Brief Record of the Advance of the Egyptian Expeditionary Force* (London, 1919); W.T. Massey: *Allenby's Final Triumph* (London, 1920); P.E. White: *The Disintegration of the Turkish Empire* (London, 1920); J. Bourelly: *Campagne d'Egypte et de Syrie contre les Turcs* (Paris, 1919).
[1068] W. T. Massey: The British Conquest of Palestine; *Current History*, vol 7; part two; pp. 98-9.

Following the fall of Jaffa, the occupation of Jerusalem became a foregone conclusion. The end of November saw Allenby closing in on the city from the north and west.[1069] Allenby's strategy had forced the Turks to carry out their defensive fighting for Jerusalem on the hills some distance from the city.[1070] The emotions preceding the capture of the city were felt throughout both Christendom and the Liberating/Crusading army. Major Vivian Gilbert, who was part of Allenby's army, in his appropriately titled: *The Romance of the Last Crusade*, wrote:

> All around me lay the soldiers of the last crusade, resting, waiting for tomorrow's dawn. Jerusalem, the sacred city of the world, was so near that one could hear the clocks striking; and, if one remained very still, one could almost imagine he could feel her heart beating too. In a few hours we should be marching forward to free her after four centuries of Turkish misrule and oppression. How totally inadequate are words to tell of such an adventure as this![1071]

General Allenby's official report stated:

> I entered the city officially at noon Dec. 11 with a few of my staff, the commanders of the French and Italian detachments, the heads of the political missions, and the Military Attaches of France, Italy, and America.[1072]

On hearing the news of the Allies success, solemn Te Deum masses were held in celebration at cathedrals in London, Paris, and other centres, and profound pleasure was expressed at the Vatican.[1073] Lloyd George had asked Allenby to capture Jerusalem as a Christmas present for the British nation. He had done so.[1074] Christendom was jubilant; Allenby now took the status of the most successful, if not the greatest, Crusader of all times.[1075] Allenby in his triumphant entry into the Holy City on 11 December 1917, declared: 'Today the wars of the crusades are completed.'[1076]

> 'When Prophecies Come True!' then wrote major Vivian Gilbert: 'At last Jerusalem was in our hands! In all the ten crusades organised and equipped to free the Holy City, only two were really successful, — the first led by Godfrey de Bouillon, and the last under Edmund Allenby.'[1077]

[1069] The Taking of Jerusalem in *Current History*; vol 7; Oct 1917-March 18; Part two; p. 95.
[1070] Major Vivian Gilbert: *The Romance of the last Crusade, with Allenby to Jerusalem*; D. Appleton and Company; New York; 1923; p. 151.
[1071] Ibid; p. 152.
[1072] The Taking of Jerusalem in *Current History*; vol VII; Oct 1917-March 18; Part two; p. 92.
[1073] Ibid.
[1074] Lord Kinross: *Ataturk*; p. 108.
[1075] R.E.C. Adams: *The Modern Crusaders* (London, 1920).
[1076] In E. Siberry: *The New Crusaders*; Ashgate: Aldershot; 2000; p. 95.
[1077] Major Vivian Gilbert: *The Romance of the last Crusade*; op cit; p. 171.

Before dawn on 26 December' the Turks launched a fierce counter-attack trying to recapture the city.[1078] Eight times they threw themselves against the 60th Division holding the Nablus road, but the British were strongly massed there, and responded with heavy fire, which decimated the Turks and forced them to retreat well beyond Ramallah to the north and out of artillery range of Jerusalem to the east.[1079]

*****

Arab Stand

> But once the Ottoman armies were defeated, the Bedouins descended on them like vultures, while the Arabs in the towns, who had given little trouble to the Ottoman government, hastened to change sides.[1080]

The substance of these lines by Mango, i.e. Arab 'Vultures' backstabbing the Turks, is not just common to him, but is found in nearly every work on that phase of history,[1081] or as is well known in films such as Lawrence of Arabia. Comparing Arabs to vultures is in fact one of the many forms and manners they are depicted these days (2020). If anyone wants to have an idea of even worse depictions, all they need to do is to pick a piece of news relating to Arabs on the internet and delve in the comments if they have the strength to read beyond the first two.

No need to dwell on this matter here as this author has already dealt with it in another of his works;[1082] our concern here is with this phase of history, and on how the British won some Arab support. From the very beginning of the war, British authorities orchestrated a propaganda campaign to win hearts and minds of the Arab rank and file, particularly focusing on the enmity between Arabs and Turks; that the Turks were Mongols who had destroyed Arab civilisation; that the Turks had slain many devout Arab figures, and so on.[1083] Indeed, British intelligence not only built relations with the secret Arab nationalist organisations well before the war, it also recruited many Orientalist scholars (such as Sir Sykes), and created an intelligence establishment better known as the Arab Bureau in Cairo.[1084] Soon these institutions and Arab nationalists worked

---

[1078] Ibid; p. 182.
[1079] Ibid.
[1080] A. Mango: *Ataturk*; p. 180.
[1081] T.E. Lawrence, *Seven Pillars of Wisdom: A Triumph* (Harmondsworth: Penguin, 1969), pp. 44–7, 49–50, 59. George Antonius, *The Arab Awakening: The Story of the Arab National Movement*, 2nd printing (Beirut: Librairie du Liban, 1969), pp. 76, 119, 149, 156–9, 186, 204, 212, 221–2, 226, 229. Alec Kirkbride, *An Awakening: The Arab Campaign, 1917–18* (Tavistock: University Press of Arabia, 1971), pp. 4, 57. Lowell Thomas, *With Lawrence in Arabia* (London: Hutchinson, 1924), pp. 112, 237. Ariel Roshwald, *Ethnic Nationalism and the Fall of Empires: Central Europe, Russia and the Middle East, 1914–23* (London: Routledge, 2002), pp. 64–72.
[1082] S.E. Djazairi: *Myth of Muslim Barbarism*; Bayt al Hikmah; 2008.
[1083] See works by British Ministry of Propaganda, such as A.J. Toynbee: *Murderous Tyranny*; op cit.
[1084] M. Uyar: Ottoman Arab Officers between Nationalism and Loyalty during the First World War; in *War in History*; Sage Publishing; vol 20; No 4 (2013); pp. 526-44; at p. 540.

together in coordination. One of the most important reasons behind the British negotiations with Shereef Hussein of Hejaz was to incite the Arab rank and file within the Ottoman military to rebel or at least refuse to obey orders.[1085] As an inducement to join the Shereef's side, officers and soldiers who showed a willingness to collaborate gained material advantages, whereas the others were punished.[1086] When taking into account the high mortality rate of Turkish prisoners (7.1 %) in comparison with Austro-Hungarian or German POWs (2.9% and 2.6%, respectively), Uyar and Erickson correctly point out, the choice of collaboration was actually a choice between life and death.[1087] In June 1916, when the Shereef needed an army, British intelligence officers sought to recruit from amongst Arab prisoners being held in India and managed in the end to carry 300 of them to the Hejaz; but except for a handful, none of these so-called volunteers was willing to fight for Shereef Hussein against the Turks, and the British authorities tried to keep this fact a secret.[1088] Arab officers, in their vast majority, fought alongside the Turks till the very end, and paid the ultimate price without once flinching from their oath of loyalty.[1089]

Mesut Uyar, who did the most formidable work on this subject, offers us a great number of instances of both Arab sacrifice for the Muslim cause, but most of all, enlightens us on the incidents and events that have served to muddle the picture of the true role of Arabs in later Ottoman military history.[1090]

Using statistical data from two typical Military Academy graduating classes, the class of 1903 (1319) and the class of 1914.C (1330.C),[1091] Uyar and Erickson show that, from the class of 1903, 740 officers were commissioned, of which 109 came from Arab provinces.[1092] Fourteen Arab officers had left the military by 1914 for a variety of reasons (chief among them was being killed in action), so 16 percent of officers from the class of 1903 were Arab officers, whilst from the class of 1914.C, 295 officers were commissioned, of which 75 came from Arab provinces.[1093] The ratio of Arab officers rose to 25 percent, and of the 95 serving Arab officers of the class of 1903, only 2 deserted, 75 of them were either killed during the war or resigned at the end of the war, 18 of them fought in the Turkish Independence War (1919-1922), and 14 of them continued to serve in the Republican Turkish military.[1094] Of the 75 serving Arab officers of the class of 1914.C, only 1 deserted, 42 were either killed during the war or resigned in 1918,

---

[1085] Ann Scoville, British Logistical Support to Hashemites of Hejaz: Taif to Maan 1916–1918, (Los Angeles: University of California Unpublished Ph.D. Dissertation, 1982), 22, 38–42, 47.
[1086] M. Uyar: Ottoman Arab Officers; pp. 541-2.
[1087] M. Uyar and E.J. Erickson: *A Military History*; p. 275.
[1088] M. Uyar and E.J. Erickson: *A Military History*; p. 276. H. V. F. Winstone, The Diaries of Parker Pasha, (London: Quartet Books, 1983), 181–184; Scoville, British Logistical Support, 73–74, 79, 81, 120–122, 126–127.
[1089] M. Uyar: Ottoman Arab Officers; p. 538.
[1090] Ibid; esp. pp. 538-540.
[1091] These statistics are derived from Military Academy cadet logbooks, Ministry of Defense Archive (Milli Savunma Bakanlığı Arsiv Mudurlugu˝) officer logbooks and several graduation anniversary publications.
[1092] M. Uyar and E.J. Erickson: *A Military History of the Ottomans*; p. 276.
[1093] Ibid.
[1094] Ibid.

and 32 fought in the Turkish Independence War, and after that served in the Republican Turkish military.[1095]

To conclude, those amongst Arabs and amongst anti Arab Turks who speak of, or celebrate, the Arab betrayal of the Turks either know nothing of history, or are just fifth columnists doing the work of the enemies of both people.

*****

The Final Blows, 1918

Following the capture of Jerusalem, the British began moving further north. The next objective appeared to be Damascus, about 140 miles to the north. The Turks put up a spirited defence, though. As the British were trying to break through modern Jordan, they were checked in front of Amman in March 1918.[1096] In three days of intense fighting, British casualties became 'alarming' as British assaults were swept by rifle, machine gun and artillery fire by well dug in Turks.[1097] Finally orders were issued for a quick retreat, which in fact was a rout:

> Our withdrawal from Amman [says Vivian Gilbert] brought home to me something of what refugees have to go through under war conditions. When the decision to evacuate the mountains of Moab was made known, it became necessary to notify our friends at Es Salt, who, had they remained, would undoubtedly have been massacred by the returning Turks for the help they gave us in our capture of the place.[1098]

In September 1918, Allenby mounted the final, and massive offensive against the Turks. By now, Turkey's military capacity had been drained, and the Allies' power was most obvious, not just in numbers, but also in superiority of military hardware, most of all artillery. The new weapon, aeroplanes, from accounts of the time, seem to have played an essential part. They located Turkish troops in the desert, thus easing their targeting by either artillery or fast cavalry envelopments.[1099] Even worse, airplanes bombed troops on the ground; and being exposed in the open, barren, landscape, the Turks could neither congregate to attack or defend, or to retreat, and so suffered heavily.[1100]

[1095] Ibid.
[1096] Major Vivian Gilbert: *The Romance of the last Crusade*; p. 198.
[1097] Ibid.
[1098] Ibid; p. 200.
[1099] A.T. Massey: Turkey's Disaster in Palestine Rout and Capture of Two Ottoman Armies by British Force. End the Turk's Power as a Belligerent; In *Current History*; vol 9; October 1918-March 1919; pp. 270-272.
[1100] Ibid.

In seeking to finish off the Turkish army, British cavalry was to cut through with all speed so as to encircle, if possible, the entire Turkish army- west of the Jordan.[1101] In the meantime the infantry would right-wheel on a sixteen-mile front, from Rafa to the sea, driving the Turks into the hills of Samaria, where their retreat would be cut off by the cavalry.[1102] General Allenby was strongly of the opinion that a decisive victory on the eastern front would greatly assist in finishing the resistance of the Central Powers in France.[1103]

For the Turks, like Mustafa Kemal, who gradually took things in hand, the main aim now was to preserve what was left of the army and its armament to fight another day. And so he began pulling his forces north to avoid the whole Turkish army being cut off and obliterated as planned by the fast advancing British.[1104] As the various Turkish units were retreating northward along the Hejaz Railway and the Pilgrim route, General Allenby informs us, they were being bombed by the Royal Air Force, harassed by the Arabs, and pursued by the Australian and New Zealand Mounted Divisions.[1105]

Quickly the British captured Haifa, Acre, Tiberias and the country to the south and west of the Sea of Galilee.[1106]

Then, on 1 October 1918, Australian cavalry entered Damascus. The Turks lost 20,000 men on that occasion, caught prisoners, as von Sanders had foolishly decided to defend the city, which could not escape encirclement.[1107] Then the British reached Homs and Tripoli and the cavalry advanced on Aleppo, which was occupied on 26 October.[1108] Wherever the British, their Arab allies, and the French passed, A.T. Massey, reports:

> People threw flowers and sprayed perfumes... Whenever a British uniform is seen the crowds surround it, shout in English, "Hooray," and clap hands. British prestige has never stood higher. The exemplary behaviour of our splendid troops is commented upon everywhere. The population regard them as the vanguard of a glorious and chivalrous army bringing a new and enlightened rule of freedom, justice, and liberty.[1109]

Which, of course, the Arabs have plentifully "enjoyed" since.

Ottoman Arabia was finished and much else beside, including Turkey's role in the war.

On 30 October 1918, after a few days of negotiations, the Allies and the Turks signed an armistice on board *HMS Agamemnon*, anchored in Mudros harbour on

---

[1101] Major Vivian Gilbert: *The Romance of the last Crusade*; p. 218.
[1102] Ibid.
[1103] Ibid.
[1104] Lord Kinross: *Ataturk*; p. 118.
[1105] General Allenby's Official Report of the Fighting North of Jerusalem up to September 18, 1918; in *Current History*; vol 9; part two; from p. 546.
[1106] Major Vivian Gilbert: *The Romance of the last Crusade*; p. 225.
[1107] M. Uyar; E.J. Erickson: *Military History*; p. 271.
[1108] Major Vivian Gilbert: *The Romance of the last Crusade*; p. 226.
[1109] A.T. Massey on the Allies triumphal advance, in *Current History;* vol 9; p. 408.

the island of Lemnos, outside the Turkish Straits.[1110] The Turkish leaders knew, of course, that the Allies had already drawn up plans to partition their country. This was confirmed by the Bolsheviks who, unlike their Tsarist predecessors, were no allies of the West, as they published the plans of partition with which they did not want to be associated. Although these plans had become invalid now that the Bolsheviks were in power, the Turks suspected that they had been merely adjusted.[1111] The Allies, true to their usual practice, made it sound that no such a thought ever crossed their mind, the British Prime Minister, Lloyd George, even declaring in January 1918 that he had no intention of depriving Turkey of Thrace and Asia Minor, 'provided that the Straits were internationalised and that Arabia, Armenia, Mesopotamia, Syria and Palestine did not revert to Ottoman sovereignty.'[1112] More importantly, the American president Wilson's Fourteen Points, which provided the basis for all negotiations to end the war, insisted (in point 12) that the Turkish portion of the Ottoman state 'should enjoy full sovereignty, on condition that subject nationalities had the right to free development.'[1113] With the Arab provinces already under British occupation, all that mattered to the Turkish leaders was to keep what they still held, i.e. Turkey proper.[1114]

It all seemed fine, indeed.

[1110] Turkey's Surrender to the Allies Text of the Terms Under Which Turkey Laid Down Her Arms; on Oct. 31, 1918; in *Current History*, vol 9; October, 1918— March, 1919; p. 399. See also accounts by Major General Vere Ferrers Townshend: *My Campaign*; p. 290 ff.
[1111] A. Mango: *Ataturk*; p. 189.
[1112] Ibid.
[1113] Bayur, Hikmet: Atatürk Hayatı ve Eseri (Atatürk's Life and Work), Vol. I (from his birth to his landing in Samsun), AKDTYK, Ankara 1990; 311.
[1114] A. Mango: *Ataturk*; p. 189.

Five

WAR OF INDEPENDENCE, 1919-1922

Turkey's War of Independence was not a war of independence, it was The War of Independence, or precisely the War for Survival. In fact, the Turkish war for survival did not begin in 1919 but in 1912. It might have even begun a century earlier. The foundation for this claim is quite simple: Any historian who knows his or her subject can easily come to the conclusion that in human history no country has ever faced final extinction as much as Turkey of today. There is no country or nation whose final removal off the map has been the object of a league of powerful nations (and its neighbours) all aiming for its final carving up/dismemberment except Turkey. The literature that justified such a removal, the policies devised to that effect, and the results on the ground, have been amply dwelt upon to be repeated here. By 1912, this carving up and mass-removal of Turks had already cut away most territories and people in Europe, and early in the Balkan Wars everyone expected the Bulgarians to be in Istanbul. It was at Catalca, principally, that Turkey was saved.

Three years later, in 1915, had the Turks been defeated at Gallipoli, the Russians and the Western Allies would have, as they had already agreed, done the final carving up of Turkey right then, and there would be no Turkey and many fewer Turks today.

The Turkish victory at Kut al-Amara in its two phases in late 1915 and then early in 1916 prevented the junction of the British and Russians threatening to take Turkey out of the war. After that the Petrograd Revolution in February-March 1917, followed by the Bolshevik Revolution later that year, took Russia out of the war scene, and once more saved Turkey. Soviet Russia dropping claims over Constantinople and other Turkish territory, although a great relief, was not the end of the story, though. Others still wanted to carve up Turkey as already agreed between them. So, when Turkey signed the Armistice Treaty in October 1918, there began the final phase: the sharing out of what had long been coveted and convened. The Final Carving up of Turkey did not, indeed, date from Sevres in 1920 as is generally claimed, but from some time before.

1. The Final Carving Up of Turkey

The Carving up of Ottoman Turkey was not just an objective. It was throughout much of the period elapsing from the early 19th century until the First World War a means of forming alliances. In other words: nations agreed alliances at the expenses of Turkey, everybody amongst the participants to be rewarded with former Ottoman territory according to their contribution. However, at times conflicting demands and interests led to war amongst the allies (such as the Crimea War and the Second Balkan War of 1913). The First World War itself resulted in large measure from squabble over former Ottoman territory and also Muslim territory (Morocco). Once this war was about to be fought, once more, Turkish territory became the lure or the prize for the fighters, meaning: 'you fight by our side (Britain and France) and when we win you get that so and so piece of Turkey.' It ought to be remembered how the issue of Istanbul/Constantinople, the Dardanelles, and one or two other spots were the sticking points between East and West for a century or more, for none in the West wanted Russia to have them. It was agreed in the West that if Russia got those Turkish territories, that would give her more power than either France, Britain, or even Austria. That's what saved Turkey throughout the 19th century and even early 20th. However, when the war began in 1914, this situation could no longer be maintained, for this time, the real enemy was the German, and unity had to be found between Britain and France on one hand and Russia on the other; compromise was a necessity.[1115] As the Russians had decided nothing would make them budge unless their demands were met, the French and British acquiesced to Russia's demands in respect to Istanbul, as usual called Constantinople, and also to give her adjoining territories commanding the Black Sea Straits.[1116] Also agreeing to Russian demands, France and Britain kept Greece out of the alliance (as Greece also wanted Istanbul), whilst Turkey was refused admission in the Allies circle, for it was precisely the prize to be shared by them. Agreement between everyone was reached in February 1915 according to Churchill;[1117] and the final settlement agreed sometime between 4 March and 10 April 1915. This agreement included the Gallipoli Peninsula and a strip along the European coast of the Marmara joining it to the Peninsula of Istanbul, all to go to Russia.[1118] This April 1915 Straits Agreement, signed by Russia, France and Britain, was in fact the inspiring model, laying out well in advance exactly how Turkey and the surrounding area would be carved up once it was beaten.[1119]

[1115] A.J. Toynbee: *The Western Question in Greece and Turkey*; Constable; 1922; p. 47
[1116] Ibid.
[1117] W.S. Churchill: *The World Crisis;* Thornton Butterworth, London; vol 2, 1923; 197-200.
[1118] A.J. Toynbee: *The Western Question;* op cit; p. 47.
[1119] Eleanor van Heyningen: *Helles; The French in Gallipoli;* The Joint Imperial War Museum / Australian War Memorial Battlefield Study; Tour to Gallipoli, September 2000; p. 1.

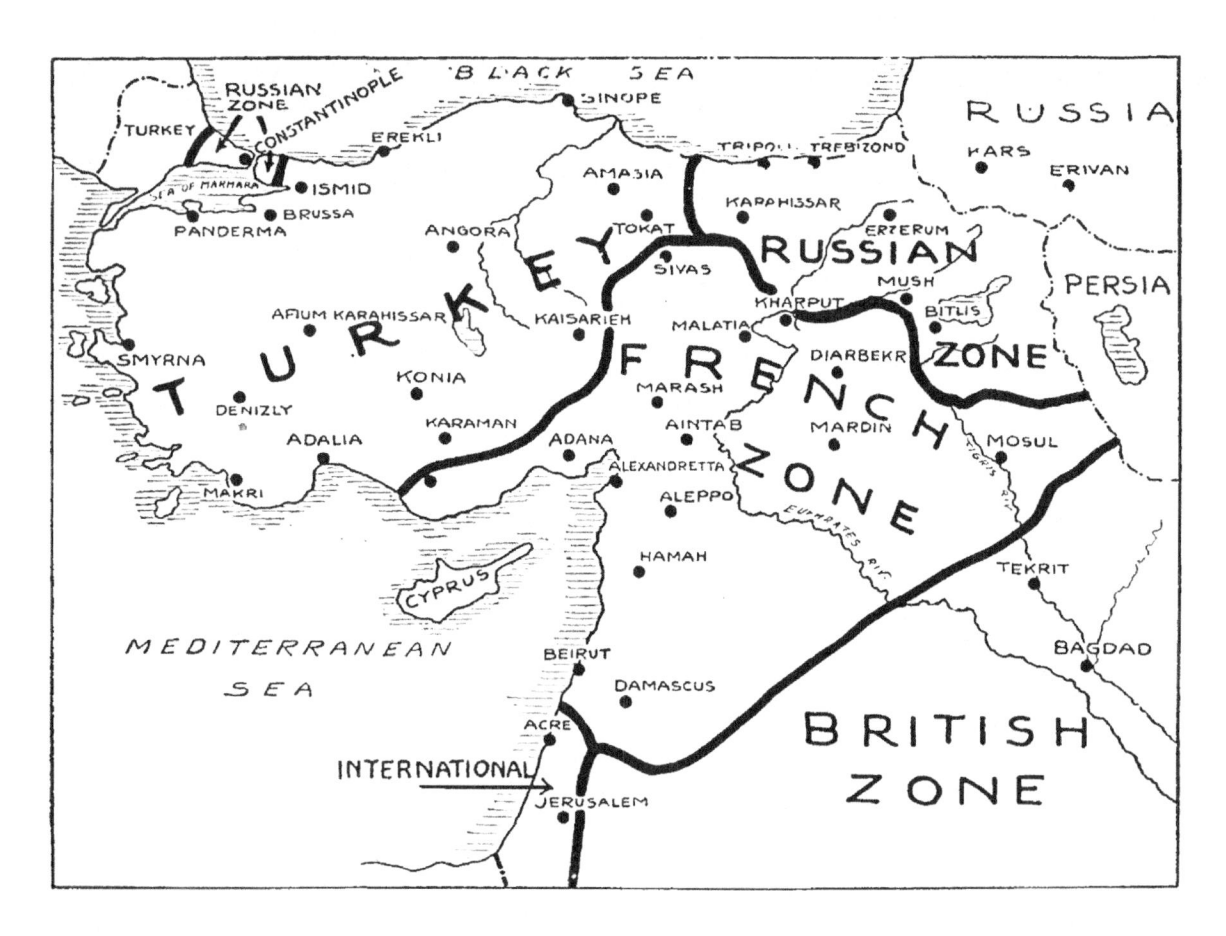

Following this, under the secret treaty of London, which was concluded precisely one day after the big landing at Gallipoli between the three powers (Britain, France, and Russia) and Italy on 26 April 1915, Italy was promised the Mediterranean region adjacent to the province of Adalia [Antalya], to the west of Cilicia, the Dodecanese Islands, and the port of Smyrna [İzmir], with much of its hinterland.[1120]

What spoiled the whole matter of carving up of Turkey then was the unexpected Turkish victory at Gallipoli. Had the Turks failed then, Turkey would have been partitioned straight in 1915 as already agreed.

Thus, the matter was postponed (after all it had been postponed by decades already), but it remained the basis of accord between all. On 26 April 1916, the first anniversary of the Treaty of London, there was signed the secret Sazonov-Paleologue Treaty, which defined everyone's territorial shares in Asiatic Turkey.[1121] Russia had gained by the force of arms the Vilayets (administrative regions) of Trebizond [Trabzon], Erzerum [Erzurum], Bitlis, and Van, a vast area which was now by right hers.[1122] For her part, France was to receive ample

---

[1120] The text of the Treaty of London between Italy and the Allies is to be found in Parliamentary Papers, 1920, No. Cmd. 671, Miscellaneous No. 7.
P. Kincaid Jensen: The Greco Turkish War, 1920-1922; in *Int. J. Middle East Stud.* 10 (1979), 553-565; at p. 553.
[1121] E. Mead: *The Baghdad Railway; A Study in Imperialism*; MacMillan; New York; 1924; p. 293.
[1122] Ibid.

'compensations' south and southwest of the Russian acquisitions, territories which were to be agreed between the French and British.[1123] And so, onto the Sykes-Picot Treaty of 9 May 1916, defining British and French political and economic interests once the former Ottoman Empire was dismembered.[1124] Britain was to obtain southern Iraq, from Baghdad to the Gulf, along with the ports of Haifa and Acre in Palestine, whilst France would receive the coastal province of Syria, the province of Adana, and all of Cilicia.[1125] Palestine would be internationalised, while the remaining Arab territories between the British and French areas would become either an Arab state or a confederation of Arab states. This area would still be divided into spheres of influence, with France controlling the rest of Syria and northern Iraq, including Mosul,[1126] while Britain would do so over the area between Palestine and Iran.[1127] Russia had to be compensated with much of eastern Anatolia, including a large part of northern Kurdistan.[1128]

Here there was a problem. The British had already agreed with the Shereef of Makkah to give him the lands they had just shared with the French. The British had indeed offered him what no ambitious monarch could refuse. These agreements planned a great Arab Confederacy of four kingdoms, where the four sons of Hussein were each to have a throne. The oldest, Ahmed, was to be heir to his father's kingdom; the second, Prince Feisal, was to be King of Syria with his capital in Damascus; the third, Prince Abdullah, was to be King of Mesopotamia with his capital in Baghdad; the fourth, Prince Zeid, a half-brother to the other Princes, was to have a kingdom in Kurdistan, with perhaps Mosul as his capital.[1129] So, whilst King Hussein was thinking that he was securing from the Allies a general undertaking, with certain reservations, the independence of the Arabs, the whole Arab land had already been staked. The result of this meant that the British and the French would have to sort out the Arabs once the messy business of war was over, which they would eventually do with a degree of force, including some gassing of Arab towns and villages.[1130] But until then, they let the Arabs do a bit of killing and conquering on their behalf. And so, happily, and unaware, the Arabs played the part seen in the previous chapter, that contributed to the German-Turkish defeat.

[1123] R. S. Baker: *Woodrow Wilson and World Settlement;* (3 volumes, Garden City, 1922), Volume I, Chapter IV, contains an excellent account of the inter-Allied negotiations of 1916-1917 regarding Asiatic Turkey, based upon the private papers of Woodrow Wilson. Cf., also, Full Texts of the Secret Treaties as Revealed at Petrograd.
[1124] E. Mead: *The Baghdad Railway;* op cit; p. 293.
[1125] S.J. and E.K. Shaw: *History;* vol 2; op cit; p. 321.
[1126] By a subsequent agreement of December, 1918, between Messrs. Lloyd George and Clemenceau, Mosul was transferred to Great Britain.
[1127] S.J. and E.K. Shaw: *History;* vol 2; op cit; p. 321.
[1128] Ibid.
[1129] *Current History;* vol xv; 98; Agreement With King Hussein (as in map pp. 97-98.) Map No. 4 presents the main features of the agreements between Great Britain and Hussein, Shereef of Mecca and King of Hedjaz. Although these agreements were made in July and October of 1915.
[1130] T.E. Lawrence; on BBC2: Saturday 6 and 13 December 2003; 8.10 p.m.

Now, there remained the Italians, who were much needed to trouble the Austrians (who were the Germans' Allies) from the south. In April 1917, by the so-called St. Jean de Maurienne Agreement, Italy was granted nearly all the southern half of Anatolia including the important cities of Antalya, Konya, and Smyrna together with an extensive "zone of influence" northeast of Smyrna.[1131] (See the map on cover and title page). Obviously, to the Italians such territories were legitimately theirs in view of past Venetian commercial influence.[1132] These inter-Allied agreements for the disposal of Asiatic Turkey, Mead remarks, 'were instructive instances of the "old diplomacy" in cooperation with the "new imperialism." The treaties were secret covenants, secretly arrived at; they bartered territories and peoples.'[1133]

Thanks to all these agreements, the Turkish state would be reduced to a few provinces in Anatolia, with only a single outlet to the Aegean.[1134]

It was all a bit complicated, but in the end everyone seemed happy, that is until 1917 when two events of major implications happened — one unexpected, the other forced — and a reshuffling of plans was needed.

The first of these events occurred early in 1917, when the Russians took two decisions to the ire of the Allies. First, they decided to quit the war, in practice from the moment the Petrograd Revolution took place in February-March 1917, but officially much later. Then, even worse, the Bolsheviks not only renounced but also denounced the carving up plans of Turkey agreed by their Tsarist predecessors, and they did not do it only once but twice.[1135] And to the further annoyance of the Allies, the Bolsheviks published secret documents which informed the Shereef of Makkah to what was afoot.[1136] Although informed, the Shereef must have decided not to believe 'the faithless, godless,' Bolsheviks, and Allah alone knows what else the Allies might have offered to entice him. He drowned in his ignorance until after the war when it became obvious that he had been fooled. By then, it was too late, of course.

The second decisive event was the replacement of Russia with Greece. Initially in 1915, as an inducement to come into the war, Sir Edward Grey had offered Greece 'large concessions on the coast of Asia Minor'.[1137] These were in principle accepted by Venizelos, her Premier, who began to nurture the customary Greek 'Grand Idea', of 'a really big Greece, to include practically all the regions in which

---

[1131] E. Mead: *The Baghdad Railway*; op cit; p. 295.
[1132] R. S. Baker, Woodrow Wilson and World Settlement (3 volumes, Garden City, 1922), vol 1 pp. 68-70. The negotiations concerning the St. Jean de Maurienne Agreement extended from the autumn of 1916 to August, 1917. The agreement appears to have been negotiated with the Italians by Mr. Lloyd George, in April, 1917, while Mr. Balfour was in America with the British Mission. It was amended in August, as a result of the insistence of the Italians that they had not received an adequate share of the spoils.
[1133] E. Mead: *The Baghdad Railway*; op cit; p. 295.
[1134] P. Kinross: *Ataturk*; op cit; p. 140.
[1135] A.J. Toynbee: *The Western Question*; op cit; p. 48.
[1136] Ibid.
[1137] P. Kincaid Jensen: The Greco Turkish War, op cit.

the influence of Hellenism has been paramount throughout the ages,'[1138] which means old Byzantium of centuries earlier. However, Greece and Russia wanted the same thing in many ways and there was room for only one amongst the two. The Russians, then, warned the King of Greece that there was nothing for Greece and that Greek troops 'would never be allowed to enter Constantinople.'[1139] Just as in 1914, when the Allies refused Turkey so as to have Russia, they quickly reached conclusion, and rejected Greece in order to have Russia. Sir Winston Churchill subsequently admitted that.[1140]

> When the collapse of Turkish resistance appeared to be imminent, the second chance of Greek intervention was thrown away, rendered unavailing through the delays introduced by the Russian autocracy, who at this critical moment, when hours counted, were occupying themselves in disputing whether Greek troops should or should not be allowed to participate in the triumphal entry into Constantinople.[1141]

In fact, had the Allies gone for the Greek option back in 1915, and had the Greeks been by their side in the attack on Gallipoli, it is fair to say that no matter how heroic the Turks had been, the operation would very likely have ended in Ally victory, for the Ally attack reinforced by Greek navy and army on a huge front with many points of contact would surely have stretched the Turks beyond their capacity for resistance.

Regardless, things always happen for a grander purpose. But now, in 1917, once Bolshevik Russia was out, Greece was courted again, except that at the helm of power there was the pro-German, King Constantine, and so he had to be kicked out of power, which the Franco-British did, before installing at the helm their ever amenable friend, Venizelos.[1142] As their condition for entering the war, the Greeks claimed, through Venizelos, the whole Aegean coast of Asia Minor and much of its hinterland, which had already been promised to the Italians, arguing that their claims were based on the ethnical factor that the Greek population formed a majority in the area. Venizelos also made similar claims for Pontus, in the Black Sea Mountains.[1143] Once satisfied, Venizelos, who like most Greeks always dreamt, and maybe still do, about the idea of a "Big Greece," enthusiastically entered his country into the war.[1144]

Thus, by the end of the war, whilst everyone was agreed to the carving up of Turkey and its disappearance, the only slight disagreements between them were some little adjustments of who should get what in some areas, and how much of

---

[1138] P. Kinross: *Ataturk*; op cit; p. 140.
[1139] H.A. Gibbons: *Venizelos*, (Boston and N.Y; Houghton Mifflin Co., 1923); p. 228.
[1140] At the Mansion House dinner, June 27, 1918.
[1141] Ibid.
[1142] On Franco-British meddling in Greek politics, the removal of the King in 1917, and all related issues, see article by Adamantios Th. Polyzoides: A review of the arbitrary acts of the Allies in Greece and of the reasons for the overthrow of Venizelos and the recall of Constantine; *Current History*; vol 16 (April-Sep 1922,) no 1; pp. 128-131.
[1143] P. Kinross: *Ataturk*; op cit; p. 140.
[1144] H.A Gibbons, *Venizelos*, op cit; p. 304.

Turkey should be left to the Turks. Here, if the Grand Greece Idea was to be applied, it would mean that most of Turkey would have to go. According to the map adopted by the Greeks, with the exception of central Turkey, i.e. three regions from north to south, as follows: Kastamonu, Ankara, and Konya; all the rest could be claimed by Greece with some accommodation for Armenia on account of the Greek/Armenian population presence.[1145] If the Armenians also got what they claimed and what subsequently America (through its president Wilson (in November 1920) generously granted them, and if the Konya region went to Italy, as already agreed, and if the Sykes Picot agreement was to be applied, that would leave Turkey a little corner in Anatolia. Turkey would end into a modern Gaza-type Bantustan, less crowded, for there would be the preliminary work of removing from life as many Turks as possible "in revenge for Turkish atrocities and centuries of oppression."

Whilst political expediency and the needs of war sufficiently justified in Allies eyes the carving up of Turkey, its removal as a nation and the removal of its people needed justifying.

2. The Intellectual/Legal/Moral Background for the Removal of Turks and Turkey

No removal of an entity takes place just out of nothing. An act of this magnitude and all the horrors it entails cannot be carried out by any officials or military men, and even in the heat of combat, mass-killing eventually dies down. Removing an entire entity in peace time is even much harder, and no amount of cruelty, inhumanity, greed, or any factor of the sort, would make that possible. To remove an entity, as has been explained in chapter one of this work, demands, indeed, intellectual, legal, and above all moral justifications, i.e. that such an entity is deemed detrimental to humanity, and only by its removal can humanity prosper, and not just that, its removal is not just a necessity but most of all right. No genocide perpetrator in history has failed to present such an argument. Even the horrid Conquistadors who slew en masse in Central and Southern America had their moral reasons and justifications (besides the lure of gold, of course), in their case citing Indian cannibalism, animal-like habits and manners, and so on.[1146] But the Conquistadors and others who did the mass-killings on the ground were not guilty, for they did not decide that their victims lacked the human pre-requisites to live. Not at all, indeed. Those who decided then, just as those who to this day decide on such matters (i.e the mass killing of others, especially after military

---
[1145] See the map in H.A. Gibbons: *Venizelos*; op cit, following page 338.
[1146] Ward Churchill: *A Little Matter of Genocide*; City Lights Books; San Francisco; 1997. W. Howitt: *Colonisation and Christianity*: Longman; London; 1838.

coups) are men (maybe a woman or two, also) who are respected for their knowledge, their status, and even 'morality.' They are intellectuals and other elites, journalists, analysts, including also Nobel Peace prize winners, and, some might think this author to be barmy: 'human right defenders' and organisations, too. In words, in the past just as today, the elimination of an entity is first justified by those whose respectability, moral and intellectual, makes any act, however seemingly abhorrent (such as mass torture and disappearances following a coup (as today in Islamic countries), a good/necessary/right act. So the torturers/slayers have nothing to reproach themselves, although everyone always throws the ball into their court, and at all times in history. Of course, there are men, and women too, amongst the latter who delight at shedding blood and inflicting physical pain, or any sort of pain, for that matter as a matter of second nature to them. Human evil, hatred, cruelty, and other vile features are limitless amongst much of earth's population, under special circumstances in particular, such as they being given the green light to do what they like most: generating pain, or humiliating the good amongst them.

Indeed, mass killing and all the vile that goes with it is a shared business, and he who applies it only comes at the bottom of the pyramid. At the top, the brains had already intellectually legitimised what would be done to their would-be victims. This was the case for Turkey around 1916 (oddly, and how a wonderfully stupid beast history is, a century later in 2016, the same type of people wished the same to be done to Turks by playing the central role in the coup of July 2016.)

Let's leave aside the devisers of the 2016 coup alone: a dangerous lot it is better not to trifle with, although all speak in low voices, and all appear constantly in the media in order to defend democracy and human rights. Let's travel back to the period 1916. Amongst the brains behind the dehumanisation of Turks and the justification for their mass removal and the phasing out of their country was Toynbee, the great historian. The Toynbee of 1916-17 would eventually in 1922 atone for his temporary blindness and turn into a great supporter/protector of Turks. The Toynbee of 1916-17, however, hated the Turks, and did his job for the British Ministry of Propaganda to win the War, and for this purpose, he completed his *Murderous Tyranny of the Turks,* where he dwelt on their barbarism, massacres of Christians, and the usual that was (and still is) associated with the Turks, and thus justified their mass-removal.[1147] The Toynbee of 1921, who was in İzmir, Bursa, Gemlik, Kumla, and Yalova (north-west Turkey) saw the very reverse of what he always believed: the Turks he formerly felt little for other than loathing, were instead, as he discovered, the real victims of barbarism at the hands of his beloved and civilised Greeks. He now realised that the evil associated with the Turks was a result of the snowballing effect of the writing and image building, devised by all sorts of opinion makers, who like him built such an image of them, and each of them inspiring and feeding the other until that image became a fact (not that there were never any evil deeds by the

---

[1147] A.J. Toynbee: *The Murderous Tyranny of the Turks*; Hodder and Stoughton, London, 1917.

Turks, for surely there were, but never as depicted by Christians; and as Jäckh puts it: all Turkish crimes in history would not equal a single one by the Christians).[1148] It must have been the mother of all shocks to Toynbee, as it is always to anyone who discovers that he who he thought was evil was not, and he who he believed to be the angel was the real evil. And so, at the risk to his career, his safety, and even his life, he did what he possibly could and saved the lives of at least thousands of Turks by literally grabbing them away from their would be Christian murderers, and saving tens of thousands more lives by reporting what the Greeks were doing to the Turks and eventually publishing that in his *Western Question*.[1149]

Prior to his transformation, Toynbee en par with many others who worked for the British War Propaganda Ministry were certainly kind, humane, people, who were doing a job so as their country would win the war. In the process, however, the same rhetoric used to win the war also served to dehumanise the Turks and justify their mass-removal. Just as Gladstone's (a zealous Christian fanatic) pamphlet in 1876-7 opened the way to the mass killing of hundreds of thousands of Turks and their exile, and just like the literature that made Greeks, Serbs, Bulgarians and Montenegrins inflict terrible atrocities on the Turks during the Balkan Wars, the works by the British Ministry of Propaganda also bore the same substance. Here we have Viscount Bryce, a rabid hater of Turks who never atoned for anything, who writing the preface for Toynbee's first work the *Murderous Tyranny of the Turks*, said:

> No one who has studied the history of the Near East for the last five centuries will be surprised that the Allied Powers have declared their purpose to put an end to the rule of the Turk in Europe, and still less will he dissent from their determination to deliver the Christian population of what is called the Turkish Empire, whether in Asia or in Europe, from a Government which during those five centuries has done nothing but oppress them. These changes are indeed long overdue. They ought to have come more than a century ago, because it had then already become manifest that the Turk was hopelessly unfit to govern, with any approach to justice, subject races of a different religion. The Turk has never been of any use for any purpose except fighting. He cannot administer, though in his earlier days he had the sense to employ intelligent Christian administrators. He cannot secure justice. As a governing power, he has always shown himself incapable, corrupt and cruel. He has always destroyed; he has never created…

[1148] Ernst Jäckh; *Deutschland im Orient nach dem Balkan-Krieg;* Chapter 7: Deutsche und französische Augenzeugen von christlichen Massakers. (Die Balkangreuel des 30 jährigen Krieges); Martin Mörikes Verlag, Munich, 1913; pp. 83-98.
See also P. Loti: *Turquie Agonisante*; Calman Levy; Paris; 1913; pp. 46-52.
[1149] A.J. Toynbee: *The Western Question;* op cit.

> As a famous English historian wrote, the Turks are nothing but a robber band, encamped in the countries they have desolated. As Edmund Burke wrote, the Turks are savages, with whom no civilised Christian nation ought to form any alliance.
>
> Turkish rule ought to be ended in Europe, because, even in that small part of it which the Sultan still holds, it is an alien power, which has in that region been, and is now, oppressing or massacring, slaughtering or driving from their homes, the Christian population of Greek or Bulgarian stock. It ought to be turned out of the western coast regions of Asia Minor for a like reason. The people there are largely, perhaps mostly, Greek speaking Christians. So ought it to be turned out of Constantinople, a city of incomparable commercial and political importance, with the guardianship of which it is unfit to be trusted. So ought it to be turned out of Armenia and Cilicia, and Syria, where within the last two years it has been destroying its Christian subjects, the most peaceful and industrious and intelligent part of the population.
>
> If a Turkish Sultanate is to be left in being at all, it may, with least injury to the world, be suffered to exist in Central and Northern Asia Minor, where the population is mainly Mussulman, and there are comparatively few Christians and those only in the cities to suffer from its misgovernment. Even there one would be sorry for its subjects, Mussulman as well as Christian, but a weak Turkish State, such as it would then be, could not venture on the Crimes of which it has been guilty when it was comparatively strong...
>
> The Muslim peasant of Asia Minor is an honest, kindly fellow when not roused by fanaticism, but the Turk, as a Governing Power, is irreclaimable, and the Allied Powers would have been false to all the principles of Right and Humanity for which they are fighting if they had not proclaimed that no Turkish Government shall hereafter be permitted to tyrannize over subjects of another faith.[1150]

Before he realised the truth in 1921, and back in 1916-17 when he was still employed by the British Ministry of War Propaganda, Toynbee completed his *Murderous Tyranny of the Turks*. First, he praises all the people living under 'Turkish tyranny,' i.e. the Greeks, Armenians, and Arabs, who all had the most admirable of qualities until the Turks arrived and indulged in slaughter, tyranny, and destruction. Even the Kurds, he tells us, were formerly good people until they, too, were turned into mass-murderers by the Turks who have massacred and expelled the Christians from their homes.[1151] Then towards the end of his book, he concludes:

[1150] Viscount Bryce: Preface, in A.J. Toynbee: *The Murderous Tyranny of the Turks*.
[1151] A.J. Toynbee: *Murderous Tyranny*; op cit; pp. 9-10; 14.

> There is no possibility of returning to the Status Quo before August 1914 first, because the Status Quo under the Turks was itself the mere perpetuation of an oppression and a misery that disgraced the civilised world, and that should have been ended long before; and secondly, because it has been made unspeakably worse during the War than it was before it. Every element of good that had maintained its existence under Turkish government, and that made less intolerable a system that in itself was too wicked to survive, is being stamped out now by deportation, spoliation, abduction and massacre. The evil has purged itself altogether of the good.
>
> It is not a question of ameliorating the Status Quo. The Status Quo in Turkey, irremediable before, is being actively changed into something infinitely worse, and this is being accomplished, behind the bulwark of Militarism, under the eyes of the civilised world. This is why the Allies' aims are drastic, but it is also why they find no difficulty in stating them in the full light of day.[1152]

And what are the Allies' aims? They stated this:

> 'The Liberation of the Peoples who now lie beneath the murderous Tyranny of the Turks, and the expulsion from Europe [including Istanbul] of the Ottoman Empire which has proved itself so radically Alien to Western Civilisation.'
>
> (Joint Note of the Allied Governments in answer to President Wilson.)

Toynbee as an employee of the British Ministry of War Propaganda was only carrying out government instructions. The Prime Minister, Lloyd George, had instructed those responsible for British war propaganda on the aim and direction of anti-Turkish propaganda:

> The Turks' inability to govern, their misrule and above all massacres of the hardworking population must be emphasized. I hardly need to point out that this should be done gradually and the articles spread over a long period so that our purpose is not too obvious. Sir Mark Sykes' article in the Times is exactly what we want to see.[1153]

Sykes even fabricated quotations by different members of the Ottoman government that it was the Turks (not the Mongols) who had invaded and destroyed Baghdad in 1258, and then, the same Ministry also published a *Blue Book*, 'chiefly,' Karlsson remarks, 'inspired by Greeks and Armenians, which expressed an open and unconstrained hatred of the Turks in racist terms.'[1154]

Besides the British, all other Allies and chancelleries, with the exception of the Italians, did absolutely the same, and at the same time. Mandelstam, the Russian

---

[1152] Ibid; 34-35.
[1153] I. Karlsson: The Turk as a Threat and Europe's Other; in *International Issues and Slovak Foreign Policy;* issue 1, 2006; pp. 62-72; at p. 68.
[1154] Ibid.

ambassador, in 1917, literally said the same that Toynbee said except in much bigger scope, again reiterating the substance of the same Ally Joint Note.[1155] Mandelstam spent a lot of effort explaining that the Turks,

> Just like other inferior races' have the chance to become civilised one day, but until then, they have to be removed entirely, and placed in some corner of Asia Minor, where they can spend a while, and like 'the Black people might then, after a few generations civilise themselves, and then find their way back amongst humans.'[1156]

He adds (in original French),

> Mais il ne saurait s'agir pour l'Entente victorieuse de rétablir sur l'Empire Ottoman Une tutelle aussi inefficace que celle qui a permis à l'Etat tuteur ottoman de massacrer ses pupilles arméniens en se jouant de ses propres tuteurs européens. Cette extraordinaire combinaison internationale de tutelles superposées a fait définitivement faillite. C'est dans le cas turc que l'intervention d'humanité doit être poussée à ses limites extrêmes et recevoir sa plus forte consécration. Cette consécration ne saurait être autre que la destruction de l'Empire Ottoman. Tout notre ouvrage tend à cette conclusion.[1157]

Which translates:

> There is absolutely no question that the Ottoman realm be allowed to survive, including under the Allies' tutelage; this tutelage that has allowed this state to murder its Armenian subjects by deceiving its European tutors. This tutelage has proved itself bankrupt. With the Turks the most extreme policies have to be applied and consecrated, and their consecration is nothing other than the utter destruction of the Ottoman state. Our entire work has worked towards this conclusion.

The novelist and writer, E.F Benson, published his *Crescent and Iron Cross* in 1918. He writes in his preface, stating:

> The Allies have pledged themselves to remove the power of the Turk from Constantinople, and to remove out of the power of the Turk the alien peoples who have too long already been subject to his murderous rule. I have, in fact, but attempted to conjecture in what kind of manner that promise will be fulfilled.

Then he elaborates at great length why the Allies have promised to undertake this task, amongst others:

> For at whatever period we regard Turkey, and try to define that monstrous phenomenon, we can make a far truer phrase than Lord Aberdeen's. For Turkey is not a sick man: Turkey is a sickness. He is not sick, nor ever has been, for he is the cancer itself, the devouring tumour that for centuries has

---
[1155] A. Mandelstam: *The Sort de l'Empire Ottoman*; Lausanne, Imprimeries Reunies; 1917; p. 573, and throughout.
[1156] Ibid; pp. 401-2 and after.
[1157] Ibid; p. 577

fed on living tissue, absorbing it and killing it. It has never had life in itself, except in so far that the power of preying on and destroying life constitutes life, and such a power, after all, we are accustomed to call not life, but death. Turkey, like death, continues to exist and to dominate, through its function of killing. Life cannot kill, it is disease and death that kill, and from the moment that Turkey passed from being a nomadic tribe moving westwards from the confines of Persia, it has existed only and thrived on a process of absorption and of murder. When first the Turks came out of their Eastern fastnesses they absorbed; when they grew more or less settled, and by degrees the power of mere absorption, as by some failure of digestion, left them, they killed. They became a huge tumour that nourished itself by killing the living tissues that came in contact with it. Now, by the amazing irony of fate, who weaves stranger dramas than could ever be set on censored stages, for they both take hundreds of years to unravel themselves, and are of the most unedifying character, Turkey, the rodent cancer, has been infected by another with greater organisation for devouring; the disease of Ottomanism is threatened by a more deadly hungerer, and Prussianism has inserted its crab-pincers into the cancer that came out of Asia. Those claws are already deeply set, and the problem for civilised nations is first to disentangle the nippers that are cancer in a cancer, and next to deprive of all power over alien peoples the domination that has already been allowed to exist too long.[1158]

Then, throughout the book he goes through the same claims of Turkish massacres of Christians, strangeness to civilisation, the same arguments as Mandelstam, Viscount Bryce, Morgenthau, Driault, and others. Then, towards the end of his work, he offers us the picture of the new Turkey the Allies envisaged to create at the end of the war, as abridged here:

> Here, then, has been outlined the effect of the Allies' declared aims. Such territories as Turkey holds in Europe, such control as she possesses over the free passage of the Straits must pass from her, and the alien peoples, who for centuries have fainted and bled underneath her infamous yoke, must be led out of the land of bondage. As we have seen throughout preceding chapters, it was the fixed policy of the Ottoman Government to rid itself of their presence, and already it has gone far in its murderous mission. Indeed the avowed aims of the Allies, when accomplished, will do that work for her, for the Allies are determined to remove those peoples from Turkey. The difference of execution, however, consists in this, that they will not remove Arabs and Greeks and Italians and Jews, as Turkey has already done with the Armenians by the simple process of massacres, but by a process no less simple, namely, of taking out of the territories of the Ottoman Empire the districts where such peoples dwell... It is no dismemberment of an Empire that the Allies contemplate, for they cannot

---
[1158] E.F. Benson: *Crescent and Iron Cross*; George H. Doran Company; New York; 1918; pp. 12-14.

dismember limbs that never belonged to the real trunk. It was a despotic military control that the Osmanlis had established, they always regarded their subject peoples as aliens, whom they did not scruple to destroy if they exhibited symptoms of progress and civilisation. Henceforth the Turkish Government shall govern Turks, and Turks alone. That for many years has been its aim, and, by the disastrous dispensation of fate, it has been largely able to realise its purpose. Now, though by different methods, the Allies will see thorough accomplishment of it... Russia, France, England, Italy, all allied nations, will be established in close proximity to the Turkish frontiers, and the New Turkey will be as powerless for aggression as she will be for defence, should she provoke attack. But within their borders there may the Osmanlis dwell secure and undisturbed, so long as they conform to the habits of civilised people with regard to their neighbours, and it is a question whether, now that the military despotism which has always misguided the fortunes of this people, has no possible fields for conquest, and no need of securing security, the nation will not settle down into the quiet existence of small neutral countries. Perhaps the last chapter of its savage and blood-stained history is already almost finished, and in years to come some little light of progress and of civilisation may be kindled in the abode where the household gods for centuries have been cruelty and hate.[1159]

Remarkably, when at San Remo in April 1920 the Allies cut Turkey's territory by 85% and its population by 16 millions, as will be seen further down, their plans and proposals were an absolute replica of what Benson had stated years earlier.[1160]

Writing at the same time (1916-1917), the Frenchman Driault, in his work on the Eastern Question went through the usual route as Mandelstam, making, however, a long historical detour, and then in his conclusion summed up his thoughts, stating amongst others (as translated from French) that like other Turkish rulers, Abdülhamid was deceiving Europe, that

> Whilst he pretended to be carrying out reforms, he was strengthening Turkey militarily. This is not what Europe, France in particular, meant by reforms.
> Other nations such as Hungary have reformed themselves and joined the club of the civilised, but they are Christians; the Turks, however, have remained Muslim, and therefore have refused to amalgamate with European culture, the Koran only inspiring them with contempt for others and hatred. In every closer contact with the Christians, it only raised in them fanaticism and accentuated their Asiatic character, and so they come

---
[1159] Ibid; pp. 220-225.
[1160] *Current History*, vol 12; Apr-Sep 1920; Dismemberment of the Turkish Empire. Terms of the Final Peace Treaty of the World War — Effects on the Map of Asia Minor p. 446; see whole article pp. 445-448..

forth as even more strange and barbaric, and could hardly comprehend Europe's revolutionary ideas. The Turk has remained the stubborn, fearless Muslim of the past; and his hatred of the Christian has remained extreme and expressed itself in lust for blood; and to the sight of his enemy's progress, he replies with abominable massacres. The Turk has been cheating Europe in regard to his true aims... Europe, tired of being duped, but also afraid of a dismemberment that might draw it into chaos, decided to reform the empire by force, even under the threat of the gun, a strong use of cautery, but the powers have never agreed on this cautery...[1161]

Then after going through Christian success in the Muslim world, Driault concludes:

> We have not refrained in this book from defining the Eastern Question by the retreat of Turkish Islam in front of the push of Christian nations: there is no other way of understanding the scale and historical greatness of this. The solution is the end of Turkey. The war will change nothing; the only thing it will do will be to designate/appoint what is now important: Who would be the inheritors of the sick man.[1162]

The vast propagandist machine that demeaned the Turk and justified his removal worked on the same lines as the Nazi propagandist machine would work about two decades later. It was not just an intellectual effort, it encompassed all other means of communication in order to impact on opinion. Just as the Nazis used cartoons to lampoon the Jews and magnify the usual stereotype of them, reducing them from humans to sub-humans, so did the Allies do with the Turks. Punch, the main satirical magazine which since the 1870s played a leading role in enhancing the image of the sanguinary, bestial, Asiatic barbarian, Turk, released at the start of the First World War, in 1914, a commemorative issue (*The Unspeakable Turk*) in which were revived all the usual stereotype images of the Turk. Drawings showing the Turk massacring Christians have already been seen in previous chapters. Here we highlight other depictions of the Turk.

[1161] E. Driault: *La Question d'Orient depuis ses origines jusqu'a la paix de Sevres;* Librairie Felix Alcan; 8th ed; 1920; pp. I-IV and p. 402.
[1162] Ibid; pp. 461-462.

The slimy Turk about to profit from European problems and divisions (Source: Punch; the Unspeakable Turk 1914)

Right: The non-human Turk (Source: Punch; the Unspeakable Turk 1914)

The cowardly bully, oppressor of Christians, now faced by Britain, France and Russia (Source: Punch; the Unspeakable Turk 1914)

So, by the time of the Armistice and when peace with Turkey was agreed in October 1918, all there was from the Ally view-point was the moral and legal justification to carve up the Turkish realm. In fact, reports of massacres by Turks of Christians (always by unspecified witnesses in unspecified places and times, but conveyed by people hundreds or thousands of kilometres away) always appeared at the same time as maps showing Turkey's carved up territory in any publication of the time. *Current History* vol. 9, dating from the time of the Armistice, is a remarkable instance that shows this link: Turkish massacre of hundreds of thousands of Greeks, thus justifying the carving up of Turkey.[1163] Incidentally, the Greeks by this time, if one perused through Western literature, had been massacred tens of times over and over, in such numbers that the population of Greece must have been at least as large as that of China today; and even more remarkably after the armistice in 1918, we find Greeks in their hundreds of thousands living amongst a majority of Turks.[1164] Anyone with the slightest bit of common sense would have thought that a community so much slaughtered would have, if it had not entirely perished by now, either fled or seized arms to defend itself. The Greeks did nothing of such; they were neither fools nor cowards not to do one or the other. Therefore the vast literature speaking of their massacres is entirely crooked.

However, whilst everyone was agreed on the carving up, there remained the final act: how to do it? The Allies were not fools. They knew that, with the exception of the few traitors and the fifth columnists within Turkey, all the Turks would fight to the death any attempt on the integrity of their land. True the Greeks had a fine army that was intact, but to take on the Turks then, in 1918, would have been an impossible thing for the Greeks to even try. And so, the Allies began to implement the method or policy by which the carving up could become possible. So what they did, in priority, was to break Turkey's fighting capacity, but step by step.

3. The Gradual Degrading of Turkish Power and Dismembering of Turkey

The primary reason why the Allies did not hurl themselves men, carts and horses, guns and whatever, tearing Turkey left, right, and centre was not, as modern, crooked, scholarship tells us: that the carving up was not their aim. They did not do it in that direct, brutal, way because then, they did not have the capacity to do it. Maybe towards 1925 that would have been possible but not in the Autumn of 1918. This was not possible for the following reasons:

[1163] *Current History* vol 9 massacres of Greeks p. 399 ff; and map 414-415.
[1164] See following headings on Greeks in Smyrna, Istanbul, Pontus, Bursa, Gemlike, everywhere in fact.

Firstly, the Turkish army was still intact in 1918. It had not disintegrated. It could still beat them, especially now that Russia was out of the game, and most particularly if the latter, under the Bolsheviks, was willing to assist the Turks against the common enemy, especially if suddenly the Turks chose to become part of the Soviet community.

Secondly, the three Great Powers interested in the carving up: Britain, France and Italy were bogged down militarily elsewhere to attempt anything. The British were busy quelling the rebellious Irish; the French were smothering the Germans once and for all, and soon were fighting the Arabs (when the latter realised they had been duped); whilst the Italians were bogged down in Libya.[1165]

Thirdly, and this applies to the French and British, both countries had paid such a heavy price in the fields of the First World War, that simply they no longer had either the will or manpower to start yet another conflict much to the east. Their populations would have never accepted it anyway, whatever the promises that it would all be dusted and over with by the end of 1918, for they had said the same thing years before when they started the war in 1914 — that it would be over by Xmas.

Fourthly, there was the Bolshevik Revolution and all its headaches, which took much of what's left of their energies, especially as they (French and British) were helping the White Russians to destroy the Revolution.

So, prudently and realistically by means of bluff, bullying, and using the usual traitors, they always manage to find and elevate, they began to cripple Turkish military power. The defeatists, the weak, the traitors, the fifth columnist, cowards, and gullible amongst the Turks assisted.

First, the Allies marked cautiously their physical presence in various parts of Turkey, not really with the aim of colonising but with the aim of preparing for it, including: eliminating people who may act as obstacle to future carving up; establishing means for that purpose; arming Greeks and Armenians; and above all disabling Turkish military capacities. Thus, the British established small garrisons, particularly on the railways, to supervise demobilisation 'and to prevent outbreaks of violence.'[1166]

In Kurdish areas, British "advisors" were also present 'should any unwelcome development occur.'[1167] Istanbul and the Straits, now, following the Soviet withdrawal of Russian claims, came under Ally control; and so on 13 November a large Allied fleet sailed through the Straits and landed in Istanbul.[1168] Military control mainly rested with the British, and overall political and administrative

---

[1165] For British and French see further down.
For Italians see, J. Wright: *Libya, A Modern History*, Croom Helm, London, 1981, p. 32 ff. See also and essentially: R. Graziani: *Cirenaica Pacificata.* Milan: Mondadori, 1932. For those who can read Arabic: Idris El-Horeir: Mawaqif Khalida Li Umar Al-Mukhtar; in *Majallat al-Buhut al-Tarikhiya;* 2; July; 1988.
[1166] P. Kincaid Jensen: The Greco Turkish War, 1920-1922; op cit; p. 553.
[1167] Dagobert Von Mikusch, *Mustafa Kemal,* trans. J. Linton (Garden City, N.Y. Doubleday, Doran & Co., 1931), pp. 210-215.
[1168] S.J. and E.K. Shaw: *History*; vol 2; op cit; p. 329.

control was given to Admiral Calthorpe as Allied High Commissioner, governing with the help of a three-man High Commission, with British, Italian, and French members.[1169]

To the south-east, on 25 November 1918, the French landed to take up the areas allotted to them, including Mersin, Tarsus, Adana, and all the Taurus tunnels.[1170] A French officer, Colonel Raymond, arrived in Adana and told the Turkish governor that French troops would occupy the city, and ordered that the Turkish troops should be immediately withdrawn.[1171] A sign of things to come became obvious when local Muslims could see that the French were accompanied by detachments of armed Armenian volunteers, and that many Armenian civilians, deported to Syria in 1915, returned, retook their old property, and tried to avenge themselves on their Turkish neighbours.[1172] Whilst the French and the Armenians were gobbling up Cilicia, the Italians were now grabbing their share in Adalia, and from there were ready to move inland.[1173]

In north-central Anatolia, measures were undertaken to establish a Greek state in the ancient Pontus region, encompassing the districts of Samsun, Amasya, and Sivas.[1174] A secret Greek society working towards forming that state had already been established as early as 1904 in Merzifon, and had now become a powerful movement thus giving the Greek government the opportunity to press its claims.[1175] On 9 March 1919, British forces landed in Samsun and went on to occupy Merzifon, thus encouraging the local Greeks to revolt openly, and whilst at it, take the opportunity to massacre their Turkish neighbours in order to clear the ground.[1176] Order was partly restored, but with immense difficulty by the Turkish police with reluctant assistance from the British.[1177] Obviously a state of chaos would feed the by now a century-old technique: that the Christians are threatened by Turkish massacre, which thus would justify occupation, territorial carving up, disarming of Turks, and further massacres of Turks.

The priority of all priorities from an Ally perspective, understandably, was the degrading-breaking of the Turkish army. The British had control officers scattered over Turkey from Thrace to the Caucasus, whose duties were the supervising or control of both demobilisation and disarmament.[1178] At this stage, in November 1918, the Turkish military, Uyar and Erickson remind, did not just run out of the battlefield.[1179] Mustafa Kemal, Karabekir and many other officers

---

[1169] Ibid.
[1170] Tevfik Bıyıklıoğlu: *Turk istiklal Harbi, I. Mondros Mutarekesi ve Tatbikat* (The Turkish War for Independence. I. The Truce of Mondros and Its Application), Ankara, 1962, henceforth; *Mondros Mutarekesi*, pp. 77-106, pp. 57-74.
[1171] A. Mango: *Ataturk*; op cit; p. 193.
[1172] Ibid.
[1173] P. Kinross: *Ataturk*; op cit; p. 142.
[1174] S.J. and E.K. Shaw: *History*; vol 2; op cit; p. 329.
[1175] Ibid.
[1176] Ibid
[1177] *Mondros Mutarekesi*, op cit; pp. 173-74.
[1178] P. Kinross: *Ataturk*; op cit; p. 142.
[1179] M. Uyar and E.J. Erickson: *A Military History of the Ottomans*; op cit; p. 283.

had kept their units and even armaments intact, and the Turkish army, although defeated, was still in the field.[1180] They, like many others, such as the commander of the 9th Army on the Caucasian front, Yakup Şevki Pasha (who had replaced Vehip Pasha) in June 1918), did his best to thwart the Ally schemes, saving the bulk of his equipment and supplies.[1181] Brigadier Kâzım Karabekir withdrew his 1st Caucasian Corps from north-western Persia, and coming across Japanese field guns and ammunition in military stores, had them secretly shipped to Trabzon.[1182] Karabekir's other immediate objective was to protect the pre-war Turkish frontier against Armenian and Georgian encroachment.[1183] Back in Istanbul, patriots in the War Ministry were backing these officers' efforts.[1184]

All this, obviously, was not to the liking of the British. Informed by their agents, the local Greeks and Armenians that is, Allenby hurriedly travelled from Palestine to Istanbul in February 1919. There he summoned the Ministers of War and of Foreign Affairs and, not even allowing them to speak, he read them out a list of demands, including the removal of the recalcitrant officers, including the commander of the Sixth Army on the Mosul front.[1185] Having read his orders/instructions in five minutes, he rushed out, and returned at once to Palestine.[1186]

Not to be outdone, the French, too, wanted to show the Turks who was the boss now. General Franchet d'Esperey, the French commander, as Allied Commander in the Near East, had paid a flying visit to Istanbul on 23 November 1918, but he made his official entry on 8 February – the day after Allenby's visit – riding into the city on a white horse, and was 'wildly cheered by local Greeks, Armenians and Europeans.'[1187] Just as the British had 'recovered' Jerusalem for Christendom, the French were now signalling the recapture of Constantinople after five centuries of Turkish rule.

Carving up Turkey in favour of Greeks and Armenians was done through a variety of other means. Everywhere Turkish and other Muslims in control of positions of importance were removed and replaced by Christians.[1188] In many parts now under occupation, especially in eastern Thrace, south-western Anatolia, Cilicia, and the eastern provinces, local authority institutions were put under local Christian responsibility as a prelude for the final partition of the country.[1189] Everywhere in public places, Muslims were discriminated against, as in

---

[1180] Ibid; p. 273.
[1181] W.E.D. Allen, and P. Muratoff: *Caucasian Battlefields* (Cambridge, 1953), 478.
[1182] Kâzim Karabekir, Istiklal Harbimiz (Our War of Independence) (Istanbul, 1960), 35
[1183] A. Mango: *Ataturk;* op cit; p. 209.
[1184] Ibid; p. 194.
[1185] P. Kinross: *Ataturk*; op cit; p. 143.
[1186] Ibid.
[1187] Sina Akşin: İstanbul Hükümetleri ve Milli Mücadele (The Istanbul Governments and the National Struggle), I–II, Cem, Istanbul 1992, I, 158.
[1188] S.J and E.K Shaw: *History*; op cit; v2; p. 328-9.
[1189] Ibid; 330.

education, for instance, for, following the reopening of state schools, Christian children were allowed in, but not Muslims.[1190] Christian missionaries were put in charge of the major orphanage institutions, and, understandably, because in Western view only the Christians could have lost their parents (to Turkish massacres,) thousands of Turkish children were turned into Armenians or Greeks unless they could prove the contrary, which was a near impossibility in a country in utter administrative chaos, with very few or hardly any records.[1191] And much worse, even, the Christians, who, during the Balkan Wars only amused themselves by jeering at the returning, defeated and wounded Turkish soldiers, now, under Ally protection, massacred large numbers of recently discharged Turkish soldiers as well as thousands of civilians without any effort by the Ally forces to interfere.[1192] Only the Italians, who had also distinguished themselves during the Balkan Wars in calling early for a commission of enquiry to stop massacres of Turks, now, in the south tried to stop Christian mobs from lynching every Turk or other Muslim they came across.[1193]

In the meantime, still hoping for Ally leniency, or maybe firmly believing in the power of haggling as one would do in a Middle Eastern Bazaar, the Turkish delegation at the Paris Peace Conference, which opened on 18 January 1919, had a rude awakening. It was literally kicked out, which caused great distress to the gullible souls in Turkey. The Istanbul government had resorted to the abominable and despicable practice of playing the usual sick card of acknowledging crimes and blaming other Turks in power before them (the CUP), who themselves had blamed Sultan Abdülhamid of the same, not realising that to the Westerners (who always use traitors but also always despise them) this is a sickening procedure. And so the Istanbul delegation received the appropriate answer:

> The attitude of the allied and associated powers had been expressed in plain and uncompromising language, which left no doubt of their belief in Turkish guilt, both in entering the war and in the matter of the Armenian atrocities, and indicated their absolute incredulity regarding Turkish promises. No formal reply to the Turkish proposals had been given, on the ground that these proposals and the Allies' plans were too far apart, and the dismissal was attributed to the fact that the solution of the problems involved would require too long a time to make the further sojourn of the Turkish delegation expedient or profitable.[1194]

The delegation was forthwith kicked out back to Istanbul.

[1190] Ibid; 329.
[1191] Halide Edib: *The Turkish Ordeal*; John Murray; London; 1928, pp. 7-11, 16-18;
[1192] S.J and E.K Shaw: *History*; op cit; v2; p. 330.
[1193] HTVD, no. 4 (June 3, 1953), nos. 64, 65, 68, 69, 71, (7, 83; Ali Fuat Turkgeldi, *Gorup İşittiklerim*, I, Ankara, 1949, p. 188.
[1194] The Passing of the Turkish Dominion; Chaos and Suffering Increase in Asiatic Turkey in *Current History;* Vol 10 April, 1919— September, 1919; part 2; p. 530.

Indeed, the great Ally plan of carving up Turkey relied precisely on the two essential ingredients: the spineless, sold out, individuals to hold power in Turkey, and the claim of massacres, or threat of massacres, of Christians.

Regarding the first, at the end of February 1919, the Sultan changed his government, and put in place the sort of government the Allies — just as the West today — like to work with in the Muslim world: docile puppets (but of the mass murdering/mass torturing sort preferably, today). Thus was appointed Damad (Demat) Ferid, as the Grand Vizier.[1195] His first deed was to track and remove any possible opponent to Ally dictate, and use summary methods of trial by court martial.[1196] He would do even more as to be seen further on.

In regard to the second means, threats or allegations of massacres of Christians, these have been the main justification for literally everything the Christians did to Muslims since the Middle Ages, from the evil to the very evil. The main thing then as today is not what happens on the ground, for it has always been the Turk and the Muslim, in general, lying stiff on the ground, and en masse. What has always mattered and still matters is what is said, believed, written, conveyed, and repeated: that the Turk/Muslim is the fiend in chief. In Post Armistice Turkey, thanks to this Turk massacring Christians ploy, any meddling, whether in arming the Greeks and Armenians, or disarming the Turks, or slaying them (the Turks) in retribution, was justified.

Buoyed by practical Ally support, the Greeks were vigorously clashing with the Turks in areas they now claimed such as the independent State of Pontus, east of Sinope.[1197] Venizelos himself, expressing Greek claims for Turkish territory in the region on 3/4 February 1919, argued Greek majority there.[1198] At first, he had proposed 'an Armenian umbrella for 'the Black Sea Greeks,' as they were the majority. Then, by the intermediary of the Archbishop of Trabzon, Chrysanthos Philippidis (whose existence seems to indicate that the Greeks had been enjoying religious freedom), the Armenian umbrella seemed to have been set aside, the Greeks wanting the place for themselves as the dominant force.[1199] Likewise, all over Turkey, the Greeks, hitherto obedient Turkish subjects, were, as in Istanbul, 'renouncing civic responsibilities as Ottoman citizens.'[1200] They were now opting for union with Greece.[1201] In Istanbul itself, it was no longer a matter of jeering at the defeated or wounded Turks as in the wake of the Balkan Wars, but even more:

> Turks shut themselves up in their houses, emerging, shadows of themselves, only to buy bread, perhaps at half a crown a loaf. Some even

---

[1195] P. Kinross: *Ataturk*; op cit; p. 143.
[1196] Ibid.
[1197] Claims of Greece; in CH Vol 10 April, 1919— September, 1919; p. 60.
[1198] M. Llewellyn Smith: *Ionian Vision*; Allen Lane; London; 1973, 71–5.
[1199] A. Alexandris: *The Greek Minority of Istanbul and Greek-Turkish Relations 1918–1974*, Centre for Asia Minor Studies, Athens 1992.
[1200] A. Mango: *Ataturk*; op cit; p. 210.
[1201] A. Alexandris: *The Greek Minority of Istanbul*, 56–7.

> pretended they were not Turks at all, shed their fezes and tried to get jobs with the Allied forces which had moved into the city.
>
> Greeks, on the other hand, swaggered through the streets, jostling the Turks to the wall. They flaunted the blue-and-white flag from their headquarters and expected the Turks to salute it, driving them to slink down the side streets to avoid the disgrace.[1202]

If the Armistice days were for the Turks their darkest, for Turkey's Christians they were the happiest of their lives.[1203]

An army that loses its chain of command for just a couple of days literally ceases to exist straight, as seen with the Russians in the wake of the February-March 1917 Revolution; when suddenly whole divisions could be seen aimlessly meandering, without discipline, equipment, or purpose. Once the Turkish army was dismantled in the wake of the Armistice, the Turkish soldiers and officer corps did not turn into a rabble of brigands and cut-throats. However, the grinding machine of the Allies and the Puppet government in Istanbul had had its toll. Just in the space of a few months, i.e. by May 1919, the Turkish army had been reduced by 338,000 men from over half a million.[1204] Many soldiers, also, without pay, commanding officers, or organised framework, just faded away; and so by this date, the Turkish regular army had been reduced to less than 20,000 effectives.[1205] This was the moment the claimants to Turkish territory began their grab; the Armenians occupied Kars (on 19 April 1919),[1206] whilst the Greeks, a month later, made their infamous landing in Smyrna/Izmir on 15 May 1919.

On 6 May, that is nine days before the Greeks landed in İzmir, Lloyd George, President Woodrow Wilson and Clemenceau in Paris, and the Italian leadership granted the go ahead to the Greeks to land.[1207] The Greeks were given a five-year administrative mandate in the 'Smyrna Zone,' with the possibility of subsequent annexation.'[1208] The Greek ownership of territory taken from Turkey would be made irreversible by a gradual exchange of populations, whereby many more Turks would have to be uprooted than Greeks.[1209] On 14 May 1919, a vast fleet made of British, American, and French warships brought an entire Greek division into the harbour of İzmir.[1210] The same day, Allied detachments occupied the İzmir forts and informed the Turkish governor that the Greeks were about to land.[1211] On hearing the news, the local Greeks began to celebrate, and then,

---

[1202] Lord P. Kinross: *Ataturk*; p. 134.
[1203] A. Mango: *Ataturk;* op cit; p. 198.
[1204] Ibid; p. 194.
[1205] A.J. Toynbee: *The Western Question*; p. 226,
[1206] W.E.Allen and P. Muratoff: *Caucasian Battlefields*; op cit; p. 498.
[1207] D. Von Mikusch: Mustafa *Kemal,* pp. 192-193. Peter Kincaird Jensen; p. 554.
[1208] A.J. Toynbee: *The Western Question;* p. 35.
[1209] A. Mango: *Ataturk*; p. 210.
[1210] S.J. and E. K. Shaw: *History*; op cit; 2; 342.
[1211] M. Llewellyn Smith: *Ionian Vision*; op cit, 88.

'It has been ready for some days. The Bandirma – at your orders.'
He would leave next day.[1218]

4. The War of Independence: From 'Smyrna' to Sakarya

It was on 19 May 1919 in Samsun that Mustafa Kemal launched the campaign for the Independence of Turkey.[1219] On the same day in a letter to the Turkish War Minister, General, Sir George Milne, Commander of the British Army of the Black Sea, reminded the minister that the 9th Army was being disbanded, and so why then was a 'Chief of Staff', accompanied by a large suite, sent to Sivas?[1220] The War Ministry replied on 24 May that Mustafa Kemal's inspectorate took in two army corps (the 3rd and 15th), and that his duties involved making sure that units obeyed War Ministry orders to remove breech blocks from guns, and to prevent public disorder, and that Mustafa Kemal's remit extended beyond Sivas, covering the whole area.[1221]

By the time Mustafa Kemal arrived in Samsun, he had the practical support of some of the early leaders of the resistance, Ali Fuat Cebesoy, and most particularly, Kâzim Karabekir, one of the greatest figures of Turkish history. Ali Fuat Cebesoy, Commander of the 20th Army Corps in Ankara, had already, in March 1919, begun to plan and organise the resistance in the area.[1222] Kâzim Karabekir, in command of the 15th Army Corps at Erzurum, and also in charge of the provinces of Van and Trabzon, had already launched the action 'for the freedom of Anatolia from enemy rule and also regain Kars, Ardahan, Batum, and the Turkish portions of the Caucasus.'[1223] He had now an army of 18,000 men and war materiel that the British were preparing to ship back to Istanbul.[1224]

From the initial moment, mosques played the leading part in gathering the people and passing on the call for the struggle for independence. When he arrived in

---

[1218] Ibid; p. 155.
[1219] For early literature on Mustafa Kemal (which in many ways is much superior to most subsequent works, see, for instance, Major General James G. Harbord, "Mustapha Kemal Pasha and His Party," in the *World's Work*, Volume 36 (London, 1920), pp. 470- 482; M. Paillares: *Le Kemalisme devant les Allies* (Paris, 1922); "The Recovery of the Sick Man of Europe," in the *Literary Digest*, November, 1922, pp. 17 et seq.; M. K. Zia Bey, "How the Turks Feel," in *Asia*, Volume XXII (1922), pp. 857 et seq., and "The New Turkish Democracy," in *The Nation*, Volume 115 (New York, 1922), pp. 546-548; Major General Sir Charles Townshend, "Great Britain and the Turks," in *Asia*, Volume XXII (1922), pp. 949-953; Clair Price, "Mustapha Kemal and the Angora Government," in *Current History*, Volume XVI (1922), pp. 790-800; Ludwell Denny, "The Turk Comes Back," in The *Nation*, Volume 115 (1922), pp. 575-577; "The New Epoch in Turkey," in the *Muslim Standard* (London), November 9, 1922.
[1220] A. Ryan: *The Last of the Dragomans* (London, 1951) 131.
[1221] Bayur, Hikmet, Atatürk Hayatı ve Eseri (Atatürk's Life and Work), Vol. I (from his birth to his landing in Samsun), AKDTYK, Ankara 1990; 305
[1222] S.J. and E.K. Shaw: *History*; op cit; v 2; p. 341.
[1223] Karabekir, Kâzım, İstiklâl Harbimiz (Our War of Independence), 2nd ed, Türkiye Yayınevi, Istanbul 1969, pp. 19-23.
[1224] Rawlinson, *Adventures in the Near East 1918-1922*, London and New York, 1923; Karabekir, Kâzım, *İstiklâl Harbimiz*, op cit; pp. 161-162.

Samsun, Mustafa Kemal arranged for meetings to be held in the principal mosque in order to rouse the people to resistance.[1225] Following a crowded service, with prayers for success, in the mass-meeting that was held in the small square of the town, the speakers emphasised that the country was in danger; therefore all Muslims must take arms lest 'they die beneath the feet of the enemy.' A religiously binding oath was sworn to this effect.[1226] This was the beginning of the armed movement, which soon brought together all sections of Turkish society, ranging from 'roving guerrilla bands' to 'regular volunteer militias attached to local political committees, soldiers, civil servants, landowners, businessmen, artisans, religious leaders, peasants, nomads, bandits, members of different parties, including the CUP, women, and children, all united in reaction to the occupation and determined to be free.'[1227]
Even in Istanbul there was great support for the national cause.[1228]

In the meantime, the carving up of Turkey was proceeding. In the western parts of the country, following their landing, the Greeks began moving into Anatolia, ravaging as they went, and the local Greek population 'taking the opportunity to join in the massacre.'[1229] Havza, where now Mustafa Kemal was, was in the middle of Greek guerrilla warfare, Greek gangs terrorising the Turkish population, robbing and killing them on the roads, burning their villages, and kidnapping their prominent citizens.[1230] The Turks could do little since the British were confiscating their arms but allowing the Greeks to keep theirs and, even more, were arming them in order to help them build their state of Pontus.[1231] In the south, the Armenians were returning not only to the areas in Cilicia and Upper Mesopotamia under British and then French occupation, but also to central Anatolia, reclaiming houses taken over by Muslim families.[1232] The problem was particularly acute in Aegean Turkey, where 113,000 Muslims, most of whom had fled from Greece in the aftermath of the Balkan Wars, had been settled in Greek houses and were now facing eviction.[1233]
Attending Friday prayers in the main local Mosque of Havza, Mustafa Kemal called the participants to be ready to sacrifice themselves for the recovery of İzmir.[1234] The local Greek inhabitants informed their Metropolitan (Archbishop) Germanos in Samsun, who reported matters to the local British officer.[1235] The Commander-in-Chief, Sir George Milne, now demanded the Turkish War Ministry

---

[1225] P. Kinross: *Ataturk*; op cit; p. 165.
[1226] Ibid; p. 168.
[1227] Midilli Ahmet. *Turk Istiklal Harbinin... Milli Mucadele*, Ankara, 1928.
[1228] A. Mango: *Ataturk;* op cit; p. 221.
[1229] S.J. and E.K Shaw: *History*; 2; 342.
[1230] P. Kinross: *Ataturk*; op cit; p. 167.
[1231] Ibid; p. 166-7.
[1232] A. Mango: *Ataturk;* op cit; p. 222.
[1233] Akşin, Sina, İstanbul Hükümetleri ve Milli Mücadele (The Istanbul Governments and the National Struggle), I–II, Cem, Istanbul 1992, I, 309–10
[1234] A. Mango: *Ataturk*; 225.
[1235] Ibid.

On 19 June 1919, Mustafa Kemal met with Ali Fuat Cebesoy, commander in Ankara, Rauf Orbay, former Navy Minister, and Refet Bele, who commanded several army corps near Samsun.[1252] After three days of consultations, on 21 June, they signed the Amasya Protocol, and also obtained agreement by telegram from Cemal (Mersinli), 2nd Army Inspector in Konya, and Kâzım Karabekir, Commander of the 15th Corps – the strongest in the army – in Erzurum.[1253] This agreement became more or less the first call for a national movement against the occupation.[1254] It called principally for 'the unity of the Fatherland and national independence,' now both in danger; denounced the Istanbul government, which was unable to carry out its responsibilities, and decided to hold immediately a National Congress in Sivas, the most secure place in Anatolia.[1255]

In the meantime, the Greeks and Armenians were pursuing their carving-up policies under armed Ally cover. The Armenians were most busy in both the East and in the South expropriating, cleansing out Turks, and using violence.[1256] In the west, the Greeks were doing the same causing wholesale destruction of Muslim property, forcing out yet another wave of Turkish refugees, their aim, of course, being to empty that whole area of its Muslim population before annexing it to Greece.[1257]

It was at this dramatic juncture, just a few days before the Amasya meeting, that an ally of immense stature came forth: Soviet Russia; that same country that had for more than a century done so much harm to Turkey, now under Soviet rule, had come to offer what Turkey needed most: alliance and material support. The reason for this, of course, was that Soviet Russia had the same foes as Turkey then: The Allies now busy carving up Turkey were also undermining Soviet Russia in its civil war.[1258] The Soviets, of course, were also hoping that Turkey would join 'The Soviet family.' Thus, just before the Amasya gathering, a Bolshevik delegation headed by Colonel Semen Budenny met Mustafa Kemal, and offered arms and ammunition in return for stemming Armenian expansionism in the Caucasus, which, obviously threatened Turkey's existence too; and equally to Turkey's interest: to close Allied access to southern Russia through the Black Sea.[1259] And so were laid the bases for the cooperation that was to be of crucial importance once the national movement was organised.[1260]

[1252] S.J. and E.K. Shaw: *History*; op cit; 343.
[1253] Erikan, Celâl, Komutan Atatürk (Atatürk as a Commander), T. İş Bankası, Ankara 1972, 374.
[1254] S.J. and E.K. Shaw: *History*; op cit; p. 343.
[1255] Ataturk: *Nutuk*, I, 30-34.
[1256] Armenian atrocities in South or east, or both source: Mango 222-25.
[1257] See Toynbee *Western Question*; A. Mango: *Ataturk;* p. 228.
[1258] To have the best idea on the Western-Bolshevik conflict, and also Western involvement, and why, and all the political military ramifications, there is, and by far, nothing better than Current History, especially vols 5-12. Although the magazine itself is rabidly anti Bolshevik, it gives a wonderful idea of the situation as was lived and experienced then.
[1259] S.J. and E.K. Shaw: *History*; op cit; p. 344.
[1260] Ibid.

The Erzurum Congress, which took place between July 23 and August 7, 1919 came as a result of the Society for the Defence of the Rights of Eastern Anatolia call for a regional meeting to be held in Erzurum in response to the threat of further Armenian aggression in the east.[1261] Thanking the delegates for electing him chair, Mustafa Kemal denounced the process of partitioning of the country, the impotence of the government in Istanbul and 'the machinations of the Allies and their dupes.'[1262] Only in Anatolia, he declared, 'could a national administration gain control over the country's fate, free from outside interference,' thus, calling for the formation of an alternative national government.[1263] On 7 August, the congress met in ultimate session, and published its final declaration, which included

> The indivisible integrity of the eastern provinces as part of the Ottoman state,... Describing realistically any Allied act of occupation and intervention as support for Greek and Armenian separatism, it declared that this would be met with the united resistance of all Muslims.[1264]

The Nationalist Congress of Sivas on 11 September 1919, somehow repeated the principles established in Erzurum, with minor additions such as that the formation of an independent Greece on the Aydın, Manisa, and Balıkesir fronts was unacceptable.[1265]

'And that whilst fair treatment would be granted to minorities, there would be no special privileges, but instead, resistance to Greek and Armenian territorial claims.'[1266]

After that, Kemal headed for what was to become the capital of Free Turkey: Ankara.

Now his support was growing fast. The people of Bursa and Edirne, among others, had joined the movement, which was growing steadily.[1267] In an interview given at this time, Mustafa Kemal, stated:

> It is our aim to secure the development of Turkey as she stood at the time of the armistice. We have no expansionist plans. It is our conviction that Turkey can be made rich and prosperous if we get a good Government. Our Government has been weakened through foreign interference and intrigues.[1268]

[1261] Ibid.
[1262] A. Mango: *Ataturk;* op cit; p. 239.
[1263] Atatürk, Atatürk'ün Söylev ve Demeçleri (ASD) (Speeches and Statements by Atatürk), original text in Ottoman Turkish, I–III (in one vol.), Atatürk Kültür, Dil ve Tarih Yüksek Kurumu (AKDTYK) [Atatürk Culture, Language and History Higher Institute], Ankara 1989, I, 1-5.
[1264] Gologlu, Mahmut, I, Erzurum Kongresi (The Congress of Erzurum), Kalite Matbaası, Ankara 1968; II, Sivas Kongresi (The Congress of Sivas), 1969;.I, 182. Gologlu., I, 187-9. Text in Gologlu; I ,201-3.
[1265] Gologlu, *Sivas Kongresi,* pp. 232-234; an English tr. can be found in E. G. Mears, *Modern Turkey,* New York, 1924, pp. 624-627;
[1266] Text in Gologlu, II, 232-4.
[1267] The Problem of Turkey: Survey of the Rival Claims of Territory and Power in Turkey. Which Menace Peace in the Near East; in *Current History;* Vol 11: October, 1919— March, 1920 Part Two; p. 270.
[1268] Ibid.

As for the Greeks, straight in the wake of San Remo, the Supreme (Allies) Council gave the Greeks authority to advance from Smyrna/İzmir.[1308] On 22 June 1920, the Greek troops marched in execution of a plan put in place on the Greek side by Commander-in-Chief, General Paraskevopoulos, and on the Allied side by Lieut. Gen. Sir George Milne, Commander of the Allied troops in Western Asia.[1309] There were four simultaneous movements:

One force advanced northwards from Manisa along the Panderma Railway towards the south coast of the Marmara Sea.[1310] Straight was Bursa occupied by the Greek cavalry, riding ahead of the rest of the army.

A second force advanced simultaneously eastwards to Alaşehir, and then in August, up to Uşak on the plateau.[1311]

A third force, further south, moved from Aydın in a parallel direction up the north bank of the Maeander, to where easy communications with Uşak and Alaşehir could be secured.[1312]

A fourth force sailed to İzmit to assist the British, whilst Mudania and Gemlik were occupied from the sea by British and Greek navy units.[1313]

At the same time, operations were launched in Eastern Thrace against the troops of Colonel Çafer Tayar, the Military Governor of Edirne.[1314]

On 21 July 1920, supported by British aerial bombardment, the Greeks entered the Sea of Marmara port of Tekirdağ with a division and an infantry regiment.[1315] Further west, another Greek column prepared to cross the Maritza River on the Greco-Turkish frontier to attack Edirne and the Turkish forces there.[1316] On 23 July, the Greeks crossed the Maritza under heavy fire, the Tekirdağ forces marching swiftly to the north and west, and two days later captured both Lule Burgaz and Edirne; Colonel Tayar amongst the many prisoners, whilst those amongst the Turks who could, were in full retreat.[1317]

Ali Fuat (Cebesoy), who had been appointed commander of the western front, had hardly any forces with which to face the powerful Greek army.[1318] Retreat was the only option.

'The Greek columns,' as Churchill described the offensive, 'trailed along the country roads passing safely through many ugly defiles, and at their approach the Turks, under strong and sagacious leadership, vanished into the recesses of Anatolia.'[1319]

[1308] P. Kinross: *Ataturk*; op cit; p. 232.
[1309] Turkey and Her Lost Dominions; Counterproposals Submitted by the Turks on Many Articles of the Treaty; CH 12; 807.
[1310] A.J. Toynbee: *The Western Question*; p. 228.
[1311] Ibid; p. 229.
[1312] Ibid.
[1313] Ibid.
[1314] Turkey and Her Lost Dominions; Counterproposals Submitted by the Turks on Many Articles of the Treaty; CH 12; 807.
[1315] P. Kincaid Jensen: The Greco Turkish War, p. 555.
[1316] *The New York Times*, July 22, 1920, p. 17.
[1317] P. Kincaid Jensen: The Greco Turkish War, p. 555.
[1318] Özerdim, Sami N., Atatürk Devrimi Kronolojisi (A Chronology of Atatürk's Reforms), Çankaya Belediyesi, Ankara 1996, 41; 43.
[1319] P. Kinross: *Ataturk*; op cit; p. 233.

In a proclamation to the nation, Mustafa Kemal appealed to the Turkish people's religious sentiment:
> We call on the whole nation to come together in unity and rise against the Greeks in total determination. The jihad, once it is properly preached, will, with God's help, result quickly in the rout of the Greeks.[1320]

The Greek successes were met with jubilation in Ally centres. The Turks according to Lloyd Georges, were 'Beaten, and fleeing with their forces towards Mecca.'[1321]

The British and Greek Premiers were laughing at the French generals 'who did not even know (or perhaps had slyly pretended not to know) their own business.'[1322]

Venizelos seemed to have done the job. He had a formidable army, intact from the war and largely supplied, and at very favourable terms, by European arms factories.[1323] In fact, throughout their advance in Thrace and in Anatolia, the Greeks were assisted by British warships along the Marmara littoral.[1324] By August, the business seemed to be done. Having already captured Gallipoli on 4 August, the Greeks took Uşak (August 29) and cut the Aydın-İzmir-Eğridir railroad, the main transportation line in the southwest (August 26).[1325] 'Against the systematic onslaught of these troops, the ragged and motley Nationalist forces had very little chance,' says Von Mikuch.[1326]

The following round was aimed at finishing the Turks. This was planned for the Autumn: October 1920.

The Greek Autumn offensive, as expected, advanced in the direction of the railway; so successful and swift, yielding large sways of land, the Allies, once more, could not hold their joy.
> 'The Turks,' Lloyd George exulted in the House of Commons, 'are broken beyond repair.'[1327]

Then, suddenly, the Greeks successful advance stopped. It was the turning point. What happened was that, in the last day or days of September, whilst watching the antics of a pair of pet monkeys, King Alexander of Greece was bitten by one of them and days later, just as the Greek offensive was proceeding, the King died from infection.[1328] This had major effects. First, understandably, it halted the military offensive. Then, it led to new elections, which brought back to Greece ex-King Constantine, who had been exiled abroad in 1917. In the elections on 14

[1320] Ataturk: Atatürk'ün Tamim, Telgraf ve Beyannameleri (ATTB) (Circulars, Telegrams and Proclamations by Atatürk), published as IV of above, separate volume, 1991; 358.
[1321] P. Kinross: *Ataturk*; op cit; p. 233.
[1322] A.J. Toynbee: *The Western Question*; p. 229.
[1323] A. Mango: *Ataturk;* John Murray; London; 1999; p. 286.
[1324] Greek Conquest of Eastern Thrace; in CH 12; p. 1077.
[1325] S.J. and E.K. Shaw: *History*; op cit; p. 358.
[1326] Von Mikusch, *Mustafa Kemal*, p. 254.
[1327] P. Kinross: *Ataturk*; op cit; p. 239.
[1328] Ibid; pp. 253-6.

November, 1920, the ex-King and his party defeated Venizelos, and on assuming power, the New King, Constantine, eliminated Venizelos' allies.[1329] This would have a decisive impact on the relations between the Greeks and the Allies. The latter hated Constantine, a formerly pro German, and hence began to cool their enthusiasm for Greece.

The halt of the Greek offensive also gave crucial time to the Turks to pursue the reorganisation of their forces. Ali Fuad, the commander of the Turkish forces in the west, was replaced by İsmet Pasha, who had fought alongside Mustafa Kemal in the southern front.[1330]

The break, more importantly, witnessed decisive developments in the Nationalist-Bolshevik relations. The new Soviet Government, facing the same Ally foes, deemed itself a natural ally of the Nationalist Turkish government, and so the first weapon consignments started arriving from Bolshevik Russia.[1331] Yusuf Kemal, who had travelled to Russia in the Summer of 1920, now returned to Ankara with a million gold roubles, together with military supplies to be shipped across the Black Sea.[1332] Subsequently, the Soviets not only rejected the Sèvres Treaty, they also ceded to Turkey the territories of Kars and Ardahan in the Caucasus region as an expression of full accord with the principles of the National Pact.[1333]

The halt of the Greek offensive also gave the Turks the possibility to deal with the Armenian military front both south and east.

In the south, the Turks had already smothered much of French power, and so the latter could no longer lend the assistance they would have otherwise given. On 15–16 October, after a month siege, Turkish irregulars stormed the Armenian stronghold of Haçin (Hadjin, now Saimbeyli) 100 miles north of Adana in the Taurus Mountains.[1334] This somehow finished the Armenian front in the south.

It was an altogether different matter in the east. The Armenians were determined to bring under their rule eastern Anatolia, thus forcing the Turks to move against them despite the more pressing Greek danger.[1335] Armenian raids on Turkish border villages had begun in May 1920. Karabekir was appointed commander of the eastern front (June 15, 1920).[1336] He soon organised an army, making an urgent request upon the Grand National Assembly to authorise an advance.[1337] Despite the Turkish woes, the Assembly dithered somehow due to the Greek

---

[1329] Lloyd George was shocked and distressed to see the results of the Greek elections.' IILRO, Lloyd George Papers, F/55/l/41, David Lloyd George to Venizelos, 17 November 1920. Michael Llewellyn Smith, The Greek Occupation of Western Asia Minor of 1919-1922, and the National Schism, (unpublished doctoral dissertation, Oxford University, 1971).

[1330] P. Kincaid Jensen: The Greco Turkish War, p. 557.

[1331] Ibid.

[1332] Altemur Kilic: *Turkey and the World* (Washington D.C.: Public Affairs Press, 1959), p. 46.

[1333] E. Mead: *The Baghdad Railway; A Study in Imperialism*; MacMillan; New York; 1924; p. 316.

[1334] For details see CH VOLUME XIII October, 1920— March, 1921; 444.

[1335] S.J. and E.K. Shaw: *History*; op cit; p. 356.

[1336] Ibid.

[1337] *Turk Istiklal Harbi*; III, 92, 273. FO 5042/E692, FO 5211/El5253, FO 5045/E2809, FO 5045/E2736, FO 4963/El4103, F05041/E357.

threat in the west, and so contended itself to raise diplomatic protests.[1338] As the Turks were preoccupied with the Greeks, in the summer, the British military advisers were putting in place an Armenian army of 40,000 men.[1339] As E.K and S.J. Shaw remark, the postponement proved very propitious, for had the Turks moved against the Armenians at the moment of the Greek Summer offensive, moving Turkish troops east could have hampered efforts in the west.[1340] Instead, things worked out with perfection. Following the Monkey's misdeed, early in October, the Greek front went quiet (elections, a new king and a new government), which gave the Turks the break needed to face the Armenians. By October, the Armenians had more than 10,000 men on the Kars front, in addition of troops in other areas.[1341] The Armenians tried to complete their occupation of Kars province by entering the district of Oltu with its overwhelmingly Muslim population, and were accused of atrocities by the Turks, who threatened strong action.[1342] On 28 October, Karabekir launched his offensive and took the upper hand, capturing Kars castle on 30 October.[1343] The fortress was so large that the Armenian generals and ministers waited for nearly two hours before the Turkish troops could find them and accept their surrender.[1344] More than 2,000 Armenian troops, including three generals, were taken prisoner; 676 guns, most of them old, were captured. Turkish losses were 9 dead and 47 wounded.[1345]

Further campaigns during November turned to the advantage of the Turks, until on 2 December, the armistice, confirmed by the treaty of Gümrü, fixed the present frontier between Turkey and Armenia.[1346]

By late autumn 1920, the regional situation had been altered beyond recognition. The Nationalists were registering great successes; the French were facing a draining war in Syria; the British the same in Iraq; and the Italians in Libya, all three countries having now to bomb the Arab tribes from the air in order to maintain control.[1347] Then, to complicate matters, in the Russian civil war, General Wrangel, who was backed by the Allies, was defeated by the Bolsheviks, who also captured Sebastopol.[1348] Now the wreck of his army was lying in Istanbul, as the Golden Horn became glutted with Russian ships from the Crimea, loaded with 150,000 refugees, many of them dying from disease and

---

[1338] *Ataturk* TTB, pp. 337-340.
[1339] R. Hovannisian: The Republic of Armenia, I–IV, University of California, 1996, III, 341
[1340] S.J. and E.K. Shaw: *History*; op cit; p. 357.
[1341] Erikan, Celâl, Komutan Atatürk (Atatürk as a Commander), T. İş Bankası, Ankara 1972, 571.
[1342] A. Mango: *Ataturk;* p. 288.
[1343] C. Erikan: *Komutan;* op cit; 577–9.
[1344] R.G. Hovannisian, op cit; IV, 259.
[1345] Hovannisian, IV, 259. Erikan gives Armenian losses in Kars as 1,100 dead and 1,200 prisoners. Halide Edib: *The Turkish Ordeal*; John Murray; London; 1928; p. 202.
[1346] R. Hovonisian, IV, 268–91, 394–8; full text of treaty in İsmail Soysal, Türkiye'nin Siyasal Andlaşmaları (Turkey's Diplomatic Treaties), I (1920–1945), TTK, Ankara 1983; 19–23. It is dated 2 December 1920. Hovannisian says that the treaty was signed at 2 a.m. on 3 December.
[1347] *Current History;* VOLUME XIII October, 1920— March, 1921; 256; refs for air bombing of Libyans and Syrians; BBC Lawrence.
[1348] CH VOLUME XIII October, 1920— March, 1921; Part Two; p. 66; Gains of the Turkish Nationalists

Adalia increasingly precarious;[1368] bypassing the Istanbul Government, just like the French, the Italian and Turkish Ministers of Foreign Affairs signed in London a separate treaty.[1369]

Thus, the two governments, which months earlier were contemplating the carving up of Turkey, were now two of the earliest to recognise its supremacy.

At just around that time, on 16 March, the Turkish Nationalist delegates at Moscow signed a treaty 'establishing fraternal relations between Soviet Russia and Turkey', Russians now 'recognize Constantinople as the capital of Turkey.'[1370] And this was accompanied by the inflow of Soviet armament.

Also from everywhere, the Nationalist ranks were being constantly reinforced by the arrival of ex-officers and young fighters drawn to the nationalist cause.[1371] One officer in particular would prove his immense commanding skills and qualities at the Battle of Sakarya, colonel Fevzi, who was straight propelled to the high functions of Prime Minister and Acting Chief of the General Staff in Ankara.[1372] Fevzi had won a great military reputation during long campaigns in the Balkans and in the First World War.[1373] Even in the Istanbul government, his successive positions in the War Ministry had proved he was no mere puppet but a strong patriot.[1374] A man of strict habits and honesty, deeply religious, he was much appreciated by all, and he was the sort of commander needed at the moment.[1375]

It was then that the Greeks decided to launch their new offensive. King Constantine, after decreeing the call under the colours of three classes of reserves, called on his people:

> Though we were hoping that peace would be re-established without further shedding of blood, a new attempt was made to reverse the order of things established by the Treaty of Sèvres, as is proved by military movements and by the concentration of troops against our front.
>
> These manoeuvres make it necessary to reinforce our troops in order to protect our population exposed to the violence of savage bands and also to obtain definitive peace in the East, an aim which Greece pursues in common with her great allies. Confident of the patriotism and heroism of the Greeks, I would appeal to the sentiment within them to reinforce the troops charged with imposing peace.[1376]

[1368] E. Mead: *The Baghdad Railway*; p. 324.
[1369] Ibid.
[1370] In CH VOLUME XIV. April — September, 1921; pp. 351-352
[1371] M. Uyar and E.J. Erickson: *A Military History*; p. 283.
[1372] A. Mango: *Ataturk*; p. 311.
[1373] P. Kinross: *Ataturk*; op cit; p. 225.
[1374] Ibid; p. 154.
[1375] Ibid; p. 225.
[1376] Greece attempts to impose the Sevres Treaty; in CH VOLUME XIV. April — September, 1921; p. 349-50.

On 23 March 1921, the Greeks' northern and southern armies advanced simultaneously from the Bursa and Uşak sectors.[1377] After initial fierce fighting, the southern army captured the railway junction at Afyon.[1378] Once again, the Greeks fought well, even spoke of a great victory and a march on Ankara, but were stopped at İnönü by fierce resistance from the Turks, who were now better supplied with artillery, and were well dug in around Eskişehir.[1379] The three Greek northern divisions at great loss sought to capture the heights which they had easily captured two months before.[1380] This time, the approaches were swept by a well-served Turkish artillery; the slopes were well defended by excellent system of entrenchment, and defended by troops who held their ground.[1381] After several days of fierce fighting the Greek 7th Division managed to carry Turkish positions, and the Greeks could look down on the plain of Eskişehir.[1382] Then, as reinforcements arrived, on 31 March, İsmet counter-attacked again. The Greek losses were heavy, but their forces escaped destruction, and were in speedy retreat.[1383]

The victory at İnönü was greeted with joy by the Turkish population, including of Istanbul, and even the Sultan had prayers read for the soldiers killed in the fighting and sent a donation to the Red Crescent for the relief of victims.[1384]

This halt of the Greek offensive, later called the Second Battle of İnönü, caused great sorrows in Athens, and the Greeks 'dourly' realised that they now faced a regular, well-organised Turkish army.[1385] General Papoulas saw that substantially more reinforcements were needed than he had originally anticipated. The Greek government authorised the formation of three divisions of conscripts to be used in the next assault.[1386] In earnest the strength of the army in Anatolia was brought up to 200,000 men.[1387]

One of the leading Greek voices then, Adamantios Th. Polyzoides, Editor of the *Greek Daily Atlantis*, sums up for us why they were fighting Turkey:

> A war for the rescue of millions of Greeks from intolerable Turkish persecutions — Historical evidence to prove that Asia Minor always has been Greek territory — Appalling facts of recent massacres (of Christians), which are among the causes of the present war.[1388]

[1377] A.J. Toynbee: *The Western Question*; op cit; p. 233.
[1378] P. Kincaid Jensen: The Greco Turkish War, p. 558.
[1379] For details of battle, see Greece attempts to impose the Sevres Treaty; in CH VOLUME XIV. April-September, 1921; p. 350.
[1380] A.J. Toynbee: *The Western Question*; p. 233.
[1381] Ibid.
[1382] Ibid.
[1383] Ibid.
[1384] Tansel, Selahettin, *Mondros'tan*; op cit; IV, 85.
[1385] P. Kincaid Jensen: The Greco Turkish War, op cit; p. 558.
[1386] H.R.H. Prince Andrew of Greece, *Towards Disaster* (London: John Murray, 1930), p. 18.
[1387] M. Llewellyn Smith: *Ionian Vision*; op cit; 222, note.
[1388] A. Th. Polyzoides: Why the Greeks are fighting Turkey; in CH VOLUME XIV. April — September, 1921; p. 761.

Then, the author repeats precisely the same arguments seen above made by Mandelstam, Bryce and others, with the Greek dimension added. Also the same claims of Turkish massacre of Christians were being made throughout the Western world, as in America, where, *Current History*, the New York Times Magazine, stated amongst other:

> Greek wounded began to arrive in Athens, and at once the papers began to print stories of Turkish atrocities. One stated that the Greek Bishop of Adalia had been arrested and carried off in chains by the Kemalists, under the eyes of the Italians, who made no effort to rescue him. Both the Venizelist and the anti-Venizelist press supported the Government in its war policy and were unanimous in considering that on Greece has devolved the task of settling the question between Turks and Christians in Asia Minor.[1389]

It just happened that precisely at the same time when the world was being swamped with stories of Turkish atrocities committed on Greeks and other Christians, Arnold Toynbee, who was on the ground reported:

> On the morning of the 25th May (1921)... Having with me a letter of recommendation from General Papulas, the Greek Commander-in-Chief in Asia Minor, and having received much kindness from him, I drafted a telegram to him explaining the situation and requesting permission for the surviving inhabitants of Yalova, Samanly, and Akkeui to embark, as well as the refugees... I then sought out the Captain (Papagrigoriu) in the café (in Yalova), asked the favour of an interview with him in his office, and handed him simultaneously my credentials and my telegram. Would he be so kind as to send the telegram off?
> "The Commander-in- Chief says that you are a Philhellene! In this telegram you are destroying Greece!..." (replied the captain.)
> Before these interviews with the Captain were over, the (Turkish) refugees had begun to gather on the beach. It was incredible how quickly they flocked in. (Akkeui was nearly two hours' distance on foot from the Yalova jetty.) They brought just themselves and their families, and whatever they could carry off at a moment's notice. A few had a cow or some poultry, or boxes loaded on ox-carts. Most had only the bundles of bedding which they could carry on their backs. Most pitiful of all were the women with children, whose men were dead and who had no one to help them. As we reckoned it out afterwards, there were something like 500 persons huddled together there like terrified animals, in sight of the steamer, and looking to us to get them into safety. The British and Italian lieutenants returned with the last arrivals. The Christian civilians (Greek and Armenian) and the Greek soldiers gathered round, half-mocking and half menacing. The sinister priest sidled up. Captain Papagrigoriu presented himself, and the leaders of the Greek chette bands now openly paraded in

---
[1389] Greece attempts to impose the Sevres Treaty; in CH VOLUME XIV. April — September, 1921; p. 351.

his company! I secured the names of five (all of them Greeks who had been living with Turks). I have already mentioned that one of them stood at Captain Papagrigoriu's elbow during the subsequent proceedings, acting as his "interpreter" and advising him as to which individual refugees should be passed or kept back. The actual embarkation lasted seven hours. It began at midday on the 25th May and continued till about seven in the evening, when Captain Papagrigoriu, after the receipt of a second telegram from General Leonardhopulos, absolutely refused to let us take any more persons on board. By that time we had succeeded in embarking about 320 out of a total of something like 500 collected on the beach, and of between 1300 and 1500 (adding inhabitants of surviving places and refugees from destroyed places together) whom we had really been authorised to evacuate. During those seven hours we had to wrestle for their lives, not only family by family, but person by person. Captain Papagrigoriu not only kept back the very few men of military age, as was reasonable; he struggled to retain in his power every individual, however feeble or defenceless or old. He separated (I have instances vividly in my mind) wives from husbands and mothers from children.

Meanwhile, we started to claim individual cases, and an indescribable confusion arose. The Captain stormed and gesticulated; we argued and expostulated; the soldiers standing at the entrance to the jetty kept on turning back persons whom the Captain had already passed for evacuation; the soldiers and the Captain shouted at each other; both soldiers and Christian civilians crowded in upon the refugees and whispered in their ears (we learnt afterwards that they had been telling them that we intended to throw those who embarked into the sea, half-way between Yalova and Constantinople!); the priest glided in and out; the Christian women looked on and gloated (we took a photograph of them laughing at the scene); the refugees sat numb and patient till their turn came to pass muster, and then the women trembled and sobbed.

I can only mention one or two of the incidents that crowd into my memory. At one moment, I heard a woman call and saw her pointing to her husband, who was being led away by a chette leader from the shore into the town. I ran after them, led the man back by the hand, and returned with another member of our party to bring the chette before the Allied officers for an explanation. We had a scuffle with him. A Greek officer rushed up from the cafe and beckoned to the Greek and Armenian crowd; they threw themselves between us, and our chette ran like a hare down the street. I do not know with which of the five gentlemen I have named I had the honour to make acquaintance, but the leaders are recognizable by the sort of cloth turban they wear. They have borrowed it from the Lazes, a Moslem tribe who do brigandage in Anatolia for their living. The object of this (a mean trick) is to be mistaken for Moslems, so that their atrocities may be put down to the other side.

The final scene was the most pitiable, perhaps, of all. We had got off all the people whom we had rescued to the steamer, on lighters, and were now gathered on the quay, with a crowd of Greek soldiers between us and the people abandoned on the shore, when we saw two old men standing in a paralysed attitude on the jetty. Their wives had been kept back, and they would not leave without them. Rallying for a last encounter with the Captain, we went on shore again and hunted out and rescued these poor women. Yet other families were separated, by pure malignity, perhaps forever. Next morning, when our steamer was lying at anchor between Scutari and Seraglio Point, we found a very old woman on board with several small children in her care. Their mother — her daughter — had been with them on the beach, but the Greeks had prevented her from embarking, and we had learnt of it too late.[1390]

Although it must seem too much, but in order to underline the fact that the Greeks, just as their allies, were using the same technique in order to legitimise their extermination of Turks, not in one place, but systematic annihilation everywhere, let's move with Toynbee onto another setting: İzmit:

I must, however, say something about the events which preceded the voluntary withdrawal of the Greek Army from the town of Ismid, at the end of June 1921. During the year that the Greek occupation of Ismid had lasted (July 1920 to June 1921), the war of extermination had gone to such lengths, and the local Greek civilians had compromised themselves so deeply by participation, that the entire native Christian population took its departure with the troops. Naturally they felt savage. Their brief ascendency had cost them their homes; they had had to leave their immovable property behind; and though they had had time for preparations and the Greek authorities had provided shipping, their prospects were forlorn. They vented their rage on their Turkish civilian neighbours, while they still had them in their power. The villages east of Ismid were evacuated first, and the Turkish peasants with their ox-carts were commandeered to transport the departing Christians' possessions. When we landed at Ismid about thirty-five hours after the completion of the evacuation, the streets leading to the jetties were heaped with the wrecks of these carts and the water littered with the offal of the oxen, which had been slaughtered on the quay in order that the flesh and the hides might more conveniently be shipped away. Corpses of Turkish carters murdered in return for their services — were floating among the offal, and one or two corpses of Turkish women. In the town itself, the Turkish shops had been systematically looted — the Christian shops being

---

[1390] A.J. Toynbee: *The Western Question*; pp. 306-310.

protected against the destroying angel by the sign of the cross, chalked up on their shutters over the owner's name. One Turkish and Jewish quarter in the centre of the town had been set on fire, and the fire had only been extinguished after the Greeks' departure by the exertions of the French Assumptionists (who have a College at Ismid, and covered themselves with honour on this occasion). Cattle had been penned into the burning quarter by the incendiaries in a frenzy of cruelty and had been burnt alive, and the smoking ruins were haunted by tortured, half-burnt cats. The mosques had not only been robbed of their carpets and other furniture, but had been deliberately defiled. In the courtyard and even in the interior of the principal mosque, the Pertev Mehmed Jamy, pigs had been slaughtered and left lying. At 1 p.m. on Friday the 24th June, three and a half days before the Greek evacuation, the male inhabitants of the two Turkish quarters of Baghcheshme and Tepekhane, in the highest part of the town, away from the sea, had been dragged out to the cemetery and shot in batches. On Wednesday the 29th I was present when two of the graves were opened, and ascertained for myself that the corpses were those of Moslems and that their arms had been pinioned behind their backs. There were thought to be about sixty corpses in that group of graves, and there were several others.[1391]

M. Gehri, the representative of the Geneva International Red Cross, who was also on the ground, saw the same scenes as Toynbee, that instead of Turks inflicting outrages on Christians as reported then in the world media, it was the reverse, indeed:

> The Mission came to the conclusion that for the last two months elements of the Greek army of occupation have been employed in the extermination of the Muslim population of the [Yalova-Gemlik] peninsula. The facts established —burnings of villages, massacres, terror of the inhabitants, coincidences of place and date— leave no room for doubt in regard to this. The atrocities which we have seen, or of which we have seen the material evidence, were the work of irregular bands of armed civilians (tcheti) and of organized units of the regular army. No cases have come to our knowledge in which these misdeeds have been prevented or punished by the military command. Instead of being disarmed and broken up, the bands have been assisted in their activities and have collaborated hand in hand with organized units of regulars.[1392]
> The whole area had been extremely quiet until March; untouched by violence; it is certain that the systematic destruction, wholesale

---

[1391] Ibid; pp. 297-8.
[1392] Gehri, M. (Delegue du Comite International de la Croix Rouge): 'Mission d'Enquete en Anatolie, 12-22 Mai 1921,' *Extrait de la Revue Internationale de la Croix Rouge*, 3em Annee, No. 31, 15 juillet 1921, pp. 721-735; Geneva, 1921 p. 723.

destruction of villages, and widespread atrocities occurred between March and 15 May, precisely in the wake of the Greek retreat.[1393]

Then Gehri describes meticulously all the atrocities he came across, and it is needless to repeat the horrible repertory of what he saw, except these very brief extracts:

> Here are some of the things I first saw in Gemlik: a refugee from Ghedelek, Katcha Hanoum, wounded by Armenian bandits and Greek soldiers with bullets and bayonet cuts; a child from Ghedelek, the jaw shattered by a fragment from a grenade thrown into a room where women and children had been locked in; a woman from Bazar Keui, Hourie Hanoum, aged 60; robbed of everything, wounded, raped by five or 6 Greek soldiers; her husband had his throat cut beside her; the Turks, in their hundreds, were left on the ground of the mosque or in the graveyards; in another place I counted in a small room 60 women and children; for a month the Turks had been left to starve, only kept alive by what other Muslims could bring to them.[1394]

Then Gehri narrates the details of the attempted mass-annihilation of the populations of Kumla, Karacaali, Narlı. In that area all Gehri could find were accounts of terror, people freshly and brutally murdered, whole villages burnt down, charred remains of people and animals, people taken to unknown destinations and disappeared (whose mass graves must still be scattered on the hills around Kumla today in 2020); men and women, survivors, running after the delegation, seeking its protection. Then, finally, the delegation returning to Narlı, found everything burnt to the ground, except an elderly Turk, wearing a hat with a rose, sitting by his smouldering house, alone. He turned to the delegates: "It is all fine here, and there is nothing for you to do."[1395]

The Lead to, and the Battle of Sakarya: August 1921

In July 1921, the Great Summer offensive began. The initial objective once more was the railway. This time, however, the Greeks decided that rather than a frontal attack by the northern group they put their emphasis on the southern column.[1396] More or less they planned a large envelopment of Turkish forces, and by capturing Eskişehir, prevent them from withdrawing north, and thus destroying them inside the pocket.[1397]

The attack was launched on 10 July. As the Turks had also brought in reinforcements, the two opposing armies were once again roughly equal in

---
[1393] Ibid; p. 724.
[1394] Ibid; p. 725.
[1395] Ibid; for old Turk p. 728; for the description of devastation; pp. 726 onwards.
[1396] P. Kincaid Jensen: The Greco Turkish War, op cit; p. 559.
[1397] Smith, *Ionian Vision*, p. 255·Kinross: *Ataturk*; op cit; p. 267.

numbers. Some 126,000 Greek troops took part in the attack on Turkish lines, which were defended by 122,000 men.[1398] But again, the Greeks were better armed. They had 410 field guns against the Turks' 160, some 4,000 machine-guns against the Turks' 700, and 20 aircraft against the Turks' four.[1399] The Greeks, advancing between Kütahya and Eskişehir, hit especially hard at the Turkish left flank in order to cut its communications with Ankara.[1400] The plan was so successful that the Turks were about to be entirely encircled, and retreat towards Ankara became a priority. Two Greek divisions were already swinging around to the east of Eskişehir.[1401] In his headquarters in a village on the outskirts of the city, İsmet was faced with the responsibility of deciding on its evacuation. He was anxious, discouraged, and indecisive. Halide Edib, retreating with a party of wounded soldiers, found him seated in a bare low-ceilinged Anatolian room. He wore, as he always did during a campaign, the khaki uniform of a private soldier. Behind his cordial manner 'his face was haggard and his eyes feverish, and the lines about his mouth and eyes had multiplied'.[1402]

Threatened with the entire destruction of the army, İsmet at last ordered a retreat, abandoning to the Greeks Afyonkarahisar, Kütahya, and Eskişehir, the Turks having decided to make a stand before Ankara, at the Sakarya River.[1403] The bulk of the Turkish troops thus escaped encirclement, but at great costs to equipment, in particular; stores were abandoned in Eskişehir, the railway line stretching east from Eskişehir to the Sakarya was left undamaged, and thousands of men deserted, joining the crowds of civilian refugees fleeing from the Greek advance.[1404] Apparently, Toynbee remarks, two Turkish divisions one weak and another strong, were left at Kütahya, with orders to retreat after fighting a delaying action for twenty-four hours. The weak division carried out the instructions, but the strong division refused, and fought on and, after inflicting heavy losses on the Greeks, most of the men died along their commander.[1405]

Now the ground was set for the great and decisive battle of Sakarya.
Just before the battle, puffed up by their recent victory, the Greeks let it be known what was going to be the final act:

> The Greeks went to Asia Minor under a mandate from the great powers to enforce, if necessary, respect for an international pledge to which the great powers had set their signatures, and which was subscribed also by the Greeks and Turks. The object of the pledge was to liberate forever non-Moslem communities under the rule of the Turk. That no other guarantee of liberation for these peoples could be secured than that of eradication of

---
[1398] A. Mango: *Ataturk*; p. 315.
[1399] C. Erikan: *Komutan*, 685.
[1400] S.J. and E.K. Shaw: *History*; op cit; p. 360.
[1401] P. Kincaid Jensen: The Greco Turkish War, op cit; p. 559.
[1402] Halide Edib: *The Turkish Ordeal*; John Murray; London; 1928; p. 271.
[1403] S.J. and E.K. Shaw: *History*; op cit; p. 360.
[1404] C. Erikan: *Komutan*, 699-701.
[1405] A.J. Toynbee: *The Western Question*; p. 237.

all Turkish dominion over, or administration of, the territories inhabited by these populations, is manifest from the long history of cruel oppression of every race which has come under the yoke of the Turks ever since that people left their Asiatic birthplace to impose the law of the sword.[1406]

Back in Ankara, it had now become clear this was a war of annihilation of the Turkish nation. Decision was taken unanimously: Mustafa Kemal was appointed by the National Assembly as the Commander-in-Chief with full powers. Straight, Mustafa Kemal issued a proclamation to the nation. The enemy, he declared, would be 'Throttled in the inner sanctuary (harim-i ismet) of the fatherland.'[1407] And he followed words by the action necessary.

As the Greeks prepared their pursuit, the Turks began immense preparations behind the Sakarya. If the Greek Army could not be stopped here, Ankara was doomed to fall.[1408] Mustafa Kemal established National Commissions for Requisitions; the population being made to contribute stocks of food, clothing, shoes, horses and any other material for the upcoming struggle.[1409]

On 12 August, Mustafa Kemal travelled with his Chief of the General Staff, Fevzi, to headquarters at Polatlı, on the railway some fifty miles to the south-west of Ankara. After inspecting the possible line of enemy advance from the top of a commanding hill, Kara Dag, as he was remounting his horse, Mustafa Kemal was violently thrown to the ground, and broke a rib, which pressed on his lung.[1410] Now, unable to ride, and in great discomfort, he would have to direct the battle from some distance.

[1406] The Greek Triumph in Turkey; in CH VOLUME XIV. April — September, 1921; p. 1068.
[1407] ATTB, 413.
[1408] P. Kincaid Jensen: The Greco Turkish War, op cit; p. 560.
[1409] Froembgen, *Kemal Ataturk*, p. 173.
[1410] P. Kinross: *Ataturk*; op cit; p. 274.

Map of the Battle of Sakarya

The following day, on 13 August, the Greek army left its positions in Eskişehir and began to march towards Ankara. Constantine's battle-cry was, 'To Angora!' and the British liaison officers were invited, in anticipation, to a victory dinner in 'the city of Kemal.' The Athens press drew a parallel with 'the noble conquests of Alexander the Great.'[1411]

The Greeks arrived in full force on 23 August.[1412] They numbered 100,000 against 90,000 Turkish troops.[1413] Half of the Greek army was composed of native Christians, that is Turkish subjects.[1414] The Greeks had vast superiority in artillery and aeroplanes. They had twenty-one aeroplanes which they used effectively. The Turks had one, used still more effectively, although the fuel was bad and the machine rotten, but this was compensated by the courage of the few

---

[1411] Ibid; p. 275.
[1412] P. Kincaid Jensen: The Greco Turkish War, op cit; p. 560.
[1413] C. Erikan: Komutan, 713; 733.
[1414] H. Edibe: *Ordeal;* 299.

Turkish airmen.[1415] The Greek central objective was to seek out and destroy the Turkish army as arrived to at a Greek council of war at Kütahya on 28 July.[1416] Once that was done, the road to Ankara would be open.[1417]

Sakarya would witness some of the most murderous fighting in history, a ferocious contest that lasted twenty-two days and nights.[1418] Entire units perished as rugged hills were bitterly fought over, lost, captured, and lost again.[1419]

Mustafa Kemal established his headquarters at Alagöz, a village overlooking the plateau from the north, and situated roughly half-way between Ankara and Polatlı.[1420] Fevzi and İsmet had their staffs in near-by houses, but they both conducted the campaign on the ground.[1421] İsmet, wrote, 'The western front headquarters was large enough for us and our staff officers... Mustafa Kemal slept even less than usual, dropping off just before dawn... The pain of his broken rib robbed him of such little rest as he had time for.'[1422]

Halide Edib, who had enrolled as a corporal and joined him at his headquarters, would eventually record what is without a doubt, at least in English, the best account of the Battle of Sakarya.[1423]

On 23 August, the Greeks engaged a division on the Turkish left, south of the stream, and forced its withdrawal after an all-night battle from the hilltop of Mangal Dağ against weak Turkish opposition.[1424] The intense artillery fire, and the mounting Turkish losses drove, on 26 August, İsmet to propose a retreat to a new line. Fevzi decided to hold on round Mount Çal, and brought in reinforcements from the northern flank.[1425]

The troops put on the most determined fight, just as in Gallipoli, dying on the spot, surrendering nothing to the enemy. The Greeks exploited their numerical advantage and most of all their immense artillery firepower. Some little but strategic hills were lost and regained by the Turks at least seven times, and each time this meant the complete annihilation of one small Turkish unit.[1426] The Greeks gained slowly and steadily, ten miles in as many days.[1427] The Turkish position was at any time threatened by Greek outflanking and an advance on Ankara.[1428] In the midst of battle, the lines shifted so much as each tried to outmanoeuvre the other that 'Their line,' Kinross explains 'had swivelled round

---

[1415] Ibid; 300.
[1416] M. Llewellyn Smith: *Ionian Vision*, 229.
[1417] P. Kincaid Jensen: The Greco Turkish War, op cit; p. 560.
[1418] *A Speech by Gazi Mustafa Kemal*, p. 522.
[1419] P. Kincaid Jensen: The Greco Turkish War, op cit; p. 560.
[1420] A. Mango: *Ataturk*; p. 319.
[1421] Ibid.
[1422] İsmet İnönü: Hatıralar (Memoirs), ed. Sabahattin Selek, Bilgi, Istanbul, I, 1985; II, 1987, I, 262
[1423] H. Edibe: *The Turkish Ordeal*, 284-310.
[1424] A. Mango: *Ataturk*; p. 319.
[1425] Ibid; p. 320.
[1426] Halide Edib: *The Turkish Ordeal*; op cit; p. 292.
[1427] P. Kincaid Jensen: The Greco Turkish War, op cit; p. 560.
[1428] P. Kinross: *Ataturk*; op cit; p. 279.

until its axis was rather from east to west than north to south, and at the eastern end of it the Greeks were now nearer to Angora than the Turks themselves at the western.'[1429]

The main Turkish stronghold was a high ridge on their left, Çal Dağ (Mount Çal), rising a thousand feet from the plain between the two strong Turkish positions, commanding the railway to Ankara and the whole battlefield.[1430] 'Flatly scored with a pattern of vertebrae like the hide of a reptile, it offered little cover and was hard to defend.'[1431]

Holding this and other protective mountains would, for the time being, safeguard the capital. Until they occupy the Mount Çal,' Mustafa Kemal would say, 'There is nothing serious to worry about; but if they do that, we had better look out – they could easily occupy Haymana, and after that they have us in a trap.'[1432]

The Greeks had realised the importance of Çal Dağ and so maintained intense fire, mounting an attack on Haymana, which the Turks resisted with the loss of as many as eighty-two officers and nine hundred men, until 'lieutenants were commanding battalions and a division of artillery was reduced to seventeen shells.'[1433]

The fighting in some places was both fierce and unequal, as in the centre, where some units had to fight three Greek divisions at once.[1434]

Then, on 2 September, after some of the fiercest close combat, the Turks were driven off the commanding heights.[1435] In the evening the news came that Çal Dağ had fallen, and that the Greeks were advancing towards Haymana. Halide Edib narrates the scene at Turkish headquarters:

> There was grim silence everywhere, and the ugliest sort of fate seemed to hang over everyone in the headquarters. Mustafa Kemal Pasha was most affected. He fumed, swore, walked up and down, talked loudly, summed up the situation with the rare lucidity of a delirium, and tormented himself with indecision as to whether he should order the retreat or not. And I sat opposite him feeling as if the iron curtain of doom, something like the fire curtain of a theatre, was coming down, ever so slowly but surely.[1436]

The fight for Çal Dağ had raged for four days.

In the small room at Alagöz staff officers were discussing final possibilities. The situation was desperate in the extreme.[1437] A retreat meant certain defeat while continued resistance meant probable defeat. Was there any alternative? Time was getting on to two o'clock.[1438] Nerves were threatening to give out. Suddenly

---

[1429] Ibid.
[1430] Ibid.
[1431] Ibid.
[1432] Halide Edib: *Turkish Ordeal*; p. 295.
[1433] P. Kinross: *Ataturk*; op cit; p. 279.
[1434] Halide Edib: *Turkish Ordeal*; p. 298.
[1435] P. Kincaid Jensen: The Greco Turkish War, op cit; p. 560.
[1436] Halide Edib: *Turkish Ordeal*; p. 297.
[1437] P. Kincaid Jensen: The Greco Turkish War, op cit; p. 560.
[1438] Ibid.

the phone bell rang. The officers roused themselves and strained themselves to catch the message.[1439]

Fevzi Pasha was on the line. He had been in the field throughout the battle.

> 'The dimly lighted landing, with the half-built ceiling from the beams of which cobwebs dangle, is like a stage-scene. The guards in their black, and the entire household behind the few officers who stand in a line--eyes glisten over their shoulders, hectic, curious, anxious-I am leaning against the door,' says Halide.[1440]

In the room opposite, Mustafa Kemal Pasha is at the telephone.

> ..... A breathless instant, then: "Mustafa Kemal speaking. Is that you, Pasha Hazretleri?"
>
> [Fevzi said something]
>
> Mustafa Kemal: "What? Did you say that the day is in our favour? Did I understand right? Haymana is nearly occupied? Do you say that the Greeks are at the end of their strength? What? A coming retreat of the Greeks?"
>
> Eyes flash fiercely from the group, standing in the dim background of the landing.[1441]
>
> "The Chal Heights regained? The enemy is at the end of their strength?" ... Mustafa Kemal sprang to his feet.[1442]
>
> Turning round: "Gentlemen, this is the great turning-point."[1443]

Fevzi's call carried the fate of the whole nation. This was the turning point of the battle. The Turks by sheer determination, willpower, courage, and exceptional leadership, had won. Ankara was saved. Now the Greeks had to be driven out of central Anatolia. Mustafa Kemal ordered a counter-offensive.[1444]

Hard fighting continued for seven more days.[1445] Halide Edib's narration of this phase of the battle, which she witnessed by the side of Mustafa Kemal, is unique both in style and substance, a precious document of one of the most decisive moments of Turkish history.[1446] Here are brief extracts:

> I saw Mustafa Kemal Pasha's face peering from a trench and laughing at me. "Come in here, Hanum Effendi; we are fighting," he said, with the delighted voice of a boy who is at his favorite game. I went toward him and jumped into the trench...
>
> "We are attacking 'Dua-Tepe,' the highest hill on the left-" Mustafa Kemal Pasha began explaining. I went along to other trenches. The hills surrounding the valley at our feet were lively with the lugubrious intonation of artillery, and the nervous *tac-tac* of the machine-guns.

[1439] Ibid.
[1440] Halide Edib: *Turkish ordeal*; p. 297.
[1441] Ibid.
[1442] P. Kincaid Jensen: The Greco Turkish War, op cit; p. 560.
[1443] Von Mikusch, *Mustafa Kemal*, p. 294.
[1444] P. Kinross: *Ataturk*; op cit; p. 280.
[1445] P. Kincaid Jensen: The Greco Turkish War, op cit; p. 561.
[1446] Halide Edib: *Turkish ordeal*, pp. 301-5.

> Through the field-glass I was seeing the game of war as it is played, and the beast in me was enjoying it as much as the rest, forgetting what its results would look like in the hospitals later on. I could see men coming nearer and nearer, and even the fall of the men in the front line, leaving it indented and broken; and the final onslaught with bayonets. Thus the ants take their exercises around the small yellow mounds of their nests. Until I realized that those who could not rise after the smoke had cleared away had had their eyes opened to reality and were scorning this clumsy, stupid game of death, I was feeling sorry for them for not having been able to continue.
> "Do you see that black pyramid, very pointed? It is called the Black Mountain [Kara-Dagh]. Look there, through that opening, and you will see the Greek retreat."
> Yes, I looked and I saw a mighty cloud of dust rising from the ground to the sunlit sky, and a dark mass flowing ceaselessly like a flood…
> "Dua-Tepe" was taken. My last vision of it was with a single Turk standing all alone against the setting sun, his water-bottle glistening against the blue-gold sky…
> The Greeks were leaving the eastern part of Sakaria as fast as they could. We would soon move to Puladli.[1447]

The order for a final Greek retreat came from Athens. The Greeks, under steady hammering of the Turkish counter-attack, and threatened with cut-off by the cavalry, were at last ordered by General Papoulas to execute a general retreat to their previous positions about the railway. The Greek Army had lost 20,000 men in the ferocious struggle.[1448] The Turks, too exhausted to mount a full-scale pursuit, paused to catch their breath.

The Greeks were trailing back to their starting-point on the rim of the plateau, scorching the earth as they went.[1449]

Mustafa Kemal, in praising his troops, ascribed their salvation of their 'sacred country to the grace of God.'

After the battle, he changed into civilian clothes and returned unannounced in his decrepit staff car to Ankara.[1450]

Walking into the Assembly he received an ovation from the people of Ankara, 'who had lived for three weeks with the sound of the guns, then had heard it recede.' Using maps, Mustafa Kemal gave the deputies a precise review of the battle and the lessons to be drawn from it. To a friend, he remarked, 'I think that what I do best is my job as a soldier.'[1451]

[1447] Ibid; 301-305.
[1448] Von Mikusch, *Mustafa Kemal*, p. 294.
[1449] P. Kinross: *Ataturk*; op cit; p. 282.
[1450] Ibid.
[1451] Ibid.

Simultaneously, Te Deums of thanksgiving were being sung in the churches of Athens.[1452]

The impact of Sakarya was considerable, not just in Turkey, but throughout the world. It was the model, the inspiration other Muslims sought and needed. The sympathy and support for Turkey was immense. From the Muslims in India, which at the time was one country (Pakistan would get its independence in 1947), came one of the most moving accolades.
From the Khilafa Committee in Bombay:
> Mustafa Kemal Pasha has done wonders and you have no idea how people in India adore his name. The honour of the Turkish nation has been once again vindicated. We are all waiting to know the terms on which Angora offers peace to the Greeks...
> The Musulmans of India – particularly the poor and middle-classes, are doing their very best in subscribing to the Angora fund... May the Great Allah grant victory to the Armies of Gazi Mustafa Kemal and save Turkey from her enemies and the enemies of Islam.[1453]

6. The Battle of Dumlupınar

Writing in the March 1922 issue of *Current History*, the Greek Prime Minister, Demetrios P. Gouranis, in his lengthy account (abridged here), entitled WHAT GREECE HAS WON FROM THE TURK, said:
> The war which we have been conducting is a war of liberation, and nothing else. It began not in 1919 but in 1821. Piece by piece, almost foot by foot, during a century of struggle we conquered back from the Turk the freedom which had been Greece's for 3,000 years. Little by little we had achieved that freedom so far as Europe was concerned, save in Thrace. Then came the World War. For a while we kept apart from it, saving our strength for the great final struggle with the Turks, which every Greek knew was bound to come... An entire nation does not give over what it has been struggling for for a century, for nothing; nor did the Greeks in this instance.
> The world shall recognize the fact that the Greek populations of Asia Minor have been freed, and that it would be a grotesque negation of the whole civilization of the past century to return them to slavery.[1454]

[1452] Ibid; p. 283.
[1453] Ibid; p. 298.
[1454] *Current History*; vol 15, March 1922; pp. 911 ff.

On 13 September, the day on which Mustafa Kemal announced that the Battle of Sakarya had been won, he ordered a general mobilisation.[1455] The main battle was not over until the last Greek had been ejected out of Turkey.

Now it was realised the Turks meant business and were no push-overs, and so the same countries which had already begun the carving up of Turkey now came to do business. On 20 October 1921, the Angora Nationalist Government and France, through its envoy, Franklin-Bouillon, agreed to the complete withdrawal of French forces from Cilicia, save Alexandretta.[1456] This was undertaken immediately, endorsed by the French Chamber in its sessions on 27 and 28 October.[1457]

> 'Politically,' the editorial of *Current History* says, 'This treaty is beneficial to France, is displeasing to Great Britain and especially to the Greeks, who are still trying to dispose of the troublesome Mustapha by force of arms. It means that France has recognized the Government of Mustapha Kemal as the ruling Government of Turkey, rather than the Government at Constantinople, recognized by Great Britain. The agreement was negotiated for the French by Henry Franklin-Bouillon, an agent of somewhat vague status.'[1458]

Shortly after the Franco-Turkish agreement, the Italians began pulling out of Antalya. Both the French and Italians, much to the ire of the British, even informally pledged to support the Nationalists in the upcoming Peace Conference.[1459]

On 21 December 1921, Turkish troops entered Adana; on 25 December 1921 Gaziantep was Turkish once again. On 5 January 1922, a 105-metre long Turkish flag was spread out from the minaret of the largest mosque in Adana to mark the arrival of the Turkish commander.[1460] Except for the district of İskenderun, the Turks had regained the territory held in the south at the end of the Great War.[1461]

The British ire with the Italians, and the French in particular, dominated the period, and led to some violent recriminations and counter-recriminations, which are needless to go into here, but which can be found detailed at great length in the media of the time, especially *Current History*, of 1921-1922 (vols 15 and 16).[1462] It was not that the British loved the Greeks and hated the Turks more than the French and Italians. It all had to do with strategic and economic interests, which the readers can glean from a perusal of the various issues of the magazine.[1463]

[1455] ATTB, 429.
[1456] *A Speech by Gazi Mustafa Kemal*, p. 527.
[1457] Editorial *Current History*; vol xv; p. 511.
[1458] Ibid; p. 511.
[1459] Lord P. Kinross, *Ataturk*, p. 341.
[1460] Tansel, Selahettin, Mondros'tan Mudanya'ya Kadar (From Mudros to Mudanya), I–IV, MEB, Istanbul 1991, IV, 52–3.
[1461] A. Mango: *Ataturk*; p. 325.
[1462] Editorial *Current History*; vol xv; p. 511.
[1463] See, for instance, H. Woodhouse: Anglo-French Discord in Turkey; *Current History*; 15; p. 652-8.

For the Greeks, despite the loss of the Allies' support, the situation was this: Their armies were still controlling vast lands in Anatolia and were strongly entrenched; this was their chance to take what they had sought for centuries. Moreover, they had spent so much in terms of lives lost and had dried their treasury — in Athens 'millions of drachmas were being absorbed by the Anatolian sponge.'[1464] They were not going to give in. Divided politically, certainly, but regarding the campaign in Anatolia, they were all united. No Greek, whether pro Venizelos or pro Constantine, was going to give up the Grand Idea.[1465]

As fixated as the Greeks were about their Grand Idea, the Turks were likewise adamant that no Greek occupation of one single square meter of Turkish territory would be allowed. Plans for an offensive had been under discussion by the Turkish commanders since the previous autumn.[1466] On 28 of July, Mustafa Kemal went back to Akşehir. Turkish senior commanders had gathered there for a secret staff meting under the pretext of watching a football match between two teams of officers.[1467]

> 'The night of 28-29 July,' says Mustafa Kemal, 'I exchanged views with them on the attack and after a further consultation with the Chief of Staff and the Commander of the Western Front, we arranged the details of the attack. Kiazim Pasha, the Minister of National Defence... also came to Ak Shehir on the afternoon of 1 August. We arranged the measures to be taken by the Ministry to complete the army's preparations. When I had ordered these preparations to be carried out and the attack to be pushed on rapidly I returned to Ankara.'[1468]

Mustafa Kemal returned to Ankara, and informed the ministers of his decision and of his belief in success. Fevzi backed him considering that there was an eighty per cent chance of it – allowing twenty per cent, for the hazards of war.[1469]

Mustafa Kemal ordered that the armies should be ready for the offensive by the middle of August.[1470]

The Turkish and Greek armies in Anatolia were of roughly equal strength, the Greeks with 225,000 men, and the Turks 208,000, but as before, the Greeks were better equipped with more machine-guns and field guns, and infinitely better motorised transport.[1471]

[1464] P. Kincaid Jensen: The Greco Turkish War, op cit; p. 561.
[1465] Ibid.
[1466] A. Mango: *Ataturk;* p. 338.
[1467] Ibid.
[1468] *Discours du Ghazi Moustafa Kemal, Oct. 1927,* Leipzig 1929, p. 528.
[1469] P. Kinross: *Ataturk;* op cit; p. 309.
[1470] Ataturk; Nutuk, 446–7; S. Tansel; op cit; IV, 1544–5.
[1471] C. Erikan: *Komutan,* 785.

Greek troops were under the overall command of General Hatzianestis, who had succeeded General Papoulas after the defeat at Sakarya.[1472] Below him in rank, General Soumilas commanded the III Army Corps, which covered the northern sector, running from the Marmara past Eskişehir to a point east of Kütahya, whilst the southern sector, including Afyonkarahisar, was held by the I and II Army Corps, under Generals Trikoupis and Digenis.[1473] Trikoupis' headquarters were at Afyon, near the point of the salient held by the Greek 12th, 4th, and 1st Divisions.[1474]

The 'sickle-shaped' Greek front, Llewellyn Smith explains, starting at Kios on the Sea of Marmara, followed a line south-eastwards, cutting the Eskişehir-Ankara railway, then turning south to Afyonkarahisar, then, from there, it ran westwards down the right bank of the Meander river to the Aegean Sea.[1475] The strongest points were at Eskişehir in the north, and at Afyon in the south. The Greeks expected a Turkish attack to come against Eskişehir, in the north, where the Turks had the largest concentrations, and where, according to Intelligence sources, which included the British employees of the liquorice factory, there was strong activity.[1476] It was the Turks' ploy as they were in fact planning an attack in the south, against Afyon, since it commanded the direct supply line by the railway to İzmir.[1477] This was the Greek stronger defensive position, so fortified that British engineers deemed it impregnable and likely to prove 'the Turkish Verdun', i.e. the German point of failure on the French front.[1478]

The Turkish Western Front Command was organised into two field armies (the First and Second), composed of 17 infantry divisions and five cavalry divisions.[1479] These were battle-hardened men, fourteen of the Turkish infantry divisions having seen active service in the First World War.[1480] The Turkish command, moreover, as Erickson remarks, was made up of highly gifted and experienced commanders.[1481] At the top was Marshal Mustafa Kemal, with Lieutenant General Fevzi (later Cakmak) as his Chief of General staff, with İsmet commanding the western front, Brigadier Nurettin Pasha (planner of the Kut al-Amara encirclement of 1915) commanding the First Army, and Brigadier Yakub Sevki (Subasi), who had a brilliant career in the Caucasus Mountains, commanding the second army; the Greek army in Asia Minor, Erickson adds, had no such kind of leadership either in terms of experience or in talent.[1482]

[1472] P. Kincaid Jensen: The Greco Turkish War, op cit; p. 561.
[1473] M. Llewellyn Smith: *Ionian Vision;* p. 284.
[1474] Ibid; p. 285.
[1475] Ibid; p. 284.
[1476] P. Kinross: *Ataturk;* op cit; p. 310.
[1477] Ibid.
[1478] Ibid.
[1479] E.J. Erickson: From Kirkilisse to the Great offensive, Turkish Operational Encirclement planning, 1912-1922; in *Middle Eastern Studies;* Vol 40; No 1; pp. 45-64; at p. 59.
[1480] E.J. Erickson: *Ordered to die;* op cit p. 202.
[1481] Ismet Gorgulu: *On Yillik harbin kadrosu…* Ankara, 1993, pp. 289-95.
[1482] E.J. Erickson: From Kirkilisse to the Great offensive, op cit; p. 59.

Moreover, the Turkish Corps and divisional command structure was equally strong with every major position filled with men of great experience from hard won battles against the British and Russians.[1483]

The Turkish plan of attack aimed at a concentrated thrust from the south against the Greek forces holding the Afyon salient; the objective was to cut off the bulk of Greek forces in and around Afyon.[1484] The sector chosen for the attack ran through difficult mountainous terrain. The Greeks held fortified positions on a series of steep and well-fortified peaks, rising to a height of some 5,000 feet.[1485] The Turks would have to come down into narrow valleys and then storm up positions, where the Greeks could literally wipe them out with heavy machine gun fire. The Turkish plan, moreover, involved not just the storming and capture of Greek hill-top positions, but also the encirclement and annihilation of the Greek southern army, Corps I and II. After studying the operational situation, the Turkish general staff determined that an encirclement operation was possible using the First and Second Turkish armies.[1486] For the plan to work there were four prerequisites:

-Moving enough men from north to south nearest the enemy's front in great secrecy.

-Attacking fast, relying on the element of surprise.

-Achieving a perfect coordination in time and space between the main army units, including cavalry, coming from different directions (east and south, primarily) so as to accomplish the encirclement.

-Delivering a sudden, brief, violent attack as to break the enemy once and for all, for there was no possibility for a second round.

All these were the elements that were missing in previous operations during the Balkans and the First World War, and all these were present at Dumlupınar. Any High Command, any army, that could achieve these four pre-requisites and also storm a number of steep hills defended by barbed wire, a deeply entrenched enemy, sweeping machine gun fire, and then shatter the enemy, who is equal in number, in hand to hand combat, capture his positions, then accomplish the encirclement and final destruction of such an enemy, in just a couple of days, is worthy of history's highest mark. No army has ever accomplished anything similar in the whole history of warfare.

The plan of the offensive demanded the massing of 12 of the 17 available divisions, and doing it discretely.[1487] In late July and early August the Turks began moving their forces from north to south, to assembly areas from which to launch

---

[1483] Ibid.
[1484] A. Mango: *Ataturk*; p. 339.
[1485] Ibid.
[1486] Gorgulu, Ismet, *Buyuk Taaruz*, (The Great offensive) (Ankara: Genelkurmay Basim Evi, 1992), pp. 80-1.
[1487] E.J. Erickson: From Kirkilisse; p. 59.

the offensive.[1488] In order to gain the element of surprise and prevent detection by aerial reconnaissance, Turkish troops were marched south by night, and during the day were made to rest inside houses or under trees.[1489] Then, a series of other tricks were used to confound the Greeks who despite aerial reconnaissance did not have the faintest idea of what the Turks were up to at the time, whilst a huge army was moving against them.[1490] If we look at the 1916 situation, the Russians were aware of the arrival of the Turkish Second Army from Thrace to the Caucasus and were able to destroy the Turkish Third Army before the Second arrived, and then they dealt with the latter. Not in this instance.

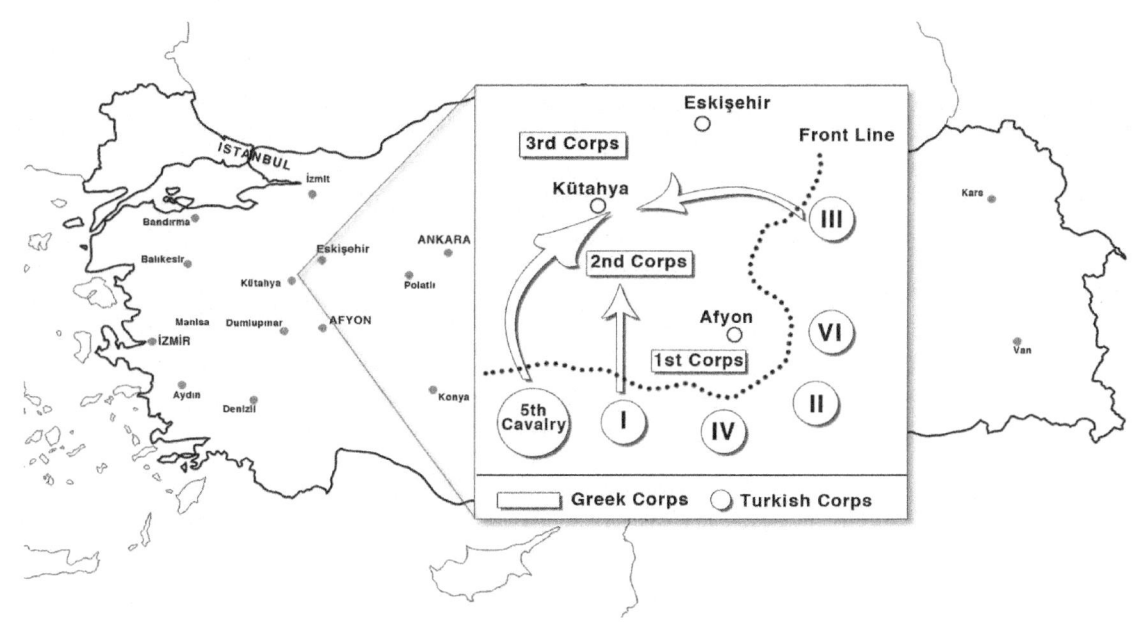

Turkish Plan of attack at Dumlupinar as inspired by, and based on, E.J. Erickson (From Kirkilisse…).

The Turkish objective was to turn the Greek right flank. This was concentrated over a front of some fifty miles, around the town of Afyonkarahisar and the supporting region of Dumlupınar, facing in two directions, east, and the south.[1491] In concept, Erickson explains, the First Army (its I Corps) would attack the Greeks from south to north, whilst V Cavalry Corps by its side would sweep behind the Greeks; at the same time, from its northerly position, the III Corps would cut horizontally from east to west, and meet with cavalry in Kütayha. This leaves the IV and VI Corps to pin the Greeks down, the IV from the south, and VI from the

---

[1488] Turkish General staff: *Turk istiklala harbi*……..(The Turkish war of independence, Western front, Great offensive preparation and the Great offensive; (Ankara, 1967, pp. 337-51; Operations Division, First Army, offensive Plans; 26 July 1922.
[1489] P. Kincaid Jensen: The Greco Turkish War, p. 566.
[1490] M. Llewellyn Smith: *Ionian Vision*; 287.
[1491] P. Kinross: *Ataturk*; op cit; p. 310.

east. II Corps was kept in reserve (see map).[1492] Inside the newly created pocket the Turks planned to trap the Greek I Corps (four divisions) and the II Corps (three divisions).[1493] The aim of the offensive was to destroy the Greek Army by eliminating seven of its twelve infantry divisions and to open the way for a complete collapse of the Greek presence in Anatolia.[1494] Suddenness, speed, decisive blunt action, and most important of all: perfect timing and utmost coordination of unit movements were utterly essential in this respect.

On 24 August, the troop concentration that had begun on 14 August was completed.[1495] During the night of 24, and on the 25, Turkish infantry had advanced to their start lines within 400 m of the main Greek lines without being seen.[1496]

On 25 August when Mustafa Kemal joined the 1st Army battle headquarters that was to lead the attack, all communications between Anatolia and the outside world were cut.[1497] He had moved his headquarters up from the plain into the mountain region next to the village of Shuhud, then to a camp behind the crest of Kocatepe.[1498]

As zero hour approached Kemal issued a battle order to the troops. It read:

> 'Soldiers, your goal is the Mediterranean!'

The first major offensive of a nation that had committed itself for the last twelve years to defence was about to begin.[1499]

In the hour before dawn on 26 August, Mustafa Kemal, Fevzi, Ismet, and Nurettin gathered on the peak of Kocatepe, which dominated the sector chosen for the breakthrough.[1500]

> Then with a thunderous roar the artillery barrage began – and the Greeks woke up. Many of them had been out at a dance in Afyon until an hour or so earlier.[1501]

The artillery barrage concentrated most particularly at the Greek positions along the ridges and flanks of Akar Dağ.[1502] The strength and accuracy of the Turkish fire delighted Mustafa Kemal. After a time, Greek guns stopped responding, because, as it became clear later, their observation posts had been knocked out.[1503] From his lookout point on Kocatepe, with Fevzi and Ismet by his side, they looked northwards at the line of hilltops, steeper and rockier, each of them

---

[1492] E.J. Erickson: *From Kirkilisse*; p. 59.
[1493] Gorgulu, Ismet, *Buyuk Taaruz*, p. 18, Overlay, 2.
[1494] E.J. Erickson: *From Kirkilisse*; p. 60.
[1495] Ibid.
[1496] Ibid.
[1497] A. Mango: *Ataturk;* op cit; p. 339.
[1498] P. Kinross: *Ataturk*; op cit; p. 311.
[1499] Ibid.
[1500] A. Mango: *Ataturk*; p. 339.
[1501] P. Kinross: *Ataturk*; op cit; p. 311.
[1502] M. Llewellyn Smith: *Ionian Vision;* p. 288.
[1503] Ismet İnönü: *Hatıralar* (Memoirs), ed. Sabahattin Selek, Bilgi, Istanbul, I, 1985; II, 1987, I, 287-293.

strongly fortified, which the Turkish infantry were to take by assault.[1504] Each of the hills was the objective of a Turkish division, to be stormed in an uphill attack until the summit was reached.

At 5.30 a.m., half an hour after Turkish artillery began firing, under a thick cloud of smoke from the artillery, the infantry and cavalry launched their assaults.[1505] It was a shattering and bloody assault as the Turks stormed uphill, 'tough Anatolian foot soldiers, in the face of deadly Greek fire' along a twenty-five mile front from Sinan Pasha to the railway east of Afyon.[1506]
The first Greek position to fall was Kamelar in the sector of the 4th Division, lost after fierce fighting, and Tilki Kiri Bel was abandoned without resistance by the 1st Company of the 49th Regiment, 1st Division at 8 a.m.[1507] In the brief but extremely bloody first phase, all but two of the objectives were in Turkish hands by 9.30 in the morning.[1508] In the meantime, the Turkish cavalry had swept round to the Greek rear, harrying them from the west and cutting the railway to İzmir.[1509] All along the front fierce fighting raged all day. The violence was such that some hilltop positions changed hands several times.[1510] The Greek II Corps sent the 7th and 13th Infantry Divisions forward to fill gaps and reinforce the I Corps holding the forward positions.[1511] By the evening of 26 August, the situation was not yet lost for the Greeks. The Turks had made significant gains, but there was no definite breakthrough.[1512]

The next day, 27 August 1922, in the early morning, the Turkish assault concentrated most powerfully on the Greek 4th Division. The Turkish IV Corps of the 1st Army, commanded by Colonel Kemalettin Sami, broke through the Greek lines, and captured the 5,000-feet high 'Saw-toothed Rock' of Erkmentepe (Kamelar).[1513] In the meantime, the Turkish V Cavalry Corps broke free of the main defensive line, and advanced over 20 km into the Greek rear area, whilst to the north-east, the Turkish III Corps broke in the Greek lines as well and advanced almost 10 km.[1514] The encirclement of the Greeks was now proceeding to its final stage. General Trikoupis realised the gravity of the situation and decided to abandon his positions and the bulk of his stores and retreat to a new line west of Afyonkarahisar.[1515]

[1504] M. Llewellyn Smith: *Ionian Vision;* p. 288.
[1505] E.J. Erickson: From Kirkilisse to the Great offensive, Turkish Operational Encirclement planning, 1912-1922; in *Middle Eastern Studies;* Vol 40; No 1; pp. 45-64; at p. 60.
[1506] M. Llewellyn Smith: *Ionian Vision;* p. 288.
[1507] Ibid.
[1508] P. Kinross: *Ataturk;* op cit; p. 311.
[1509] Ibid.
[1510] A. Mango: *Ataturk;* p. 340.
[1511] E.J. Erickson: From Kirkilisse; p. 60.
[1512] M. Llewellyn Smith: *Ionian Vision;* Allen Lane; London; 1973; p. 288.
[1513] M. Llewellyn Smith: *Ionian Vision;* p. 289. A. Mango: *Ataturk;* p. 340.
[1514] E.J. Erickson: From Kirkilisse to the Great offensive, Turkish Operational Encirclement planning, 1912-1922; in *Middle Eastern Studies;* Vol 40; No 1; pp. 45-64; at p. 60.
[1515] M. Llewellyn Smith: *Ionian Vision;* p. 290.

Meanwhile, the Greek 1st and 7th Divisions under General Frangou, which had been fighting hard all day to hold their positions on Akar Dağ, recognising in the afternoon that the position was untenable, also retreated in order to take up new positions on the heights of Bal Mahmout.[1516]

The two sudden retreats took place in such confusion that the two armies lost contact with each other.[1517] Moreover, the Turks had succeeded in driving a wedge into the Greek southern army at a vital point that the two Greek forces could not converge towards each other.[1518] By the end of the day, it became obvious that the Turkish breakthrough in the mountains south-west of Afyon on 27 August had 'knocked out the Greek army in Anatolia at one blow.'[1519]

On the night of 27-28 August, brigadiers Nur Ettin and Ismet decided to renew their attacks on the following (28th) morning.[1520] At dawn, whilst the Turkish attack was beginning to unfold, the Greeks, now retreating, 'pushed their weary bodies into motion again. They had been fighting and marching now for forty-eight hours.'[1521] By now there no longer was any cohesion in their ranks. The shock and violence of the Turkish attack had their toll. Instead of an army, Llewellyn Smith notes, there were scattered groups of soldiers, 'some frightened and anxious to run, others held together by dynamic commanders or a sense of necessity in this hostile environment.'[1522]

In the meantime, Mustafa Kemal had moved his headquarters to the municipal offices of the newly liberated town of Afyonkarahisar, 'the black fortress perched on its towering rock.'[1523] There he received reports that the bulk of the Greek 1st and 2nd Corps was grinding round Dumlupınar, some thirty miles to the west.[1524] Here Halide Edib, whom he had summoned back to his side, saw him gesticulating and poring over a map with Fevzi by the light of two lamps.[1525]

> He [Mustafa Kemal] 'seems to be blinking at a hundred suns all rising over his head, so exalted and radiant he seems.'[1526]
>
> "Welcome, Hanun Effendi," he said; the ring of his voice and the shake of the hand made you feel his excitement – the man with the will-power which is like a self-fed machine of perpetual motion.[1527]
>
> "Come, Hanum Effendi, let us eat."
>
> Fevzi Pasha sat opposite-he is patting his right shoulder, as he usually does in moments of satisfaction.[1528]

[1516] Ibid.
[1517] Ibid.
[1518] Ibid; p. 291.
[1519] A. Mango: *Ataturk*; p. 340.
[1520] E.J. Erickson: From Kirkilisse; p. 60.
[1521] M. Llewellyn Smith: *Ionian Vision;* p. 292.
[1522] Ibid.
[1523] A. Mango: *Ataturk;* p. 340.
[1524] Ibid.
[1525] H. Edibe: *Turkish Ordeal*; op cit; p. 354.
[1526] Ibid.
[1527] Ibid.
[1528] Ibid.

Mustafa Kemal discussed the options with Fevzi, İsmet and Nurettin, and decision was taken for the encirclement of the Greeks at Dumlupınar, and go for the kill.[1529] Fevzi moved to the north to command the right arm of the pincer movement, while Mustafa Kemal took personal command of the forces massed in the south and west, leaving İsmet behind at Afyon. It took a day for Turkish troops to complete the encirclement.[1530]

Now Trikoupis and Frangou realised that the main objective was to escape entire encirclement.[1531] In the meantime, Turkish heavy artillery fire was having its toll, adding to the confusion in Greek ranks.[1532] Whilst Frangou's group was marching west towards Uşak, Alaşehir, İzmir and the sea, under cover of darkness, the Trikoupis army was marching towards where Frangou had just left.[1533]

On the night of 29-30 August, Mustafa Kemal summoned his Chief-of-Staff and army commanders and ordered them to destroy completely the encircled enemy forces.[1534]

On the morning of 30 August he moved his headquarters forward to a low hill, since named Zafertepe (Victory Hill), rising just above the railway line, a little to the east of Dumlupınar, to direct the final assault on the encircled Greeks.[1535] The small town of Dumlupınar, around which the Greeks had built up a fortified position, lies in an upland valley hemmed in by mountains – Murat Dağ in the north and Ahır Dağ in the south.[1536] The valley affords a passage for the single-track railway from Afyon to İzmir, which the Greeks sought to use for their retreat.[1537] Just as they were marching, they suddenly came under Turkish intense artillery fire and then infantry bayonet charges. Their troops disintegrated.[1538] On this day, 30 August, the Turks fought what they would later call the battle of the Supreme Commander, which destroyed most of the Greek forces remaining in the pocket.[1539] In the course of the fighting and artillery pounding that took place on that day, the Greek 1st and 2nd Corps were annihilated as effective fighting forces, and amongst the troops which had evaded death or capture round Dumlupınar, only one thought remained: to escape from Anatolia as quickly as possible.[1540] Thus, all in all, by the end of 30 August, four days after the initial attack, half the Greek army had been either annihilated or

---

[1529] Ismet İnönü, op cit; I, 290-1. C. Erikan: *Komutan*; 808.
[1530] A. Mango: *Ataturk;* John Murray; London; 1999; p. 341.
[1531] E.J. Erickson: From Kirkilisse to the Great offensive, Turkish Operational Encirclement planning, 1912-1922; in *Middle Eastern Studies*; vol 40; No 1; pp. 45-64; at p. 60. M. Llewellyn Smith: *Ionian Vision*; p. 292.
[1532] P. Kincaid Jensen: The Greco Turkish War, op cit; p. 563.
[1533] M. Llewellyn Smith: *Ionian Vision;* Allen Lane; London; 1973; p. 293.
[1534] Gorgulu, Ismet, *Buyuk Taaruz*, p. 106.
[1535] A. Mango: *Ataturk;* p. 341.
[1536] Ibid; p. 340.
[1537] Ibid; p. 341.
[1538] M. Llewellyn Smith: *Ionian Vision;* p. 294.
[1539] E.J. Erickson: From Kirkilisse; p. 61.
[1540] A. Mango: *Ataturk*; p. 341.

taken prisoner, with the loss of all its war material.[1541] The scene looked to Halide afterwards

> Like a disordered dream... Forsaken batteries glistened in the sun; rifles and ammunition in huge piles, endless material of all descriptions lay huddled in a great mass all over the valley. And amidst it all corpses – of men and animals – lay as they had fallen.[1542]

In the meantime, the surviving Greek army was in headlong flight to the coast, out of range of its pursuers, a fighting force no longer, but still burning villages and crops, murdering men, women and children as it fled, 'for this, according to the Greek soldiers' orders, was a 'war of extermination.'[1543]

All through 31 August, the main group of Greek survivors marched on, snatching a little, and dangerous rest as the Turks were in pursuit.[1544]
On the Turkish side, meanwhile, Mustafa Kemal, Fevzi and İsmet met in the yard of a village house near Dumlupınar discussing what they should do next.[1545] Mustafa Kemal's tent was pitched on the roof of a stable; peasant women gathered around, staring at him, begging him to avenge the sufferings which they had endured at the hands of the Greeks.[1546]

> 'One of them with burning eyes said to Mustafa Kemal Pasha:
> "Thou must avenge our wrongs, if thou ever catchest their women; thou must see that they are treated as we were treated... Oh, the dogs, the pigs... they have treated us as if we were mire, abomination under their heel ..."
> She went into details, in their grimmest form, and she produced a discordant sound in her choking throat that gave one creepy feelings in one's back. I felt that their wounds would never be healed with time; they would brood over them, they would probe them ever in the same passionate way. Yes, this mood was absolutely Western in its fixedness and its vindictiveness; it lacked the mellowness, the subtle understanding and forgiveness of the real Eastern soul. These women had learned the lesson of ugly hatred which the West had been trying so hard to teach the East.[1547]

On 1 September Mustafa Kemal issued an army order, announcing for the first time that victory had been won. The order ended with the words:

> 'Armies! The Mediterranean is your immediate objective. Forward!'[1548]

The Mediterranean was 250 miles distant from Dumlupınar.

About noon on 2 September, what remained of the Trikoupis group (5,000 men) came near Uşak, only to realise that the town was now occupied by the Turks,

---

[1541] P. Kinross: *Ataturk*; op cit; p. 313.
[1542] Halide Edib: *Turkish ordeal;* op cit; pp. 356-7.
[1543] P. Kinross: *Ataturk*; op cit; p. 314.
[1544] M. Llewellyn Smith: *Ionian Vision;* Allen Lane; London; 1973; p. 295.
[1545] A. Mango: *Ataturk*; p. 341.
[1546] P. Kinross: *Ataturk*; op cit; p. 314.
[1547] Halide Edib: *Turkish Ordeal;* op cit; p. 360.
[1548] ATTB, 473-4.

who had arrived there only hours before.[1549] Trikoupis' troops were completely surrounded in a steep valley with a Turkish division before them and another two at their rear.[1550] Choosing between surrender and certain annihilation, Trikoupis ordered the raising of the white flag.[1551] Their surrender was accepted by a Turkish captain. In all, nearly 500 Greek officers and 5,000 men were taken captive; hundreds of machine-guns and 12 field guns passed into Turkish hands.[1552]

Elsewhere, to the north, III Army Corps, upon hearing of the disaster which befell Trikoupis, retreated toward Bandırma and Mudanya for evacuation.[1553] To the south, to the surviving divisions, pressed closely by the Turks from behind, fast flight was the only recourse. Greek officers made for safety, each to save his own skin, whilst soldiers, discontented, homesick, without heart for the fight, made off as fast as they could.[1554] The men could no longer care for military discipline or even self-defence, many throwing away their rifles for the sake of speed, whilst at the same time, they burned and ravaged what lay in their path.[1555]

7. Recovery of İzmir, Istanbul, and Thrace

In Ankara and Istanbul, little was known of the progress of the battle until it was virtually won. Mustafa Kemal, still intent on security, issued only brief daily communiqués, which announced a series of forward movements without elaborating on their scale.[1556]

Ankara, which was closer to the front than Istanbul knew a little more of the situation, and when it was heard that operations had started, anxious crowds moved to and fro between the Ministry of War and the Assembly, seeking news and speculating on the brief reports which were read out to the deputies in secret sessions.[1557] On the second day, when the battle had been virtually won, there was no communiqué, then came the news of the capture of Afyon, which drew great crowds into the streets, celebrating the Gazi, the army, and the Turkish people, firing joyful salvoes into the air.[1558]

In Istanbul, to many the Anatolian offensive seemed a foolhardy enterprise, as Greek communiqués belittled the Turkish successes and hinted at a Turkish retreat.[1559] The Greeks drank champagne in the clubs of the city, 'to the

---

[1549] P. Kincaid Jensen: The Greco Turkish War, op cit; p. 563.
[1550] Ibid.
[1551] Lord Kinross, *Ataturk*, p. 357.
[1552] C. Erikan; *Komutan*; 827.
[1553] Lord Kinross, *Ataturk*, p. 362.
[1554] Armstrong, *Grey Wolf*, pp. 159-160.
[1555] M. Llewellyn Smith: *Ionian Vision;* Allen Lane; London; 1973; p. 296.
[1556] P. Kinross: *Ataturk*; op cit; p. 316.
[1557] Ibid.
[1558] Ibid.
[1559] Ibid; p. 317.

destruction of Mustafa Kemal,' and a rumour had spread that he had been taken prisoner.[1560] When the first real news was heard that the Greek armies were defeated and in full retreat, the crowd before the newspaper offices was such that it blocked the doors and the papers had to be thrown from the windows.[1561]

Whilst the Turks celebrated, the Greeks, both the army and the local Christians fleeing with it, vented their anger on the population, and all that stood, finding the strength, the time and the resources to burn and kill, whilst their enemy was just behind them. Most of the towns that stood in the Greek's army path were left in ruins. One third of Uşak no longer existed; Alaşehir was 'a scorched cavity, defacing the hillside.'[1562] There, 4,300 out of 4,500 houses were destroyed with the loss of 3,000 lives, whilst in Manisa (ancient Magnesia) only 1,400 out of 14,000 houses remained standing.[1563] In Afyonkarahisar, the Turks were able to put out the fires started by the retreating Greeks.[1564] But hundreds of villages and a whole string of market towns – from Uşak to İzmir – were burned down.[1565] In the north, the neighbourhood round the railway station in Eskişehir was destroyed.[1566] The Turkish population was subjected to horrifying atrocities by the retreating troops and accompanying civilian Christian mobs.[1567] Here, we must briefly return to Toynbee, who gives one principal reason why he decided to publish his accounts of Greek crimes of 1921, for he could then foresee what was going to happen:

> These details are as horrible as those which I have withheld, but I have recorded them with a purpose. The rabies that broke out among the Greeks at the moment of quitting Ismid (April 1921) was a warning of what might happen on a much larger scale if the statesmen whose policy was responsible for this war of extermination in Anatolia should altogether fail to retrieve the mischief which they had made. But if hostilities were still going on at the time when the Greeks, with their taghmatarkhs and their sindaghmatarkhs, their khorofilakl and their armosiis, one and all, bag and baggage, cleared out from the province they had desolated and profaned, then the horror which I have deliberately described was almost bound to be repeated through the length and breadth of the occupied territory, from Brusa to Aidin and from Eski Shehir to Smyrna.[1568]

Indeed, events were now proving him right.

[1560] Ibid.
[1561] Ibid.
[1562] P. Kincaid Jensen: The Greco Turkish War, op cit; p. 563.
[1563] A. Mango: *Ataturk*; p. 343.
[1564] Atatürk, Atatürk'ün Söylev ve Demeçleri (ASD) (Speeches and Statements by Atatürk), original text in Ottoman Turkish, I–III (in one vol.), Atatürk Kültür, Dil ve Tarih Yüksek Kurumu (AKDTYK) [Atatürk Culture, Language and History Higher Institute], Ankara 1989, I, 274.
[1565] A. Mango: *Ataturk*; p. 343.
[1566] S. Tansel: op cit, IV, 173.
[1567] P. Kincaid Jensen: The Greco Turkish War, op cit; p. 563.
[1568] A.J. Toynbee: *The Western Question*; pp. 298-9.

The Turkish forces were hurrying on towards İzmir striving to overtake the Greeks before they could decimate all western Anatolia 'by fire and sword'.[1569] On 2 September, Eskişehir was recovered by the Turks, and the same day, the Greek government begged Britain to arrange a truce that would keep Greek rule in İzmir at least, which Mustafa Kemal categorically rejected.[1570] Bahkesir was retaken on 6 September, then the following day the Turks reached Aydın and Manisa, which they found turned into ashes by the fleeing Greeks.[1571]

Everywhere the Greek troops took with them Christian families 'that their quarters too might be burned and not a roof left for the advancing Turks.'[1572] 'They tore up the railway between İzmir and Aydın. They pillaged and destroyed and raped and butchered. "They went to pieces altogether," as Rumbold recounted to Curzon on the basis of reports from his consul in Smyrna. It was 'a sickening record of bestiality and barbarity.'[1573]
Filling the atmosphere, as the Turks advanced down the valleys, was the stench of unburied bodies, of charred human and animal flesh.[1574]
As early as February, the British representative in İzmir, Sir Harry Lamb, had warned:
> The Greeks have realized that they have got to go, but they are decided to leave a desert behind them, no matter whose interests may suffer thereby. Everything which they have time and means to move will be carried off to Greece; the Turks will be plundered and burnt out of house and home...[1575]

For Western powers, though, what mattered were the Christians. In their views, the massacres of Turks were mere expressions of Greek anger or excesses, whilst the Turkish push, on the other hand, would, they were certain, end in massacres of the Christians. A personal telegram for Mustafa Kemal had arrived from the Allied powers, relayed through the French cruiser Edgar Quinet in the harbour of İzmir, stating that they hoped he would protect the Christian population.[1576] At once surprised by the speed of the Turkish advance and also seeking to mellow the reaction towards Christians, the Allies swiftly renewed their plea for an armistice, which was passed on to Mustafa Kemal.[1577] His reply on 5 September said that, since the Greek army in Anatolia had suffered a total defeat,

> There was no longer any need to negotiate an armistice there; negotiations, instead, should, therefore, be confined to the return to Turkish rule of Thrace up to the 1914 Ottoman boundaries.[1578]

[1569] P. Kinross: *Ataturk*; op cit; p. 318.
[1570] S.J. and E.K. Shaw: *History*; op cit; p.; 363.
[1571] Ibid.
[1572] P. Kinross: *Ataturk*; op cit; p. 318.
[1573] Ibid.
[1574] Ibid.
[1575] M. Gilbert, (Sir Harold Rumbold): *Portrait of a Diplomat*, Heinemann, London; 1973, 251.
[1576] P. Kinross: *Ataturk*; op cit; p. 318.
[1577] A. Mango: *Ataturk*; p. 344.
[1578] Ibid.

This area, he insisted,
> Should come under the military and civil authority of the Ankara government within fifteen days of the conclusion of the armistice, and that Greece should free all Turkish prisoners and guarantee to pay compensation for the damage it had inflicted in the previous two and a half years. The Turkish offer to negotiate these conditions would remain valid until 10 September.[1579]

In İzmir, meanwhile, the situation was at its paroxysm. From villages and towns in the hinterland the Greeks began to crowd the roads down to the city, fully realising that the Greek occupation was at an end.[1580] A British eye-witness described the refugee trains as
> A wonderful sight: passengers standing all along the footplates and others swarming on the roof. In the carriages the passengers were so crowded that dead bodies were passed out at stations on their way to Smyrna.[1581]

After the refugees came those parts of the army which did not bypass the city:
> Then the defeated, dusty, ragged Greek soldiers began to arrive, looking straight ahead, like men walking in their sleep... In a never ending stream they poured through the town toward the point on the coast to which the Greek fleet had withdrawn. Silently as ghosts they went, looking neither to the right nor the left. From time to time some soldier, his strength entirely spent, collapsed on the sidewalk, or by a door... And now at last we heard that the Turks were moving on the town.[1582]

On the 7th, the Greeks reached the line which had long been recognised as the last defence of 'Smyrna.' The city itself was only some 25 kilometres away.[1583] The Asia Minor National Defence League started to issue rifles to the citizens, hoping still to join with the retreating army in defending the city and its surroundings.[1584] The army, meanwhile, was unconcerned; General Polymenakos, his first loyalty to the defeated army, moved himself and his staff from the barracks on shore onto a Greek warship, ready to move down the peninsula to Çesme where the bulk of the Greek army was now concentrated.[1585] The frightened inhabitants of Smyrna saw the main Greek columns, 'their only protection against the Turks,' bypass the city and rush towards the sea and their homes in 'Old Greece.'[1586] The Metropolitan Chrysostom had sent a message of despair from himself and his Armenian colleague to the Archbishop of Canterbury

---
[1579] Ibid.
[1580] M. Llewellyn Smith: *Ionian Vision*; p. 300.
[1581] Admiral Sir Bertram Thesiger, *Naval Memories*, privately printed.
[1582] G. Horton: *Recollections Grave and Gay*, Indianapolis 1927; pp. 119-120.
[1583] M. Llewellyn Smith: *Ionian Vision*; p. 298.
[1584] Ibid.
[1585] Ibid. 303.
[1586] Ibid. 298.

appealing to him to use his influence with the British Cabinet to help 'keep Kemal out of the city.'[1587]

Time for loving the Greeks had gone, though. Nobody cared for them now.

The Great Powers sent ships to protect their own: the British sent in the *Iron Duke, George V, Cardiff,* and *Tumult.* French, Italian and American ships were also there.[1588]

8 September dawned, and the Greeks crowded down to the quay once more, as on 15 May 1919, when the Greek army had first set foot in Asia Minor. All hoped for a pass on one of the remaining boats to leave İzmir.[1589]

Mustafa Kemal, meanwhile, who had moved his headquarters forward in the wake of his army – from Uşak to Salihli, to Nif, on the hills above İzmir, had taken military steps should the Greeks make a final stand before the city itself.[1590] The French had instructed their consuls to negotiate with him so as to hand over the city to the Turkish army, and had asked him to fix a time and place for a meeting.[1591] In response, he offered to meet them in Nif on 9 September.[1592]

The last of the Greek troops, but for a few stragglers, had left the day before – forty thousand of them in a convoy of Greek warships, together with all the Greek civil servants and police. They left behind them fifty thousand prisoners in the hands of the Turks, according to Kinross' overestimates.[1593]

The same day, 9 September, an Allied force, primarily British, entered the city 'to prevent looting and arson before the arrival of the Turks,' says the New York Times.[1594] In truth, had that been their intention, they ought have entered the city long before the Greeks had committed their final atrocities there, the Allies' entry really aiming at the usual they had done for nearly a century, bullying the Turks into accepting their military presence in one form or another. They would soon realise, though, that this, just as the days when they ran the Turkish economy the way they liked, and when their citizens were above Turkish law, and Christians had a special status, were now over.

The First Turkish soldier to reach the Mediterranean was a young cavalry lieutenant. On the deserted quay of İzmir he was greeted by a French colonel, 'who delivered to him a long speech, advising him to see to the protection of the Christians,' and as he spoke a Christian bomb fell from a window and a Christian rifle fired, wounding the lieutenant.[1595]

[1587] Ibid; 300.
[1588] Ibid. 300.
[1589] Ibid; 303.
[1590] P. Kinross: *Ataturk*; op cit; p. 318.
[1591] Ibid.
[1592] Ataturk: Nutuk, 449-50.
[1593] P. Kinross: *Ataturk*; op cit; p. 320; the true, official figure was a maximum of 35,000. See below.
[1594] *The New York Times,* September 11, 1922, p. 1.
[1595] P. Kinross: *Ataturk*; op cit; p. 320.

Witnesses agree on the proper demeanour and the relative order of the Turks' entry into İzmir at 11 o'clock on 9 September. The British chaplain was on his way to the British Consulate when he first saw them.[1596]

On 10 September, Mustafa Kemal and his troops entered the city and were greeted with wild enthusiasm by the Turkish population.[1597] It was three years, almost to a day, since the proclamation of the National Pact at the Sivas Congress (9th September 1919). At the entrance to the city the procession was met by a regiment of cavalry, which was to act as escort. The soldiers had been in the saddle, fighting almost without a break for nine days. When weeks earlier Mustafa Kemal had promised his cavalry food in plenty, he had not then reckoned with 'the enemy's scorched earth tactics.'[1598]

The Turkish War of Independence was won. In three years of warfare, the Turkish army lost just over 13,000 officers and men killed and 35,000 wounded.[1599] In the final offensive, the Turks lost 13,000 men killed, wounded and missing. Greek losses amounted to nearly 70,000, including 35,000 prisoners.[1600] The Greeks left behind half their guns and most of their stores.[1601]

Captain Thesiger, subsequently Admiral Thesiger, wrote his memories, as here summed up by Lord Kinross:
> In command of a detachment of British marines and bluejackets – who formed the bulk of the force, since the French and the Italians contributed little – was Captain Bertram Thesiger of HMS King George VI Guards had been posted at the Consulate and at the gasworks, and were now needed at the stores of the railway station, where he could see, as he later recalled, "about three thousand Greeks, some armed, cheerfully looting everything." At this moment there was a general scream and a rush. Shots were being fired, and there were yells of 'the Turks are coming" They came in his direction – a unit of Turkish cavalry, advancing in extended formation across open ground. They galloped towards the captain with drawn swords and a swashbuckling air.
> Foreseeing unnecessary bloodshed, he determined to halt them. Getting between Greeks and Turks, he held up his hand, looking, as a British eyewitness put it, "for all the world like a London policeman," feeling none too confident since his white uniform was like that of a Greek naval officer.

[1596] M. Llewellyn Smith: *Ionian Vision;* Allen Lane; London; 1973; p. 306.
[1597] P. Kincaid Jensen: The Greco Turkish War, op cit; p. 564.
[1598] P. Kinross: *Ataturk*; op cit; p. 321.
[1599] Özakman, Turgut, Vahidettin, Mustafa Kemal ve Milli Mücadele (Vahidettin, Mustafa Kemal and the National Struggle), Bilgi Yayınevi, Istanbul 1997, 464–5, correcting Selek, 92–3.
[1600] A. Mango: *Ataturk;* John Murray; p. 345.
[1601] C. Erikan: *Komutan;* op cit, 838.

The Turkish commander, however, halted his men and dismounted. Captain Thesiger went up to him. In awkward French he explained to him that the Allies had landed troops to keep order and that if he would refrain from firing there was little danger of trouble. The Turkish officer, who bore the rank of colonel, replied that he did not intend to fire but wished to enter the city. He suggested doing so by a side street, but the captain advised him to follow the sea-front. He agreed to do this. Thesiger asked the colonel to leave a patrol to guard the railway stores. This was done. The cavalry then rode on into town, and Thesiger returned to the *Iron Duke* to report.[1602]

A few days later a fire destroyed half the city; the authorship of the deed is disputed, a matter which has been studied by Heath Lowry.[1603] Tens of thousands of Christians fled to the waterfront. A large fleet of Allied warships and transports had assembled in the harbour to evacuate the citizens of the Allied Powers which had theoretically been neutral in the Greek-Turkish war.[1604] In all some 213,000 men, women and children – the majority of the population of the city – were evacuated.[1605]

Western Powers waited to see what the victorious Turks would do next.
'It was,' wrote Vansittart, 'as if a boxer, after being counted out, had risen from the ring, stunned his opponent, knocked the referee through the ropes and levanted with the purse.'[1606]
Even though the Greeks had been routed and Anatolia recovered, the work, in Turkish eyes, was not yet complete: Eastern Thrace was under Greek occupation, and Istanbul was still in Allied hands.[1607] The Turks intended to cross the Straits to enter Eastern Thrace, but the Allies had established a neutral zone along each side of the waterway.[1608] In a series of press interviews in İzmir, Mustafa Kemal clearly stated that he was seeking both places, Thrace and Istanbul, by immediate negotiation, but as he declared to an American journalist he would be in Istanbul within eight days and would proceed to occupy eastern Thrace.[1609]
A show of force seemed unavoidable as already before the Turks' entry into "Smyrna" Lloyd George's Cabinet had declared that

> Any attempt by the Turks to cross over to the European shore should be met by force,' and that 'an invasion of the Straits, Constantinople and

---

[1602] Thesiger: Naval Memories; op cit; in P. Kinross: *Ataturk*; op cit; pp. 320-1.
[1603] Heath. W. Lowy: Turkish History, on whose sources will it be based; A case study on the burning of Izmir; in *The Journal of Ottoman Studies;* vol IX; 1989; pp. 1-29.
[1604] A. Mango: *Ataturk;* p. 346.
[1605] David Walder, *The Chanak Affair* (London: Hutchinson & Co. Ltd, 1969), 177.
[1606] In P. Kinross: *Ataturk;* op cit; p. 330.
[1607] P. Kincaid Jensen: The Greco Turkish War, op cit; p. 564.
[1608] Ibid.
[1609] P. Kinross: *Ataturk;* op cit; p. 330.

> Thrace by the Turks was a danger to Europe and to the Christian population of Turkey – moreover an affront not to be borne. Defeat is a nauseating draught; and that the victors in the greatest of all wars should gulp it down, was not readily to be accepted.[1610]

The days passed, and the Turks were about to move into Thrace. In view of Italy's and France's recent support of Mustafa Kemal, the British realised neither of them would resist a Turkish 'encroachment' on the Straits.[1611] The British army prepared for war, requesting reinforcements,[1612] but the General Staff reported that:

> The time of year would be "most unpropitious for field operations, and the hardships to which the troops will be subjected will be much more trying to the British than the Turks, who are more or less inured to them."[1613]

The British cabinet decided instead to resist the Turks at the Dardanelles, and with French and Italian support, enable the Greeks to remain in eastern Thrace.[1614] However, neither French nor Italians were keen on dying for the Greek cause, and they had signed agreements with the Turks, and so on 19 September, they abandoned their positions at the Straits, leaving the British alone to face the Turks 'if they wished to do so.'[1615]

On 24 September, Mustafa Kemal's troops, despite British warning, moved into the Straits zones and refused to leave.[1616] As tension soared, the British General Harrington, now Allied commander in Istanbul, and possibly the only cool head about, warned the cabinet in London, and persuaded Mustafa Kemal that the best way forward was through negotiations.[1617] In London, Lord Curzon, who could not contain himself at what he saw French abandonment, rushed to Paris, where he and the French president, Poincare, after a heated exchange, still agreed to ask the Nationalists to attend a meeting which would determine lines of demarcation between Greece and Turkey.[1618] Their declaration 'viewed with favour' Turkey's desire to recover Thrace as far as the Meriç (Maritza) river, including Edirne, but the area had to remain neutral for the time being. Likewise, the Turks could have Istanbul, but only after peace was signed.[1619] It was, in other words, a proposal for an Allied-mediated armistice.[1620] On 27 September, the Greeks were persuaded to withdraw their fleet from Istanbul, and their troops to withdraw behind the Maritza in Thrace.[1621] Now satisfied, Mustafa Kemal agreed to a truce

---

[1610] Ibid; p. 332.
[1611] P. Kincaid Jensen: The Greco Turkish War, op cit; p. 564.
[1612] S.J. and E.K. Shaw: *History*; op cit; p. 363.
[1613] David Walder, *The Chanak Affair* (London: Hutchinson & Co. Ltd, 1969) 281.
[1614] Ibid.
[1615] S.J. and E.K. Shaw: *History*; op cit; p. 363.
[1616] Ibid.
[1617] Ibid.
[1618] P. Kincaid Jensen: The Greco Turkish War, op cit; p. 564.
[1619] D. Walder: *The Chanak Affair*, 222; 229.
[1620] Ibid; pp. 281-2.
[1621] S.J. and E.K. Shaw: *History*; op cit; p. 363.

with the British and peace talks.[1622] In the name of the Grand National Assembly Mustafa Kemal sent his acceptance to the meeting to be held in Mudanya.[1623] His representative was İsmet Pasha, and the main demand was Eastern Thrace and the ending of the Greek occupation (the Allies had already accepted to surrender Istanbul).[1624] The preliminary meeting at Mudanya was announced for 3 October.[1625]

In Mudanya, for four days, the British, Turkish, French, and Italian delegations wrangled over several details, then finally agreement was reached. It stipulated amongst others, that the withdrawal of Greek troops from eastern Thrace would start immediately and would be completed within fifteen days; Allied troops would take over from the Greeks and would then hand over the territory to the Ankara government within thirty days; Turkish troops would withdraw to a distance of 15 kilometres from the Dardanelles and 40 kilometres from the Bosphorus, whilst all hostilities between Greece and Turkey would cease.[1626]

Eastern Thrace was now back in Turkish possession, and the Greek troops, and countless Greek civilians, began their westward move
'Whole (Greek) families tramping, laden with trunks, beside ox-drawn waggons piled with household goods, while their flocks trooped before them and at night their camp-fires dotted the earth like stars in the sky.'[1627]
Now they were doing what the Turks had been doing for decades.

On 19 October, General Refet (Bele) arrived in Istanbul as the special representative of the Ankara government.[1628] The Muslim population of the city welcomed him enthusiastically. The following day, the first detachment of Turkish troops disembarked as a military band played.[1629]
The handover of Eastern Thrace proceeded smoothly and was completed by 26 November.[1630]

In Greece, in the meantime, King Constantine was overthrown and a new regime established in Athens.[1631] After a trial, among those subsequently executed for treason were Prime Minister Gounaris and General Hatzianestis.[1632]

[1622] Ibid.
[1623] P. Kincaid Jensen: The Greco Turkish War, op cit; p. 564.
[1624] M. Llewellyn Smith: *Ionian Vision*, p. 318.
[1625] P. Kinross: *Ataturk*; op cit; p. 337.
[1626] Text in S. Tansel: *Mondros'tan Mudanya'ya Kadar*; op cit; IV; 216-18; n. 216.
[1627] P. Kincaid Jensen: The Greco Turkish War, op cit; p. 565; quote: P. Kinross: *Ataturk*; op cit; p. 338.
[1628] A. Mango: *Ataturk*; p. 355.
[1629] E. Aybars: Türkiye Cumhuriyeti Tarihi (History of the Turkish Republic), I, 3rd ed., Dokuz Eylül Üniversitesi, Ankara 1994 I, 350.
[1630] S.N. Ozerdim: Ataturk; 68-9.
[1631] S.J. and E.K. Shaw: *History*; op cit; p. 363.
[1632] H.A. Gibbons, *Venizelos*, p. 399.

The Lausanne Conference began on 21 November 1922, and from its onset, the Allies tried to treat İsmet as representative of a defeated nation.[1633] İsmet rose to the occasion. Whenever inappropriate proposals were made, he simply pretended he heard nothing.[1634] He would not budge one inch, insisting that Turkey had to be treated as an independent and sovereign state, equal with all others at the conference.[1635] The Allies, as in the old times, tried to bring forth the usual old matters by which Turkey was kept under their dictate for nearly a century, or maybe even more: control of Turkish finances and justice, protection for the Christian minorities, the Capitulations, the Straits, and similar issues; İsmet would have none of it.[1636] Calm and patient by nature, stubborn and firm, he did not flinch one iota. Lord Curzon, the British representative, 'often assumed the role of a weary schoolmaster admonishing a stupid pupil,' İsmet cared very little.[1637] Lord Curzon yelled, and hit the wall with his cane; İsmet, who had been involved in hard military fighting and leading from the front, was not going to be bothered by that. He stood for one thing: complete Turkish sovereignty. A British representative reported that

> Ismet Pasha, who was well-attended by a phalanx of forbidding... looking Turks, seemed impervious to all argument on the subject, and his obtuseness and obstinacy put the patience of the Allied delegates to a severe test.[1638]

In the meantime, Mustafa Kemal sent the Conference a huge volume chronicling the Greek atrocities in Thrace and Anatolia.[1639]

After long months of stalemate, the Lausanne Conference paused on 4 February 1923. The Grand National Assembly then drew up its own peace proposals (8 March 1923).[1640] İsmet came back armed with these when the conference reconvened on 23 April.[1641] Three more months of tough negotiating followed, with İsmet as imperial as ever, whilst the Allies press and public became more and more anxious for peace.[1642]

Then, on 24 July, at last, the articles of the Treaty of Lausane were signed, confirming Turkey's integrity as specified by the National Pact.[1643]

It was, Kinross remarks,

> The only peace settlement signed after the First World War in which one of the Central Powers (the others were Germany, Austria and Bulgaria) was

---

[1633] S.J. and E.K. Shaw: *History*; op cit; p. 365.
[1634] Ibid.
[1635] Ibid.
[1636] Ibid.
[1637] Ibid. 366.
[1638] *Documents on British Foreign Policy, 1919-1939,* First Series, XVIII, London, *1972,* no. 478, p. 690.
[1639] S.J. and E.K. Shaw: *History*; op cit; p. 366.
[1640] Turk Istiklal harbi II/6; kp 4; p. 213.
[1641] S.J. and E.K. Shaw: *History*; op cit; p. 366.
[1642] *Documents on British Foreign Policy,* First Series, XVIII, 688-1064;
[1643] S.J. and E.K. Shaw: *History*; op cit; p. 366.

able to demand her own terms from the Allies, and the only one to survive the second as an instrument of peace for the future.[1644]

[1644] P. Kinross: *Ataturk*; op cit; p. 373.

CONCLUSION

Educated Osmanlis [wrote Toynbee in 1922] are aware that the Spanish-speaking Jews who are so prominent in the principal cities of the Levant, are descended from the Jews of Spain, who were expelled by the Spanish and given asylum by the Ottoman Government at the close of the fifteenth century. Following up this clue, they have studied the martyrdom of the "Moriscos", the Moslem population of the Moorish states in the Peninsula reconquered by the Christians. They have read in Western histories how this civilised and industrious Middle Eastern people (Spanish Muslims) was forcibly converted, driven by oppression into desperate revolts, and then massacred, despoiled, and evicted by its Western conquerors, at the very time when in the Near East the Osmanlis were allowing conquered non-Moslems to retain their cultural autonomy and were organising Orthodox, Armenian, and Jewish millets as official departments of a Moslem state. I have heard Turks express ironical regret that they did not Westernise in the fifteenth century after Christ. If they had followed our example then, they would have had no minorities to bother them to-day![1645]

The Turks, long before anybody else, not only welcomed the persecuted but also allowed whatever minority to dwell amongst them in the respect and safety of its possessions and faith, when others slew and burnt at the stake whoever believed differently. The Turks went even further, granting to minorities roles and status, which none other did, and everyone derided them for that: Here is Schem, (in 1878) pouring his scorn on the Turks for this sort of policy:

> The Mussulmans recede before the non-Mussulmans wherever the two come in contact. All of the enterprise, all of the progressive force that exist in the Empire are the results of Christian or Jewish energy. Even before the Greek Revolution, the commercial and naval fleets of Turkey were manned by Greeks and commanded by Greek officers. The maritime commerce of the East is still controlled by Greeks, and all the important trade of the commercial ports is managed by Greek and Armenian merchants. The experience of the French traveler, Choisy, who went to Constantinople from Trieste in a ship of Turkish nationality, but manned by Greek and Dalmatian sailors, is the rule at most Turkish ports. The Christian populations are most numerous all along the seacoasts, wherever any enterprise exists or any progress is visible. This is most conspicuously true of the towns of the Macedonian and Thracian coasts, but the non-Musulmans are also a power at Alexandria and even at Constantinople,

---

[1645] A.J. Toynbee: *The Western Question in Greece and Turkey*; Constable; 1922; p. 267.

while Smyrna and Beyrut have come largely under foreign influences, and several recent writers speak of the whole west coast of Asia Minor as steadily undergoing a Grecianizing process.

Now, there are a large number of Christian officers employed in every ministry; and in some bureau, as in those of Customs and Foreign Affairs, the Christians have numerically half the appointments, and an overwhelming majority of those which require capacity. In all the provinces where the Christians form a considerable fraction of the population, are Christian higher officers. Within ten years an Armenian has been Minister of Public Works; in 1877 an Armenian was Minister of Trade; Greek under-secretaries were employed in the Ministries of Foreign Affairs and Instruction, an Armenian in the Ministry of Justice; the under-Governors in Crete and Epirus, and the Governor-General of the Archipelago, were Greeks; and the Governors of the Lebanon since 1860 have been Catholics. The same work from which we have just quoted proceeds, in illustration of the growing sterility of the Turkish official aristocracy, to show how, with only a few exceptions, those persons in high positions who have distinguished themselves by their intelligence, talents, and capacity, are not of the "Stamboul race," as follows: The father of Ahmed Vefik Pasha was a Jew converted to Islam, his mother a Greek; Grand Vizier Edhem Pasha is a Greek, who fell into the hands of the Turks when a boy, at the catastrophe of Scio in 1822; Subhi Pasha is of Morean or Peloponnessian stock, and is the son of a Greek woman; Munif Effendi, Minister of Instruction, is an Arab from Aintab; the deceased Grand Vizier, Meheraed Pasha, was of Cypriote descent; the ex-Grand Vizier, Mehemed Rushdi Pasha, was from Sinope; Midhat Pasha, from Widin; the family of the Khedive of Egypt from Kavala in Macedonia.[1646]

So this openness, which is today the sign of an advanced, civilised society, was the norm amongst the Ottoman Turks centuries earlier. It shows a Turkish optimism and faith in humanity, and a lack of cynicism towards human nature, for, here, we return to the first point by Toynbee: Had the Turks done like everybody else, and followed the reverse policy, they would have just slaughtered and burnt at the stake and would have avoided themselves a hell lot of problems. After all, to this day, we find amongst scholars those who forgive Christian Spain for having wiped out its 'Moriscos.' They do not just forgive, they fully support it. Lapeyre, for instance, the Grand Specialist of the Morisco question, possibly the most referred to 'scholar' over the issue, and the most celebrated, too, admits that the Muslim population was en masse ethnically cleansed, but as he puts it, it was:

[1646] A.J. Schem: *The War in the East between Russia and Turkey*; H.S. Goodspeed & Co; New York; 1878; pp. 560-562.

> A brutal solution, perhaps, but it simplified things. The power of resistance of strong minorities is not to be demonstrated, especially when this is a faith as tenacious as Islam.[1647]

The same position is adopted by Perez:
> Once the reconquista was completed, there was no reason to keep such a situation. Spain had now become a nation like others in Christian Europe... The Moors, descendants of the Mudedjares, had refused to assimilate; they had to be expelled in the early 17th century.[1648]

According to Cardaillac and Dedieu:
> Why expulsion? Why now? Political considerations won, and the decision was justified by the rising threat and the fears just described.[1649]

Conrad goes even further, conceiving, just as Menendez Pidal in his *Historia de Espana* did, that:
> After many centuries of forced neighbourhood with the Christians, this exotic race never integrated into Spain, neither to its faith nor to its collective ideals, nor to its character, the Moors never assimilated and lived like a cancerous growth in the Spanish flesh.[1650]

Indeed, any thinking person today, with good knowledge of history, would instinctively agree. Had the Turks done like everybody else, had they adopted the same approach as just stated and held by most modern scholarship of Spain, with the exceptions of a the usual few (T. Glick and A. Castro, for instance) they would have saved themselves much agony in subsequent centuries as seen in this work.

The Turks, however, despite whatever defects they had, still have, and will always have, still had, and certainly still have, and will always have, a sense of humanity that others did not have, do not have, and will never have.

The Turks, for centuries, even amongst the bad ones amongst them, had to observe fundamental precepts of Islam, whether the Sultan or the Vizier liked such precepts or not. Amongst the most fundamental rules was the security and rights of minorities. This, no true Muslim can transgress. No other people would have tolerated the scenes which M. Pickthall, Seppings Wright, or Ashmead Bartlett, saw and described (in chapters one and three of this work,) when during the Balkan Wars, the Christian minorities living amongst the Turks were insulting and jeering returning wounded Turkish soldiers, or conniving with the invaders, or when despite what the Greeks did to the Turks in Macedonia, in the same war,

---

[1647] H. Lapeyre: H. Lapeyre: *Geographie de l'Espagne Morisque*; SEVPEN, 1959; pp. 119-120.

[1648] J. Perez: Chretiens; Juifs et Musulmans en Espagne; Le mythe de la tolerance religieuse (VIII-XV e siecle); in *Histoire*, No 137; October 1990.

[1649] L. Cardaillac; J.P. Dedieu: Introduction a l'Histoire des Morisques; in *Les Morisques et l'Inquisition*: *Les Morisques et l'Inquisition*: edited by L. Cardaillac; Publisud; Paris; 1990 pp. 11-28; p. 25.

[1650] P. Conrad: *Histoire de la Reconquista*; Que Sais je? Presses Universitaire de France; Paris; 1998; R.M. Pidal: *Historia de Esapana dirigida por Ramon Menendez Pidal*; Vol 2; Madrid; 2nd edition; 1966; p. 41.

there were still hundreds of thousands of Greeks living scattered amongst the Turks during the First World War (the figures are from the Greeks themselves), unmolested. No other nation would have shown the same fortitude as the Turks did. True, the Turks were not always angels, and there were excesses in their reactions, and excesses and defects can never be avoided on this earth except in fiction. Should we, however, peruse through history, and unfold its darkest pages, then, so many white images today would be indeed immensely tarnished. The repertory of the crimes committed through the continents by those who today lecture civilised behaviour is huge, and a vast literature exists.[1651] It is not, however, that the Turk was born angelic and others responsible of vile deeds were born on the same side of the devil. All the Turk did, just as a true Muslim, was to abide by the Islamic precepts, and that was it.

And it was not just because Islam imposes rules regarding the minorities or others that the Turks showed their excessive fortitude, it was also for another simple, and yet powerful foundation in Islam, which is this:

> 'And it may be that you dislike a thing which is good for you and that you like a thing which is bad for you. Allah knows but you do not know.'
> (Qur'an 2: 216)

[1651] Ward Churchill: *A Little Matter of Genocide*; City Lights Books; San Francisco; 1997.
-J.W. Draper: *A History of the Intellectual Development of Europe*; 2 vols; Revised edition; George Bell and Sons, London, 1875.
-J.W. Draper: *History of the Conflict Between Religion and Sciences;* Henry S. King and Co; London; 1875.
-R. Garaudy: *Comment l'Homme devint Humain,* Editions J.A, 1978.
-R. Garaudy: *Appel aux vivants*, Le Seuil, Paris, 1979.
-W. Howitt: *Colonisation and Christianity*: Longman; London; 1838.
-D. E. Stannard: *American Holocaust; The Conquest of the New World;* Oxford University Press; 1992.

BIBLIOGRAPHY

1. Turkish Primary sources (of Participants and Military) through translated extracts

Kemal Atatürk. Edited by Ulu Idemir. Anafartalar Hatiralari (Recollections of Gallipoli) (Istanbul, 1955).

Kemal Atatürk, Letters to Corinne Lütfü. Milliyet, Istanbul. November, 1955.

K. Atatürk: A Speech. Delivered at Angora, 15th–20th October, 1927. English translation (Leipzig, 1929).

K. Ataturk Nutuk (Speech), original text, AKDTYK, Ankara 1989, Vesikalar (Documents), 1991.

(Fevzi) M. F. Cakmak: Buyuk Harpte Sark Cephesi Hareketleri, Sark Vilayetlerimizde, Kafkasyada ve Iranda (Ankara, 1936,: Genelkurmay Matbaası).

Ali Fuat Cebesoy, Milli Mücadele Hatiralari (Recollections of the National Struggle) (Istanbul, 1953).

Ismet Inönü, Recollections. Akis, Istanbul. January–September, 1959.

Ismet Inönü, Negotiation and National Interest (in Perspectives on Peace, 1910-60) (New York, 1960).

K. Karabekir 1937-38) Cihan Harbine Neden Girdik, Nasıl Girdik, Nasıl Idare Ettik?, vol. I–II (Istanbul: Tecelli Basımevi).

Kâzim Karabekir, Istiklal Harbimiz (Our War of Independence) (Istanbul, 1960).

ATASE [Military History Department of Turkish General Staff], 1911–1912. Military History Commission, Turkish General Staff. Askeri Mecmua (Military Journal) (Istanbul, 1939).

2. Secondary sources, Turkish (translated extracts)

Sina Akşin: İstanbul Hükümetleri ve Milli Mücadele (The Istanbul Governments and the National Struggle), I–II, Cem, Istanbul 1992.

Celal Bayar, Atatürk'ten Hatiralar (Recollections of Atatürk) (Istanbul 1955).

Tevfik Biyiklioglu, Atatürk Anadolu'da (Atatürk in Anatolia) (Ankara, 1959).

Tevfik Bıyıklıoğlu: *Turk istiklal Harbi, I. Mondros Mutarekesi ve Tatbikat* (The Turkish War for Independence. I. The Truce of Mondros and Its Application), Ankara, 1962,

Hikmet Bayur: Atatürk Hayatı ve Eseri (Atatürk's Life and Work), Vol. I (from his birth to his landing in Samsun), AKDTYK, Ankara 1990.

Mahmut Gologlu: I, Erzurum Kongresi (The Congress of Erzurum), Kalite Matbaası, Ankara 1968; II, Sivas Kongresi (The Congress of Sivas), 1969.
Ismet Gorgulu: *On Yillik harbin kadrosu...* Ankara, 1993.
Uluğ İğdemir: Atatürk'ün Yaşamı (Life of Atatürk) (Vol. I 1881–1918), AKDTYK, Ankara 1988 (1st impression TTK, Ankara 1980)-
Selahettin Tansel: Mondros'tan Mudanya'ya Kadar (From Mudros to Mudanya), I–IV, MEB, Istanbul 1991.

3. Primary sources including unpublished sources, originals and translations

Current History, The New York Magazine: 1914-1923.
Foreign Office Reports; such as F.O. 195-1185; No 73. F.O. 195-2438, no 6650; Lamb to Lowther, Salonica 3 December 1912.
Foreign office reports; such as F.O. 195-1185; No 73; Layard to earl of Derby, 26 July 1877.
FO. 371-1762, no 55161; Greig to Crackanthrope, Monastir, 19 November 1913.
M. Gehri (Delegue du Comite International de la Croix Rouge): 'Mission d'Enquete en Anatolie, 12-22 Mai 1921,' *Extrait de la Revue Internationale de la Croix Rouge*, 3em Annee, No. 31, 15 juillet 1921, pp. 721-735. (Geneva, 1921.)
Lausanne Conference on Near Eastern Affairs, 1922–23 (H.M.S.O., London, 1923).
The Guardian (Manchester).
Naval Memoirs of Admiral Sir Bertram Thesiger, 1875–94. Private.

4: Contemporary sources, including politicians, army commanders, war correspondents and other witnesses of events

G.F. Abbott: *The Holy War in Tripoli*; Edward Arnold; London; 1912.
General Allenby: *Soldier and Statesman* (London, 1946).
E. Ashmead Bartlett: *With the Turks in Thrace*; George H. Doran Company; New York; 1913.
H.F. Baldwin: *War Photographer in Thrace; An Account of Personal Experiences During the Turco-Balkan War 1912;* Fisher and Unwin, London, 1913.
Commodore W.H. Beehler: *The History of the Italian Turkish War*; Annapolis; 1913.
E.N. Bennett: *With the Turks in Tripoli* (London, 1912).
Ernest N. Bennett: *Among the Cretan Insurgents*, Blackwood's Edinburgh Magazine, February 1898; pp. 166-169.
A. Cemal: *Memoirs of a Turkish Statesman* (London, 1922).
Rear Admiral Chester: Turkey Reinterpreted; *Current History* Vol XVI, No 6, Sep 1922, pp. 939-946.

W.S. Churchill: *The World Crisis: The Aftermath* (London, 1929).
W. S. Churchill: *The World Crisis, 1915*, (New York: Charles Scribner's Sons, 1923).
Gustav Cirilli: Journal du siege d'Adrianople; Paris, 1913.
Lord Curzon: *The Last Phase* (London, 1934).
Major Edwin W. Dayton: Military Operations of the War; CH Vol 6; pp. 502-3.
H. Edib: *Memoirs* (London, 1926).
H. Edib: *The Turkish Ordeal*; John Murray; London; 1928.
G. Ellison: *An Englishwoman in Angora* (London, 1924).
General von Falkenhayn: *The German General Staff and its Decisions 1914-1916;* Dodd, Mead and Company; New York; 1920.
Sir Philip Gibbs: *Adventures in Journalism* (London, 1923).
Phillip Gibbs and Bernard Grant: *The Balkan War,* Boston, Small, Maynard and Company; 1913.
T. Gordon, *History of the Greek Revolution,* 2 vols; Edinburgh, William Blackwood, 1832.
General C. Harington: *Tim Harington Looks Back* (London, 1940).
A. Haidar: *A Angora Auprès de Mustapha Kemal* (Paris, 1921).
K. Holmboe: *Desert Encounter,* London, 1936.
Ernst Jäckh; *Deutschland im Orient nach dem Balkan-Krieg;* Chapter 7: Deutsche und französische Augenzeugen von christlichen Massakers. (Die Balkangreuel des 30 jährigen Krieges); Martin Mörikes Verlag, Munich, 1913; pp. 83-98.
E. Jäckh: *The Rising Crescent* (New York, 1944).
P. Loti: *Turquie Agonisante*; Calman Levy; Paris; 1913.
F. McCullagh: *Italy's War for a Desert;* Herbert and Daniel; London; 1912.
A. Ostler: *Arabs in Tripoli*; John Murray; London; 1912.
A.A. Pallis: *Greece's Anatolian Venture – and After* (London, 1937).
M. Pickthall: *With the Turk in Wartime*; J.M. Dent &Sons; London; 1914.
M. Philips Price: *War and Revolution in Asiatic Russia*, George Allen & Unwin Ltd, London, 1917.
G. Ward Price: *Extra-Special Correspondent* (London, 1957).
A. Rawlinson: *Adventures in the Near East* (London, 1923).
Sir A. Ryan: *The Last of the Dragomans* (London, 1951).
C. Ryan: *Under the Red Crescent*; Charles Scribner's Sons; New York; 1897.
Liman von Sanders: *Five Years in Turkey*; tr. from German by C. Reichmann, United States Naval Institute; 1927.
H.C. Seppings Wright: *Two Years Under the Crescent*; Small, Maynard & Company; Boston; 1913.
Rear-Admiral Sir Adolphus Slade: *Turkey and the Crimean War*; Smith, Elder &CO; London, 1867.

W.T. Stead: *Tripoli and the Treaties or Britain's Duty in this War;* London; 1911.

Major General Vere Ferrers Townshend: *My Campaign;* The James A. McCann Company; vol 2; 1920.

A.J. Toynbee: *The Western Question in Greece and Turkey;* Constable; London, 1922.

5. Other primary sources and studies

M. Aksakal: Defending the Nation: The German-Ottoman Alliance of 1914 and the Ottoman Decision for War. Princeton: Princeton University Unpublished Ph.D. Dissertation, 2003.

E.J. Erickson: From Kirkilisse to the Great offensive, Turkish Operational Encirclement planning, 1912-1922; in *Middle Eastern Studies*; Vol 40; No 1; pp. 45-64.

I. Karlsson: The Turk as a Threat and Europe's Other; in *International Issues and Slovak Foreign Policy;* issue 1, 2006; pp. 62-72.

P. Kincaid Jensen: The Greco Turkish War, 1920-1922; in *Int. J. Middle East Stud.* 10 (1979), 553-565.

Salahi R. Sonyel: Disinformation, the Negative factor in Turco-Greek Relations, *Perceptions,* March-May 1998, pp. 39-48.

Syed Tanvir Wasti: The 1912-13 Balkan wars and the Siege of Edirne; in *Middle Eastern Journal*; 40 (2004); pp. 59-78.

Pinar Ure Immediate effects of the 1877-1878 Russio-Ottoman War on the Muslims in Bulgaria, in *History Studies;* vol 13; pp.153-170.

M. Uyar: Ottoman Arab Officers between Nationalism and Loyalty during the First World War; in *War in History*; Sage Publishing; vol 20; No 4 (2013); pp. 526-44.

6. Secondary sources

W.E.D. Allen, and P. Muratoff: *Caucasian Battlefields* (Cambridge, 1953).

E. Brémond: *La Cilicie en 1919–20* (Paris, 1921).

E.J. Erickson: *Defeat in Detail*; Praeger; London; 2003.

E.J. Erickson: *Ordered To Die, A History of the Ottoman Army* in *the First World War.* Westport, CT: Greenwood Press, 2000.

E.J. Erickson: *Ottoman Army Effectiveness in WW1: A Comparative Study;* (London: Routledge, 2007).

Lord Eversley: *The Turkish Empire, its Growth and Decay;* Dodd, Mead & Company; New York; 1917.

Lord P. Kinross: *Ataturk: The Rebirth of a Nation*; Weidenfeld and Nicolson; London; 1964.

M. Llewellyn Smith: *Ionian Vision;* Allen Lane; London; 1973.

J. McCarthy: *Death and Exile: The Ethnic Cleansing of Ottoman Muslims, 1821-1922;* The Darwin Press; New Jersey; 1995.

J. McCarthy: *The Ottoman Peoples and the end of Empire;* Bloomsbury; 2001.
A. Mango: *Ataturk;* John Murray; London; 1999.
E. Mead: *The Baghdad Railway; A Study in Imperialism*; MacMillan; New York; 1924.
M. Philips Price: *A History of Turkey: From Empire to Republic*; London, Allen and Unwin, 1956.
J. Salt: *The Unmaking of the Middle East*; University of California Press, 2008.
S.J. Shaw and E.K. Shaw: *History of the Ottoman Empire and Modern Turkey*; vol 2; Cambridge University Press; 1977.
Sutherland Menzies: *Turkey Old and New*, 2 vols; Allen Lane; London; 1880.
M. Uyar and E.J. Erickson: *A Military History of the Ottomans from Osman to Ataturk*; ABC and Clio, Santa Barbara, California, 2009.
David Walder: *The Chanak Affair* (London: Hutchinson & Co. Ltd, 1969).
Ahmet Emin Yalman: *Turkey in My Time*, University of Oklahoma 1956
A.E. Yalman: *Turkey in the World War;* Yale, 1930.

Printed in Great Britain
by Amazon